Geoffrey Sampson and Anna Babarczy
Grammar Without Grammaticality

Trends in Linguistics
Studies and Monographs

Volume 254

Geoffrey Sampson
Anna Babarczy

Grammar Without Grammaticality

Growth and Limits of Grammatical Precision

DE GRUYTER
MOUTON

ISBN 978-3-11-048806-7
e-ISBN 978-3-11-029001-1
ISSN 1861-4302

Library of Congress Cataloging-in-Publication Data
A CIP catalog record for this book has been applied for at the Library of Congress.

Bibliographic information published by the Deutsche Nationalbibliothek
The Deutsche Nationalbibliothek lists this publication in the Deutsche Nationalbibliografie;
detailed bibliographic data are available in the Internet at http://dnb.dnb.de.

© 2014 Walter de Gruyter GmbH, Berlin/Boston
Typesetting: RoyalStandard, Hong Kong
Printing and binding: Hubert & Co. GmbH & Co. KG, Göttingen
♾ Printed on acid-free paper
Printed in Germany

www.degruyter.com

Preface

This book sets out to explain and give evidence for a distinctive view of the nature of human language, a view which contrasts sharply with assumptions that are taken for granted by many or most linguists publishing today. The book has had a long gestation, but the bulk of it emerges from collaborative work carried out at Sussex University in England, where one of us (Sampson) was Professor of Natural Language Engineering, and the other (Babarczy) was assisting him as Research Fellow.

Some chapters of the book are primarily conceptual in nature, aiming to make as clear and explicit as possible what we think language is like, where we disagree with others, and how we answer their objections to our point of view. Other chapters go into details of the empirical, quantitative researches that have led us to those conceptual conclusions. (Some chapters mix these modes of discussion.)

We realize, of course, that many readers are more comfortable with conceptual discussion than with the nitty-gritty of numbers and statistics. Some might have preferred us to leave out the second kind of material, feeling that they could trust us to get that part right and give them just the conclusions which emerge. We believe that it is important not to omit the quantitative material. There is a style of linguistic publication which is quite influential nowadays, that might be described as a pastiche of scientific writing. General statements are expressed in words, but here and there one sees a sprinkling of algebraic notations or other formalisms which create an impression of hard scientific analysis underlying the generalities – only, if you press, that analysis never seems to be forthcoming. (The kind of intellectual charlatanry skewered by Alan Sokal and Jean Bricmont (1997) is familiar in modern linguistics, although it happened that none of the individual academics Sokal and Bricmont discussed was a linguist.) We want it to be clear to readers that our work is not like that. If some passages of the book seem hard going, we hope that readers will be patient with them for the sake of receiving a sense of the detailed research which, in our eyes at least, has entitled us to assert the conclusions we have drawn.

If some parts of the book may seem dry, in another respect the book may offer *more* human interest than the average work on linguistics. Since language is an aspect of human behaviour, and an important one, any fresh insights on the nature and structure of language will be of some interest to human beings – but often those insights are rather abstract. Linguistics is frequently seen as a subject which does not have the weighty practical or moral implications for society that commonly attach to fundamental theorizing in other human sciences, such as economics or politics. But we believe that the contrasting views about language structure discussed in this book – ours, and the current majority view with which we disagree – do indeed entail contrasting consequences for how societies should be organized and lives should be led. The central aim of our book is to establish a truth about language, but professional academics have a duty to society to spend some time discussing the practical implications of their work. We take this issue up in our final chapter.

Some of our chapters are based on papers previously published in academic journals or conference proceedings, with redrafting and additional material to fit them into a volume that reads coherently as a whole. Only in this way can separate small-scale investigations be appreciated as contributing to a single novel and consistent model of the nature of language. Other chapters are newly published here.

Where material was published previously, this was sometimes done under one of our names, sometimes the other, and sometimes we published as co-authors. That creates a problem about pronouns for this book. It would be tedious for readers if we chopped and changed between "I" and "we", depending on details of the original published version of different passages here. Furthermore, even when Sampson published under his sole name, often his writing drew on work done by Babarczy.

Luckily, in English the authorial "we" is vague between singular and plural: for the sake of readability, we shall be "we" throughout this book, even in contexts where the reference is obviously singular. For instance, at the beginning of chapter 1 we mention "our copy" of an old book by John Meiklejohn: of course the book belongs to only one of us, and we have separate bookshelves, now in different countries – but we spare the reader the need to wade through irrelevant references to "one of us", "the other co-author", and so forth.

The exception is that at a few points it matters which of us is which. For instance, in chapter 2 we describe an experiment in which we played separate roles and where it could have been relevant that GRS but not AB is an English native speaker. In such contexts we identify ourselves by initials, as we have just done. Broadly, as will commonly be the case when a senior academic collaborates with a full-time researcher, the bulk of the hard quantitative work tended to be done by AB, and the general conclusions, together with the ways to make them engage with the ongoing context of debate that constitutes the discipline of linguistics, tended to be settled by GRS. But each of us contributed at each level; the book is a genuine collaboration.

The programme of research from which this book emerges has centred round various English-language "corpora" – samples, held in electronic form, of different genres of the language. Since many chapters will refer to one or another of these resources, we list here those which are relevant to our book, with access details. (Sampson and McCarthy 2004 contains papers discussing these and many other corpora, and illustrating various ways in which they are used for linguistic research.)

The "raw" English corpora mainly relevant to our work – where "raw" means that the electronic files contain the wording of the language samples but little more[1] – are the *Brown Corpus*, the *Lancaster–Oslo/Bergen (LOB) Corpus*, and the *British National Corpus*. Brown and LOB are the resources which first enabled corpus linguistics to get off the ground: they are matched collections of one million words each of published writing in, respectively, American and British English of the 1960s. The British National Corpus is a more recent collection comprising one hundred million words of British English, of which ninety million is written language but ten million is spoken, and of the latter about 4·2 million words are "demographically sampled" speech – broadly, the spontaneous conversational talk of a cross-section of the UK population. For Brown and LOB Corpora see e.g. <khnt.hit.uib.no/icame/manuals/>; for the British National Corpus, <www.natcorp.ox.ac.uk>.

Initially as a member of the corpus research group at Lancaster University led by Geoffrey Leech, and later as leader of his own research group of which AB became a key member, GRS has used these and similar materials in order to generate a maximally refined and comprehensive structural taxonomy for written and spoken English, attempting to do for the grammar of the English language something akin to what Linnaeus in the eighteenth century did for plant life. (On this analogy, cf. Sampson 2000a.) In practice this entailed using subsamples of the raw corpora as testbeds to uncover and resolve shortcomings in a scheme of structural annotation for the language, making the scheme ever more adequate to record and classify the grammatical detail that occurs in samples of the language in practice – a process which can never be complete. The resulting annotated subcorpora, or "treebanks", then became research resources in their own right:

- the SUSANNE Corpus comprises 64 files drawn from four genre categories of the Brown Corpus, for a total of about 130,000 words of written American English
- the CHRISTINE Corpus comprises about 80,500 words, plus many ums and ers and the like, of spoken British English (taken from the demographically-sampled speech section of the British National Corpus)

---

1 In fact, for these resources, recent versions of the files do also include wordtags, i.e. part-of-speech classifications of the individual words.

– the LUCY Corpus comprises 165,000 words of written British English representing a spectrum of genres ranging from polished published writing to the writing of young children.

(The name SUSANNE was chosen to stand for "surface and underlying structural analyses of natural English", and also to celebrate links with the life of St Susanna. The names CHRISTINE and LUCY likewise refer to saints whose reputed careers were in different ways appropriate to the language genres in question.)

These research resources are freely available for others to download and work with (and many researchers internationally have done and are doing so). For details of access, and documentation of these resources, see <www.grsampson.net/Resources.html>.

The structural annotation scheme which emerged from this programme of research, called the SUSANNE Scheme after the earliest of the treebanks listed, was published in the form of a 500-page book (Sampson 1995). Various refinements to that published scheme which derived from work since 1995, particularly to handle the special features of spontaneous speech, are covered in the electronic documentation files for the corpora.

Geoffrey Sampson
University of South Africa

Anna Babarczy
Budapest University of Technology and Economics

Acknowledgements

We thank Alan Morris for his work on the electronic resources used in the research discussed in this book, and Anna Rahman for permission to use the material on which chapter 6 is based, of which she was a co-author. For discussion of various of our ideas, we are grateful to Anders Ahlqvist, John Carroll, Gerald Gazdar, Adam Kilgarriff, and the late Larry Trask, as well as numerous participants at conferences and anonymous referees for journals. We ask anyone whose name we have overlooked to forgive us.

Much of the research presented here was sponsored by the Economic and Social Research Council (UK), whose support we gratefully acknowledge.

The origin of the various chapters is as follows:

Chapter 1 is new material.

Chapter 2 is based on a paper in the *Journal of Natural Language Engineering*, vol. 14, pp. 471–494, 2008, reprinted with permission of Cambridge University Press.

Chapter 3 is based on a paper in the *Proceedings of the Workshop on Linguistically Interpreted Corpora, LINC–2000*, Luxemburg, 6 Aug 2000 (ed. by Anne Abeillé et al.), pp. 28–34.

Chapter 4 is based on a "target paper" which appeared in *Corpus Linguistics and Linguistic Theory*, vol. 3, pp. 1–32 and 111–129, 2007.

Chapter 5 is new material.

Chapter 6 is based on a paper in J. M. Kirk (ed.), *Corpora Galore*, 2000, pp. 295–311, reprinted by permission of Rodopi of Amsterdam.

Chapter 7 is based on a chapter in *Empirical Linguistics*, © Geoffrey Sampson 2001, reprinted by permission of Continuum Publishing, an imprint of Bloomsbury Publishing plc.

Chapter 8 is based on a paper in Sylviane Granger and Stephanie Petch-Tyson (eds), *Extending the Scope of Corpus-Based Research*, 2003, pp. 177–193, reprinted by permission of Rodopi of Amsterdam.

Chapter 9 is new material.

Chapter 10 is based on a paper in Mickael Suominen et al. (eds), *A Man of Measure: Festschrift in honour of Fred Karlsson on his 60th birthday*, 2006, pp. 362–374, reprinted with permission of the Linguistic Association of Finland.

Chapter 11 is based on a paper in *English Language and Linguistics*, vol. 6, pp. 17–30, 2002, reprinted with permission of Cambridge University Press.

Chapter 12 is based on a paper in the *Journal of Natural Language Engineering*, vol. 9, pp. 365–380, 2003, reprinted with permission of Cambridge University Press.

Chapter 13 is based on a paper in the *International Journal of Corpus Linguistics*, vol. 10, pp. 15–36, 2005.

Chapter 14 is new material.

Chapter 15 is based on a keynote address to the International Association for Dialogue Analysis workshop (IADA 2006), Mainz, September 2006, published in Marion Grein and Edda Weigand (eds), *Dialogue and Culture*, pp. 3–25, 2007, and reprinted with kind permission of John Benjamins Publishing Company.

Table of contents

Preface —— v
Acknowledgements —— ix
List of figures —— xvi
List of tables —— xvii

1   **Introduction** —— **1**
1.1   Grammar before linguistics —— **1**
1.2   All grammars leak —— **6**
1.3   No common logic —— **8**
1.4   "Chicken eat" —— **9**
1.5   The case of Old Chinese —— **13**
1.6   It cuts both ways —— **18**
1.7   Vocabulary differences —— **19**
1.8   What can be said about grammar —— **21**
1.9   The computational viewpoint —— **24**

2   **The bounds of grammatical refinement** —— **26**
2.1   An experiment —— **26**
2.2   The experimental material —— **29**
2.3   The analytic scheme —— **31**
2.4   Measuring similarity of analyses —— **34**
2.5   Text complexity —— **35**
2.6   Overall similarity results —— **36**
2.7   Dividing overall discrepancy between annotation categories —— **37**
2.8   Assigning responsibility for discrepancies —— **40**
2.9   Monitoring for bias —— **46**
2.10   Implications of the experiment —— **47**
2.11   New research techniques yield novel perspectives —— **52**

3   **Where should annotation stop?** —— **53**
3.1   Another way to survey indeterminacy —— **53**
3.2   Detailed v. skeleton analytic schemes —— **53**
3.3   The trainability criterion —— **55**
3.4   Limits to expert decision-making —— **55**
3.5   Some examples of indeterminacy —— **56**
3.6   Annotation practice and linguistic theory —— **61**
3.7   A disanalogy with biology —— **62**

4   **Grammar without grammaticality —— 64**
4.1   Strangers or unmet friends —— 64
4.2   Unfamiliar does not imply ungrammatical —— 66
4.3   Statistics of construction frequencies —— 70
4.4   A range without boundaries —— 75
4.5   Can intuition substitute for observation? —— 78
4.6   How intuitions have misled —— 81
4.7   Is English special? —— 84
4.8   The analogy with word meaning —— 86
4.9   Grammar as an expression of logical structure —— 90
4.10   Realistic grammatical description —— 92

5   **Replies to our critics —— 95**
5.1   Is our idea controversial? —— 95
5.2   Geoffrey Pullum's objections —— 96
5.3   No virtue in extremism —— 98
5.4   Stefanowitsch versus Müller —— 99
5.5   Trees have no legs —— 101
5.6   Law versus good behaviour —— 103
5.7   Conceptual objections to our thesis —— 104
5.8   Do we really mean it? —— 105
5.9   Grammaticality implied by Universal Grammar —— 107
5.10   The downfall of Universal Grammar —— 109
5.11   Economic growth and linguistic theory —— 112
5.12   Discipline should not contradict discipline —— 116
5.13   Language is not "special" —— 117

6   **Grammatical description meets spontaneous speech —— 119**
6.1   The primacy of speech —— 119
6.2   An example —— 120
6.3   Wordtagging —— 123
6.4   Speech repairs —— 124
6.5   Syntactically Markovian constructions —— 125
6.6   Logical distinctions dependent on the written medium —— 127
6.7   Nonstandard usage —— 128
6.8   Dialect difference versus performance error —— 130
6.9   Transcription inadequacies —— 132
6.10   Dropping the paradigm —— 133

7   **Demographic correlates of speech complexity** —— 136
7.1   Speech in the British National Corpus —— **136**
7.2   Measuring speech complexity —— **138**
7.3   Classifying the speakers —— **141**
7.4   Demographics and complexity indices compared —— **144**
7.5   "Critical period" or lifelong learning? —— **148**
7.6   Individual advance or collective retreat? —— **153**

8   **The structure of children's writing** —— 155
8.1   Moving from spoken to adult written norms —— **155**
8.2   The language samples —— **155**
8.3   The suitability of the child-writing sample —— **156**
8.4   Writing "wordier" than speech —— **157**
8.5   Width v. depth in parse-trees —— **158**
8.6   Interim summary —— **161**
8.7   Phrase and clause categories —— **162**
8.8   Use of phrase categories —— **163**
8.9   Use of subordinate clause categories —— **165**
8.10   The complexity of the relative constructions —— **168**
8.11   Simple v. complex relatives —— **169**
8.12   Unanswered questions —— **171**

9   **Child writing and discourse organization** —— 172
9.1   A fixed grammatical programme? —— **172**
9.2   New information about a previously identified object —— **172**
9.3   The new study: data and methods of analysis —— **173**
9.4   Context frequency —— **175**
9.5   Syntactic patterns —— **176**
9.6   Mistakes with relative clauses —— **179**
9.7   The upshot of the analysis —— **182**

10   **Simple grammars and new grammars** —— 184
10.1   Pidgins and creoles —— **184**
10.2   Old Chinese as a counterexample —— **187**
10.3   Old Chinese not a creole —— **187**
10.4   Examples of structural vagueness —— **188**
10.5   Lack of word classes —— **190**
10.6   Logical indeterminacy —— **191**
10.7   McWhorter's diagnostics —— **193**
10.8   No tone in Old Chinese —— **193**
10.9   No inflexion in Old Chinese —— **194**

10.10   Derivational morphology in Old Chinese —— **194**
10.11   An accident of history —— **196**
10.12   "Hidden" versus "overt" structure —— **197**
10.13   Deutscher on Akkadian —— **199**
10.14   Diverse paths of evolution —— **199**

11   **The case of the vanishing perfect** —— **201**
11.1   Losses as well as gains —— **201**
11.2   The Perfect aspect and spontaneous speech —— **202**
11.3   The standard system and nonstandard alternatives —— **203**
11.4   Verb qualifiers in CHRISTINE —— **205**
11.5   Past and Perfect —— **207**
11.6   *got* for *HAVE got* —— **209**
11.7   Casual subject-auxiliary omission —— **209**
11.8   Modals + *of* —— **210**
11.9   Nonstandard verb forms —— **212**
11.10   A possible explanation —— **214**
11.11   If one feature can go, what cannot? —— **217**

12   **Testing a metric for parse accuracy** —— **218**
12.1   The need for a metric —— **218**
12.2   Alternative metrics —— **219**
12.3   The essence of leaf-ancestor assessment —— **220**
12.4   The experimental material —— **222**
12.5   Calculation of lineage similarity —— **224**
12.6   Are the metrics equivalent? —— **226**
12.7   Performance systematically compared —— **229**
12.8   Local error information —— **234**
12.9   Authority is fallible —— **236**

13   **Linguistics empirical and unempirical** —— **237**
13.1   What went wrong? —— **237**
13.2   Two kinds of empiricism —— **237**
13.3   Universal Grammar versus empiricism —— **239**
13.4   Arguments against empiricism —— **241**
13.5   How empirical should linguistics be? —— **243**
13.6   How intuition has led linguists astray —— **243**
13.7   Were our intuitions correct after all? —— **246**
13.8   Can intuitions be empirical? —— **248**
13.9   Is our characterization of generative linguistics
         misleading? —— **251**

13.10   New possibilities —— **252**
13.11   The Hirschberg survey of computational linguistics —— **253**
13.12   The literature sample —— **255**
13.13   Evidence-based, intuition-based, or neutral —— **255**
13.14   How much evidence counts as "evidence-based"? —— **257**
13.15   Explicit authenticity claims —— **259**
13.16   Raw and smoothed counts —— **260**
13.17   The match between statistics and history —— **263**
13.18   A rearguard action? —— **265**
13.19   Empiricism reasserted —— **266**

14   William Gladstone as linguist —— 269
14.1   Ducking an intellectual challenge —— **269**
14.2   What Gladstone didn't say —— **271**
14.3   Gladstone's positive contributions —— **280**
14.4   Intellectual advance depends on a receptive audience —— **294**

15   Minds in uniform —— 296
15.1   Trivializing cultural differences —— **296**
15.2   An earlier consensus —— **296**
15.3   Globalization concealing cultural diversity —— **297**
15.4   Generative linguistics as a theory of human nature —— **299**
15.5   Cognitive constraints and cultural universalism —— **302**
15.6   "Universal grammar" means European grammar —— **303**
15.7   Honest and dishonest imperialism —— **305**
15.8   Vocabulary and culture —— **307**
15.9   Universalist politics —— **310**
15.10   Abandoning the touchstone of empiricism —— **313**
15.11   Intuition-based politics —— **314**
15.12   New evidence for language diversity —— **318**
15.13   Conclusion —— **319**

References —— 320
Index —— 335

List of figures

Figure 1:   Meiklejohn's structural diagram of a William Morris couplet — 3
Figure 2:   Meiklejohn's diagram recast in tree format — 3
Figure 3:   A SUSANNE tree structure — 32
Figure 4:   Locations of analytic discrepancy — 39
Figure 5:   Causes of analytic discrepancy — 42
Figure 6:   Noun-phrase expansion frequencies in SUSANNE — 71
Figure 7:   Tree structure of a CHRISTINE speaker turn — 121
Figure 8:   Embedding scores of words in a CHRISTINE extract — 140
Figure 9:   Embedding indices plotted against age — 150
Figure 10: Frequencies of clause types in conducive contexts, by genre — 176
Figure 11: Frequencies of clause types by clause-function of anaphor
            and by genre — 177
Figure 12: Frequencies of clause types by phrase-function of anaphor
            and by genre — 179
Figure 13: Frequencies of clause types by antecedent position and
            by genre — 180
Figure 14: GEIG/unlabelled v. LA parse scores — 226
Figure 15: GEIG/labelled v. LA parse scores — 227
Figure 16: Corpus-based computational linguistics papers
            (after Hirschberg 1998) — 254
Figure 17: Raw 3-way classification of *Language* articles — 261
Figure 18: Evidence-based as % of non-neutral *Language* articles
            (smoothed) — 263

List of tables

Table 1:   Complexity figures for the sample texts —— 35
Table 2:   Inter-analyst agreement on sample text analyses —— 36
Table 3:   Results of discrepancy resolution —— 47
Table 4:   Mean embedding indices by region —— 144
Table 5:   Mean embedding indices by social class —— 145
Table 6:   Mean embedding indices by sex —— 146
Table 7:   Mean embedding indices by age —— 146
Table 8:   Mean adult embedding indices by sex —— 147
Table 9:   Mean adult embedding indices by age —— 147
Table 10:   Incidence of phrase categories in different genres —— 164
Table 11:   Incidence of subordinate-clause categories in different
            genres —— 166
Table 12:   Incidence of relative-clause types in different genres —— 171
Table 13:   Effects of context type on relative-clause selection —— 182
Table 14:   Verb qualifier frequences —— 206
Table 15:   Perfect and Past marking by region —— 207
Table 16:   *got* for standard *HAVE got* by region —— 209
Table 17:   Ranking on either metric of parses ranked lowest by
            the other metric —— 230
Table 18:   Leaf-ancestor scores for individual words in a parse tree —— 235

List of Tables

Chapter 1
Introduction

1.1 Grammar before linguistics

Grammar (or "syntax", as American linguists often prefer to call it) has lain at the heart of linguistic theorizing for decades now.[1] Rightly so: although grammar is often seen as a dry topic, it is grammar which provides the architecture of conscious, explicit thought and communication, so anyone who turns to linguistics in hope of gaining a clearer understanding of how human minds work should accept grammar as central to the discipline.

Pick up almost any issue of a mainstream modern linguistics journal, and you will find articles which analyse particular aspects of the grammar of particular languages by contrasting grammatical and ungrammatical word-sequences (with asterisks labelling the ungrammatical examples), by defining rules which aim to produce ("generate") the grammatical examples while excluding the ungrammatical sequences, and by displaying tree structures that show how the rules group the words of particular grammatical sentences into multi-word units of various sizes nested within one another – phrases and clauses of various types.

But of course, grammar was studied before modern linguistics was inaugurated early in the twentieth century, by Ferdinand de Saussure's lectures at the University of Geneva. If we look at how grammar was discussed before there was a subject called "linguistics", we shall find much in common with present-day assumptions – but also, one important difference. We believe that on the rare occasions when that difference is noticed nowadays, its significance is seriously misinterpreted.

As one representative treatment of grammar before Saussure, consider the grammatical section of John Meiklejohn's book *The English Language*, first published in 1886.

---

1 Traditionally, "grammar" has referred to the patterns of word inflection (in inflecting languages) together with the patterns in which words are grouped into larger structures such as phrases, clauses, and sentences (in any language). Americans sometimes use "grammar" more broadly to refer to *all* aspects of language structure, including for instance the patterns in which speech-sounds are organized into syllables; that leaves "syntax" as the only one-word term available to cover the bulk of grammar in the traditional sense, while the remainder is rather clumsily called "inflectional morphology". Because we see syntax + inflectional morphology as a natural class of phenomena meriting a simple one-word label (and also because neither of us is American), we use "grammar" in the traditional sense.

John Miller Dow Meiklejohn (1830–1902) was a remarkable man, whose career would be hard to parallel in the academic world of today. A Scot, Meiklejohn worked as a schoolteacher and a war correspondent, until in 1876 he became the first professor of education at St Andrews University. To supplement his salary he produced what one writer (Graves 2004: 15) calls "a veritable torrent" of textbooks on various school subjects, including history, geography, and English, which were widely distributed, and in some cases remained in use for many decades after his death. (He also produced what is still probably the most widely-read English translation of Immanuel Kant's *Critique of Pure Reason*.) Our copy of *The English Language* is the 23rd edition (1902), which is one indication of its influence. The book was intended primarily for trainee teachers; among other things it includes 41 pages of specimen question papers from the exams taken to gain teaching qualifications. It seems safe to infer that Meiklejohn's approach to English grammar was uncontroversial and representative by the standards of his day.

In its style or flavour, Meiklejohn's treatment of English grammar certainly feels different from modern linguistics writing. Notably, rather than aiming to make all his examples represent the colloquial English of his time, Meiklejohn tended to draw examples from literature, and often from quite high-flown genres far removed from everyday usage. But that is a superficial difference. In other respects, Meiklejohn covered much the same topics as one would find in a modern treatment of English grammar. He first examined the parts of speech and the inflection patterns of the language; then he went on to look at the various ways in which words can be grouped into simple and complex sentences. We often think of tree-structure diagrams as a speciality of modern linguistics, but Meiklejohn had them too, though they look superficially quite different from modern notation. Figure 1 is his structural diagram (p. 109) for a couplet from William Morris's *Jason*:

And in his hand he bare a mighty bow,
No man could bend of those that battle now.

Meiklejohn glosses the single and double lines as representing respectively a preposition, and a "conjunction or conjunctive pronoun". He does not explain his use of bold face for the words *He*, *bare*, *bow*, and *those*, but bold v. plain seems to correspond to the head/modifier distinction (which is ignored in the phrase-structure tree notation of modern linguistics, but recognized in the rival, "dependency grammar" notation). It seems to us that Meiklejohn's diagram might be translated into a combination of modern dependency and phrase-structure notation as Figure 2 (where NP, PP, and S mean respectively "noun phrase", "prepositional phrase", and "clause").

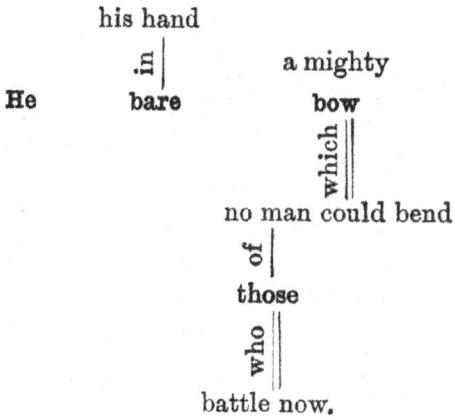

Figure 1: Meiklejohn's structural diagram of a William Morris couplet

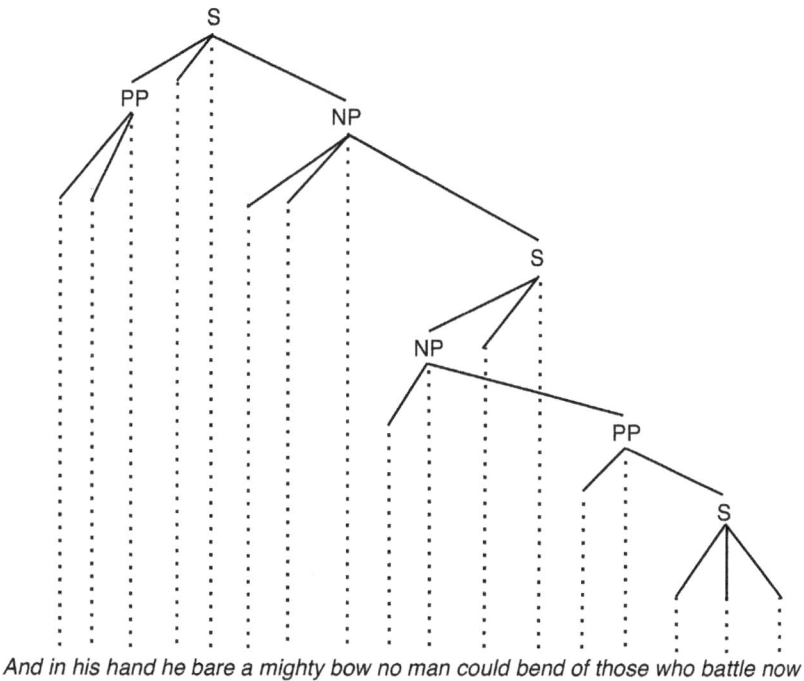

And in his hand he bare a mighty bow no man could bend of those who battle now

Figure 2: Meiklejohn's diagram recast in tree format

Where Meiklejohn's approach differs fundamentally, rather than just cosmetically, from what would be normal today is that Meiklejohn's examples are all positive. He only describes what *does* happen in English, he never contrasts this with hypothetical ungrammatical possibilities.

And so, naturally, Meiklejohn has no generative rules for producing the range of positive examples while excluding the ungrammatical. When he identifies a grammatical unit intermediate between the entire couplet and the individual words, say the phrase *in his hand*, he recognizes it as a unit not because in the process of using rewrite rules to derive the couplet from an initial symbol these three words are dominated by a single nonterminal symbol, but because the words fit together as a unit with a meaning.

Meiklejohn does, fairly often, identify some turn of phrase as to be avoided. Readers who think of late-nineteenth-century British society as imbued with snobbery and social anxiety might perhaps expect that those cases will be examples of socially-deprecated usage, such as double negatives. In fact Meiklejohn never mentions any examples of that sort. But there are two other categories of usage which Meiklejohn describes as not properly part of the language.

Often, Meiklejohn quotes obsolete usages from older authors and comments that they are not used in the modern language. An example would be Shakespeare's use of *as* to introduce a relative clause in the context *that kind of fruit/ As maids call medlars* (*Romeo and Juliet* Act 2, scene 1), where Meiklejohn (p. 75) comments "This usage cannot now be employed". Occasionally he objects to a usage as illogical:

> The Adverb ought to be as *near* as possible to the word it modifies. Thus we ought to say, "He gave me *only three* shillings," and not "He only gave me three shillings," ... (p. 83)

Neither of these usage categories correspond to the way modern linguistics uses asterisks. Meiklejohn is not saying that these constructions will not be found in English; he is saying that they *will* be found, but are not to be imitated for different reasons – either because they are illogical or because they are too old-fashioned.

In more than one hundred pages of the book which deal with grammar, we have found just one case that seems directly comparable to the modern use of asterisks. On p. 23 Meiklejohn questions the idea that a "pronoun" is a "word that is used instead of a noun", pointing out that this definition "hardly applies to the pronoun *I*. If we say *I write*, the *I* cannot have *John Smith* substituted for it. We cannot say *John Smith write*." This does perhaps correspond neatly to a starred example **John Smith write* in a modern linguistics publication. But even this case is included by Meiklejohn in order to query a part-of-speech definition – not in order to help draw a dividing line between word-sequences that are and are not grammatical in the language.

At least to a close approximation it is fair to say that Meiklejohn is not in the business of specifying word-sequences which cannot occur in English. He describes in considerable detail various syntactic structures which *do* occur in the language; he is not interested in contrasting these with other hypothetical word-sequences which do not occur.

When present-day academic linguists notice this absence in pre-modern accounts of grammar (we do not know of any recent linguist who has discussed Meiklejohn in particular), it seems to us that they standardly see it as exemplifying a pre-scientific approach to language description. Karl Popper has taught us that the hallmark of empirical science is falsifiability: a theory is empirical to the extent that it predicts a range of events which will not occur, so that it can be tested by seeing whether any potential falsifiers are in fact observed. Modern linguistics, or at least the central branch of linguistics concerned with grammar, is thought to have become a respectable science precisely by adopting a formal approach which allows a grammatical description to define a range of non-sentences alongside the range of well-formed sentences. The term "generative grammar", used for the style of linguistics with which we disagree, refers to the idea that a central goal of grammatical research is to devise formulae which "generate" all and only the grammatical sentences of a language, as a circle or other geometrical curve is said by mathematicians to be "generated" by an algebraic equation that defines all and only the points comprised in the curve.

We on the other hand want to argue that Meiklejohn's failure to define a set of non-sentences makes his description *more* faithful to the fundamental nature of human language than a theory that specifies a contrast between "grammatical" and "ungrammatical" word-sequences could be.

We have little doubt that, if it were possible to ask him, Meiklejohn would readily agree that his description of English was not a "scientific theory" comparable with the theories of the hard sciences. We doubt whether Meiklejohn would have taken that as a criticism of his work; but, whether he would have done so or not, we do not see it as such. If science requires potential falsifiers, then we do not believe that a good grammatical description of a human language can be truly "scientific".[2]

---

2 Early generative linguistics envisaged grammars which simply divided strings over a vocabulary into two classes, of grammatical and ungrammatical sentences, so that a "potential falsifier" would be an individual sentence. More recent approaches have often incorporated variable rules or similar mechanisms, which associate strings with probabilities rather than merely classifying them as well- or ill-formed. Popper's equation of science with falsifiability applies to probabilistic as well as to absolute theories: for a probabilistic theory, a potential falsifier will often be an observed distribution of frequencies over types of event, rather than observation of an individual event. We question whether grammatical description can be scientific even in this sense.

Not all worthwhile discourse has the characteristics of scientific theorizing, after all (and Popper knew this as well as anyone). Think for instance of literary analysis. It is a normal enough activity to discuss the various genres of prose or poetic writing found in the literature of a language. In the case of some poetic genres (the sonnet, for instance) the definitions may be quite precise and formal. But it would be strange for an aspiring writer to describe a hypothetical genre of writing having some novel feature or features, and to ask "Would that be a valid kind of literature?" A question like that seems to misunderstand the kind of enterprise literature is. The only reasonable answer, surely, would be along the lines "Try it and see – write that way and discover whether you can attract a readership and, perhaps, imitators: if you can, then it's a valid new literary genre". There are no rules which allow or disallow a form of writing in advance as a candidate for literary consideration.

Grammar is rather like that. There are ways, in English or in another language, in which we know we certainly can put words together to produce successful structures of meaning, because utterances of those kinds occur specially often. But there is no particular range of ways in which it is *not* open to us to put words together – we can try anything, though if we speak idiosyncratically enough we may not succeed in getting through to our hearers. Human languages have grammar, but they do not have "grammaticality".

1.2 All grammars leak

One reason to deny the reality of the "grammaticality" concept is the simple fact that no linguists have ever succeeded in plotting the boundary between the grammatical and the ungrammatical, for any language, despite many decades of trying. Edward Sapir ([1921] 1963: 38) famously stated that "All grammars leak", and this remains as true now as when he wrote, almost a century ago. As David Graddol (2004) put it: "No one has ever successfully produced a comprehensive and accurate grammar of any language". Even if we date the enterprise of developing formal generative grammars not to Sapir but, more realistically, to Noam Chomsky's *Syntactic Structures* (Chomsky 1957), that book appeared more than half a century ago: time enough, surely, to have approached within sight of the goal for a few languages, if the goal were meaningful and attainable.[3] In reality, the most comprehensive grammars developed by linguists

---

3 Ivan Sag (2010: 487) notes that the attempt to develop large-scale generative grammars (for any language) was in practice abandoned soon after it was defined; the most recent example known to him is the Stockwell, Schachter, and Partee grammar of English discussed in the next paragraph.

invariably turn out to have holes as soon as their predictions are checked against small samples of real-life usage. (That is true even when the samples represent edited written language; spontaneous speech, of course, is more anarchic still.)

One of the most serious attempts at a comprehensive generative grammar of English that has ever been published was Stockwell, Schachter, and Partee's 854-page *Major Syntactic Structures of English* (1973). Those authors summarized their view of the ultimate feasibility of the exercise by quoting as a motto to their book a passage by the seventeenth-century grammarian James Howell (1662: 80, orthography modernized):

> But the English ... having such varieties of incertitudes, changes, and idioms, it cannot be
> in the compass of human brain to compile an exact regular syntaxis thereof ...

French culture is considerably more interested than that of Britain or the USA in the concept of linguistic correctness, which ought to make it a relatively favourable case for generative description – national newspapers commonly include columns responding to readers' worries about whether this or that construction is good French. However, at the end of an attempt lasting more than a decade by a team of French linguists to construct a generative grammar for that language, Maurice Gross (1979) concluded, in a thoughtful paper which received surprisingly little attention, that the enterprise was hopeless.

(Indeed, it is not just difficult to plot a boundary dividing the whole range of possible sequences of words of a language into grammatical and ungrammatical subsets: it can be surprisingly hard even to find cast-iron examples of individual ungrammatical sequences of English words. A word-sequence which at first sight looks clearly bad very often turns out to have a plausible use in some special circumstance. F.W. Householder 1973: 371 observed that it is necessary to "line up several articles and several prepositions in such examples, otherwise they become intelligible as some kind of special usage".)

Commenting on Graddol's paper quoted above, Anne Dalke (2010) compares his picture of grammar with "the sort of friendly adjustment that happens when we hang out w[ith] one another: there is a range of possible behaviors, but no rules." Behaviour patterns but no binding rules: that is a good summary of how we see grammar.[4]

---

4 Throughout the period since *Syntactic Structures* there have been sporadic expressions of related points of view. Charles Hockett's *The State of the Art* (1968) has never, it seems to us, received the level of attention it deserved. More recently, remarks we find congenial have come e.g. from the "emergentist" school of linguists; for instance, Nick Ellis and Diane Larsen-Freeman (2006: 562) refer to "systematicity despite persistent instability", and Paul Hopper (2011) writes that "structure ... is unstable ... and is constantly being created and recreated". We do not necessarily agree with all views of the writers quoted, but there is undoubtedly a

1.3 No common logic

It is not merely the fact that no-one has done it which causes us to doubt that grammaticality can be defined. More important, we see the grammaticality concept as founded on a false conception of the job which grammar does. Linguists often seem to imagine that the range of articulated ideas is somehow fixed and given to us prior to individual languages; the grammar of a particular language is seen as a device for clothing independently-existing structures of thought in pronounceable words. People have often seen logic as a realm, like mathematics, comprising structure that is eternal and independent of human culture, and have thought of individual languages as encoding that structure. The nineteenth-century Harvard professor Charles Carroll Everett wrote ([1869] 1891: 82) that "the laws of grammar, which seem at first sight so hard and arbitrary, are simply the laws of the expresson of logical relations in concrete form." Sometimes a language may provide alternative grammatical devices to express the same thought-structure, for instance *a tidy room* and *a room that is tidy* use different constructions to say the same thing; and often the historical evolution of a language will lead to it containing arbitrary grammatical irregularities. Both of these considerations mean that the grammar of a human language is likely to be much more complicated than the grammars of the artificial "languages" developed by mathematical logicians, such as the propositional calculus and the predicate calculus (which are designed to be thoroughly regular, and as simple as their functions permit). But, since the range of thought-structures is given in advance and therefore, presumably, finitely definable, it seems to follow that the range of grammatical structures in a language should be definable also, even if the definition has to be rather long.

The trouble with this is that it just is not true that English and other human languages express a common range of thought-structures which are independent of particular languages. Not merely the modes of expression, but the structures of thought expressed, vary from language to language.

In the first place, the thought-structures underlying a natural language cannot be equated with the expressions of a logical calculus. To see this, consider for instance that in both of the present authors' native languages (and many others) there is an important contrast between *and* and *but*. (We are native

---

family resemblance between their pictures of grammar and ours. Nevertheless, our central point, that there are "good" word-sequences in a language but no starred, "bad" sequences, does not seem to have appeared on the menu of generally-recognized alternative linguistic doctrines before now – and indeed, in chapter 5 we shall show evidence that this has *not* been a recognized idea.

speakers respectively of English and Hungarian, members of the Indo-European and Finno-Ugric families; the Hungarian words for "and" and "but" are *és* and *de*.) Yet in mathematical logic those different words translate into the same symbol, which some logicians write as & and others as ∧.

Some philosophers of logic have argued that natural-language distinctions which have no expression in their artificial symbolic calculi cannot be real intellectual distinctions. Gottlob Frege ([1918] 1967: 23) wrote:

> The word "but" differs from "and" in that with it one intimates that what follows is in contrast with what would be expected from what preceded it. Such suggestions in speech make no difference to the thought.

For a logician it may perhaps be appropriate to use the word "thought" that way, but as linguists we are not interested in such a narrow definition. *P and Q*, and *P but Q*, clearly say different things in English – they are not interchangeable, as *a tidy room* and *a room which is tidy* perhaps are – so for us they express different "thoughts". The same point could be made about many other English-language distinctions that have no parallel in formal logic.

The logician's predicate calculus certainly is a system with a clear concept of grammaticality: certain sequences of its symbols are "well-formed formulae", which can appear within proofs demonstrating that given conclusions follow from given premises, while other, random, permutations of the same symbols are ill-formed and can play no part in proofs. Within a particular logical system, the distinction between the two classes of symbol-sequence is entirely clearcut and predictable. But English and other natural languages cannot be mapped into the symbols of mathematical logic without (large) loss, so the fact that there are clear boundaries to well-formedness in a logical system does not imply that such boundaries exist in natural languages.

(Because formal logic is in this way a misleading guide to the nature of human language, we prefer to write about grammar encoding "thought-structures" rather than "logical structures".)

1.4 "Chicken eat"

Furthermore, the conceptual distinctions which various natural languages express in their grammars can be very diverse. This is concealed from 21st-century Westerners by the fact that European civilization has historically been moulded by two languages, Latin and Ancient Greek, both of which had grammars that made certain conceptual distinctions extremely explicit, and which were so influential that modern European languages have all been developed so as to make much the same distinctions almost equally explicit. (This involved large changes to some European languages as they existed in the mediaeval period; see e.g. Utz Maas (2009: sec. 3) on the case of German. Latin was actually the official language of Hungary as late as 1844.) Because of the dominant cultural role played by European-descended societies on the world stage from the nineteenth century onwards, many non-European languages have by now been similarly remoulded to express European thought-structures.

But there are or have been other languages. Within the total history of human speech, languages influenced in their grammar by Latin or Greek – although to us they may seem all-important – have certainly been only a tiny minority.

Consider for instance the dialect of Malay/Indonesian spoken in the Indonesian province of Riau (east-central Sumatra), as described by David Gil. Gil (2001) writes as follows. (We replace Gil's example numbering with our own, to avoid confusion with later examples in the present book.)

> Ask a speaker of Riau Indonesian to translate the English sentence "The chicken is eating", and the answer might be as follows:

> (1) *Ayam   makan*
>   chicken eat
>
>   "The chicken is eating"

> ... *ayam* "chicken" is unmarked for number, allowing either singular or plural interpretations; and in addition it is unmarked for (in)definiteness, permitting either definite or indefinite readings. Similarly, *makan* "eat" is unmarked for tense and aspect, allowing a variety of interpretations, such as "is eating", "ate", "will eat", and others.

> So far, not too surprising, but this is only the tip of the iceberg. Arbitrarily keeping constant the singular definite interpretation of *ayam* and the present progressive interpretation of *makan*, the above construction can still be interpreted in many different ways, some of which are indicated below:

> (2) *Ayam   makan*
>   chicken eat
>
> | | |
> |---|---|
> | (a) | "The chicken is being eaten" |
> | (b) | "The chicken is making somebody eat" |
> | (c) | "Somebody is eating for the chicken" |
> | (d) | "Somebody is eating where the chicken is" |
> | (e) | "The chicken that is eating" |
> | (f) | "Where the chicken is eating" |
> | (g) | "When the chicken is eating" |
> | (h) | "How the chicken is eating" |

Gil points out that Riau Indonesian grammar allows *ayam*, "chicken", to be understood as playing any conceivable thematic role vis-à-vis the act of eating – it could be the eater, the thing eaten, the cause of eating (2b), the beneficiary (2c), etc. etc.; and, looking at (2e)–(2h), we see

> that the construction as a whole may be associated with an interpretation belonging to any ontological category: an activity, as in (1); a thing, as in (2e); a place, as in (2f); a time, as in (2g); a manner, as in (2h), and others.

Gil tells us that when he began learning Riau Indonesian, he assumed that any particular utterance of *ayam makan* must be intended in one of these interpretations and not others, but he came to see this assumption as a consequence of wearing European mental blinkers. Because European grammars require these interpretations to be distinguished, he at first took for granted that they must be exclusive alternatives for Riau speakers; later, he came to see the situation otherwise. There is a difference between ambiguity, and vagueness. For instance, in English the sentence *The chicken is ready to eat* is ambiguous between an interpretation in which the chicken will do the eating, and one in which the chicken will be eaten:

> in any given utterance of the sentence, the speaker will have only one of these two interpretations in mind … Now consider the fact that, under the latter interpretation, the chicken could be fried, boiled, stewed, fricasseed, and so on. Although in many situations the speaker might know how the chicken is prepared, in many other situations he or she may not. But in those situations, the speaker simply would not care, and the sentence could still be appropriately uttered. Clearly, in such cases, we would not want to characterize *chicken* as ambiguous with respect to mode of preparation.

Rather, with respect to mode of cooking the English sentence is not *ambiguous* but just *vague*. In Riau Indonesian, Gil argues, *ayam makan* is vague (not ambiguous) between the various interpretations given in (1–2) above (and others). In a European language, one cannot be vague about most of those distinctions, because our grammars require us to express them, but in Riau Indonesian one can be and often is vague about them.

Standard Malay/Indonesian, which is one[5] of the many modern non-European languages that has been heavily influenced by European models, is significantly less vague and more "normal" (to Western eyes) than Riau dialect, having adopted grammatical apparatus allowing it to express various logical distinctions that speakers of European languages take for granted. But Riau Indonesian is indisputably a natural human language; it is less clear that Standard Malay

---

5 Or two, if the standard languages of the two countries are counted separately.

can count as more than an artificial construct. According to McKinnon et al. (2011: 716), it has "almost no native speakers".

We have quoted Gil at length because he expresses with unusual clarity the unfamiliar idea that the structures of thought expressed by the grammar of one language may be incommensurable with those expressed by another language's grammar. ("Incommensurable" is perhaps not the ideal word here; we have not found a better one, and we hope that the example will show readers what we mean by it.) If that is so, then evidently different languages do not merely provide alternative methods of verbalizing a fixed range of thought-structures which are prior to any individual language. Languages define the structures of thought which they offer means of expressing, and different languages may define different thought-structures.

In that case, there is no obvious reason why we should expect a language to cease developing new thought-structures at a particular point in its history, any more than we would expect its literary tradition to cease evolving novel genres. Rather, we might expect the grammar of a language to remain open to innovation, and we might expect individual speakers to combine a great deal of imitation of other speakers' grammar with at least a modicum of grammatical innovation. To quote John Taylor (a linguist whose views have much in common with ours):

> ... speakers are by no means restricted by the generalizations that they may have made [from their linguistic experience]. A robust finding from our investigation is that speakers are happy to go beyond the generalizations and the instances that they sanction. Speakers, in other words, are prone to innovate with respect to previous usage, using words in ways not already sanctioned by previous experience, extending the usage range of idioms and constructions, thereby creating new words, new idioms, and new constructional patterns ... (J. Taylor 2012: 285)

No doubt some individuals will be more innovative than others, in their linguistic usage as in other respects; and some communities will be more receptive to grammatical innovation while others are more conservative. Perhaps there could be cases where some thoroughly hidebound community at a particular time gives up all grammatical innovation, and from then on limits itself slavishly to using only word-sequences that have clear grammatical precedents – and in a case like that it might make sense to draw a line between grammatical and ungrammatical word-sequences. But it seems to us that a case like that would be an exception requiring special explanation (and we wonder whether it could really happen). Certainly English and Hungarian in the 21st century are far from being such languages.

1.5 The case of Old Chinese

This way of looking at grammar and thought conflicts with assumptions that are deeply engrained in the modern discipline of linguistics. Many readers may feel that we are resting a great deal on one scholar's understanding of the functions of two words in the dialect of an out-of-the-way corner of South-East Asia. Even in Indonesia, the dialect described by Gil has low prestige relative to Standard Indonesian (the grammar of which has been influenced by and is more commensurable with European grammars); and as we understand the situation, Riau Indonesian is used only in informal spoken communication. Some may feel that it is not all that surprising if a form of language limited to face-to-face chat among inhabitants of a remote backwater is strikingly vague – after all, the speakers will commonly know each other and be able to see what they are talking about, so background knowledge and the evidence of their senses might compensate for lack of verbal explicitness.

We therefore want to stress that although Gil happened to be discussing a low-prestige spoken dialect, a similar level of incommensurability with European grammar can be found in written languages of high civilizations.

Consider the following passage from the Confucian *Analects*. We quote the passage (chapter 23 of Book IX – a fairly typical example of Chinese of the classical period) in a romanization of the modern Mandarin pronunciation. (We do not show the Chinese script; for those who cannot read Chinese its impenetrability is offputting, while those who can read it can easily look the passage up in the original.) Classical Chinese, like Riau Indonesian, is an isolating language – its words do not vary to mark parts of speech, distinctions of tense or case, etc. – so for instance the word *néng*, glossed by us "be.able", could equally be glossed "is.able", "was.able", "ability", and so on – for each word we choose as neutral a gloss as English allows. Many words are polysemous, for instance the first word, *zǐ*, originally meant "son" but acquired the alternative senses "you" and "sir, master"; in such cases our gloss keeps things simple by giving only the sense relevant to the context in question.[6] Word-order rules are essentially like English, so in principle the glosses give readers all the information needed to understand the text – we have not left any clues to interpretation

---

6 In our glosses, the symbol Q represents a particle which turns a statement into a question. ATTR is an attributive particle (in X ATTR Y, Y is a head and X modifies it), and 3 represents a third-person pronoun ("he/him", "she/her", "it", or "they/them") – in Chinese this is a case of polysemy, the same word *zhī* is used for both ATTR and 3. ASSERT is a particle making what precedes into a definite assertion, and particles glossed FINAL suggest that what precedes is "it and all about it", there is nothing more to be said.

unstated. Readers might like to check how far they can make sense of the text, before looking at the translation below.

(3) *Zǐ yuē*   master say

    fǎ yǔ zhī yán   law talk ATTR speech

    néng wú cóng hū   be.able not.have follow Q

    gǎi zhī wéi guì   reform 3 do/be valuable

    sùn yǔ zhī yán   mild concede ATTR speech

    néng wú yuè hū   be.able not.have pleased Q

    yì zhī wéi guì   unfold 3 do/be valuable

    yuè ér bù yì   pleased and not unfold

    cóng ér bù gǎi   follow and not reform

    wú mò rú.zhī.hé yě yǐ yǐ   I there.isn't what.about.3 ASSERT FINAL FINAL

Here is the translation offered by James Legge, the nineteenth-century interpreter of the Chinese classics to the English-speaking world:

> The Master said, "Can men refuse to assent to the words of strict admonition? But it is reforming the conduct because of them which is valuable. Can men refuse to be pleased with words of gentle advice? But it is unfolding their aim which is valuable. If a man be pleased with these words, but does not unfold their aim, and assents to those, but does not reform his conduct, I can really do nothing with him."

Comparing Legge's English with the glosses, one can see correspondences, but these fall far short of any one-to-one matching of structural elements between the two languages. For instance, although the two opening words form a subject–verb structure, other words translated as verbs often have no subject – in the third line, who or what might "be able" to do something? (In this case Legge supplies the very general subject "men", but it is not that Chinese omits subjects only where a European language might use a general term like French *on*, German *man* – subjects very commonly do not appear even when, if they did appear, they would probably be quite specific.) The last three lines are translated as an "if ... (then) ..." structure, but nothing in the Chinese marks them as such.

In the last line, *rú zhī hé* is an idiom, meaning something like "what about it/him?" (the three words could be glossed literally as "as 3 what?"); the English "can do [anything] with him" is far more specific than the original. Following that are three words all of which have the force of making what precedes a definite and complete assertion. (The two words romanized *yǐ* are different words, beginning with different consonants in Old Chinese, which happen to fall together in modern Mandarin pronunciation.) This piling-up of assertive closing particles is typical of Classical Chinese prose, which often gives European readers the impression that it is very explicit about making an assertion but far from explicit about what is asserted.

With a language as structurally different from English as this, "translation" cannot be a simple replacement of elements of one language by corresponding elements of the other, as translation between modern European languages often is. What Legge has done (and all that a translator can do) would be better described as inventing wording that Confucius might have used, if Confucius had been an English-speaker.

We have discussed a Classical Chinese example at length in order to counter any suggestion that the kind of phenomena discussed by David Gil (what we might call "*ayam makan* phenomena") are restricted to low-prestige local spoken vernaculars. The *Analects* is one of the "Four Books" which have provided the canonical philosophical underpinnings to one of the longest-lasting and most successful civilizations that have ever existed on Earth. It might not be a stretch to say that the Four Books fulfilled much the same functions for China as Plato's dialogues and the New Testament fulfilled for Europe. The Classical Chinese in which they are written remained, with some development, the standard written language of China for millennia, until it was replaced early in the twentieth century by a written version of the modern spoken language (which is structurally rather different). Any suggestion that a language needs to offer structural equivalences to the grammar of modern European languages in order to serve the needs of a high civilization is just wrong.

To say that logic is universal and independent of individual cultures may be true, but it is not very relevant. Unlike the ancient Greeks, Chinese thinkers of the classical period had very little interest in logical matters. A persuasive discourse for them was not one whose successive statements approximate the form of syllogisms, but one in which they exhibit parallelism of wording (as in the *Analects* extract, e.g. *fǎ yǔ zhī yán ... sùn yǔ zhī yán; gǎi zhī wéi guì ... yì zhī wéi guì*). Charles Everett's claim that the laws of grammar reflect logical laws is grossly simplistic with respect to the European languages he was discussing; as a generalization about the languages of the world, it would be absurd.[7]

---

7 A defender of the relevance of logic might urge that it is *desirable* for languages to encode the universal structures of logic fairly directly, so that the languages of the world "ought" ideally to resemble one another in that respect. Whether or not that is so, our point is that in fact they don't.

A sceptic might claim that the structural differences between Classical Chinese and modern European languages are smaller than they seem at first sight. We once read a paper in an academic journal[8] which argued that a human language could not be as lacking in explicit grammar as written Classical Chinese, so there must have been grammatical apparatus in the spoken language which was not recorded in writing. Chinese script is not phonetic but (simply put) assigns a distinct graph to each word; the suggestion was that when the language was a live spoken language, the words must have been inflected, but the script recorded only the roots, ignoring the inflexions.

If that were true, it would be remarkable that modern spoken Chinese preserves no remnants of the putative inflexion patterns;[9] and it would be mysterious how written Classical Chinese could have functioned as a successful communication system. And there are other reasons why it cannot be true. For instance, the language had contrasts between full and reduced forms of pronouns, as English *you* in unstressed positions can be pronounced *ya*, and the script distinguished these (cf. 10.9 below). Is it credible that a writing system would carefully distinguish pronunciation variants with no semantic significance, yet ignore aspects of pronunciation which were crucial for meaning?

Another possible sceptical line is to say that European languages as well as Chinese are often inexplicit about items that can unambiguously be recovered in context, and seeming vagueness in Chinese grammar results from taking this principle to an extreme.

The English verb "see" is transitive, but if someone draws our attention to something that has just happened in our presence, we can reply either "I saw it" or just "I saw". The object of "see" is apparent from what was just said, so we will not spell it out; often, in English, we will nevertheless represent the object by an empty placeholding pronoun, but we do not have to do that. Languages differ in the extent to which they have the option of omitting the obvious; in Hungarian, the verb inflects differently for specific versus unspecific objects, so that *látom* means "I see it" while *látok* means "I see some unspecified object" or just "I have my sight", and there is no possibility of neutralizing

---

8 Unfortunately we have not succeeded in retrieving the specific reference we have in mind, though for instance Creel (1936: 125–126), Rosemont (1974), and Mair (1994: 708–712) made similar claims less explicitly. We do not know of any Chinese scholars who have accepted this point of view.

9 A possible exception is the handful of pairs of words (e.g. *hǎo* "good" versus *hào* "to love") which are related in meaning but differ in tone, where the difference is believed to reflect an earlier derivational suffix. But these cases are far too few to undermine the point made above (and in any case derivation is only marginally part of "grammar").

the contrast. Classical Chinese went the other way: much more often than English, it represented what was obvious by silence. Walter Bisang (2009) uses this strategy to challenge Gil's account of *ayam makan* phenomena, with respect to Classical Chinese and various other languages of East and South-East Asia, though we are not sure whether Bisang would want to claim that the whole contrast in structural explicitness between Classical Chinese and European languages can be explained by reference to a Chinese preference for omitting the obvious.

We do not believe the contrast can be explained that way. Where Chinese is silent about something which European grammar would require to be explicit, frequently it is *not* obvious what is intended. Consider the fact that verbal elements often lack subjects. Those who translate Chinese poetry are familiar with the problem that it is often unclear whether the poet is describing his own activities, or reporting his observation of things done by others. A translation into a European language must opt for one or the other. If the view we have associated with Bisang applied to this, we would have to say that in the poet's mind it was clear whether he was thinking "I did ..." or "*X* did ...", but that, as written, the poems are ambiguous between well-defined alternatives. This is not the view taken by Chinese commentators themselves. James Liu uses a poem by the eighth-century-AD writer Wang Wei to discuss this issue. The poem begins:

(4) *Kōng shān   bú jiàn rén*
     empty mountain not see people

   dàn wén rén   yǔ xiǎng
   only hear people talk sound

and Liu (1962: 41) comments:

> The poet simply says "not see people", not "I do not see anyone" or even "One does not see anyone"; consequently no awkward questions such as "If no one is here, who is hearing the voices?" or "If you are here, how can the mountains be said to be empty?" will occur to the reader ... the missing subject can be readily identified with anyone, whether the reader or some imaginary person. Consequently, Chinese poetry often has an impersonal and universal quality, compared with which much Western poetry appears egocentric and earth-bound.

The possible aesthetic advantages of this feature of Chinese grammar are not our concern here. Our point is that, for Liu, the subjectless clauses are *not* ambiguous, in the way that Gil describes "the chicken is ready to eat" as ambiguous – it is not that "see" and "hear" have subject slots which contain specific entries in the poet's mind but which the reader is unable to identify, rather the subject role is genuinely blank for poet as well as readers, in the same way that an English statement about a cooked chicken being ready may be vague about cooking method.

1.6 It cuts both ways

If a sceptic, who believes that the range of possible thought-structures is prior to particular languages, continues to press the point that prose like the *Analects* extract must have been understood as meaning something more fully articulated than it appears at the surface, comparable to the Legge translation, because only a structure of thought with that degree of articulation "makes sense", then another response is to confront the sceptic with cases where an exotic grammar is *more* specific than English. It is not that languages independent of the European classical heritage always differ from European languages in the direction of structural vagueness. Sometimes it is the other way round. Franz Boas gave many examples where the grammars of various American Indian languages require speakers to be explicit about issues which European languages commonly leave open. He takes as an example the English sentence "The man is sick":

> We express by this sentence, in English, the idea, *a definite single man at present sick.*
> In Kwakiutl [a native language of British Columbia, nowadays called Kwak'wala] this
> sentence would have to be rendered by an expression which would mean, in the vaguest
> possible form that could be given to it, *definite man near him invisible sick near him
> invisible.* ... In Ponca, one of the Siouan dialects, the same idea would require a decision
> of the question whether the man is at rest or moving, and we might have a form like *the
> moving single man sick.* (Boas 1911: 39)

If we say that someone is ill (or, in American English, sick), are we happy to agree that we have spoken ambiguously, because the hearer might understand us to be referring either to someone we can see or someone out of sight (or, to someone moving or someone at rest)? The present authors do not have any feeling that, in English, the utterance is "ambiguous" in these ways – commonly, if we say that someone is ill, there will be no thought in our mind about whether he is visible or not; we may not even know whether he is moving. "*X* is ill" represents a thought complete in itself.

If the sceptic agrees with that, and sees Kwakiutl and Ponca as requiring specificity about issues which the pre-existing range of possible thought-structures allows to be left vague, while at the same time insisting that the *Analects* passage must have been interpreted by its original Chinese readers with a degree of explicitness that resembled the Legge translation more than the surface Chinese wording, because that wording is "too vague to make sense", then it is fairly clear that "making sense" is being understood as "translatable without much loss or addition into the language I speak". Surely we cannot take very seriously the idea that just those languages which *we* happen to speak are languages whose grammars are neither unnecessarily specific nor unduly vague but, like Goldilocks's porridge, just right?

We take it, rather, that the grammars of different languages are fairly good guides to the structures of thought available to their respective speakers. "I there.isn't what.about.3" would not be a complete thought for us as speakers of modern English or Hungarian, but for a Chinese of 2500 years ago it was. "The man is ill" would not be a complete thought for a Kwakiutl or Ponca speaker, but, for us, "The man is ill" in English, or *A férfi beteg* in Hungarian, is a complete thought.

Consequently, we shall take for granted from now on that the grammar of a language is a system which has to be evolved by the community of speakers, along lines which are not set in advance and do not lead towards any natural terminus; so that different languages may have developed structurally in different directions, and it is open to individual speakers of a language to play their part in the continuing process of grammatical development.

(Even the most central, "core" constructions must have begun as novel cultural developments once. Guy Deutscher (2000) has shown that in the case of the very early written language Akkadian we can actually witness the process by which it equipped itself for the first time with complement clauses, by adapting a grammatical element previously used for a different purpose; see p. 199 below.)

1.7 Vocabulary differences

Incidentally, this picture of how languages behave in the domain of grammar, which many linguists find intuitively difficult to countenance, would seem very normal in the domain of vocabulary. Most people recognize that individual languages will often develop vocabulary items that cannot straightforwardly be translated into the vocabulary of other languages, and that innovation in vocabulary is a bottom-up process in which any individual speaker can participate, though no doubt some individuals do much more of it than others. (When we think about incommensurability of vocabulary, probably most of us think first of words for sophisticated cultural abstractions, but plenty of examples can be found at the level of simple concrete everyday words. Ernst Leisi, whose book *Der Wortinhalt* is enlightening on vocabulary incommensurability between German and English, discusses for instance the difficulty of finding good English translations for the concrete nouns *Zapfen* and *Scheibe*, neither of which relate to culture-specific phenomena (Leisi 1974: 30).)

Furthermore, those of us who are parents are surely familiar with the idea that grammar acquisition tends to lag behind acquisition of vocabulary – a small child will typically have mastered many words for concrete objects, animals, food, and so on, at a stage when his or her grammatical production seems very impoverished relative to what it will be in later years. If people accept that learning lexical items is genuinely a matter of acquiring concepts as well as verbal forms which are not given in advance, it might seem odd that they are so attached to the idea that acquiring grammar is about merely learning how to verbalize pre-existing structures of thought. Would we not expect progress to be faster where more is predetermined?

The explanation, we suggest, is that once one has mastered the grammar of one's mother tongue, the fact that its structures provide the architecture of one's articulate thinking makes it near-impossible to conceive that those structures could be otherwise – they become the structures which "make sense" to us. We can fairly easily imagine what it would be like not to have the concept "elephant", but we cannot imagine what it would be like not to have a past tense. That is why grammar *feels* as if it were predetermined; but if we look at grammatical differences between languages, we see that it cannot be.

It is true that there have been linguists who believe that even vocabulary is in some sense predetermined. Notably, Jerry Fodor's book *The Language of Thought* (1975) argued that any first language is acquired by learning how to translate its forms into those of a common, innately given "language of thought"; and Fodor focuses mainly on the vocabulary side of languages. Fodor believes that although the vocabularies of languages cannot always be put into a one-to-one correspondence with each other, they are commensurable in the sense that any vocabulary item in any language has a perfect translation into the "language of thought", which itself has a finite vocabulary – some of the translations might equate individual words with multi-word structures, but one will be able to get from any language via the language of thought to perfect equivalents in any other language. However, Fodor's argument is wholly aprioristic. He never compares elements of English with those of any other language, and he says very little about what he envisages the hypothetical "language of thought" to be like.[10] We do not believe that questions about relationships between the world's languages can usefully be addressed without looking at any languages.

1.8 What can be said about grammar

Of course, while ours may be a minority position, we are by no means the first linguists in the past half-century to have questioned the concept of "grammaticality". We have discussed that issue in this introductory chapter in order to provide a background for the detailed studies in later chapters; the main point of the book is not merely to argue against the grammaticality concept, but to present a range of concrete positive findings about grammar that emerge when one gives that concept up. The fact that grammaticality may be a myth does not imply that there is little to say about grammar in general, above the level of studies of particular constructions in individual languages. It might well be desirable for the division of effort in linguistics to be rebalanced towards a larger share for research on individual languages, dialects, language-families, etc., and a smaller share for general linguistics, but a smaller share should certainly not be a zero share. There is plenty to say about grammar in general. This book aims to say some of it.

Our way of thinking about "grammar in general", though, does not involve advocating some novel way of defining grammars of human languages, as some readers may be expecting. For decades, theorists of grammar have been arguing the toss between formalisms such as "X-bar theory", "lexical-functional grammar", "tree-adjoining grammar", "relational grammar", and many others. We shall not be adding a new candidate to this list of rival ways of defining grammars, nor shall we be taking sides in the debates between existing candidates – we do not see much point in those debates.

We recognize that there are some structural generalizations to be made about grammar in any human language. People have been aware for a very

---

10 In over 200 pages we have found just one place where Fodor mentions a specific element of a language other than English: on p. 105 he claims that "the dog" translates into French as *le chein* (sic). But even if this were correct, it does nothing to support Fodor's theory of relatedness between languages; he does not, for instance, use the example to discuss differences between French and English use of articles, or to say whether the "language of thought" uses articles the English way, the French way, or some other way. Even authors who strongly support the idea that languages have fixed grammatical rules which are largely innate no longer seem to take Fodor's idea seriously; see e.g. Margolis and Laurence (2012: sec. 5), Berwick and Chomsky (forthcoming: footnote 6).

long time that *hierarchy* – tree structure – is central to grammar. Words group into small units such as phrases, the small units group into larger units, and so on up to the largest units having structural coherence, complex sentences containing subordinate clauses which may in turn themselves contain clauses at lower levels of subordination. When grammatical constructions involve shifting groups of words from one position to another (say, as questions in English involve shifting the questioned element from its logical position to the front – "*Which brush* did you paint it with? I painted it with *that brush*"), the words moved will typically be a complete unit in the tree structure, rather than (say) comprising the last word or two of one unit and the opening word(s) of the following unit.

We do not need the linguistics of the last century to tell us about the centrality of tree structure in grammar, though it was perhaps only in the twentieth century that anyone thought to ask why this particular abstract type of structure should be so important. That question was answered in 1962 by the psychologist, artificial intelligence expert, and economics Nobel prizewinner Herbert Simon. Simon's essay "The architecture of complexity" (Simon 1962) showed that any complex products of gradual (cultural or biological) evolution are, as a matter of statistical inevitability, overwhelmingly likely to display hierarchical structure. (On the implications of Simon's ideas for linguistics, see Sampson 2005: 141–150.) It is just much easier to develop small units and then build on them stepwise in developing larger structures, than to move from no structure to complicated structure in one fell swoop. The fact that we each learn our mother tongue by building up from small to large in this way is why we, like Meiklejohn, can recognize sub-sentential word sequences such as *in his hand* as meaningful units.

Human languages are culturally-evolved institutions, so Simon's argument explains why tree structure is commonly found in them – though we shall see in chapter 6 that even this rather weak generalization about human-language grammar is not without exceptions. The idea that grammatical theory should be about detailed descriptive formalisms stems from a widespread belief that the languages of the world share universal structural properties which are much more specific than a mere tendency to assemble large units out of smaller ones. As Steven Pinker (1995: 409) has put it:

> the babel of languages no longer appear to vary in arbitrary ways and without limit. One now sees a common design to the machinery underlying the world's language, a Universal Grammar.

The formalisms serve as a way of codifying the alleged universal grammar: the idea is that the correct formalisms will provide a definition for any structure which obeys the universal constraints on language diversity, but a hypothetical "unnatural" language which violates the constraints would be one that is not definable within the formalisms.

We, on the other hand, see no mechanism that could constrain ever-changing languages scattered across the face of the planet all to share detailed structural features – and so far as we can tell, contrary to Pinker's claim they do not in fact do so (a point to which we shall return in chapter 5). Consequently we are not interested in descriptive formalisms. We (like Haspelmath 2010) believe that linguists should be encouraged to describe the diverse language structures of the world using whatever descriptive techniques they find clear and convenient.

The sort of questions which seem to us worth asking about grammar in general are questions like these:

- If the grammatical structure of a language is developed by the community which uses it, and acquired by individual speakers, along lines that are not prescribed in advance, how refined does that structure become?
- Are there particular areas of grammar which are less, or more, precisely defined than other areas?
- Do the answers to some of these questions differ as between written and spoken modes of language?
- Can we make any generalizations about the path taken by children towards the levels of grammatical refinement achieved by adults? (Many linguists have studied the early stages of child language acquisition, as children take their first steps away from one-word utterances and begin to put words together – later stages have been less studied, perhaps because to linguists who believe that the endpoint of the process is in some sense given in advance, those stages seem less interesting.)

As phrased here, these questions are general, in the sense that they do not relate to particular constructions in individual languages, which might not have counterparts in other languages. They arise for all languages (except that the question about written and spoken modes applies only to languages which possess both modes).

However, the questions can only fruitfully be studied by reference to a particular language or languages. It is reasonable to hope that the findings for one language will be at least suggestive for other languages, but how similar languages are with respect to these issues could emerge only from comparison of separate studies. Since the questions are rather new, we have had the opportunity of researching aspects of them for only one language: modern English, the language which both co-authors share.

Thus, to summarize, we have set out to enquire into *the growth and limits of grammatical precision* in English.

1.9 The computational viewpoint

The direction from which we have approached the topic is computational linguistics. Both co-authors have spent years developing so-called *treebanks* – structurally-annotated electronic samples of real-life English of various written and spoken genres – intended largely as sources of data for computational natural-language analysis and processing systems. For some readers, this may seem a specialist discipline remote from their own interests. However, the work has features which give its results particular relevance for the pure academic study of language as an aspect of human cognition and behaviour.

When we set out to equip samples of real-life language with annotations identifying their grammatical structures, we have to deal with everything the samples contain; we cannot pick and choose. We have to use a scheme of annotation which provides means of logging any structural phenomena that crop up, and we must develop explicit guidelines specifying how the annotation applies to debatable cases – in order to ensure that the statistics extracted by our computers reliably count apples with apples and oranges with oranges. The point has been well put by the computational linguist Jane Edwards of the University of California, Berkeley (J. Edwards 1992: 139):

> The single most important property of any data base for purposes of computer-aided research is that *similar instances be encoded in predictably similar ways.*

These imperatives of comprehensiveness and consistency give us (we believe) a clearer perspective on the degrees of structural complexity actually present in various areas of the language than is commonly achieved by non-computational approaches. A linguist whose goal is to develop rules reflecting speakers' linguistic competence, as an aspect of their psychological functioning, will quote examples that clearly bear on known issues about grammar rules, but may overlook or avoid discussing examples containing messy little turns of phrase whose implications for the overall grammar are not clear one way or the other.

In principle that might be a reasonable thing to do. A scientist will often be justified in looking for an equation which accounts well for the bulk of his data-points, discarding a few anomalous readings where the data may somehow have been corrupted. The trouble is, with language it is not a question of a handful of anomalies: in our experience, a very high proportion of real-life usage contains oddities which one might be tempted to set aside – only, as computational linguists, we cannot set them aside. The picture of grammar which emerges from non-computational approaches tends to be neater and simpler than the reality, to an extent that (we believe) seriously distorts our understanding of what kind of phenomena languages are. Languages are often seen as artificially schematic, Esperanto-like systems, whereas in reality they are grainy, irregular accumulations of complication and inconsequentiality.

(Ironically, there is one class of languages which really are of the former, schematic kind: computer programming languages. But our computational research teaches us that human languages are not at all like programming languages.)

The proof of the pudding is in the eating. Some of the findings we discuss in later chapters should be of interest, we believe, to anyone who cares about the subtle human ability to speak and understand language. We would not have been led to these findings if we had not been working within a computationally-oriented intellectual framework. But, irrespective of how we came to them, the findings speak for themselves. They have things to say to linguists working in almost any framework.

Chapter 2
The bounds of grammatical refinement

2.1 An experiment

The first issue we wish to address is: how refined is English grammar?

Any linguist recognizes that a classification of English grammatical structures must distinguish, say, between prepositional phrases (such as *in his hand*) and nominal clauses (such as (*I knew*) *that you could do it*) – these are structures with different internal constituency and fulfilling different functions. But how far can this process of delimiting and classifying tagmas be taken?[1] If an individual were invited to assign structure to language-samples at whim, the process of identifying tagma boundaries and inventing ever-subtler grammatical categories might be restrained only by his fancy, but the question is about the degree of refinement which is objectively meaningful enough to be applied the same way by independent grammatical analysts. And, when analysts disagree about the grammar of particular examples, is this a limitation of the analytic scheme, or a limit in individual human beings' ability to apply it?

For an analogy to this last question, consider the idea of measuring the size of clouds. When we see a cumulus cloud sailing through a blue sky, it surely makes sense to ask how large it is – we could certainly quote a number of cubic metres which is clearly far too low, and a much larger number which is clearly far too high. But it is not obvious what determines how precisely the size could be measured. Clouds have irregular shapes, so one would have to try to measure all the bulges and hollows, not just on the side we can see from the ground but the other side too – even with 21st-century technology this would surely be a challenging task. But also, clouds are fuzzy things, so it is not clear how precise a figure would even be meaningful. We surmise that no reasonable way of defining cloud boundaries would make a figure meaningful to the nearest cubic

---

1 Linguists commonly use the term *constituent* for a grammatical unit – a sequence of one or more words dominated by a single node at some level within a tree structure. But a "constituent" is by definition part of a larger unit (so the entire word-sequence below the topmost node in a tree is not a constituent), and a single word will be a constituent of some larger unit. We are assuming that (at least to a rough approximation) the breakdown of sentences into words is given; what interests us are the higher units into which words are grouped, including the most comprehensive multi-word units of all, such as sentences. The term for wording dominated by a non-terminal tree node is *tagma*.

metre – surely cloud-size is inherently vaguer than that? But, if we knew how precise a figure for cloud sizes could in principle be achieved, does that limit on precision stem from limits of our measuring technology, or limits to the exactness of the property measured?

For cloud sizes, the present authors have no idea what the answer is. But for English grammatical analysis we have begun to uncover answers to analogous questions.

To address the issue, we need a detailed and comprehensive scheme for registering the grammatical properties of samples of the English language (a "grammatical annotation scheme"); and we need to compare the results when this scheme is applied independently to the same set of samples by separate analysts. In our case, an annotation scheme was already available when we began studying the issue under consideration. The independent application to common samples and comparison of results was an experiment carried out for the purpose of the study.

The annotation scheme we used was the *SUSANNE scheme*, defined in the book *English for the Computer* (Sampson 1995). This scheme was developed and refined over a period of many years beginning in 1983 at the University of Lancaster, for use in creating and doing statistical research on "treebanks" as defined in the Preface. In fact the first treebank developed using this scheme was so far as we know the earliest treebank created anywhere in the English-speaking world (and the term "treebank" itself, though now in universal use, was a Lancaster coinage); the SUSANNE scheme was developed in connection with the SUSANNE Corpus. (For access details on the corpus resources to be discussed in this book, see the Preface.)

The SUSANNE scheme aims to represent a consensus point of view about English grammar, recording facts which linguists of different theoretical persuasions would so far as possible all be happy to interpret in their own terms. (Although the initiative to create the scheme was led by GRS, it is important to make clear that it was very much a team effort – a chief contributor in the early, intensive phase of scheme development was Geoffrey Leech, one of the world's most distinguished authorities on English grammar, and at different times the scheme was worked on by some fifteen to twenty people.) At the same time the scheme aims to be comprehensive, providing a way of recording any grammatical distinction that is likely to be seen as significant by more than the odd one-off maverick linguist; and above all it aims at rigorous explicitness, so that ideally the published definition of the scheme should never leave room for doubt about how a given English-language form should be annotated. (How close that ideal can be approached in practice is part of the issue we aim to study.)[2]

Since the early work from which the SUSANNE scheme emerged, other groups of computational linguists have developed their own annotation schemes and applied them in creating other English-language treebanks. Notably, the Pennsylvania group led by Mitchell Marcus have used their own scheme to develop treebanks which in terms of wordage dwarf the SUSANNE Corpus and any other samples to which the SUSANNE scheme has been applied. But it is fair to say that the Pennsylvania initiative is characterized by different priorities. The aim there is to maximize the quantity of language samples analysed, so that statistical counts can deliver numbers large enough to be usable for automatic language-processing purposes. The SUSANNE priority, by contrast, was to maximize the delicacy and definitional rigour of the annotation scheme. This, certainly, is how the respective schemes are seen by independent third parties. Lin Dekang (then Professor of Computing Science at the University of Alberta, now Staff Research Scientist at Google) commented that "Compared with other possible alternatives such as the Penn Treebank ... [t]he SUSANNE corpus puts more emphasis on precision and consistency" (Lin 2003: 321). Terence Langendoen wrote, shortly before he became President of the Linguistic Society of America, that "the detail [of the SUSANNE scheme] is unrivalled" (Langendoen 1997).

Because computing technology is capable of processing very large quantities of material almost instantaneously, there is a standing temptation for researchers who use this technology to treat close study of individual instances as too small-scale an activity to take seriously. We recognize that large-scale research on overall aggregates has a valuable role, but we also believe that, in the domain of language, painstaking attention to individual examples is a source of insights that cannot be arrived at in other ways, and deserves its share of research effort irrespective of whether language samples are stored and retrieved using computers or manually. We hope that what follows will illustrate that principle.

---

2 The bulk of the published scheme definition is contained in the book *English for the Computer*, already cited. In online documentation it has subsequently been extended, to cover spoken English more fully than was possible in the 1995 book (www.grsampson.net/ChrisDoc.html), and to cover the writing of unskilled writers (www.grsampson.net/LucyDoc.html). However, these extensions were not relevant to the language samples used for the experiment described below. The only additions and revisions to the 1995 version of the scheme that were treated as operative for this experiment were the relatively small collection listed in sections 14–15 of ChrisDoc.html.

2.2 The experimental material

The analysts who independently applied the annotation scheme to a common set of language samples were the present co-authors. As samples we used a set of ten extracts from diverse written documents in the British National Corpus ("BNC") each 2000+ words long (i.e. each containing at least 2000 words, but beginning and ending at natural breaks, hence in practice rather longer); all were categorized as "polished" (edited published) writing, as opposed to informal or ephemeral documents.

The choice of polished writing, rather than informal writing or speech, was in practice a necessary consequence of the fact that we needed to use corpus material that we had on hand, and which one analyst had already annotated but the other was known not to have looked at (so that there could be no "contamination" of one analyst's judgements by the other). However, it would in any case have been the right choice. Annotating informal writing or speech introduces many issues about how to handle writer errors, unclarities of speech transcription, and so forth, which are additional to the issues about well-definedness of the notation scheme for English language structure, and obscure the latter. These additional issues are interesting and important in their own right (and some of them will be considered in later chapters), but for an initial exploration such as that reported here it was advisable to restrict the problem domain by focusing on polished writing.

The following listing of the genres of the source documents gives an impression of the range covered; we also give brief mnemonics used below to refer to the individual samples, since the identifiers used internally in our work are not transparent. When, later in this chapter, we quote individual passages from our samples, these mnemonics will be followed by five-digit numbers locating the passages within their BNC files in terms of the BNC division into "s-units" (roughly speaking, sentences).[3]

---

3 The samples were ones that had been annotated by GRS as part of the LUCY treebank, which applies the SUSANNE annotation scheme to passages of written English; all the LUCY files used for this experiment were derived from the written section of the British National Corpus. It may be worth mentioning that when the LUCY treebank was created, we took the source for "Legion" to be a work of fiction, but it later emerged that it was published as a non-fictional memoir; hence the sample-set is weighted even more heavily to non-fiction than we intended. We doubt that this has significantly affected the experiment.

genre of source file	mnemonic
book on librarianship	Librarian
City material from *The Guardian* newspaper	City
cookery book	Cook
art magazine	Art
women's magazine	Women
law reports	Law
two reviews of books on literary linguistics	Ling
Irish bank staff association newsletter	Bank
memoir of life in the French Foreign Legion	Legion
novel set in India	Novel

Ideally, an experiment of this kind would involve more than two analysts, and a body of analysed material larger than 20,000-odd words. But this is a case where the ideal must bow to what is practical. We were not aiming to study the process by which newcomers learn an annotation scheme, but to study how accurately it can be used by individuals who have already mastered it thoroughly; for a scheme of this level of complexity, that means that the analysts had to be people who had years of experience of working with it, and in the circumstances of university research there are never likely to be more than a tiny number of individuals meeting that requirement available at any time.[4] Also, because of the intricate nature of the annotation scheme and the degree of detail in which it was necessary to scrutinize individual annotation discrepancies, even the

---

[4] It is that point which justifies the strategy of using an annotation scheme for which the experimental subjects' own research group was responsible. Some readers may feel that it would have been preferable to ask experimental subjects to apply some independent group's scheme of grammatical analysis; in principle we might agree, but that would imply requiring subjects to devote several years of their working lives to acquiring adequate mastery of a system which would be of no further use to them after the experiment was over. Clearly that is unrealistic.

Incidentally, in case it should be suggested that the fact of one analyst not being a native speaker of English undermines the validity of our experiment, we do not agree with that. It has often been shown that educated non-native language users tend to make more accurate judgements about subtle aspects of language structure than the average native speaker (e.g. Chipere 2003: 3, 178–180). For what it is worth, in several years of face-to-face collaboration GRS does not recall AB ever manifesting sub-native-speaker competence in English.

quantity of material we used represented a serious research challenge; and it proved sufficient to yield a number of rather clear and interesting findings.[5]

2.3 The analytic scheme

In order to follow our quantitative findings on inter-annotator agreement, it is necessary to know something both of the general nature of the SUSANNE annotation scheme, and of the metric we used to assess the similarity of pairs of analyses of the same texts.

To give the reader an impression of the analytic scheme, we begin with a simple example: a brief, artificial text chosen to include the main scheme features. The example is the one-sentence paragraph:

(5)   *Mr Jones expected her to admit it.*

This would be assigned the labelled bracketing:

[O [S [Nns:s *Mr Jones*] [Vd *expected*] [Nos:O123 *her*] [Ti:o [s123 GHOST] [Vi *to admit*] [Ni:o *it*]]].]

which is a typographically compact representation of the tree structure displayed in Figure 3. These equivalent annotations say symbolically that the whole is a paragraph, O, consisting of one main clause, S, and the full stop. The main clause has four immediate constituents (ICs):
- *Mr Jones*, which is a proper noun phrase, Nn, in singular form, s, functioning as surface and logical subject, :s, of the main clause
- a verb group, V (consisting in this case just of one word, *expected*) marked for past tense, d
- *her*, an object-marked singular pronoun, Nos, which is surface but not logical direct object of its clause, :O, and which is linked by an index 123 to its logical counterpart elsewhere in the structure
- an infinitival clause, Ti, functioning as logical object, :o, of the main clause

and the infinitival clause in turn contains:

---

5 The following sections describe our experiment in terms intended to be accessible to outsiders to this research area. It omits various technicalities which newcomers might find confusing; readers wishing to check our findings in detail are recommended to consult our original research report (Sampson and Babarczy 2008).

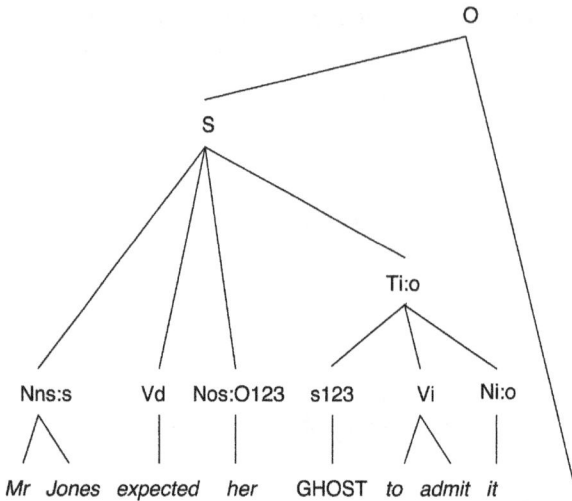

Figure 3: A SUSANNE tree structure

- a "ghost" element (some linguists would call it a "trace") functioning as logical subject, :s, and co-referential with *her* in the main clause, but realized by no verbal material of its own
- *to admit*, an infinitival verb group, Vi
- a noun phrase headed by (and in this case consisting entirely of) the word *it*, Ni, functioning as surface and logical object of the subordinate clause, :o

(Note that, in our annotation scheme, the term *verb group* refers to the unit consisting of the main verb of a clause together with any auxiliaries that may precede it: *expected* is a one-word verb group, but sequences such as *will expect, to expect, had been expected*, and so forth are also verb groups. We say "verb group" rather than "verb phrase" to distinguish this unit from the "VP" tagma recognized by generative linguists, which comprises not only verb(s) but also object and/or other complements – e.g. *expect a letter* would be a VP for generative theory. Our analytic scheme does not treat "verb phrases" as units; subject, verb group, and object are three sister constituents of a clause.)

In this example :s, :O, :o, and the s which labels the ghost node are called *functiontags*, identifying the functional role of the element within its clause; the other label-elements (apart from the index) are called *formtags*, classifying the elements they label formally. Under the SUSANNE scheme, each tagma receives a formtag, and most constituents of clauses additionally receive a functiontag. The system of formtags recognizes 32 main classes of constituent, together with

64 subcategories, various combinations of which can apply to various main categories. Additionally, certain types of multi-word sequence can be marked as grammatically equivalent to single words of particular classes. The function-tag system recognizes 23 roles for constituents of clauses. The scheme provides for "ghost" or null tokens which identify the logical place and role of items that in surface grammar occur elsewhere ("guests"); numerical indices (here, "123") are used to show which ghost element is represented by which surface guest element, since in a long passage there may be many such pairs.

The purpose of the 499 pages of *English for the Computer* is to provide guidelines which so far as possible eliminate all ambiguities about how this system of symbols should be applied, so that for any form of words found in real-life English usage there should ideally be one and just one annotation that conforms to those guidelines. The scheme aims to represent all features and distinctions which are commonly recognized by grammarians, and it seeks to embody uncontroversial, consensus conceptions of language structure; but it makes no claims to be the "correct" analysis (in terms of speakers' psychological models of their language or in other respects). It is explicitly a classification system imposed on the English language, rather than a scientific theory about the nature of the language; the principle that there should always be a single, predictable notation available for any form of words is given precedence over the aim that the notations of the scheme should mirror theoretical linguists' analyses.

Since most readers will be unfamiliar with the details of SUSANNE notation, in what follows we shall as far as possible discuss our experimental findings using the ordinary grammatical terms which are used in *English for the Computer* to gloss the SUSANNE symbols. But it will be important to grasp that the scheme explicitly eliminates the vagueness or ambiguity which inhere in many of these traditional terms. For instance, the SUSANNE functiontag :i is glossed as "indirect object". For some grammarians, an "indirect object" is a noun phrase which, like a direct object, is marked by no preceding preposition; other grammarians would describe *Harry* as indirect object not only in *I gave Harry a cup of tea* but also in *I gave a cup of tea to Harry*. Again, some grammarians restrict the use of the term to "second objects" in clauses which also contain a direct object; others call a sole object "indirect", if the semantic relationship between it and the verb is characteristic of indirect rather than direct objects (as in e.g. *I paid Harry*). §§5.22–28 of *English for the Computer* are designed to remove these and other ambiguities from the use of the SUSANNE :i symbol, and other passages do likewise for each of the other elements of the notation. References beginning with "§" in what follows will refer to the numbered subsections of *English for the Computer*.

2.4 Measuring similarity of analyses

To assess how far independent analyses of our sample texts diverge from one another, we need a way to quantify similarity or difference between alternative labelled tree structures over the same sequence of words. For computational linguists this is a familiar issue: the performance of automatic parsing systems is assessed by comparing the parse-trees they output with "gold-standard" trees representing the desired analyses of the respective language samples. Our situation differs from that, in that we are comparing pairs of trees neither of which is regarded as more authoritative than the other; but this does not affect the calculations to be performed.

The metric we used was the *leaf-ancestor metric*. In chapter 12, below, we shall discuss experimental evidence to show that this is a successful operationalization of pre-theoretical ideas of parse accuracy – more successful than a more widely-known alternative. We shall not give a detailed definition of the leaf-ancestor metric at this point, but in essence it measures similarity between trees by comparing the *lineages* within the respective trees of successive words. The "lineage" of a word is the list of node-labels on the path linking that word to the topmost node of the tree: for instance, in the small-scale example of Figure 3 above, the lineage of the word *admit* is:

Vi] Ti:o S O

(A left or right bracket within a lineage marks the highest point in the tree where the word in question is respectively the first or the last word of a tagma: *admit* is the last word of the Vi to *admit*. Including these elements within lineages is necessary in order to ensure that identity of lineages implies identity of tree structures.)

The metric computes similarity between the lineages of a given word in alternative trees in terms of the edit distance between the respective label-sequences (that is, the minimum number of deletions and insertions needed to change one sequence into the other), computed in a fashion whereby 1 represents identical lineages and 0 represents no relationship between the respective lineages. Figures for the lineages of successive words are averaged to give an overall figure for a text.[6]

---

6 Strictly, the elements at the terminal nodes of SUSANNE parse-trees are not always "words", for instance we saw in 2.3 that the full stop at the end of the example sentence has a terminal node of its own. But the term "word" is so much simpler than more precise alternatives such as "leaf-node label" or "terminal element" that we have preferred to use "word" here.

2.5 Text complexity

Before examining the similarity or otherwise of the two analysts' annotations, it is worth looking at the relative complexity of the various samples. One might expect that the ability of independent analysts to produce matching annotations would correlate with the complexity of the texts analysed: the more there is to say about the structure of a language sample, there more chances there are for analysts to say different things. Table 1 presents measures of the complexity of our ten sample texts, where "complexity" is used in the schoolroom sense of the incidence of clause subordination. For each word we count how deeply embedded within main and subordinate clauses it is (that is, how many elements in its lineage are symbols for main or subordinate – finite or non-finite – clauses); for instance, the word *admit* in the above example would score 2, for the "main clause" symbol S and the "infinitival clause" symbol Ti in its lineage. Then we average over the words of a text to give an overall complexity figure for the text as a whole. In the present experiment we had two figures for each word, one from each analyst, so we averaged over the union of the two sets of figures for a text to give an overall complexity measure for that text: this figure is shown in the middle column of Table 1. The right-hand column gives the maximum complexity count for any word in the respective texts (the maximum counts were always identical for the two analysts' output). It was surely predictable that by far the largest average and maximum complexity figures are for the law-reports text, where the average word is evidently more deeply embedded than within a clause immediately subordinate to a main clause. It seems plausible enough that the lowest average should be for the cookery book.

Table 1: Complexity figures for the sample texts

text	mean complexity	maximum complexity
Library	1·50	5
City	1·82	5
Cook	1·16	4
Art	1·58	6
Women	1·22	4
Law	2·49	9
Ling	1·63	5
Bank	1·53	4
Legion	1·74	6
Novel	1·56	5

Table 2: Inter-analyst agreement on sample text analyses

Text	Mean leaf-ancestor score	Words with identical lineages
Library	0·950	74·8%
City	0·953	74·8%
Cook	0·944	76·5%
Art	0·954	77·2%
Women	0·901	75·2%
Law	0·934	61·1%
Ling	0·938	66·8%
Bank	0·956	77·5%
Legion	0·970	82·0%
Novel	0·955	75·9%
mean	0·945	74·2%

2.6 Overall similarity results

Table 2 shows, in the second column, average leaf-ancestor scores for the ten texts; each figure is close to 1, so the analysts' outputs are predominantly in agreement. (If that were not so, our research could scarcely get off the ground.) The third column gives the percentage of words whose lineages are identical in both analysts' trees. As one would expect, the most complex text has the lowest percentage of identical lineages: the longer the lineages are, the more elements there are in them which may disagree.

Among the mean scores, 0·901 for "Women" is a clear outlier. On examination the reason turned out to be that the lively typography of a long feature in a popular magazine, full of sidebars, coloured headings printed continuously with the text, etc., had stretched the techniques used by the British National Corpus for representing document formatting up to and perhaps beyond their limits, creating a complex file structure that the analysts had interpreted in diverging ways.

These typographical issues are rather separate from the topic of our investigation, so when we give numerical results in what follows these are taken from the set of nine texts omitting Women. (In all but one case, noted below, the figures are very little different whether this text is included or excluded; both sets of figures are available in our original research report.) If the leaf-ancestor score is averaged over nine texts, omitting Women, it rises from 0·945 to 0·950.

In themselves the similarity scores are not very informative, since we have no basis of comparison. It will be more instructive to look at how the discrepancies are divided between different sources of error. There are two questions here:

(i) are there particular aspects of English grammar which lead to disproportionate numbers of discrepancies? and (ii) how is responsibility for the discrepancies shared between inadequacies of the annotation scheme, and human limitations?

2.7 Dividing overall discrepancy between annotation categories

We examined how various aspects of the annotation scheme contributed to the observed level of inter-annotator discrepancy by recomputing the agreement figures while relaxing in various ways the requirements for labels in the respective trees to count as matching, or while discounting failures to match by particular classes of label.

Thus, we can expect many discrepancies to arise from different choices of formtag by the analysts, the formtag system being by far the richest and most complex part of the complete annotation scheme.

Most SUSANNE formtags are classified either as clause or as phrase labels; for instance, in the structure for example (5), Ti and S are clausetags, Nns and Vi are phrasetags. (There are also two minor groups of formtags, "rootrank" and "wordrank" tags – for instance O for "paragraph" is a rootrank tag. We shall discuss those groups later, for the moment we shall examine just the clause and phrase labels.) If agreement figures are recomputed with pairs of phrase or clause labels counted as matching whenever they agree with respect to any features other than formtags (that is, a pair of such labels are treated as matching if either both labels lack a functiontag or they share the same functiontag, and either both lack an index or both have an index, but one may be formtagged as, say, a plural noun phrase while the other is formtagged as a relative clause), then agreement figures for texts naturally rise. The overall mean agreement figure rises from 0·950 to 0·963.

For any one text, we compute the proportion of discrepancy attributable to aspect X of the annotation scheme as:

$$\frac{\text{agreement ignoring differences with respect to } X - \text{overall agreement}}{1 - \text{overall agreement}}$$

On this basis the mean proportion of discrepancy attributable to clause and phrase formtagging is 24·3 per cent.

It seems likely *a priori* that analysts will be more consistent in deciding main form categories (whether a tagma is a noun phrase, an adverb phrase, a relative clause, a nominal clause, an infinitival clause, etc.) than in deciding subcategories (whether a verb group is perfective, whether a noun phrase is a proper name, and so on; whether a tagma of any main category is co-ordinated with, or in apposition to, what precedes; etc.). We tested this by recomputing agreement figures ignoring just subcategory information in clause and phrase formtags. We find that on average 70·7 per cent of the total clause/phrase formtag discrepancy figure is attributable to discrepancies in subcategories.

Apart from formtags, the other elements that may occur in a tagma label are functiontags, and indices. If we relax the definition of label-matching so that labels which are identical except for having different functiontags match, we find a mean agreement figure of 0·965; on average 29·9 per cent of total discrepancy in a text is accountable for in this way.

If indices are ignored, so that otherwise similar labels match despite one having and the other lacking an index, then the mean agreement figure is 0·951; the mean proportion of total discrepancy accounted for in this way is 1·8 per cent.

Apart from phrasetags and clausetags, as already mentioned there are two further classes of formtags. Rootrank formtags include O "paragraph" and Oh "heading", one or the other of which labels each root node, together with labels for the categories "title", "quotation", "interpolation", "tag question", "technical reference". Wordrank formtags cover "grammatical idioms" such as *up to date*, treated by the scheme as orthographic word-sequences that function grammatically as single words, together with co-ordinations between single words.

For these classes of tag it seems likely *a priori* that discrepancies would relate less to different labels for corresponding tree-nodes, than to whether nodes bearing the relevant labels are postulated at all. Where a tagma is regarded as, say, an interpolation, it will be a constituent of some grammatical class and will be formtagged accordingly, but the node bearing that formtag will be dominated by a higher node labelled I, for "interpolation". Thus a typical inter-annotator discrepancy would be, not an I node in one tree corresponding to a node with another label in the other tree, but an I node in one tree having no counterpart node in the other tree, because one analyst does not regard the tagma in question as "interpolated". Likewise, what one analyst treats as an idiom the other analyst may regard as a sequence of words used in their normal senses, and hence not a tagma at all.

Accordingly, the method of relaxing conditions on label-matching is not suitable for investigating discrepancies relating to these aspects of annotation. Instead, we computed agreement figures by relaxing the requirement that labels

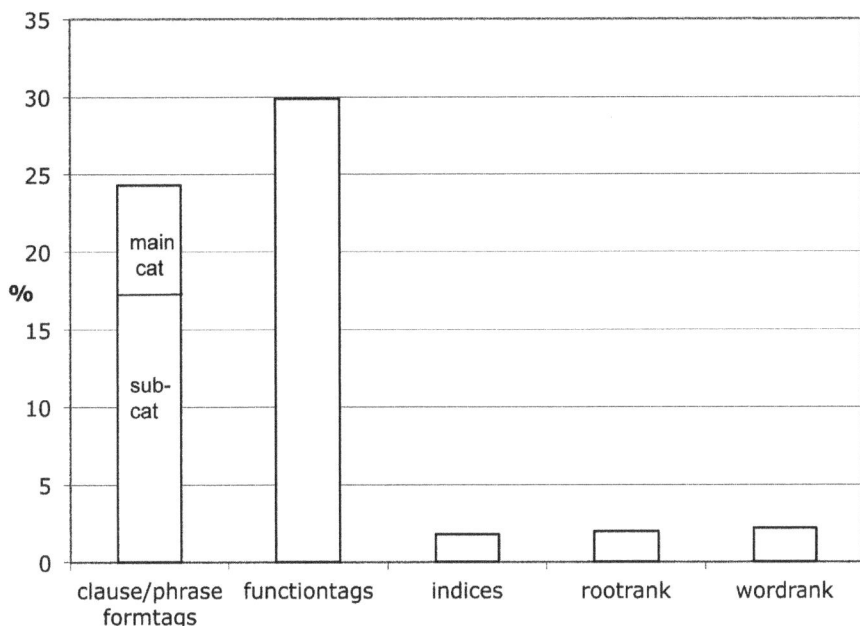

Figure 4: Locations of analytic discrepancy

of the relevant class in one lineage need to match any label in the counterpart lineage. The score for a partial mapping from labels in one lineage into labels in the other lineage is computed as the total number of labels in the two lineages which are *either* mapped onto identical labels *or* belong to the class whose contribution to inter-annotator discrepancy we are examining (or both), divided by the total number of labels in both lineages (and the score for a lineage-pair is then as usual the highest possible score for any partial mapping between the two sets of labels).

Computed in this way, the mean agreement figure ignoring rootrank discrepancies is 0·952, and the mean proportion of overall discrepancy attributable to rootrank discrepancies is 2·0 per cent.[7] The mean agreement figure ignoring wordrank discrepancies is 0·952; the mean proportion of overall discrepancy attributable to wordrank discrepancies is 2·2 per cent.

The above findings are displayed graphically in Figure 4.

---

7 The unusual structural feature of the Women text already discussed relates to rootrank labels, so it is not surprising to find that in this one case inclusion of that text makes a large difference to the overall figure, which rises from 2·0 per cent to 3·6 per cent – for Women alone, 17·5 per cent of total discrepancy (almost nine times the average in the other texts) is attributable to rootrank discrepancies.

The various categories of analytic discrepancy examined above account between them for about sixty per cent of the total discrepancy figures. A small proportion of the remaining forty per cent could be due to node-labels simultaneously failing to match in two or more respects: if counterpart labels differ with respect both to formtag and to occurrence of an index, relaxing the matching requirements for either of these annotation elements alone will not convert failure to match into a successful match. But it seems likely that the great majority of the unexplained forty per cent of total discrepancy relates to the multifarious ways in which analysts' trees may differ not just in labelling but in structure and number of nodes. We have not devised insightful ways of classifying discrepancies of that kind that would allow us to break the forty per cent figure down into meaningful categories.

Considering the results for the discrepancy categories we have examined, it is no surprise that the figure for formtagging should be relatively large; almost every node of a parsetree has a formtag (the only exceptions being ghost nodes), and as already said the formtag system provides for far more potential distinctions than any other aspect of the annotation scheme. So there is plenty of room for inter-annotator disagreement in the area of formtags. (On average, 97·8 per cent of nonterminal nodes in a sample text contain a formtag; because of the various constraints on combinations of main category and subcategory symbols, it is hard to say exactly how many distinct valid formtags would be available in principle, but our sample texts contain 461 distinct formtags, which is certainly only a fraction of the total possibilities.)

On the other hand it is more remarkable that the proportion of total discrepancy attributable to functiontagging is even larger: under the SUSANNE scheme only a minority of nodes are assigned any functiontag, and the distinctions between functiontags are far fewer. (On average, 37·8 per cent of nonterminal nodes in a sample text contain a functiontag, and functiontags are single characters selected from a range of 23 possibilities.)

2.8 Assigning responsibility for discrepancies

The next question to ask is how far inter-annotator discrepancies arise from human error as opposed to vagueness or inadequacy in the explicit annotation scheme. Where we disagree in our cloud measurements, as it were, is that because we are not sufficiently skilled at measuring clouds or because the concept of cloud-size is ill-defined?

This question can be addressed only through close attention to specific discrepancies between the two analysts' annotation decisions. To examine every discrepancy in our data in the necessary degree of detail would be a larger task than we could undertake, so we looked at a sample subset. For this purpose, a sample was constructed by considering every twentieth discrepantly-parsed word. (A word is "discrepantly-parsed" if there is any difference between its lineages in the respective analysts' parse-trees.) This gave a sample of 310 discrepancies to be scrutinized in detail.

A handful of cases in this sample were set aside for special reasons. For instance, analysts were expected to correct clear misprints in a text before annotating it, and there were two debatable misprints each of which had been corrected by one analyst and not the other, leading to discrepant parse-trees. The ability of analysts to agree on what is or is not a misprint, while an interesting issue, is not the issue we are concerned with here. Altogether, sixteen cases in our sample were eliminated from analysis as irrelevant to the main research topic.

The 294 remaining discrepancies are classified as follows:

A   Discrepancy resulting from violation by an analyst of an explicit rule of the annotation scheme: 173 (58·8%)

   A.i   Correction chiefly requires close attention to detail(s) of the scheme: 113 (38·4%)
   A.ii   Correction chiefly requires close attention to the meaning of the text: 35 (11·9%)
   A.iii Error represents a typing mistake or careless slip: 25 (8·5%)

B   Although the meaning of the text is clear, the scheme does not yield a single, unambiguous annotation decision: 58 (19·7%)

   B.i   The scheme is vague about the boundary between alternative annotations: 57 (19·4%)
   B.ii   The scheme is contradictory: separate guidelines explicitly require incompatible annotations: 1 (0·3%)

C   Discrepancy corresponds to structural ambiguity in the text; either construal is defensible: 63 (21·4%)

   C.i   The contrast between alternative interpretations corresponds to a "real", humanly-significant difference: 23 (7·8%)
   C.ii   In context the contrast is a logical distinction without a significant difference: 40 (13·6%)

Figure 5 displays these proportions graphically.

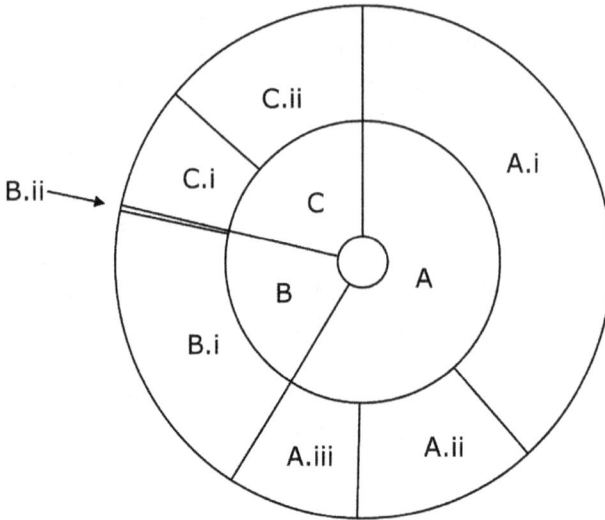

Figure 5: Causes of analytic discrepancy

Some examples will clarify these categories, and should at the same time give readers a sense of the level of analytic detail at which annotation predictability breaks down:

A.i, discrepancies depending for resolution on details of annotation scheme

(6) ... *put your skincare creams into small, non-breakable, plastic bottles,* ...
     (Women 00865)

The comma following *small* implies that that adjective is co-ordinated asyndetically with what follows; but one analyst treated *small, non-breakable* as a tagma modifying the phrase *plastic bottles*, while the other treated *small, non-breakable, plastic* as a three-way co-ordination. Arguably, the former analysis better represents the sense, but §4.517 makes the comma after *non-breakable* decisive in favour of the latter analysis.

(7) *Nor is the procedure under section 7(5) "the hearing of complaint."*
     (Law 00096)

The placing of the closing inverted commas after the sentence-final stop is a common publishers' convention, if an illogical one. Our annotation scheme normally treats sentence-final punctuation marks as sisters rather than daughters of the sentence tagmas they bound, but treats paired inverted commas as sisters below the same mother node. In this case, one analyst has placed the sentence boundary before the full stop, the other has placed it after the inverted commas. §4.77 is decisive in favour of the former analysis.

A.ii, discrepancies depending for resolution on subtleties of meaning

(8) *Her dress stuck to the back of her legs with perspiration* ... (Novel 00843)

The analysts have functiontagged the *to* phrase respectively as an adjunct of Direction or as a prepositional object. For a car passenger's dress to stick to the back of her legs does not imply movement of the dress towards the legs; the word *to* is determined by the verb *stuck* here rather than carrying an independent meaning of its own, i.e. the phrase is a prepositional object.

(9) ... *whether the justice had power to adjourn the proceeding before her under section 7(5) of the Bail Act 1976 to the following Monday.* (Law 00117)

One analyst treats *before her under section 7(5) of the Bail Act 1976* as a whiz-deleted relative clause postmodifying *proceeding* – "[which was] before her under ...".[8] The other treats the object of *adjourn* as just *the proceeding before her*, and treats the *under* phrase as an adjunct of *adjourn*. In context it appears that the reference to the Bail Act is intended as a potential source of authority for the act of adjourning, it does not describe the proceeding or how it comes to be before the J.P.

A.iii, typing mistakes and careless slips

(10) *It is very rare to have this feeling with another person.* (Novel 00947)

The phrase *this feeling* should be labelled Ns:o, as a formally singular noun phrase which is functioning as direct object of its clause; one analyst has accidentally omitted the colon separating formtag from functiontag, resulting in a notation which is invalid within the scheme.

(11) *But managing director Mr Peter Jarvis admitted* ... (City 00343)

---

8 A "whiz-deleted" relative clause is a relative clause in which the main verb is a form of *BE* and in which that verb, and the relative pronoun, are "understood" rather than included explicitly.

The subject of *admitted* is the noun phrase *managing director Mr Peter Jarvis*. One analyst has placed the left-hand boundary of the noun phrase so that it includes the word *But*, which in reality is obviously an IC of the sentence.

B.i, discrepancies arising from scheme vagueness

(12) *Bookings can be made at the Society's Offices, 42 Merrion Sq. Dublin 2. tel. 01767053.* (Art 00154)

One analyst has included the "proper name" subcategory symbol (Nn) in the label for the noun phrase *the Society* (which in context refers to the Irish Georgian Society), the other has not. The rules for deciding when a noun phrase consisting of words that have uses as common nouns should take the Nn subcategory are subtle, and depend heavily on typography, namely whether capitalization would be recommended by a named standard house-style manual (§4.144, and see also §4.153). In the present context it is not clear whether the capital *S* is required; and the capitalization of *Offices* is non-standard, suggesting that the style of the document tends to overcapitalize so that the capitalization of *Society* should perhaps be discounted.

(13) *Last time the Democratic-controlled Congress sought* ... (City 00313)

The form *Democratic-controlled* (which by the scheme is divided into three "words", the hyphen being assigned a terminal node of its own in the parse-tree) is a past-participle clause, within which *Democratic* is functiontagged as Agent of the verb *controlled*. The analysts differ on whether *Democratic* is formtagged as an adjective phrase (J) or as a noun phrase with adjective rather than noun head (Nj, as in e.g. *the poor*). The agent in a clause will normally be a nominal rather than adjectival element, and *Democratic* here appears to be a reference to the Democratic Party; on the other hand the word is uncontroversially an adjective rather than a noun, and within a hyphenated compound there is inevitably no surrounding material such as a definite article to show that *Democratic* is functioning as a noun phrase. The wording in fact seems slightly unexpected (arguably, *Democrat-controlled* would be the expected usage), and this perhaps excuses the failure of the scheme to resolve the annotation issue.

B.ii, discrepancy arising from scheme contradiction

(14) *An evening had been set aside for a get-together of the Branch's top 50 clients* ... (Bank 00204)

One analyst labels the *for* phrase as a Contingency adjunct, the other as a Benefactive adjunct. If considered in isolation, the reference to "purpose" in §5.158 would justify the Contingency classification, and the *for*-phrase examples in §5.184 would justify the Benefactive classification; but by the rules of the scheme only one of the two can be selected.

C.i, significant structural ambiguities

(15)   *Sterling lost ground against a buoyant German mark as dealers took fright at the prospect of a fall in exports leading to a widening of the current account deficit last month.* (City 00259)

This sentence contains two C.i cases: the *as* clause was marked alternatively as a Time or a Contingency adjunct (*as* = "while" or *as* = "because"); and the phrase *last month* was either an IC of the *leading* clause, or a postmodifier of *deficit* – if the former, the feared widening would have occurred last month, but if the latter, the fear was that last month's deficit would widen at a later date. Each of these contrasting interpretations seems reasonable.

(16)   *I had set my sights on getting a good position in training so that I would be sent* ... (Legion 00933)

The phrase *in training* was either an IC of the *getting* clause, or a postmodifier of *position*. This makes a real difference: the former structure implies that the aim during training was to get a good position (for the future, after training), the latter would be the appropriate analysis if a "position in training" is itself something which may be favourable or unfavourable. Perhaps someone more familiar than the present authors with life in the Foreign Legion could reliably resolve this ambiguity, but for us either reading is plausible.

C.ii, non-significant structural ambiguities

As pointed out in *English for the Computer* (§4.34), structural ambiguities which are real enough logically can often be "distinctions without a difference" in practice. Consider the following examples:

(17)   *At one point the Nawab reached across Olivia to pull down the blind on her window, as if wanting to spare her the sight of all that parched land.* (Novel 00836)

The *as if* clause was an IC either of the *reached* clause or the *pull* clause. Since reaching across to pull down the blind was a single action with a single purpose, in human terms there is no significance in the question whether the reaching or the pulling seemed intended to spare Olivia.

(18)   *The good news is for members in the Republic of Ireland where no premium*
       increases are proposed during 1993. This means that members in the
       Republic of Ireland who are over twenty five years of age ... have had no
       increase in premium for over three years and for all other policyholders there
       has been no increase for over two years. (Bank 00109–10)

The clause *and for all other policyholders there has ...* was co-ordinated alternatively with the *This means* main clause, or with the *have had* subordinate clause. In the former case, only the three-year-plus premium stability for Irish over-25s is claimed to be an entailment of the first sentence, and the two-year lack of increase for other policyholders is an independent assertion; in the second case, both lacks of increase are claimed to follow from the good news in the first sentence. Logically, these interpretations are clearly distinct, but no policyholder will care which is intended; the financial implications are identical.

One might be tempted to feel that the incidence of C.ii-type discrepancies merely demonstrates that aspects of the SUSANNE annotation scheme are too fine-grained, and do not correspond to distinctions that have any reality in the language as used by its speakers. But it would be hard to sustain that argument. What appear to be, structurally, the very same contrasts that in some contexts lead to a C.ii discrepancy, in other contexts make large differences to the sense of examples. The prevalence of C.ii cases, in our view, is telling us something significant about language, not just about a specific annotation scheme. We return to this point below.

2.9 Monitoring for bias

The process by which discrepancies were classified as analyst errors or limitations in the annotation scheme is open to criticism, in that it involved one co-author (GRS) referring to the definition of the scheme in order to resolve differences between his own and the other co-author's annotation decisions.

As one check on whether the results represented mere bias in favour of one's own views (in which case they would tell us little), we looked at how often resolutions of the 173 type-A cases sided with the respective analysts. The answer was that 109 cases were resolved in agreement with GRS's original decisions, 62 were resolved in agreement with AB's original decisions, and in two

Table 3: Results of discrepancy resolution

	Sb	S?	Ss
Bb	2	3	1
B?	7	9	10
Bs	1	9	15

cases it appeared on reconsideration that neither analyst's original annotation was correct. There is an imbalance in these figures; but that is to be expected, when one considers that GRS had been the researcher primarily responsible for the annotation scheme for two decades, and the compiler of *English for the Computer*, while AB had been working with it for about four years. The fact that in more than a third of these cases GRS concluded that his own original decision was wrong and AB's correct suggests that personal bias was not a major factor in the classification process described in this section.

Nevertheless, as a further check, a random subset of 57 of the discrepancies were independently resolved by AB. The two analysts' resolution decisions are compared in table 3, in which Bb stands for "AB regarded her own original annotation as correct and GRS's as incorrect", B? for "AB regarded neither analyst's original annotation as clearly more correct than the other", Bs for "AB regarded her own original annotation as incorrect and GRS's as correct", and Sb, S?, and Ss similarly classify GRS's discrepancy-resolutions. If bias by an analyst in favour of his or her own original decision were an important factor, one might expect to find Bb > Sb and Ss > Bs (using these symbols to stand for the totals in the rows and columns they label). In fact, Bb = 6 and Sb = 10, a large difference in the other direction; and Ss = 26 and Bs = 25, where the difference is in the predicted direction but proportionally very small. We believe that personal bias can be discounted as a factor affecting our findings.

2.10 Implications of the experiment

The above findings yield three broad conclusions.

2.10.1 Human fallibility more significant than definitional limitations

In the first place, it is clear that (for these analysts and this scheme) the limitation on annotation predictability is due far more to human fallibility than to the limited precision of the scheme. Type A discrepancies are almost three times as numerous as those of type B. It is of course logically possible that other individuals, or the same individuals after accumulating even more years of experience, might succeed in reducing their incidence of type-A discrepancies. But, assuming that we shall not encounter people willing to dedicate entire careers to honing their grammatical-annotation skills, we question whether the A versus B differential could be much reduced. It seems that (as it were) our ability to make the size of clouds a well-defined property runs well ahead of our ability to measure cloud size in practice.

(This matches the findings of an earlier experiment (Babarczy, Carroll, and Sampson 2006) which looked at the rather simpler issue of classifying the grammatical uses of words in context – what computational linguists call "wordtagging". From that research it was rather clear that the constraints on wordtagging reliability stem less from difficulty in defining a detailed and consistent scheme of classification than from human inability to apply the scheme reliably.)

The picture which emerges from these findings is not a picture of grammar as a fixed set of structures determined by universal logical principles, with which mature, competent speakers of a language are fully familiar. It is a woollier picture, in which individual speakers agree in their structural understanding much of the time but feel their way uncertainly at the margins (and where the reliable solid ground runs out surprisingly soon in certain areas, see 2.10.3 below). If even professional linguists with years of experience in applying the most precise extant analytic scheme to real-life language samples cannot agree perfectly, how can we see the language as possessing a particular scientifically-valid grammar which, if the discipline of linguistics could only succeed in discovering it, would specify a "correct" analysis for any sample?

It would be easy, of course, to claim that inter-annotator discrepancies in an experiment like this are the consequence of shortcomings in the particular analytic scheme used. But if so, where is the superior scheme which would enable analysts to avoid discrepancies? We find it quite implausible that the situation we have examined is a case of examples of a well-behaved language being hard to fit into a messy or ill-thought-out analytic scheme. Surely it is rather a case of real-life language being too anarchic, and speakers' internal language models being too imprecise, to permit them always to fit examples neatly into the pigeonholes of any scheme, however well-defined.

2.10.2 Structural ambiguity often pragmatically nonsignificant

The second general conclusion is that, not only is genuine structural ambiguity quite common in English, but (more surprisingly) there is often no reason to resolve ambiguities because in practice either interpretation amounts to the same thing. Instances of type C.ii are almost twice as numerous as those of type C.i.

This generalization might seem to imply that the annotation scheme is over-refined, postulating artificial structural distinctions that lack real linguistic validity. But the finding cannot be explained away so easily. In these particular contexts the relevant structural distinction is non-significant; but in other contexts, with different vocabulary, the same distinction may make a large difference. Compare example (17) above (... *the Nawab reached across Olivia* ...) with the following invented examples:

(19)   *he crawled out of the tent to mount his horse, as if leaping onto a royal throne*

(20)   *he limped up the aisle to lead the prayers, as if suffering from gout*

The relevant aspects of grammar are the same in all three cases; but in these latter examples, one structural interpretation is clearly correct and the other wrong – *as if leaping* must be an adjunct to the *mount* clause, *as if suffering* must be an adjunct to the *limped* clause. (Or, more precisely, under the alternative structural construals the examples would be saying something quite different and implausible: the crawling would somehow resemble leaping onto a throne, something about the way prayers were led would indicate gout.)

We believe this is representative for the range of C.ii-type discrepancies in our data. The structural differences are ones which a satisfactory annotation scheme must recognize, because they sometimes correspond to important meaning-differences; but in many contexts they do not. Grammar appears to be a tool like, say, a ruler marked off in 32nds of an inch which is commonly used simply to check whether one has picked up a seven-inch or an eight-inch bolt. So far as we are aware, this is not a consideration that has been much noticed by linguists.[9]

The objection that the annotation scheme may be over-refined has sometimes been expressed to us in a different way. Consider the example:

(21)   *Scatter the brioche cubes in six small gratin ... dishes. Place four slices of pear on top, then cover each one ...* (Cook 00918–9)

---

9 Though cf. Edward Sapir's analogy of a dynamo that is capable of powering a lift but used mainly to supply a doorbell (Sapir [1921] 1963: 14).

– where the analysts have functiontagged *on top* respectively as a Place and as a Direction adjunct. In order to place pear slices on top of a dish of brioche cubes, it is evidently necessary that the pear slices are moved towards the dish (Direction); on the other hand, arguably the focus here is on the static end-point of that movement (Place). No example in the relevant scheme sections seems to offer a good precedent for this case, so we classified it as a type-B.i discrepancy. But, the objection runs, if we understand the English word *place* and the phrase *on top* in this example, it is not clear that there remains any further question to answer about the meaning of the clause; the annotation system is forcing us to create spurious facts, rather than merely recording facts that exist independently of the scheme.

At root this seems to be an objection to the general concept of grammatical annotation. Clearly, a speaker of a language will normally understand examples of that language, and this understanding surely involves something beyond knowledge of the meanings of individual words (otherwise the words of a sentence could be freely permuted without affecting meaning). If so, then there must surely be *some* way of modelling symbolically the aspects of meaning that relate to relationships between successive words, rather than to the meanings of the words in isolation. The SUSANNE scheme for English may well not be the ideal approach, but in that case it presumably needs to be replaced by a better scheme – rather than by no scheme at all.[10]

2.10.3 Functiontagging specially problematic

Thirdly, it seems that assigning functional categories to clause constituents is a specially problematic area of structural classification. The functiontag bar in Figure 3 is considerably higher than the clause/phrase formtag bar, despite the fact that the range of distinct clause and phrase formtags is massively larger than the range of functiontags, and that many more tagmas are formtagged than functiontagged (both of which points should tend to make discrepancies more frequent in the former case).

Although on the face of it these numerical considerations make the share of discrepancies attributable to functiontags startling, that share in fact came as no

---

10 As it happens, computational linguists have recently found it worth devoting intensive study to the area of "semantic role labelling", from which the above example is taken – though it seems fair to say that this research has focused on the task of devising algorithms to assign labels automatically, rather than on the problem of defining adequate sets of labels and watertight boundaries between them. On this research trend see e.g. Gildea and Jurafsky (2002), Xue and Palmer (2004), Màrquez et al. (2005).

surprise to us who have worked with the SUSANNE scheme over a long period. It has been clear from the outset that developing a satisfactory set of functional categories with watertight boundaries was an unusually troublesome aspect of scheme definition. (Cf. similar findings by Levin and Rappaport Hovav 2005: 46.) Nevertheless, it is difficult to understand how the English language works, if some such category-set does not apply to it.

Mathematical logicians distinguish the arguments of a predicate in terms of numerical order, but that cannot be the crucial factor deciding the semantic relationship between an English verb and its arguments: in *he travelled to Wells by car* and *he travelled by car to Wells* the relationship between Wells and travelling, and the relationship between the car and travelling, are the same (Wells is always the destination, the car always the means) rather than interchanged as they would be if numerical order were decisive. But prepositions such as *to* and *by* do not identify argument-relationships unambiguously either; *by* expresses a different relationship in *he stood by the door*, and *to* in *he gave the box to Julie* expresses the same relationship which is alternatively expressed by position in *he gave Julie the box*. Many linguists, from Charles Fillmore's "The case for case" (Fillmore 1968) onwards, have believed that the most plausible way to define semantic verb/argument relationships in English and other natural languages is via a limited set of "cases" or functional categories, onto which prepositions and positional roles can be mapped in a predictable though not straightforwardly one-to-one way. The SUSANNE functiontag set was in fact developed from the most fully worked out version of Fillmorean case theory that we could find when we began work (namely the Stockwell, Schachter, and Partee book discussed on p. 7 above), "debugged" through the process of applying it to the text samples of the SUSANNE treebank.

If numerical sequence is not crucial, prepositions are frequently ambiguous, and (as our experience suggests) a satisfactory set of case roles cannot be found, there will be a large unanswered question about how English-speakers understand the relationships between verbs and their arguments. Within the information-technology discipline of natural language processing, the question is crucial for systems that aim to incorporate an inferencing function. But it is a challenging question for pure linguists too, because it implies a mystery about a quite central aspect of language structure.[11] How do we understand clauses?

---

11 Scholars associated with Charles Fillmore have recently developed his case theory into a system of "frame semantics" independent of and more elaborate than the SUSANNE function-tag scheme; see particularly Ruppenhofer et al. (2006). We have not attempted – we are not qualified – to check whether this FrameNet scheme yields closer inter-annotator agreement on unseen language samples than we have obtained for SUSANNE functiontagging, and we are not aware that the FrameNet researchers have studied this issue.

2.11 New research techniques yield novel perspectives

The data-set produced by the experiment discussed here is necessarily modest in size. Nevertheless, even these limited findings suggest perspectives, and raise questions, which merit the attention of anyone interested in the nature of human language. These perspectives, and the related questions, could scarcely have emerged from more traditional linguistic research techniques.

Chapter 3
Where should annotation stop?

3.1 Another way to survey indeterminacy

In chapter 2 we looked at the problem of grammatical indeterminacy by examining how much agreement or disagreement one finds in practice when expert analysts are set to annotate the same language samples using the same annotation scheme. There, the focus was on numbers of instances in a sample, so our tendency was to consider at length issues which are frequent, and allot less attention to rare problems. In this chapter we turn things round and consider indeterminacy from the point of view of defining a comprehensive annotation scheme. Where should annotation stop? Although this chapter will not involve precise numerical quantification, as chapter 2 did, the natural tendency of this approach is to distribute attention across problems more in proportion to the amount of overall guidelines they affect. (Compare generalizations about words based on word-tokens on the page with generalizations based on word-types listed in a dictionary: they may give very different results, for instance initial *th-* is frequent among English word-tokens but rare among English word-types.) If we find that both approaches lead to broadly similar findings, we can surely be confident that these are telling us something real about the nature of language.

3.2 Detailed v. skeleton analytic schemes

Any scheme for structural annotation of corpora must embody decisions about how much detail to include.

Some groups explicitly aim at "skeleton parsing", marking much less grammatical detail than linguists recognize a language as containing. In many circumstances, this will be a sensible strategy. If one's chief goal is to have as large as possible a quantity of analysed material, from which reliable statistics can be derived, then skeleton parsing is more or less unavoidable. Automatic parsers may be able to deliver skeleton but not detailed analyses, and human analysts can produce skeleton analyses quickly. Furthermore, for some natural language processing applications skeleton analysis may be all that is needed.

But attention also need to be given to detailed structural analysis. All the grammar in a language, surely, serves some function or another for users of the language – it is not just meaningless ornamentation. If some minor details of structure might be significant for research in the future, then the sooner we begin devising standardized, explicit ways of registering them in our treebanks (structurally analysed corpora) the better, because the business of evolving usable, consistent schemes of structural classification and annotation is itself a challenging and time-consuming activity.

To draw an analogy from the biological domain, much of the range of very lively research developments currently taking place in genetics and cladistics depends on the fact that biologists have a detailed, internationally-recognized system for identifying living species, the foundations of which were laid down as long ago as the eighteenth century. Linnaeus and his successors could not have guessed at the kinds of research revolving round DNA sequences which are happening in biology nowadays, but modern biology would be hampered if their species-identification scheme were not available.

Our SUSANNE structural-annotation scheme for English aims at rigorous explicitness and maximum completeness of detail. For us as computational linguists, these goals are particularly salient; our work is heavily informed by Jane Edwards's principle quoted above (p. 24): "The single most important property of any data base for purposes of computer-assisted research is that *similar instances be encoded in predictably similar ways*". But linguists who aim to study grammar systematically rather than merely anecdotally need to acknowledge these goals whether or not their research happens to need computers. Hence, to quote the documentation file of the SUSANNE Corpus:

> The SUSANNE scheme attempts to provide a method of representing all aspects of English grammar which are sufficiently definite to be susceptible of formal annotation, with the categories and boundaries between categories specified in sufficient detail that, ideally, two analysts independently annotating the same text and referring to the same scheme must produce the same structural analysis.

Comprehensiveness and rigour of analytic guidelines are ideas which can never be perfectly attained, but we saw on p. 28 above that there is some evidence that the SUSANNE scheme is recognized as having made a useful advance.

If one's aim is a comprehensive detailed rather than skeleton analytic scheme, then a question which arises and which does not seem to have been much discussed to date is where to stop. How does one decide that one has exhausted the range of grammatical features which are "sufficiently definite to be susceptible of formal annotation"?

3.3 The trainability criterion

In practice, one factor that may impose limits on detail is what it is practical to teach annotators to mark reliably. Even if an annotation scheme is limited to standard, traditional grammatical categories, it is hard to overestimate the difficulty of training research assistants to apply it to real-life language samples in a consistent manner. Some annotation projects are explicit about ways in which training considerations shaped their notation scheme. Meteer et al. (1995), defining the dysfluency annotation scheme of the Switchboard Corpus, make remarks such as "annotators were basically unable to distinguish the discourse marker from the conjunctive use of *so*", "*actually* also proved impossible for the annotators to mark consistently and was jettisoned as a discourse marker part of the way through".

But, although what one can and cannot train annotators to do is obviously an important consideration in practice, it is hard to accept it as a principled boundary to detail of annotation. Sometimes, annotators' failure to apply a distinction consistently may be telling us that the distinction is unreal or inherently vague. But there are certainly other cases where the distinction is real enough, and annotators are just not good at learning it (or a principal investigator is not good at teaching it). Usually, leaders of annotation projects are senior and more linguistically experienced than the annotators employed by the projects, so taking trainability as decisive would mean systematically ascribing more intellectual authority to the inexpert than to the expert.

3.4 Limits to expert decision-making

In principle, what junior annotators can learn to do is a secondary consideration, which is likely to depend on factors such as time available for training and individual educational background, as much as on the properties of the language itself. More scientifically interesting is the fact that sometimes it seems difficult or impossible to devise guidelines that enable even linguistic experts to classify real-life cases consistently.

If some grammatical distinction is hard for an expert to draw in a majority of cases, then probably we would all agree that that distinction is best left out of our annotation scheme. An example might be the distinction, among cases of the English pronoun *they*, between the original use referring to plural referents, and the newer use, encouraged recently in connexion with the "political correctness" movement, for a singular referent of unknown sex. This probably deserves to be called a grammatical distinction; note for instance that "singular *they*" forms a reflexive as *themself* rather than *themselves*, as in the following British National Corpus examples:

(22) *Critics may claim inconsistency, but the person involved may justify themself by claiming total consistency.* FA9.01713

(23) *... the person who's trying not to drink so much and beats themself up when they slip back and get drunk!* CDK.02462

(These are not isolated oddities; traditionalists may be surprised to learn that 23 of the 4124 BNC texts each contain one or more tokens of the form *themself*, which seems quite a high number considering that singular *they* is unquestionably far less frequent than plural *they*.) But (although we have not checked this) it seems likely that in a high proportion of cases where *they* is in fact being used for "he or she", there will be few or no contextual cues to demonstrate that it is not used with plural reference – sometimes even for the speaker or writer it may be intended as nonspecific with respect to number as well as sex. So we would not want to add a distinction between singular and plural *they* to our annotation scheme, and we imagine few colleagues would advocate this for general-purpose linguistic annotation schemes. (If an annotation scheme is devised for some specialized purpose, there is obviously no saying what distinctions it may need to incorporate.)

More problematic are the many grammatical distinctions which can often be made easily, and which may seem to the linguistic expert (and perhaps to less expert annotators) rather basic to the structure of the language, but which in particular cases may be hard to draw. What proportion of instances of a distinction need to be indeterminate, before we regard the distinction as too artificial to include in our annotation scheme?

3.5 Some examples of indeterminacy

In chapter 6, below, we shall look at various problems that arise in applying an annotation scheme to spontaneous spoken language. But it is important to understand that the problem of this chapter is not confined to speech. Some may feel that the structural ambiguities in spoken language are something of a side issue, since applying any annotation scheme to spoken language inevitably leads to numerous unclarities caused by the nature of speech rather than the nature of the scheme. (Analysts typically work from recordings with little knowledge of the situation in which a conversation occurred or the shared assumptions of the participants. Often, patches of wording are inaudible in the recording; speakers will mis-speak themselves, producing wording which they would not themselves regard as good examples of their language; their "body language" will be invisible to the analyst; and if analysts work from transcriptions, even intonation cues to structure are unavailable. In these circumstances there will often be doubt about how to apply even a very limited, skeleton annotation scheme.)

In fact, many of the problems in applying structural analysis to spoken language are more "systematic" than this (the vague distinction between direct and indirect quotation discussed on pp. 127–128 in chapter 6 would be one example). But the important point is that unclarities arise even in applying an annotation scheme to published written language, where the wording is as well disciplined as writer and editor can make it, and the only background assumptions shared by writer and reader are those common to members of their society and hence available to annotators too.

Let us illustrate via a range of examples drawn more or less at random from one written BNC text, EE5, taken from a popular book about life in the French Foreign Legion. (This is the text identified as "Legion" in chapter 2. As English prose, we would judge it to be well-written.)

There are in the first place various passages which are genuinely grammatically ambiguous, e.g.:

(24) *I had set my sights on getting a good position in training so that I would be sent to the* 2ème Régiment Étranger de Parachutistes. EE5.00933

– is the *so that I ...* sequence a constituent of the *set* clause or the *getting* clause (was being sent to the *Deuxième Régiment* the motive for setting sights, or the potential result of getting a good position)?

(25) *They were kicked senseless and then handed over to the Military Police who locked them up in the roofless regimental prison before they were handed over to the Colonel of the Regiment for interrogation and questioning.* EE5.00912

– is the *before* clause part of the *locked* relative clause, or is it a constituent of the *then handed over* clause near the beginning (is the handover to the Colonel described as following the prison spell or as following the handover to the Military Police)? In both cases, the alternative interpretations would correspond to different annotation structures in the SUSANNE scheme, and surely in any other plausible linguistic annotation scheme.

Where a passage is genuinely ambiguous, we *expect* an expert to be unable to choose between alternative annotations – that is what "ambiguous" means in this context. Consequently, inability to choose in these cases is not a ground for suspecting that the SUSANNE scheme is over-refined. Notice, though, that even though many linguists would agree that the examples are genuinely ambiguous, these are not the kinds of ambiguity which might be resolved by asking the writer "what he really meant" – in the second case, for instance, the handover to the Colonel in fact followed *both* the handover to the Military Police *and* the prison spell, and there is no reason to suppose that the writer intended one interpretation to the exclusion of the other. This is a frequent situation in real-life usage.

In many other cases, the SUSANNE annotation scheme requires the analyst to choose between alternative notations which seem to correspond to no real linguistic difference (and where the choice is not settled by the rather full definitions of category boundaries that form part of the scheme), so that one might easily conclude that the notation is over-refined – except that the same notational contrast seems clearly desirable for other examples. Here are a handful of instances:

Passive v. BE + predicative past participle

The SUSANNE scheme (§4.335) distinguishes the passive construction, as in *I doubt ... whether the word <u>can be limited</u> to this meaning ...*, from cases where *BE* is followed by a past participle used predicatively, as in *... the powers ... <u>were</u> far too <u>limited</u>.* What about the following, in a context where earth is being shovelled over a man:

(26)   *When his entire body was covered apart from his head, ...* EE5.00955

We see no distinction at any level between a passive and a *BE* + predicative particle interpretation of *was covered* here; does that mean that it was a mistake to include the distinction even in connexion with "clear cases" such as those previously quoted?

Phrase headship

The SUSANNE system classifies phrases in a way that depends mainly on the category of their head words, which is commonly uncontroversial. In the example:

(27) *If we four were representative of our platoon,...* EE5.00859

it is clear that *we four* is a phrase, subject of the clause, but we see no particular reason to choose between describing it as a noun phrase headed by *we*, or a numeral phrase headed by *four*.

Co-ordination reduction v. complete tagma

In the example:

(28) *He had wound up in Marseilles, sore and desperate, and signed on at Fort St Nicholas.* EE5.00855

the first clause contains a pluperfect verb group *had wound*. It is normal for repeated elements optionally to be deleted from conjoined tagmas, so *signed* might be either the past participle of another pluperfect form from which *had* was deleted, or a past tense forming the whole of a simple past construction. This again seems in this context a distinction without a difference. Yet simple past v. pluperfect, and past tense v. past participle, are elementary English grammatical distinctions likely to be recognized by any plausible annotation scheme.

Interrogative v. non-interrogative how

A subordinate clause beginning with an interrogative is commonly either an indirect question (*I know why* ...) or a relative clause (*the place where* ...). But if the interrogative form is *how*, there is also a usage in which the clause functions like a nominal clause, with *how* more or less equivalent to *that*:

(29) *... shouting about the English and how they were always the first to desert* ... EE5.00902

(30) *It was frightening how hunger and lack of sleep could make you behave and think like a real bastard.* EE5.00919

The shouting in the first example was presumably not about the manner of English legionnaires' early desertion but about the fact of it. The second example is more debatable; it might be about either the fact of hunger and no sleep affecting one's psychology, or about the insidious manner in which this occurs.

This is an instance where the SUSANNE scheme avoids recognizing a distinction which is arguably real; the scheme does not allow *how* to be other than an interrogative or relative adverb, and therefore treats the *how* clauses as antecedentless relative clauses with *how* functioning as a Manner adjunct, even in the former example. But we could not give a principled reason for failing to recognize a distinction here, when other distinctions that are equally subject to vagueness are required by the annotation scheme.

Multi-word prenominal modifiers

Where a sequence of modifying words precedes a noun head, if the SUSANNE scheme shows no structural grouping then each word is taken as modifying the following word or word-sequence (Sampson 1995: §4.9). But a noun can be premodified by a multi-word tagma, in which case the modifier will be marked as a unit: cf. *He graduated with* [Np [Ns *first class*] *honours* [P *in oil technology*]] ... GX6.00022 – *first class* is a noun phrase, the word *first* is obviously not intended as modifying a phrase *class honours*. However, consider the examples:

(31)   *the nearby US Naval base at Subic Bay* EE5.00852

(32)   *... handed over to US Immigration officials ...* EE5.00854

The words *US Naval* could be seen as the adjectival form of *US Navy*, which is a standard proper name; and *US Immigration* is perhaps also current as a way of referring to the respective branch of the American public service. Yet at the same time, the base at Subic Bay is a naval base, and among naval bases it is a US one; and similarly for US immigration officials. If there are no grounds for choosing whether or not to group premodifying words in these cases, does that make it over-refined to recognize such a distinction in cases like *first class honours*?

(In fact the SUSANNE annotation scheme contains an overriding principle that only as much structure should be marked as is necessary to reflect the sense of a passage, and this principle could be invoked to decide against treating *US Naval*, *US Immigration* as units in the examples above. But ideally one would hope that an annotation scheme should give positive reasons for assigning a particular structure and no other to any particular example, rather than leaving the decision to be made in these negative terms.)

It would be easy to give many more examples of structural distinctions which are clear in some cases but seem empty in other cases. Perhaps the examples above are enough to illustrate the point.

We have no definite solution to the problem posed by cases like these. We do not believe that any neat, principled answer is available to the question of how refined a useful general-purpose structural annotation scheme should be; it seems to us that the devising of such schemes will always be something of a "black art", drawing on common-sense rules of thumb and instinct rather than on logical principles.

But, if that is true, it is as well that those of us involved with corpus annotation should be aware that it is so. People who work with computers tend often to be people who expect a logical answer to be available for every problem, if one can find it. For treebank researchers to put effort into trying to establish the "right" set of analytic categories for a language would lead to a lot of frustration and wasted resources, if questions like that have no right answer. The main purpose of this chapter is to urge any readers who doubt it that, unfortunately, there are no right answers in this area.

3.6 Annotation practice and linguistic theory

One group of academics might suggest that there are right answers: namely, theoretical linguists. For theoretical linguists it seems axiomatic that what they are doing in working out the grammatical structure of a language is not devising a useful, workable set of descriptive categories, but *discovering* structure which exists in the language whether linguists are aware of it or not. What makes the structure "correct" is either correspondence to hypothetical psychological mechanisms, or (for linguistic Platonists such as Jerrold Katz, e.g. Katz 1981) the fact that languages are seen as mathematical objects with an existence independent of their users. For some of the problem cases discussed above, it is plausible that linguistic theorizing might yield answers to classification questions which we described as unanswerable. It would not surprise us if some linguistic theory of headship gave a principled reason for choosing one of the words of the phrase *we four* as head. (It would also not be surprising if another linguist's theory gave the opposite answer.) For some other cases it is less easy to envisage how linguistic theory might resolve the issue.

But linguistic annotation ought not to be made dependent on linguistic theorizing, even in areas of structure where theoretical linguists have answers. That would put the cart before the horse. The task of linguistic annotation is to collect and register data which will form the raw materials for theoretical linguistics, as well as for applied natural language processing. If linguistic theory is to be answerable to objective evidence, we cannot wait for the theories to be finalized before deciding what categories to use in our data banks.

The most we can reasonably ask of an annotation scheme is that it should provide a set of categories and guidelines for applying them which annotators can use consistently, so that similar instances are always registered in similar ways; and that the categories should not be blatantly at odds with the theoretical consensus, where there is a consensus. We cannot require that they should be the "correct" categories. To return to the biological analogy: studies of DNA sequences at the turn of the 21st century are giving us new information about the theoretically correct shapes of the "family trees" of animal and plant kingdoms. It would have been unfortunate for the development of biology if Linnaeus and his colleagues had waited for this information to become available before compiling their taxonomic system.

3.7 A disanalogy with biology

We have alluded to the analogy with biological systematics; questions about how many and what grammatical categories treebankers should recognize have many parallels with questions about how many and what taxa should be recognized by biologists. Since our treebanking enterprise is rather a new thing, it is good to be aware of old-established parallels which may help to show us our way forward.

But although the classification problem is similar in the two disciplines, there is one large difference. We are worse placed than the biologists. For them, the lowest-level and most important classification unit, the species, is a natural class. The superstructure of higher-level taxa in Linnaeus's system was not natural; it was a matter of common-sense and convenience to decide how many higher-order levels (such as genus, phylum, and order) to recognize, and Linnaeus did not pretend that the hierarchy of higher-order groupings corresponded to any reality in Nature – he explicitly stated the contrary (cf. Stafleu 1971: 28, 115ff.). But for most biological purposes, the important thing was to be able to assign individual specimens unambiguously to particular species; the higher-order taxonomy was a practical convenience making this easier to achieve. And species are real things: a species is a group of individuals which interbreed with one another and are reproductively isolated from other individuals. There are complications (see e.g. Ayala 1995: 872–873, who notes that in some circumstances the objective criteria break down and biologists have to make species distinctions by "commonsense"); but to a close approximation the question whether individuals belong to the same or different species is one with a clear, objective answer.

In grammar, we have no level of classification which is as objective as that. So far as we can see, whether one takes gross distinctions such as clause v. phrase, or fine distinctions, say infinitival indirect question v. infinitival relative clause, we always have to depend on unsystematic common sense and *Sprachgefühl* to decide which categories to recognize and where to plot the boundaries between them.

It feels unsatisfying not to have a firmer foundation for our annotation activity. Yet anything which enables us to impose some kind of order and classification on our bodies of raw language data is far better than nothing.

Chapter 4
Grammar without grammaticality

4.1 Strangers or unmet friends

The realization that a typical human language allows the construction not just of very many but actually of infinitely many distinct utterances was a key intellectual advance in twentieth-century linguistics. However, although languages came to be seen as non-finite systems in that respect, they were seen as bounded systems: any particular sequence of words, it was and is supposed, either is well-formed or is not, though infinitely many distinct sequences are each well-formed. As said in chapter 1, we believe that the concept of "ungrammatical" or "ill-formed" word-sequences is a delusion, based on a false conception of the kind of thing a human language is.

Think of the remark sometimes made by hail-fellow-well-met types: "There are no strangers, only friends I haven't met yet" – that is, rather than the world being divided into two sorts of people with respect to our mutual relationships, namely friends and strangers, inherently all people are of the same friendly sort, though in a finite lifetime one has the chance to establish this only for a subset of them. Whether or not this is a good way of thinking about human beings, we believe it is a good way of thinking about word-sequences.

In chapter 1 we adumbrated this point of view about grammar, which we believe was taken for granted (without necessarily being explicitly stated) by nineteenth-century linguists, such as Meiklejohn, but which has been lost sight of since. In the present chapter the time has come to spell out our position more clearly and concretely.

The point of view we are arguing against was put forward (for the first time, so far as we know) fifty-odd years ago, by Noam Chomsky in *Syntactic Structures*:

> The fundamental aim in the linguistic analysis of a language L is to separate the grammatical sequences which are the sentences of L from the ungrammatical sequences which are not sentences of L and to study the structure of the grammatical sequences. (Chomsky 1957: 13)

After this principle was stated in 1957, it quickly became central to much of what happened in theoretical linguistics. It continues to be so. Writing in 2010, Carson Schütze comments that *a priori* one might have expected linguistic theory to be concerned with properties of word-sequences such as whether native speakers can interpret them, but that

As it turns out, linguistic theory has devoted virtually no attention to [such] questions ... Rather, its focus has been on ... delineating well-formed or "grammatical" versus ill-formed or "ungrammatical" sentences and explaining various properties of the grammatical ones (Schütze 2010).

It is true that, as Cedric Boeckx (2006b: 217) put it, "The idea expressed in Chomsky (1957) that it is possible to bifurcate the set of sentences into the grammatical and ungrammatical and define theoretical adequacy on the basis of that distinction was quickly abandoned"; but what this means is that Chomsky and his followers came to see formalizing the distinction as an insufficient goal for linguistics. Apart from doing that, they hold that a "descriptively adequate" grammar (Chomsky 1965: 24) should also do things like assigning correct structural descriptions to those strings which are grammatical, and so forth. Boeckx was not saying that the idea of bifurcation into grammatical and ungrammatical strings was abandoned; it was not, indeed most of the additional goals set for generative linguistics depend on it.

In order to confirm our (and Schütze's) impression that Chomsky's principle retains its influence, we looked through the few introductory grammar textbooks which are seen by the linguistics department of Sussex University (not by any means regarded by other linguists as a strongly "Chomskyan" or "formal" group, we understand) as basic and up-to-date enough to be placed in the Reserve section of the university library. We quickly encountered the following:

To really get at what we know about our languages (remember syntax is a cognitive science), we have to know what sentences are *not* well-formed. That is, in order to know the range of what are acceptable sentences of English, Italian, or Igbo, we *first* have to know what are *not* acceptable sentences in English, Italian, or Igbo. This kind of negative information is not available in corpora ... (Carnie 2002: 10–11, emphases in original)

This particular remark goes further than Chomsky, by making the status of ill-formed sequences even more fundamental than that of well-formed sequences to the definition of a language ("*first* have to know"). Although other items in the Reserve collection of textbooks did not express Chomsky's principle so explicitly, many of them contained passages in which it seemed more or less implicit (and certainly we found nothing in any of them contradicting it).

Contrary to Carnie, we do not believe that getting at what we know about the things we can say in our language requires us to study a range of things we cannot say (let alone to give that study priority). We do not believe that there is in an interesting, relevant sense a "range of things we cannot say".

4.2 Unfamiliar does not imply ungrammatical

Consider one particular example of a word-sequence of questionable status. We quote this particular case just because it happened to catch GRS's eye in a novel he was reading when he began drafting the original version of this chapter, namely John Mortimer's *Dunster*, but we believe it would be easy to find any number of comparable examples:

(33)   ... *Dunster seemed to achieve, in the centre of this frenzied universe, an absence of anxiety which I had never known. But then, as I have made it clear to you, I worry.* (Mortimer 1993: 21)

When GRS read this it seemed to him that, if he had written it, he would have omitted the *it* in *made it clear.* Yet John Mortimer's spoken and written output has as good a claim as anyone's to be a model for the kind of English GRS thinks of himself as aiming to speak and write. Mortimer (who died in 2009) was highly educated (Harrow and Brasenose) and lived by the spoken and written word, combining a career at the Bar with a prolific and successful output of intelligent fiction, notably the Rumpole series, and frequent broadcasting on current affairs. His style was direct and unpretentious. And Penguin books normally seem to be carefully copy-edited. On the face of it the present co-authors would expect that if Mortimer and Penguin between them let a sentence into print, we ought to be happy with it from a grammatical point of view. Of course we are told that even individuals from the same regional and social dialect background may have odd differences between their personal idiolects (and random slips of the pen and misprints can always occur). So we tried to work out what the basis was for GRS's adverse reaction to this passage, which he certainly *understands* perfectly well.

Subordinate clauses introduced by *as* are of (at least) two kinds. Sometimes *as* means roughly the same as *because*, and in that case the quoted clause would be grammatically unremarkable (but would not make sense in the context – making something clear was not a reason for worrying). The other kind of *as* clause, which is the one we are evidently dealing with here, introduces an appositive relative clause which modifies not a noun phrase but the proposition expressed by the higher clause to which it is attached. A straightforward example would be *As you know, I have to leave by four* – meaning "I have to leave by four, and you know that I have to leave by four". In relative clauses it is usual, at least in "good" English, to omit the relativized element (unless it is represented by a relative pronoun at the beginning of the clause) – thus, *know* is a transitive verb, but the clause *As you know* does not itself contain an object.

This is undoubtedly the reason why GRS felt surprised when he read *as I have made it clear to you*. But on the other hand, this is a more complicated clause; recast in main-clause form it could very easily contain an extraposition structure – *I have made it clear to you that I worry*, in which the pronoun *it* anticipates the complement-clause object *that I worry*. So, whether we would expect to find *it* in the *as* clause depends on whether the relativized object to be deleted is counted as covering both parts of the extraposition structure, *it ... that I worry*, or only the "substantive" part, *that I worry*. But there seems to be no obvious way in which one could infer the expected answer to that question from more common sorts of relative clause, because those will not contain extraposition of the relativized element. We can say *I worry, which I have made clear to you* – but in that case the propositional object of *made* is represented by a relative pronoun and no possibility of extraposition arises. So, although GRS would not himself have written as Mortimer wrote, we have no grounds for regarding Mortimer's usage as contrary to the norms of usage recognized by GRS.

The issue is further complicated by the fact that there are socially-deprecated varieties of English in which relativized items are *not* omitted – one hears phrases like *that girl which you know her*. While we are sure that neither Mortimer nor we would dream of using that language variety in our writing, it seems normal enough that a grammatical feature which has special social implications in one environment might entirely lack those implications in a different environment. For instance, it is socially frowned on to reduce a possessive pronoun + *house* phrase to a bare possessive pronoun in a non-contrastive situation but perfectly acceptable to do so in a situation of contrast: someone who says *she'll be coming round to ours* rather than *... to us* or *... to our house/place/ ...* categorizes himself socially, whereas someone who says *she looked at several houses and decided to buy ours* does not. The social connotations of non-deletion of relativized items could similarly fail to apply in the case of extraposition structures.

The upshot of this rather lengthy consideration of a commonplace example is that it seems inappropriate to explain GRS's response to John Mortimer's usage by saying that GRS and Mortimer have slightly different idiolects. What the preceding analysis suggests to us is that Mortimer's usage is in fact quite all right in English as *GRS* speaks and writes it – only GRS had not realized that before. It is rather as if one had got into the habit of walking to work one way but there was another equally suitable way that one happened not to take; perhaps, now one's attention has been drawn to it, one will sometimes in future go that way. It may be that some would argue that this is all that is meant by "different idiolects", but it seems to us that the term is normally used with an implication of something more like a block on the paths not taken: if Mortimer and GRS word *as*-relatives differently, that is because they are walking through towns with similar but non-identical streetplans, and the lane Mortimer has gone down is not there in GRS's town. The truth is, surely, that both are walking through the same town, and GRS had never before noticed the possibility of going Mortimer's way.

If this sounds too metaphorical to mean very much, consider a non-grammatical example. If someone asks GRS to name the days of the week, he lists them beginning with Monday. Many people (we have no idea what the relative proportions are) begin with Sunday. Would one say that we have different idiolects? Surely it would be unreasonable to say that we are speakers of even slightly different languages, because of a difference of habits like this. We understand each other perfectly well; we might quite readily adopt the other sequence, and probably would if there were ever some practical reason to do so; we just happen to have fallen either into the Sunday-first or into the Monday-first habit and never had a reason to change. This does not seem at all like the fact that some people are English-speakers and others are Italian-speakers. It is more like the fact that some English-speakers take tea at breakfast and others prefer coffee.

If that is fair comment about the alternative ways of listing days, our suggestion is that what are commonly regarded as idiolect differences are often much more akin to the Sunday-first versus Monday-first contrast than to actual differences of language. Furthermore, it is not just that each of us individually has got into the habit of using only a proper subset of a fixed set of grammatical strctures which the language as a whole makes available to us, so that we may individually expand the range of things we say without the language expanding: using a language means putting words together in more or less novel ways, so that as a language community uses its language it will very frequently happen that uses are found for sequences of words which had no use previously. Calling such phenomena "changes in the language", comparable to the changes studied by historical linguists such as the Great Vowel Shift, seems as misguided as treating Sunday-first versus Monday-first as an idiolect difference. The community is simply progressively discovering more and more ways to achieve rhetorical goals by putting words together, and although this is a process that unrolls through time so that not all possibilities are well-established at any given date, there is no reason to think that any particular sequences of words are definitely "out of bounds" at a given date – perhaps in fact it will not happen to be for several decades before someone first finds a use for sequence X, but it could be this afternoon.

Our example of two ways of forming *as*-relatives illustrated the questionable nature of the "idiolect" concept, but did not illustrate the idea that language-users find new things to do with their language. As a very simple example of the latter, we offer a phenomenon which has become very frequent in English in the last decade or two but was unheard-of not long ago: *Whatever* used as a one-word conversational response. GRS is not sure when he first encountered this usage, though he is fairly sure it was after, probably well after, 1970 (it was already established by the time AB first lived in Britain in the 1990s).[1] GRS's own attempt to make explicit how the usage now functions, when the question arose in connexion with his work as a panelist for the Ask-a-Linguist public information service, was that it was a way of saying something like "You are such a loser that you mustn't expect me to put effort into giving you a considered answer". More recently, we read a journalist's attempt to explicate the same usage; she understood it as something like "You are correct, but I am unwilling to admit it explicitly". These glosses do not coincide but they have a family resemblance. They agree in interpreting the usage as expressing an attitude of scorn towards the conversational partner, while avoiding any commitment on the speaker's part to a position distinct from the hearer's.

The point relevant here is that (so far as we are aware) there was no previous recognized form of words that did quite the same job. If the interpretations quoted are correct, then one could have used similar wording to spell one's attitude out explicitly – but the point of saying "Whatever", as we understand it, is in large part to demonstrate one's aloofness by making a minimal response: it would be uncool and defeat the object to say something in many words.

But although the usage was new, it was not an arbitrary invention, as if teenagers had decided to start saying *Yonk*, or *Potato*, to express their attitude. The fact that we could interpret the usage, at least approximately, stemmed from the fact that this new use of the word *whatever* has recognizable links to long-established uses of the word within fuller utterances. In the 1960s there was no known use for the word *whatever* in isolation, it was a word that would only occur as a part of a few fairly specialized constructions; if GRS, who was a linguistics teacher by the end of that decade, had been asked to give an example of an ill-formed English sentence he could easily have suggested *Whatever.[2] Yet although there was no recognized use for this utterance, someone, somewhere, found a use for it, hearers understood (at least roughly) what that person was doing with it, and it caught on. This was not most usefully seen, we suggest, as

---

1 Randall Mann (2013: 121) claims that he personally initiated this usage in 1996, but Hugo Williams (whom we thank for the reference) and GRS are rather sure that the usage was older than that.

2 The main reason why GRS would probably not have chosen that example in practice is not that he anticipated in the 1960s that it might have a use, but that people who ask for examples of "starred sentences" are usually hoping for multi-word examples.

a change in the English language. It was the exploitation of a possibility that had been latent in the English language before anyone thought to use it.

Since Chomsky's principle became influential in linguistics, it has often been pointed out how difficult it seems to be to identify specific word-sequences which one can confidently predict to be unusable. (Cf. the Householder quotation on p. 7.) And, before *Syntactic Structures* appeared in 1957, the concept of dividing the range of all possible word-sequences into well-formed and ill-formed subsets does not seem to have occurred in the linguistic literature. The asterisk notation, which theoretical linguists now use to mark strings as ill-formed, was adapted by them from a notation used by historical linguists to mean something quite different. (Historical linguists asterisk reconstructed forms to show that, although they are postulated to have occurred, they are not actually attested.) It is not clear to us precisely what Sapir meant by his famous remark "All grammars leak", quoted on p. 6, but it would be difficult to interpret it in its context as a statement that every real-life grammar generates some set L' of strings which includes some strings that are not members of the target set L of well-formed strings, and/or excludes some members of L – this idea of a language as a precisely-bounded set of strings simply does not seem to be present in the pages which lead up to the remark.

4.3 Statistics of construction frequencies

So far our discussion has been mainly conceptual and anecdotal. To make it more concretely empirical, let us introduce a piece of statistical analysis. Figure 6, below, displays statistical properties of the alternative realizations of the high-frequency nonterminal category "noun phrase" in the SUSANNE Corpus.[3]

SUSANNE comprises grammatical parse-trees for 64 texts totalling 131,302 words of published written American English. The question addressed by the present analysis is: how diverse are the alternative realizations of a particular category, and in particular is there any objective evidence for a contrast between "well-formed" realizations that recur repeatedly thanks to their normative status, and one-off or rare "performance deviations"? Chapter 2 offered objective evidence that the SUSANNE annotation scheme approaches the limit of humanly-possible grammatical-annotation precision. Thus, grammatical diversity in the

---

3 The analysis summarized in Figure 6 replicates an experiment discussed in Sampson (1987), but that early work was less robust: it used a treebank which was less than one-third the size of SUSANNE, and was annotated at a period when the rigorous SUSANNE scheme was not yet fully developed, so that its annotation decisions may have been less consistent.

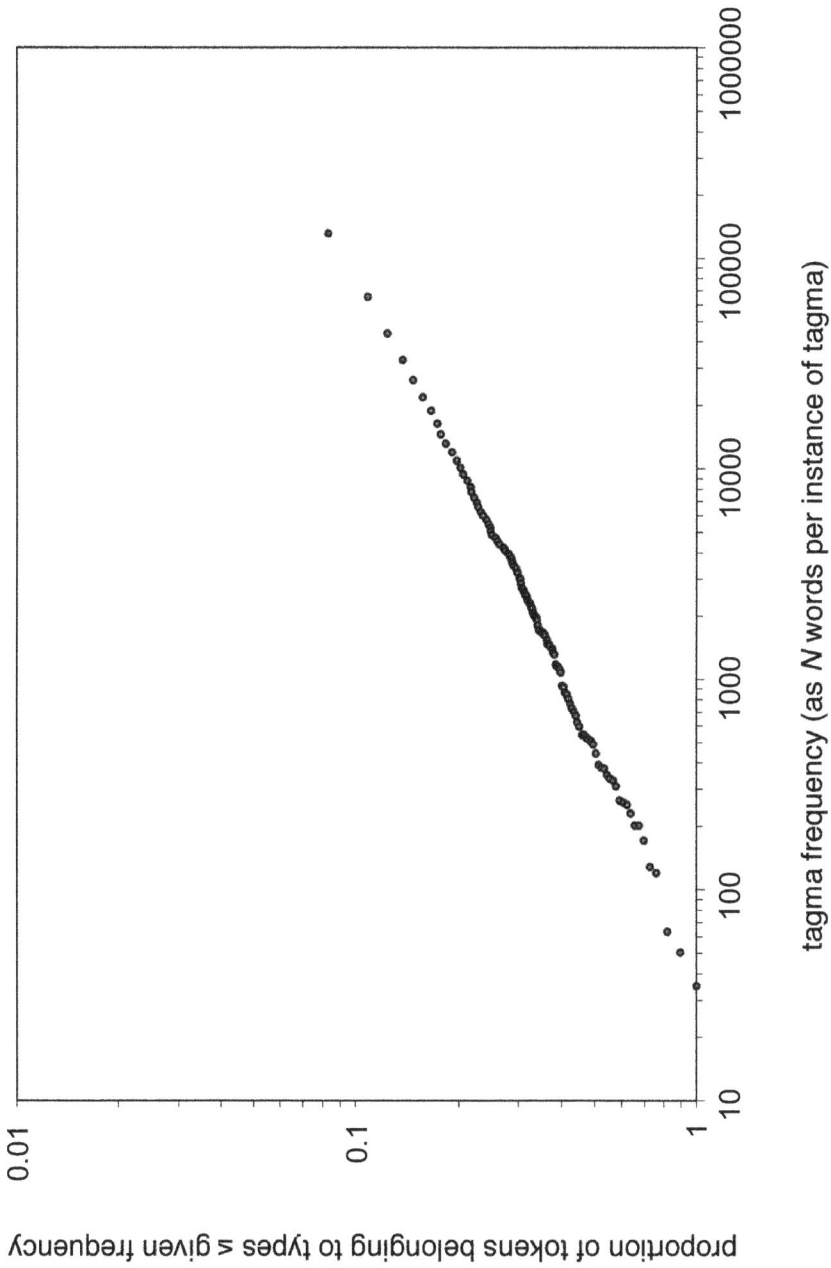

Figure 6: Noun-phrase expansion frequencies in SUSANNE

SUSANNE treebank is likely to be genuine, rather than a product of inconsistent annotation behaviour by analysts.

Our analysis examined the incidence, in Release 5 (dated 2000) of the SUSANNE treebank, of various daughter-label sequences below mother nodes labelled as noun phrases.[4] Within the SUSANNE scheme, any mother node in a parse-tree dominates a sequence of one or more daughter nodes whose labels may include tagmatags, wordtags, or both.[5] The SUSANNE labelling system makes distinctions which are often more refined than it is useful to include in the present investigation, so we collapsed groups of related labels into single labels by the rules which follow. For the sake of accountability, we specify each label-merging rule in terms of specific changes to the codes defined in the SUSANNE scheme, but for the sake of readers unfamiliar with the scheme we add in brackets a statement that seeks to give a sense of what these changes mean in terms of retaining or ignoring particular grammatical distinctions.

Rules for merging tagmatags:

tags beginning F... or T... (finite or non-finite subordinate clauses) are reduced to that character and one immediately-following lower-case character (thus e.g. relative clauses are distinguished from nominal clauses, and infinitival clauses from past-participle clauses, but e.g. functiontags (p. 32) are ignored)

tags beginning V... (verb group) are reduced to that character, followed only by i, g, or n if one of those characters appears in the unreduced label (verb groups beginning with infinitives, present participles, and past participles are distinguished from finite verb groups, but contrasts e.g. of tense or person among finite verb groups are ignored)

all other tagmatags are reduced to their first character, followed only by q or v if one of those characters appears in the unreduced tag (basic tagma categories such as main clause, noun phrase, adjectival phrase, are distinguished from one another, and phrases including *wh-* or *wh ... ever* elements are distinguished from non-*wh-* phrases, but e.g. number distinctions in noun phrases, or person and case in pronouns, are ignored)

Rule for merging wordtags:

wordtags beginning V ... (verbs) include all capital letters found in the unreduced tag (grammatically-distinct verb forms are distinguished)

other wordtags are represented by their first two letters, together with the characters 1, 2, and/or Q if these appear in the unreduced tag (parts of speech are distinguished, and explicitly singular or plural forms, and *wh-* forms, are marked as such)

---

4 In terms of the SUSANNE labelling scheme, noun-phrase nodes are all nodes whose labels begin with the letter N, not followed by a second capital.

5 "Tagmatags" are labels for nonterminal nodes (cf. note 1, p. 26). Apart from nodes labelled with tagmatags or with wordtags, there can also be "ghost nodes" (pp. 32–33), representing the logical position of elements which in surface structure are deleted or appear below other mother nodes. For the present analysis, ghost nodes are ignored.

The consequence of this process of label simplification is that the vocabulary of labels found in daughter sequences below the 34,914 SUSANNE noun-phrase nodes comprises exactly one hundred distinct items: 29 distinct tagma-tags, and 71 distinct wordtags.

Various sequences of elements drawn from this vocabulary occur with different frequencies as daughter-sequences of noun-phrase nodes. Thus, the commonest and second-commonest expansions of the category "noun phrase" are PP1 (singular personal pronoun – 3749 instances) and AT NN1 (either *the* or *no*, followed by singular common noun – 2605 instances). At the other extreme, there are 2904 distinct daughter-sequences which are each represented once in the data; an example is the sequence NP1 NN1 YC Fr, i.e. singular proper noun + singular common noun + comma + relative clause (the SUSANNE instance being *Fulton County, which receives none of this money*). Figure 6 plots the various frequencies observed (expressed as average words of text per instance of a daughter-sequence) against the proportion of noun-phrase tokens in the data that represents types of that or a lower frequency; both scales are logarithmic.

Thus, the leftmost data-point in Figure 6 is at $(35 \cdot 0, 1 \cdot 0)$: 3749 instances of the noun-phrase type PP1 in the 131,302 words (not counting punctuation marks) of SUSANNE is one per $35 \cdot 0$ words, and since this is the highest frequency in the data, all noun phrases in SUSANNE belong to types of that frequency or less. The rightmost data-point is at $(131302, 0 \cdot 083)$; $8 \cdot 3$ per cent of SUSANNE noun-phrase tokens (i.e. 2904 out of 34,914) belong to types occurring just once each in the treebank, i.e. once per 131,302 words.

The significance of Figure 6 lies not just in the fact that on a log–log scale it is linear, without notable discontinuities, but in the shallowness of the slope. Although the data-points towards the right represent low frequencies for particular label-sequences, so many different types of label-sequence occur with those low frequencies that the proportion of noun-phrase *tokens* accounted for by low-frequency types is nevertheless quite high.[6]

The trend line to which the data-points approximate is $y = 3 \cdot 1 x^{-0 \cdot 3}$. If this linearity were maintained in larger samples of text, permitting lower frequencies to be observed than is possible with SUSANNE (where the lowest observable frequency is one instance in 131,302 words, since that is the size of the corpus), then substantial proportions of noun-phrase tokens would be accounted for by types of truly minute frequencies. One in twenty noun phrases would represent types that occur individually not more than once in a million words. One in 160

---

[6] Somewhat comparable findings, looking at all constructions (rather than just noun phrases), but within a smaller corpus (of Dow Jones newswire stories), were published by Krotov, Gaizauskas, and Wilks (1994).

or so noun phrases would represent types occurring not more than once in a billion (10^9) words. One in 1300 noun phrases would represent types occurring not more than once in a trillion (10^{12}) words (and the figure of one in 1300 suggests that a couple of dozen of the one-off types in SUSANNE may be as rare as this).

In other words, constructions too individually rare for their existence to be reliably confirmed by observation would collectively form too large a proportion of what happens in the language for a grammatical description which ignored them to be satisfactory.

Many of the one-off constructions in SUSANNE, such as the *Fulton County* example quoted above, are clearly "normal" although they happen not to recur within this data-set. But there are other cases where low frequency seems to correlate with oddity. Consider for instance the sequence of daughter labels AT S NN1 YC S, that is: (*the* or *no*) + main clause + singular common noun + comma + main clause. Is that sequence a valid way to realize the category "noun phrase"? Considered in the abstract, one might well feel confident in saying no. But now look at the SUSANNE instance (we show the preceding context within square brackets): [*One can meet with aloofness almost anywhere:*] *the Thank-Heaven-We're-not-Involved viewpoint, It Doesn't Affect Us!* The oddity of the tag sequence turns out to stem largely from the way in which a quoted sentence being used to modify the noun *viewpoint* has in part been postposed after that noun. Before we read this example, we are not sure that we would have been alive to the possibility of realizing an idea like this in quite that way (just as GRS was not aware of the possibility exemplified by the Mortimer example quoted earlier before he read Mortimer's novel); but now that we see the SUSANNE example, we cannot regard it as "wrong". It was written by an English native speaker, and as English L_1 and L_2 speakers respectively we understand it perfectly well; furthermore, we understand and sympathize with the writer's motive in postposing the second quoted clause (if the entire quotation had been included in the ordinary modifying position before *viewpoint*, a reader could easily lose the thread before reaching the point at which he discovered that the long quotation was functioning as a modifier to a following noun). This seems to be an example of what we shall call a "*Dunster* construction": a construction which, before we encountered it, we would not have thought of as available in English, but which after confronting a real-life example we come to see as a valid possibility which had been available to us all along. It is not likely that the leftmost parts of Figure 6 contain *Dunster* constructions (if a construction recurs often enough, a speaker of the language will surely recognize it); but the right-hand side of Figure 6 includes some *Dunster* constructions alongside clearly normal constructions.

4.4 A range without boundaries

The picture we take from Figure 6 is that the grammatical possibilities of a language are like a network of paths in open grassland. There are a number of heavily used, wide and well-beaten tracks. Other, less popular routes are narrower, and the variation extends smoothly down to routes used only very occasionally, which are barely distinguishable furrows or, if they are used rarely enough, perhaps not even visible as permanent marks in the grass; but there are no fences anywhere preventing any particular route being used, and there is no sharp discontinuity akin to the contrast between metalled roads and foot-made paths – the widest highway is only the result of people going that way much more often and in far greater numbers than in the case of narrow paths.

We do not say that, for a given language, there are *no* word-sequences which genuinely will never find a use. We are not claiming that every member of the set of all possible strings over the vocabulary – or even, every member short enough to be utterable in practice – will sooner or later acquire some communicative function. It may be that some never will, even if the language continues to be spoken indefinitely. That would mean that instead of one boundary, between grammatical and ungrammatical sequences, there might in principle be two boundaries: (i) a boundary between the set of sequences which feel familiar to a speaker, and the set of sequences which are unfamiliar either because they include *Dunster* constructions or because they will never have any use; and (ii) a boundary between sequences destined never to have a use, and those which will in due course be useful.

But boundary (ii), between those word-sequences which are destined never to have a use, and those which have not found a use so far but will do so at some time in the future (whether we are discussing the language of a community or that of an individual speaker), is an unknowable thing, as inaccessible to scientific enquiry as questions about what technological inventions will be made in the future. (If we knew precisely what invention would be made next year, we would have made it now.) And boundary (i), between the word-sequences for which an individual, or a language-community, has already found a use, and the sequences which have not come into use yet but are destined to do so in due course, while it might be scientifically checkable (though to do so accurately for the more marginal constructions would require an impractically comprehensive range of observations), is a purely contingent thing of no real scientific interest. If the only reason why GRS has not been saying things like *as I have made it clear* is that, before reading Mortimer, he had not realized that it is equally as compatible with the norms of his language as the alternative *as I have made clear*, then plotting the boundary between things a speaker does say, and things he has not said yet but will, would in effect mean listing a long series of chance pieces of linguistic experience. It would be as tedious as listing what a man was given to eat each time he visited friends for dinner; it would just be a set of contingent facts, with little system or principle underlying them.

Frederick Newmeyer (2003) has argued that "grammar is grammar and usage is usage": the two are different, and not to be confused. In a sense we agree with Newmeyer: a description of usage, whether an individual's usage or that of a wider speech-community, does not define a grammar in his sense of the word. But we would add that grammar in Newmeyer's sense is a fiction. Usage is a reality in the world, which can be described more or less accurately, but there is no separate reality corresponding to Newmeyer's "grammar".

How might a defender of the distinction between normal and deviant (or "grammatical" and "ungrammatical") strings hope to justify that distinction, if constructions occur at a range of frequencies which vary smoothly down to a lowest observable level where clearly-normal constructions are mingled with *Dunster* constructions? Would anyone argue that the problem will be solved by enlarging the data-set? Since our analysis here is based on the largest extant data-set which we believe to be adequately accurate, we must concede that it is logically possible that a very much larger body of data, enabling substantially lower frequencies to be registered, could show a discontinuity in the distribution of construction-frequencies, with a gap between the range of "normal" construc-tions and a scattering of much-lower-frequency deviant constructions. But the 1987 analysis cited in note 3, based on a 40,000-word sample, gave a linear plot. SUSANNE more than triples the quantity of wording and gives an equally linear plot. We venture the prediction that, no matter how far the database is expanded, the statistics corresponding to Figure 6 will continue to be about equally linear. (As a matter of fact, although the earlier analysis of Sampson (1987) was criticized, by L. Taylor et al. 1989, Briscoe 1990, and Culy 1998, the critics do not appear to have made or suggested a prediction contradicting the one we have just offered.)

Clearly, other linguists might well disagree with the particular scheme for annotating grammatical structure from which the data in Figure 6 are derived. A linguist might urge that the one hundred symbols into which the SUSANNE label-set has been collapsed make too few distinctions in some areas, and/or too many (irrelevant) distinctions in others – and not just the limited alphabet of 100 symbols, but the far larger range of symbols in the full, uncollapsed SUSANNE scheme, might be criticized in similar ways. Not only the label-set, but the shapes of the SUSANNE trees (and hence the identity of the word-sequences which are recognized as constructions), may be called into question; generative linguists tend to draw much "deeper" trees than those assigned by the SUSANNE scheme to given sentences, i.e. their analyses recognize more con-structions per sentence and their constructions on average have fewer daughters.

We would be the first to agree that the analytic scheme from which Figure 6 derives is not to be seen as "the right scheme" for annotating English grammar – we are sceptical about the concept of a particular "right" scheme. If the SUSANNE text-samples were re-annotated in conformity with some other analytic scheme, the shape of Figure 6 would change.

But although numbers derived from a re-annotated treebank would certainly differ in detail from those of Figure 6, again our prediction would be that for any reasonable analytic scheme (any scheme that was not deliberately gerrymandered to give a contrary result with the SUSANNE text-samples) the significant features of Figure 6 would be unchanged: the new plot would continue to show data-points distributed smoothly and approximately log-linearly along a gentle slope. This is a fallible hypothesis, of course, as scientific statements should be; but at present we do not have the impression that this is a direction in which critics see our position as vulnerable.

We realize also that those who believe in a clearcut grammatical/ungrammatical contrast make no claim that grammatical constructions all occur with equal or even similar frequencies. Many would emphatically reject that idea. Presumably they would say that ill-formed constructions occur only at frequencies substantially lower than those of the commonest well-formed constructions (this is not a point which we have seen discussed in the literature, but it is unclear to us what it could mean to describe some of the most usual turns of phrase in a language as not well-formed in that language – unless "not well-formed" meant "unacceptable in high-prestige discourse", which is not the sense relevant here). But saying that ill-formed constructions are less common than the commonest well-formed constructions is compatible with saying that different well-formed constructions occur at very different frequencies, with some being fully as rare as the ill-formed structures that occur as sporadic performance errors.

Indeed, as already mentioned, many linguists favour schemes of analysis which yield "deeper" trees than those of the SUSANNE scheme, so that constructions which SUSANNE treats as minimal subtrees (pairings of a mother node with a set of immediately-dominated daughter nodes) often have several or many intermediate nodes in those analyses. If the frequency predicted for an overall sentence structure were identified with the product of the relative probabilities of each production contained in the parse tree (that is, for each non-terminal node, the probability of its sequence of daughter labels given its own label), then (since relative probabilities are fractions of one), a SUSANNE construction which in one of these analyses contains many intermediate nodes would be assigned a probability representing the product of many fractions, i.e. a low probability. In other words, someone who favours that style of grammatical analysis would *expect* various SUSANNE constructions to occur over a wide range of frequencies extending down to very low ones. (The critiques listed above of Sampson (1987) each included comments along these lines.)

But if one reconciles data like Figure 6 with the grammatical/ungrammatical distinction in this way, by saying that grammatical constructions occur at many different frequencies, and the lower areas of their frequency range include frequencies at which various specific types of performance deviation also occur, then the question arises how someone constructing a grammatical description is to distinguish between well-formed but rare constructions, which the grammar should generate, and performance deviations, which it should exclude? What evidence could this distinction be based on? If a significant proportion of constructions occur on the order of once per trillion words (p. 74), it would seem unrealistic to think that candidate grammars could adequately be checked against the data of observation. How could one hope to argue that one particular grammatical description of a language was more or less accurate than another?

4.5 Can intuition substitute for observation?

A number of linguists would answer the question about how we are to establish a grammatical/ungrammatical distinction by arguing that it is not a matter of observed frequencies at all, but a matter of what speakers of a language know *qua* speakers to be allowable versus deviant – a matter of "introspection" or "speaker intuition". Andrew Carnie, quoted on p. 65 above, writes (2002: 11) that as grammarians "we have to rely on our knowledge of our native language (or on the knowledge of a native speaker consultant for languages that we don't speak natively)", eliciting this unconscious knowledge via "grammaticality judgment task[s]". Terence Nunnally, reviewing a corpus-based account of one aspect of English grammar, puts the point specially forcefully (2002: 177): "it is intuition that signals ill-formedness, not frequency of formations per million words". Frederick Newmeyer (2003: 689–692) makes various claims about judgements which he claims English-speakers can make introspectively, independently of experience, about what can and cannot be said. Linguists have been making similar comments since the beginning of the generative movement. Sometimes they have claimed that speakers have introspective or intuitive access to aspects of grammar extending far beyond the fundamental issue of whether given word-sequences are well- or ill-formed; in an early textbook, Terence Langendoen (1969: 9–11) claimed that fluent speakers not only can do this but can identify the parts of speech to which the words of a well-formed sentence belong, and the constituent structure into which those words fit.

It is startling to find twentieth- and 21st-century scientists maintaining that theories in any branch of science ought explicitly to be based on what people subjectively "know" or "intuit" to be the case, rather than on objective, interpersonally-observable data. Surely we would think it strange if, say, physicists based their laws of motion on the fact that they "knew" without experiment that balls of different weights released from a tower simultaneously would hit the ground at the same time, or "knew" that they would hit at different times (and we would think it even stranger if they ignored contrary experimental findings as irrelevant).[7] But language is an aspect of human behaviour, while the motions of inanimate objects are not, so there is perhaps superficial plausibility in the idea that people might have access to reliable intuitions about their native language, whereas no-one today would claim reliable intuitive knowledge about the laws of motion.

However, plausible though the former idea might be to some, it is obviously wrong.

Its chief flaw is not the fact that different individual speakers of the same language regularly differ when asked about the grammaticality or well-formedness of particular strings of words – though the fact that they do is by now so well-known that it is not worth quoting examples here. That *could* reflect merely the fact that individuals induce slightly different sets of rules when exposed during childhood to different finite samples of the same language. Wayne Cowart (1997) has shown us that the chaotic appearance of an individual speaker's grammaticality judgements may be misleading: one can sometimes tease out systematic patterns underlying the apparent chaos. The real issue is that there is no reason to assume that patterns in a speaker's intuitive grammaticality judgements reflect realities of his language.

---

7 It is odd also to find Carnie, in the passage quoted on p. 65, claiming that corpus data cannot enable linguists to distinguish between grammatical and ungrammatical sequences on the ground that corpora do not contain "negative information". If that were a barrier, natural science would be impossible. Carnie is saying here that a grammar of a language must tell us what sequences do occur in a language and what sequences do not, but that a finite corpus shows us only that certain sequences do occur – the fact that no example of some type of sequence happens to turn up in a particular corpus does not imply that sequences of that type cannot occur in the language in general. However, a scientific theory tells us what phenomena do occur and what do not, with respect to some aspect of the natural world (a theory which ruled no possibility out would be empty); yet a scientist can observe only a finite sample of the phenomena that do occur, he can never observe an impossible phenomenon. Clearly, natural science manages to advance despite this asymmetry in its data, and likewise the asymmetry of corpus data is no hindrance to empirical linguistics. This issue is well understood by philosophers of science, though Carnie is far from the only linguist to imagine that it is problematic. The issue has been discussed at length in Sampson (2002: 94–97), Sampson (2005: 89–91), and we shall not repeat the discussion here.

There are plenty of other factors which they may reflect. The realities of some other, socially significant dialect or language can often give a speaker false intuitions about his own usage. (Consider for instance William Labov's discussion (1975: 34–36) of Philadelphia speakers who insisted, with every appearance of sincerity, that they had not encountered "positive *any more*" sentences such as *John is smoking a lot any more*, and had no idea how to interpret them, yet were observed to use the construction themselves in the way that is normal for their dialect area though it does not occur in general American English.) Speakers' linguistic intuitions may be heavily moulded by a tradition of teaching the national language which happens to be erroneous in various respects (as schoolroom teaching about the English language for centuries misrepresented it in terms of models based in part on Latin and on Hellenistic Greek rather than on English itself). A speaker who is an academic linguist may unconsciously permit his intuitive response to examples to be moulded by the desire to produce evidence supporting and not disconfirming his grammatical theories; it was cases where this seemed to have happened that led Labov to urge ([1970] 1978: 199) that "linguists cannot continue to produce theory and data at the same time". Indeed, a speaker's linguistic intuitions can in some cases be controlled by some purely private, and mistaken, theory which that speaker has formulated. We have discussed elsewhere (Sampson 2001: 140 n. 1) the case of an English-speaking computing engineer who insisted that the English *a/an* alternation rule implied the choice of *an* rather than *a* before e.g. *good egg* – he realized that the choice depended on whether a later word began with vowel or consonant, but he wrongly believed that the relevant word was the head noun of the phrase rather than the immediately-following word, where these are not the same. (He surely had not heard people regularly saying things like *an good egg*.)

It may be that many speakers do have reasonably accurate intuitions about at least the high-frequency, "core" constructions of their language. But even if that were true, it would not help theoretical linguists much, because their controversies tend to turn on the grammatical status not of straightforward core examples but of unusual word-strings which would probably be infrequent in practice even if "grammatical". One could argue that whereas intuitive methods might often have been satisfactory in practice for linguistics in the pre-generative period, when the grammatical phenomena discussed were commonly high-frequency ones for which speakers' intuitive judgements may be accurate, generative syntactic research has a much greater need of corpus or other empirical data, because speakers cannot be expected to make reliable judgements about the status of the unusual word sequences which are often crucial to its theoretical debates.[8]

And in any case, the only way that we could ultimately know speaker intuitions to be reliable, even with respect to core usage, would be to check a language-description based on intuitions against one based on empirical observation. But, if we had the latter, the former would be redundant and uninteresting.

4.6 How intuitions have misled

It is understandable that grammarians of the 1960s and 1970s made heavy use of subjective intuition, because before the widespread availability of computers and language corpora it was often quite difficult in practice to gather relevant empirical data. In such circumstances it might perhaps be scientifically respectable to base theories on impressionistic data (provided that it was made explicit that such theorizing was provisional and liable to reconsideration as better data became available). But linguists' intuition-based claims were often so extravagant that one suspects those making the claims cannot have realized how soon advances in technology were destined to make it easy to check and refute them.

One example that we have discussed elsewhere (Sampson 2005: 71–72) is a claim made originally by J.R. ("Haj") Ross in a 1974 lecture, following which it was reasserted by Mark Aronoff (1976), by Thomas Roeper and Muffy Siegel (1978), by Greg Carlson and Thomas Roeper (1981: 123–124), and (according to Laurie Bauer 1990) by others since. The claim is that if a verb in English has a prefix it cannot take a non-nominal complement; various of the linguists cited developed subtle grammatical theories in the attempt to explain this "fact".

There is a story that when Charles II founded the Royal Society, he asked its scientists to explain to him why a pail of water does not become heavier when a live fish is added to it. After the scientists eventually confessed themselves baffled, the king roared with laughter and pointed out that in fact the pail does become heavier. Ross's "fact" is one of a similar order. Bauer gives a series of examples that Carlson and Roeper predict to be impossible, but which in reality seem perfectly normal: two of them are *Sam has a tendency to overindulge in chocolate*, and *Chris reaffirmed that everything possible was being done* (with verbs containing the prefixes *over-* and *re-*, two of those listed by Carlson and Roeper). It seems questionable whether any linguist would continue to maintain the quoted generalization, if he considered Bauer's potential counterexamples. In case any would, here are a few real-life counterexamples we found using Google on 17 October 2005:

---

8 We believe that this point is not original with us but was made somewhere by William Labov; however, we have not succeeded in tracking it down in his writings.

(34)   *If you tend to overindulge in tasty, high-sugar and fatty foods, try the Raw*
       Food or Macrobiotics diet.

       I want to overindulge in you.

       The only way to be happy is to overindulge in food and drink.

       His fellow monks thought he'd overindulged in turnip wine when he told
       them about it.

(35)   *New rules reaffirm that it is illegal to give out state secrets on the Internet.*

       New U.S. Geological Survey (USGS) science reaffirms, with strong genetic
       evidence, that the northern spotted owl is a separate subspecies from
       California and Mexican spotted owls.

       We recognised that maintaining this growth is a challenge, and reaffirmed
       that each of our countries must play its part to support long-term
       sustainable growth.

       The U.S. side reaffirmed that the U.S. has always been open to dialogue
       in principle.

How would a believer in intuition-based linguistics respond to a case like
this? We take it that he would not argue that the various Google quotations
represent ungrammatical "performance deviations". They made sense to the
writers, they make sense and feel normal enough to us (and, we suspect, to our
present readers); why should we agree to classify them as "deviant", merely
because a number of linguists said that such constructions do not occur in
English? Can anyone announce off the cuff that some ordinary-looking construction is ungrammatical, and are we under some obligation to agree? Surely no-one
would go as far as that.

But if a defender of intuition says that in this case Haj Ross, and the various
linguists who repeated his claim, were mistaken, then the obvious question
arises as to how we distinguish between reliable, veridical linguistic intuitions
and mistakes. It is not, evidently, that occasional mistakes are made by individual linguists in the heat of the moment but once an intuitive claim is considered and reaffirmed over a period by a range of linguists we can safely take
it as veridical; the latter did happen in this case. (In chapter 13 we shall look at a
case which has been discussed even more intensively, but where again linguists'
intuitions have proved misleading.)

If intensity of discussion is no guarantee of reliability of linguistic intuitions,
would it be said that reliability is to be assessed in terms of the standing of the
person whose intuitions they are? Margaret Boden notes that Noam Chomsky
has been willing to assert that his own intuitions should be given greater

authority than the considered usage of other competent speakers; he objected to the use of corpus data already in 1962, before any corpus in the modern sense had been compiled. We quote Boden (2008: 1955), adjusting her citation format to match the conventions of this book:

> [Chomsky wrote]: "The trouble with using a corpus is that some authors do not write the English language. Veblen, for example, speaks of 'performing leisure', and the verb *perform* cannot take such an object [i.e. a mass-word]" (Hill 1962: 28). In other words, any actual usage recorded in a corpus can be ignored if it doesn't fit Chomsky's theory. And this applies not just to the false starts and unintentional mistakes common in spontaneous speech, or the syntactic 'solecisms' committed by the unschooled, but even to the carefully considered constructions of experienced native-speaker writers such as Thorstein Veblen. In defence of his remark about the grammar of *perform*, Chomsky said: "How do I know […]? Because I am a native speaker of the English language" (Hill 1962: 29).

Noam Chomsky and Thorstein Veblen were both sons of recent immigrants to the USA from non-English-speaking countries, and it is true that Veblen did not speak English until he started going to school; properly, Margaret Boden should not have called him a "native" speaker, since his first language was Norwegian. But we take it that Chomsky's point was not merely a crude boast that he had mastered English better than Veblen (to which the obvious riposte by a corpus linguist would be that part of the art of corpus research is to seek to ensure that the material collected is produced by the speakers whose language is under study). More plausibly, Chomsky was accepting that in his published writings Veblen was a competent user of the English language (as he surely was), and Chomsky was saying that competent language-users are apt to use their language in ways that they know to be invalid – so one should study the knowledge (by asking speakers about their intuitions) rather than the usage.

But is it plausible that a distinguished author who chose to use an innovative form of words, such as *perform leisure*, would agree if challenged that "yes, I realize I shouldn't have written that, but I stretched a point"? Surely a much more likely response would be along the lines "The people I was writing for don't seem to have any trouble with the phrase; whatever you think of it, it's English now".

It is true that, while Veblen and Chomsky were or are both competent users of English, Chomsky is a professor of linguistics while Veblen's academic expertise lay in a field unrelated to language. Perhaps Chomsky was suggesting that the intuitions of a speaker who is a professional linguist ought to be accorded more authority than those of someone who is "only" a competent speaker. But William Labov (1975: 28–30) has quoted passages from Chomsky's writings which imply that *other English-speaking linguists'* intuitions are merely fallible opinions, while his own intuitions are veridical linguistic data. Yet surely no-one, Chomsky included, would seriously and explicitly put this forward as a principle for assessing linguistic data?

Linguists who want to treat speakers' intuitions rather than interpersonally-observable evidence as the basis of linguistic description are simply choosing to turn their back on science, and reverting to the pre-modern pattern of "arguments from authority". Up to the early modern period, people "knew" that the Sun goes round the Earth. The Pope and other leaders of the Church proclaimed it, and Giordano Bruno was burned at the stake partly because he held a different opinion. If one's priority is to have fixed theories which everyone accepts, this may be an efficient approach to achieving them; but what the seventeenth-century development of the scientific method showed us was that as a way of arriving at truth it was severely unsatisfactory. If linguistics is to be taken seriously as a knowledge-generating enterprise, it simply must base itself on empirical, interpersonally-observable data. And if it does so, we question whether it will give us a basis for drawing a distinction between "grammatical" and "ungrammatical" word-strings.

4.7 Is English special?

One way in which our point of view might be criticized would be by arguing that it is unduly influenced by the fact that the language we are studying, English, happens to fall close to the isolating extreme of linguistic typology. We saw that Householder commented how difficult it is to line up English words in a way that cannot be assigned any sense at all; but arguably it is easier to do this for a language with a richer inflexion system. In Latin or French, for instance, one can produce clearcut ungrammaticality by violating gender agreement between adjective and noun, or person and number agreement between subject and verb.

Even English has some rules as categorical as this. A third-person singular verb form should not take a first- or second-person subject; or, consider the word-order rule cited against us by Christopher Culy (1998), that a definite article precedes rather than follows the noun with which it is in construction. We agree that we can find no case of *the* following its noun in the hundred million words of the British National Corpus.

In responding to Culy (Sampson 2001: 177), we suggested a contrived but, we believe, realistic situation in which *the* would occur after its noun in a meaningful English utterance: describing a foreign language, one might easily say something like *Norwegians put the article after the noun, in their language they say things like bread the is on table the.* Describing how other languages work is one valid use of a language, alongside innumerable other uses, so this response to Culy's objection was fair. And we believe it might be possible to construct comparable scenarios in which it would be natural to utter sentences of a more highly inflected language with violations of the normal rules governing inflexions – though as the number of such violations was increased, no doubt the scenarios in which the resulting utterances might occur would quickly become very tortuously contrived indeed.

However, we need not press this defence of our thesis. If the reader is unpersuaded by our resort to scenarios where one language is used to imitate the structure of another, we can offer a less extreme fallback position. Ultimately, we do believe one can sustain the strong claim that there is *no* well-defined contrast between grammatical and ungrammatical; but at the same time, we have some instinctive sympathy with those who find our appeal to examples like the *Norwegians* sentence to be an unsatisfactory, almost cheating way of shoring up that claim.[9]

So let us concede that word-sequences containing violations of inflexional agreement rules, or of word-order rules as fundamental as the English rule that the definite article precedes its noun, might have a status distinct from the kinds of word sequence which speakers commonly use in discussing everyday topics other than language itself. We could accept the term "ungrammatical" to describe those abnormal sequences. The idea that only the most extreme version of a doctrine is worth advocating is naïve – truth does not always lie at extremes.

We repeat, though, that this weaker position is not the one we ourselves hold. It is all very well to say that using English to imitate the structure of Norwegian does not "count" as normal English, but where are the boundaries of normal usage to be set? Does a parent's deliberately playful use of language with a young child "count"? If one made a serious attempt to answer questions like these, it might be difficult to end up with a better answer than "normal usage is usage which limits itself to standard, well-recognized grammatical structures" – in which case the grammatical/ungrammatical contrast has been imposed on language by fiat rather than emerging as an observed finding about the nature of language.

---

9 Anatol Stefanowitsch comments (2007: 58) that when he uses the *Norwegians* example to make our point against the "ungrammaticality" concept, reactions usually range "from incredulity to outright profanity, with occasional threats of physical violence." Although we have some sympathy with these negative responses, our sympathy is limited: the intemperate nature of the reactions reported by Stefanowitsch are an index of the remarkably doctrinaire ethos in modern linguistics, where the response to new ideas seems commonly to be hostility.

Nevertheless, we know from experience that many readers are not ready to go the whole hog and accept *Norwegians*-type examples as refutations of absolute grammatical rules, so we offer the weaker form of our thesis as one which those readers might be willing to countenance, and which still comes closer to the truth about language than the ideas about syntax which are current in the discipline.

It would be a mistake to take this concession as undermining the whole thesis of our book. Even with the concession, our position on "grammaticality" would remain very distinct from the standard view. Linguists who understand grammatical description in Chomsky's terms as partitioning the set of all strings over the vocabulary of a language into two subsets, a grammatical and an un-grammatical subset (whether or not they also attribute different probabilities to members of the grammatical subset), do not, surely, think of the grammatical subset as comprising all strings other than those which contain oddities as striking but superficial as an agreement failure, or (in the English case) an article following its noun. That would be a thin, impoverished concept of grammar, relative to the concept which has motivated the large volume of effort which has been devoted to syntactic description over the past fifty years. Linguists have been assuming that there are contrasts between well-formed and ill-formed also with respect to the larger syntactic architecture of clauses and sentences: for instance, with respect to the positions in a matrix clause where it makes sense to introduce a subordinate clause.

Whether a language is of isolating or inflecting type does not seem very relevant to those "architectural" aspects of sentence structure. It is with respect to those aspects that we are mainly aiming to deny the reality of the grammatical/ungrammatical contrast.

4.8 The analogy with word meaning

Let us try to make the view of grammar we are advocating more palatable, by drawing an analogy with another area of natural language where the corresponding point of view may be less controversial, namely word meanings.

Grammar is about which assemblages of words have uses in a language. Semantics is about how one can move inferentially from one usable word-sequence to another. What it means to say that an English speaker knows the meaning of the word *father*, for instance, is that he is capable of drawing various inferences involving that word: e.g. from the statement *this person is my father* he can infer *this person is male*.

That suggests a scenario in which someone who masters a language has access to a fixed set of inferential relationships among its sentences. With a logical system such as the propositional calculus, that is very much what mastery implies: for any particular set of its well-formed formulae, taken as premisses, there is some particular set of well-formed formulae which can be derived as conclusions from those premisses, and someone who learns the system will be more or less capable of working out which those latter formulae are in particular cases. But if there is one point on which philosophers of the later twentieth century came to agree, at least in the English-speaking world, it is that natural languages are not like that.

The point was usually argued in terms of the limiting case, where the premiss-set is of size zero. In a logical system, for any set of N premisses there is some set of valid conclusions, and in particular there are certain well-formed formulae which can be obtained as valid conclusions from the empty set of premisses: those formulae are called "theorems" of the system. In a natural language, one speaks of "analytic statements" which are true by virtue of their meaning (that is, they can be inferred from the empty set of premisses), versus "synthetic statements" whose meaning does not give us their truth-value – we need one or more factual premisses before we can establish whether a synthetic statement is true or false. Thus one might see *My father is male* as an analytic truth of English, whereas *My youngest cousin is male* would be either a synthetic truth or a synthetic falsehood. The idea is that merely understanding the former statement suffices to tell us that it must be true, whereas we need more information before we can tell whether or not the latter statement is true.

From the Second World War onwards, a central preoccupation of English-speaking philosophy (it might be fair to say "*the* central preoccupation") was language, and the central point about language as actually used in everyday life ("ordinary language", as philosophers call it) was that there is in fact no distinction between the analytic and the synthetic: language and the realities it is used to describe are both so fluid that it is impossible to allocate particular statements to one side or other of the analytic/synthetic boundary. For instance, if one feels that it is safe to describe *My father is male* as necessarily true by virtue of its meaning, then what does one say about a case where a man fathers children and then changes sex (for which there are plenty of precedents nowadays)? Uttered by the children, the statement is a falsehood. (This example is discussed more fully in Sampson 2001: 195–197.)

Philosophers usually discussed the issue in terms of the limiting case of analytic versus synthetic statements, but the point they were making was more general: a natural language does not embody fixed inference relationships between its statements, such that from a given set of N natural-language premisses (whether N is zero or a larger number) there is some definite set of conclusions which can be validly drawn from them. Properties flick unpredictably between being defining features of a word and being merely contingently associated with that word, as an individual's or society's experience develops: the advent of sex-change operations changed masculinity from a defining feature of fathers to a very highly-probable correlate. To quote Ludwig Wittgenstein (1953: 37e–38e), "what to-day counts as an observed concomitant of a phenomenon will tomorrow be used to define it" (and *vice versa*).

In Britain the leading proponent of this view was Wittgenstein, whose ideas dominated British philosophy in the 1950s, 1960s, and 1970s with few rivals. In the USA, essentially the same view was argued independently by Morton White (1950) and Willard Quine (1951), and again their position was accepted with very little disagreement. In the closing decades of the century philosophers' attention tended to shift away from language to other topics, but that did not mean that the discipline had changed its mind about the analytic/synthetic distinction – a new generation simply found it more worthwhile to study areas such as ethics or politics rather than language, but they did not contradict what their predecessors had said about language. Indeed, refutation of the analytic/synthetic distinction in ordinary language is arguably an unusually clear counterexample to the frequently-heard complaint that philosophy is a subject where little real progress is made and the same ranges of alternative answers to the same questions continue to be canvassed down the centuries. Since the mid-twentieth century, we have attained a better understanding of how meaning in natural language works than people had before.

If the reader accepts that the idea of fixed inference-relationships between natural-language sentences, while perhaps superficially tempting, must in fact be given up, he may find it easier to accept the analogous point that in the domain of grammar the idea of a fixed set of well-formed or "grammatical" sentences may be intuitively appealing but is in reality a delusion. Earlier in GRS's career he accepted Wittgenstein's and Quine's arguments against the analytic/synthetic distinction, but he believed that grammar was different: he supposed that there really is a well-defined set of valid English sentences, although definite rules prescribing how we can move inferentially among them do not exist. More recently, he has come to see the grammatical/ungrammatical distinction as resembling the analytic/synthetic distinction: they are inventions imposed without scientific basis on intrinsically fluid realities to which they fail to apply.

It should be said that there have been linguists who have discussed word-meaning in a fashion which implies that Wittgenstein and Quine were wrong on the analytic/synthetic issue. Within the generative school, the earliest and for years the most influential publication on meaning was Katz and Fodor (1963). But Katz and Fodor began by simply rejecting the possibility of a connection between linguistic accounts of meaning in language and philosophers' discussions of the subject:

> Philosophical inquiry into the meaning and use of words has neither drawn upon nor
> contributed to semantic investigation in psychology and linguistics. Correspondingly,
> accounts of meaning proposed by linguists and psychologists cannot in any obvious way
> be connected with theories current in philosophy or with one another.

And Katz and Fodor went on to develop a formal theory of word-meaning which treats the definitions in ordinary published dictionaries such as the *Shorter Oxford English Dictionary* as definitive, complete accounts of the meanings of the respective words (although the lexicographers responsible for compiling the dictionaries would certainly not make such large claims for the nature of their work), and which among other things implies that the class of analytic sentences, such as *Bachelors are unmarried*, is well-defined. Katz and Fodor (1963) were less concerned with the analytic/synthetic distinction than with formalizing ways in which word-ambiguities, e.g. between *bachelor* as unmarried man and *bachelor* as holder of a university degree, are resolved in context; but Katz (1964) argued that their theory actually offered a "solution to Quine's problem" about analyticity. However, all Katz actually showed was that, *if* the Katz/Fodor formalism were accepted as capable of accurately representing meaning relations in English (hence, if Quine was wrong about analyticity), then the formalism could be used to define a clearcut distinction between analytic and synthetic sentences. Katz (1964) entirely missed the point that, if Quine was right, then no formalism akin to that of Katz and Fodor (1963) could accurately represent meaning relations in a natural language.

A critique which misses the target as widely as that surely cannot be taken as a serious rebuttal of an established position. And, although some linguists have continued to discuss word meanings within the generative framework since that early period, so far as we have seen these discussions have paid little heed to earlier ideas about the topic, including ideas about how constantly evolving realities, and constantly evolving human knowledge of realities, prevent a natural language from having fixed meaning relations between words.[10] We have seen nothing in the literature of linguistic semantics which leads us to doubt Wittgenstein's and Quine's view of inference in natural language as too fluid and unpredictable to be described by fixed rules.

If the Wittgenstein/Quine view of word meaning is right, then it is surely at least plausible that "grammaticality" in natural languages is similarly ill-defined.

---

10 We saw on pp. 20–21 that Jerry Fodor later moved towards the belief that word-meanings in natural languages depend on an innate, universal "language of thought" for which he offers no empirical support and about which even other members of the generative school express scepticism.

4.9 Grammar as an expression of logical structure

Formal logic is relevant to our topic in a further way, relating to "structural meaning" as opposed to "word meaning" – i.e. to those aspects of meaning which in a natural language are expressed by the ways words are grouped together into larger structures, and by inflexions and closed-class "grammar words", as opposed to open-class content words such as nouns, verbs, and adjectives.

As we saw in chapter 1, one factor helping to explain the plausibility of the view that grammaticality is a well-defined property of word sequences is that many people see natural languages as irregular and sometimes cumbersome or imperfect devices for realizing, through the medium of speech-sound, structures of meaning which are given in advance of the evolution of particular natural languages and are common to all mankind – whether because they are a matter of logical necessity, independent of human thought, or because the meaning structures form a Universal Grammar which is part of the genetic endowment of our particular species even though, logically speaking, other grammars would be possible. The first of these two ideas, that meaning structures are universal as a matter of logical necessity, does not usually feature as more than an inexplicit assumption in the writings of linguists but has been asserted explicitly by some philosophers, for instance Bertrand Russell (e.g. Russell [1957] 2001: 245). The second idea, that a contingent rather than necessary range of meaning structures is inherited genetically, has obviously been a key element of mainstream generative linguistics for most of its history.[11]

If it were true that natural-language utterances were tools for expressing logical structures which were independent of particular languages, then it might follow that, within any one natural language, there would be a distinction between word-sequences which are the conventional expression of some formulae of the universal logic (and are therefore grammatical), and word-sequences which do not conventionally correspond to any formula of the universal logic (and are therefore deviant). The only grey areas would relate to cases where the conventional method of expressing a logical formula changed, or differed from person to person. There would be no cases akin to *Whatever!* where speakers would bend language to express novel meanings. If the structure of language were determined by our genetic inheritance, or even determined independently of our species by eternal principles, comparably to the way that the distribution

---

11 However, some of Noam Chomsky's recent writings, e.g. the comparison between language and a snowflake in Chomsky (2007a: 20), seem to swing away towards the "logical necessity" idea.

of prime numbers is determined, then there could be no possibility of individuals developing grammatically-novel meanings.

But this way of thinking about meaning in natural language is grossly unpersuasive. It is very difficult to argue that natural-language grammars are naturally-evolved and imperfect devices for expressing thought-structures which the formulae of mathematical logic express in a more direct and perfect way, because (as we saw in chapter 1) natural languages which have not been influenced by the European tradition are so diverse in the meaning structures they express, and even European languages encode basic sense-distinctions (such as *and* versus *but*) that have no equivalent in standard formal logics. Both in terms of history (natural languages came first) and in terms of the comprehensiveness of the meaning-categories expressed, it is more reasonable to see formal logical systems as partial attempts to capture meaning in the natural languages native to those who developed the logical systems, rather than *vice versa*.

Some linguists in recent decades have suggested that natural languages do not differ in the range of thought-structures they can express, for instance Ray Jackendoff claimed (1993: 32) that "the earliest written documents already display the full expressive variety and grammatical complexity of modern languages"; but this is simply not true (and Jackendoff quotes no evidence in support of his claim). Guy Deutscher (2000) has shown that complement clauses evolved within a particular ancient language that previously lacked them, namely Akkadian, after that language had already been reduced to writing. Dan Everett (2005) has given considerable evidence (though in this case it is perhaps reasonable to regard the debate as remaining open) that a language spoken by a remote South American tribe in our own time, Pirahã, entirely lacks clause subordination of any kind, and contrasts with European languages in other fundamental semantic respects also, for instance it lacks any method of expressing quantification. (We shall return to this issue in chapter 15.)

If linguistics has been slow to grasp how different from one another natural languages can be in terms of the ranges of thought-structures which they encode, part of the explanation is provided by David Gil's work on Riau Indonesian, quoted at length in chapter 1. In the case of Malay/Indonesian, the high-prestige variety of the language whose structures map fairly closely onto those of European languages, and which is thought of by present-day speakers as their "real" language, is structurally rather different in kind from lower-prestige varieties which the same speakers actually use spontaneously in ordinary life. When an exotic-language informant gives a Western linguist a picture of his language that makes it seem to be just an alternative system of coding conventions for expressing more or less the same range of meanings as a European language, this may often be because the informant is responding to the linguist's elicitation questions by using an artificial variety of his language which has been developed under the influence of European languages. One can escape this Eurocentrism, by soaking oneself in experience of a language which is remote from European influence in space (e.g. Riau Indonesian or Pirahã) or in time (e.g. Akkadian or Classical Chinese); but not too many linguists these days try to do that.

Diversity of meaning structures applies not just between languages, but between speakers of one language: individuals seem to differ in the extent to which they master the range of structural possibilities provided by their common mother tongue. Ngoni Chipere (2003) has begun to investigate differences between individuals with respect to their ability to deal with grammatical complexity.

By now the misguided nature of the concept of grammaticality has percolated even into novels for a general readership. David Lodge's *Deaf Sentence* contains a passage remarking that

> structural and transformational linguistics had lost their allure since people had come to realise the futility of trying to reduce the living and always changing phenomenon of language to a set of rules illustrated by contextless model sentences often invented for the purpose (Lodge 2009: 31).

Only within university Departments of Linguistics, perhaps, is grammaticality still widely and sincerely believed in today. But, there, it still is.

4.10 Realistic grammatical description

Finally: if natural languages do not comprise well-defined sets of grammatical sentences, what then is left for grammatical description to aim at? For half a century, many linguists have found the formulation of that task in *Syntactic Structures*, namely that it consists of separating the grammatical from the ungrammatical sequences of the language, to be a compelling one. What is there to replace it with?

Consider again the metaphor of a language as an unfenced prairie in which people have made tracks frequented to different extents and hence of different sizes. Describing the grammar of a language, we suggest, is like describing the network of tracks down to some size threshold below which fainter paths are ignored. Someone who buys a road atlas of Great Britain does not complain and ask for his money back if he sees a man walking his dog along a field path which is not registered in the atlas. The analogy is not perfect, because in modern Britain there are sharp cutoffs, physically between routes which are metalled and those which are not, and legally between routes which are publicly available for vehicular use and those which are private, or publicly available as footpaths or bridleways only. A modern road atlas will probably attempt to depict all and only the routes meeting one of these clearcut criteria – very likely the legal one. But there could be road atlases in cultures lacking the invention of tarmacadam, and where laws of access were vaguer than in modern Britain; the atlas compilers would have to make some kind of decision about how far to go, in marking routes on their maps, down the scale from crowded, well-beaten highways to occasional footpaths. Whatever cutoff point they chose would be arbitrary.

In a literate society there is even a kind of linguistic analogue for the legal cutoff between public highways and other tracks. Writing, particularly published writing, is held to public standards of grammatical normality by institutions such as writing-skills education, copy-editing of manuscripts, and so forth, which have the effect of discouraging many of the quirkier, one-off turns of phrase that people who speak in informal contexts are free to deploy. If, instead of the SUSANNE treebank, we had based the analysis of Figure 6 on the CHRISTINE treebank of spontaneous spoken English, we might have encountered a richer variety of *Dunster* constructions. (We did not use CHRISTINE, because speech data would have raised complex issues relating to dialect differences, difficulties of interpreting utterances out of context, and many others which would inevitably have taken over our exposition and diverted attention from its central theme.) But although copy-editors, for instance, encourage writers to keep to the wider grammatical highways rather than obscure footpaths, they do not really possess a tacit or explicit language model that is sufficiently well-defined to allow one to specify "all and only" the sentence-structures which count as editorially-acceptable English. (And even if they did, what linguists are primarily interested in is language as an aspect of human beings' natural behaviour, including spontaneous speaking, rather than a well-behaved subset of ordinary language that has been promulgated for "official" purposes.)

Traditional grammar description, it seems to us, was carried out in a spirit similar to road-atlas compilation in a pre-modern society as we envisaged it above. Before the middle of the twentieth century not just authors of grammars for schoolchildren's use, such as Meiklejohn, but more heavyweight grammarians such as Jespersen or Zandvoort, aimed to describe the more usual ways in which utterances are constructed in the language under description, but without any stated or tacit rider that "these *and only these* constructions are grammatical" in the language. The cutoff between constructions well-established enough to describe, and turns of phrase so unusual that the grammar is silent about them, would have been determined by the resources available to the grammarian – his own time, the size of book acceptable to his publisher, or the like – rather than by a concept of ungrammaticality.

This is still, in our view, the right way to construe the task of grammatical description. (Frederick Newmeyer might prefer to call it "usage description"; but if usage is all there is, then we take it that the work of describing it will be called grammar, as it was before *Syntactic Structures*.) Computerized corpus techniques help us find out facts about usage today which grammarians of fifty years and more ago might not have been able to ascertain because it would have taken too much effort, so in some respects we can improve on their grammatical descriptions; but the essential point, that the cutoff in delicacy of grammatical description is an arbitrary one, is as true now as it was then.

This suggests consequences which may be uncongenial to many linguists. The generative concept of an ideal grammar which succeeds in defining "all and only" the sequences constituting an individual's language is easily interpreted as a system which is psychologically real for that individual; by coinciding perfectly with the speaker's usage, the structure of the grammar might succeed in reflecting aspects of the structure or functioning of the speaker's mind. It does not seem tempting to suppose that a grammar which identifies the constructions used most frequently (by an individual, or by a speech community) down to some arbitrary cutoff could tell us much about speaker psychology.

But then, over the half-century during which the generative conception of grammar has been influential, it does not appear that the possibility in principle that grammars could tell us about minds has led to many specific discoveries about mental functioning or mental structure. So perhaps relinquishing the hypothetical possibility of defining "psychologically real" grammars is not really giving much up.

Whether that is a large renunciation or not, we believe that the conception of grammatical description outlined here is the most that scientific linguistics can realistically hope to achieve.

Chapter 5
Replies to our critics

5.1 Is our idea controversial?

When people have been living with a range of ideas as long as we have lived with the ideas about grammaticality developed in chapter 4, they can begin to seem so inevitable that one wonders whether they need lengthy public defence – perhaps almost everyone except a few diehard theorists already sees grammar in the same way that we do? After all, we said in chapter 1 that before the twentieth century our picture of grammar appears to have been uncontroversial; and in note 4 to that chapter we identified a (non-exhaustive) list of scholars who had made comments harmonizing with our view in recent decades. Are we merely pushing at an open door?

Luckily it is particularly easy to answer this question, because the original version of chapter 4 was written as the "target article" for a journal special issue, to which a wide range of other relevant scholars were invited to offer responses. Those responses, together with comments which have appeared elsewhere since the special issue was published, give us a convenient survey of what the scholarly world makes of our position.

It is extremely clear that the door we are pushing at is *not* yet an open one. Stefan Müller (2008: 23) calls our idea that there is no such thing as ungrammaticality "absurd". Geoffrey Pullum, the first of the special-issue commentators, begins (Pullum 2007: 33) by ridiculing our "extraordinary" claim. (Pullum's opening gambit, which he apparently sees as a telling blow, consists of writing a long sentence backwards and suggesting that we imply there is nothing odd about it. As an argument, this seems about on a par with someone who encounters the idea that the world is round rather than flat and responds "So how come the Australians don't fall off? – ha, bet you never thought of that one!")

Pullum and Müller are distinguished scholars; and others, while expressing themselves less forcefully, also disagree with us. So, since we continue to believe that we are in fact right about ungrammaticality, putting effort into advancing our point of view is evidently not redundant.

We shall discuss Stefan Müller's objections in a later section, but here let us take up some of the points made by Geoffrey Pullum.

5.2 Geoffrey Pullum's objections

To Pullum it is just obvious that ungrammaticality is a real thing (indeed he believes that "almost all" random sequences of English words are ungrammatical); and he is convinced that this has always been the accepted position – the target article, he says,

> gives us not a shadow of a reason for doubting the standard view, millennia old: that the whole point of a grammar is to tell you what is well formed in a given language, and by implication what is not (Pullum 2007: 45).

"Millennia old" is strong wording, when we had explicitly argued that this view is less than sixty years old, and we wonder how Pullum would support his claim about the traditional understanding of grammar. (He does not offer support in the paper we cite; the passage just quoted is its closing peroration.) The problem lies in the words "by implication". We agree of course that grammars have always aimed to show readers various things they *can* say or write, but we do not believe that traditionally they also aimed to identify things that one *cannot* say or write (apart from the special, irrelevant case of things like split infinitives or double negatives, which people *do* produce and which are meaningful, but which happen to be socially deprecated). The former does not imply the latter, and we have not seen evidence that traditional grammarians held the latter view of grammar. We believe they did not.

It is clear that Pullum does not grasp this point. He writes (op. cit.: 41) that how a scientifically well-founded grammar distinguishes between grammatical and ungrammatical expressions "is a deep and difficult question ... [which] is not to be resolved by just asserting that nobody ever follows any rules" – suggesting that we assert that. We don't, of course. We believe that speakers commonly conform to rules of grammar in constructing utterances, only the rules are positive: they say "you can do this", they never say "you cannot do that".

Whether the grammatical tradition shared our view of grammaticality is one question; the more important question is whether that view is correct. The main passage in which Pullum addresses our arguments about grammaticality, rather than our interpretation of the traditional view, is a passage (pp. 35–36) in which he claims that we have failed to answer an objection by Christopher Culy (1998) to the conclusions we draw from Figure 6 (p. 71).[1] Culy argued that data like those of Figure 6 do not refute the concept of formal grammars which divide

---

[1] More precisely, Culy's objection was to an earlier version of essentially the same argument which appeared as Sampson (1987).

strings into grammatical and ungrammatical, because he was able to contrive an artificial probabilistic context-free grammar that treats many strings as ungrammatical but generates a probability distribution over its grammatical strings which is fairly similar to that of Figure 6.

One response to Culy appeared in Sampson (2001: 175–177), and, since Pullum found this insufficient, Sampson (2007: 124–126) gave a further response. In a book which aims to be reasonably self-contained it would be tedious to grind through the details of objection, response, rebuttal to response, etc. (among other things they depended on comparing Figure 6 with other graphics not reproduced here); we encourage readers keen to pursue the debate in detail to consult the sources just cited. The central point (as we see it) is that while it may well be possible to construct grammars that preserve the concept of ungrammaticality for some strings and at the same time generate a realistic frequency distribution over other strings, if the low end of that distribution extends towards figures of the order of one in a trillion words, there can never be good empirical evidence to establish the validity of one of those grammars rather than alternatives. The point about Figure 6 is not the precise shape of the plot, but the fact that it points smoothly, without noticeable discontinuities, towards an area of the frequency scale which is beyond the reach of observation. This seems to us a good response to Culy; his artificial grammars are an interesting mathematical curiosity rather than a substantial argument in favour of ungrammaticality. Readers must decide for themselves whether our response is adequate.

Although Pullum sees himself as defending standard conceptions of grammar against a strange new heresy, it emerges from close reading of his piece that Pullum himself holds a view of grammar which is as unorthodox in its way, if not more so, than ours. In the passage leading up to the remark quoted above about "a deep and difficult question", Pullum tells us:

> I take linguistics to have an inherently normative subject matter. The task of the syntactician is exact codification of a set of norms implicit in linguistic practice.

Undergraduates who take introductory linguistics courses are commonly told at an early stage that there is an important difference between *descriptive* and *prescriptive* linguistics; discussions of usage by laymen are commonly prescriptive ("Avoid double negatives", "Don't say *ain't*", etc.), but linguistic science is descriptive – it tells us how language is used, not how it should be used. Pullum's use of the word "normative" means that, for him, something like prescriptive linguistics is all there is – linguistics is composed of statements which, if they are not of the simple form "You should say X", are nevertheless "should"-statements, perhaps typically of the form "Speakers think that they should say X".

Agreed, one might choose to study languages in that spirit. To our mind, though, such a study would be of far less human significance and interest than linguistics in a descriptive spirit, which aims to say how language users do behave rather than how they should behave or how they think they should behave. And Pullum's rejection of the descriptive approach to linguistics makes it odd for him to complain that our view of linguistics is idiosyncratic; can Pullum quote anyone who agrees with him that linguistics is a normative study?[2]

In any case, we should make it clear that when we say we do not believe in ungrammaticality, we mean that the concept has no place in linguistics as a descriptive discipline. Whether it would be a useful concept in a linguistics concerned with norms rather than behaviour is not a question we are tempted to concern ourselves with.

5.3 No virtue in extremism

Pullum feels that our point of view is not just misguided but actually self-contradictory. Referring to the "target article" concession (see p. 85 in this book) that things like violations of gender or person agreement might be categorized as truly ungrammatical, Pullum comments "Conveniently for critics ... his paper contains a rejection of its own thesis".

Certainly the point is a softening of our thesis, relative to the strongest form in which it might be held. We offered it as a fallback position rather than one we insisted on; Anatol Stefanowitsch (2007: 59) saw it as an unnecessary concession. But even with the concession, there is plenty of the thesis left, and what is left clearly contradicts the assumptions of generative linguistics. Generativists

---

2 Pullum says little in detail about what his preferred style of linguistics would be like in practice. The closest he comes to addressing his "deep and difficult question" is a reference to an account by the philosopher Norman Daniels (2003) of the "method of reflective equilibrium". Reading Daniels, although there are brief allusions to value-free topics such as logic, it is clear that the "method of reflective equilibrium" is proposed essentially as a recipe for arriving at satisfactory moral judgements; we just do not see how any such method can be of much help to the linguist. (In any case, Daniels's exposition depends heavily not on arguments of his own but on repeated appeals to the authority of John Rawls; since we see Rawls as an overrated figure among recent moral philosophers (Sampson 1984: 194–195), we do not find Daniels particularly persuasive.)

Our vision of linguistics is a non-standard one; but we acknowledge this, and in the present book we have set out to clarify it and to give reasons for believing in it, despite its unfamiliarity. To propose an equally or more radical revolution in the foundations of linguistics in a few almost throwaway remarks, based largely on third-hand philosophizing, is not easy to take seriously.

assign asterisks to word-strings not just because of local agreement failures but also because the overall architecture of the strings is abnormal: they cannot be analysed into clauses and phrases which fit together in a standard way. Chomsky's classic example *Furiously sleep ideas green colourless* does not contain any concord error.

For Pullum to suggest that by offering the concession we are as good as surrendering (rejecting our own thesis) represents an approach to scholarship which we think of as characteristically American. It is not a desirable scholarly stance. The implication is that engaging in scholarly debate is a kind of warfare, where the aim is to blow the enemy out of the water. To admit any weakness is folly. But scholarship is not warfare. Of course all of us would like to see our particular pet ideas flourish within the intellectual ecosystem, but our higher allegiance is (or should be) to helping the truth to emerge. If we have an idea which we believe is essentially correct but which has areas of weakness, we ought to be the first to identify the weak points as well as the evidence in favour of the basic thesis. That is an ideal, and, being human, we will not always fully live up to it. But actually to satirize one's intellectual opponent for being frank enough to make an open concession implies a depressing interpretation of the scholar's mission.

5.4 Stefanowitsch versus Müller

Not all contributors to the journal special issue cited above are hostile to our point of view. Anatol Stefanowitsch strongly supports it, and offers arguments in its favour that had not occurred to us. In particular, Stefanowitsch takes issue with Stefan Müller, who regards our argument (p. 84) from the *Norwegians* example as "absurd", on the ground that "this way you could turn every language in the world into a component (*Bestandteil*) of the English language" (Müller 2008: 23; translations of Müller's German are our own). Not just sentences involving word-for-word translations of foreign languages (such as the *Norwegians* example) would count as English, but so too would sentences quoting foreign wording in the original, e.g. "I think that Germans say '*weil ich diesen Ansatz komisch finde*' ", and

> Likewise all historical stages of German, all data of language evolution, all language errors in German (and of course in other languages) would become components of English, since English-language publications deal with these topics.

Müller sees this as a *reductio ad absurdum* of our point of view (and we have little doubt that many linguists will agree with Müller). Stefanowitsch sees it as no such thing.

In the first place, Stefanowitsch points out that using one language to illustrate the structure of another by mimicking it, as in the *Norwegians* example, is by no means the only or even the most "natural" way in which structures that one might think thoroughly ungrammatical (such as determiner following rather than preceding its noun) get used in practice. Another way is in language-contact situations (Stefanowitsch 2007: 59):

> To a speaker of Old English, the constituent order [ADJ N] would have appeared as fixed in stone as the order [DET N] does to speakers of Modern English. Yet in the Middle English period, when large numbers of Norman French texts had to be translated into English, it seems that it did not seem unusual to translators to mimic the Norman French order [N ADJ] and this order even entered Middle English texts that were not translated from Norman French

– Stefanowitsch quotes the opening line of the *Canterbury Tales*, "Whan that Aprille with his *shoures sote* ..." (i.e. showers sweet). In general, Stefanowitsch points out (his pp. 61–62; footnote omitted):

> Influences of language contact and the need to invent motivated sublanguages [the latter being a further source of apparently-ungrammatical real-life usage discussed by Stefanowitsch] can arise in any speech community at any moment, and it thus seems warranted to abandon a simple distinction between grammatical and ungrammatical. Instead, we might view the grammar of a language as a vast possibility space ... Which values from this space are chosen by the speakers of a language in a given situation, and which values are more likely to be chosen in a given language in general (and are thus "conventionalized"), depends on a variety of factors ... For a given language, this possibility space does indeed contain any historical or developmental stage of any language, absurd as Müller and others may find this. Of course, it makes sense for linguists to focus on those choices from that space that are conventionalized beyond a certain threshold in a given language ... But it does not make sense ... to assume any absolute distinction between rules/constructions that are part of a given grammar and rules/constructions that are not.

For Müller, it is self-evident that German is German and English is English, and examples of one are no part of the other. But that is a naive way of thinking about the reality of language. Consider an analogy which will be clear to many academics. The management of universities, and the organization of library shelving, assume for convenience that the world of learning can be chopped up into discrete "subjects"; but practising academics know that boundaries between subjects are usually fiction. Who can say where the border lies between History and Politics, or between Linguistics and Psychology, or between many other neighbouring disciplines? Likewise it is convenient for many purposes to treat English, German, Hungarian, and so forth as discrete "languages"; but in reality they are only different distributions of degrees of conventionality over a possibility space that embraces all conceivable utterances. The picture Stefanowitsch draws is more abstract than we might have chosen, and we may have overlooked some of its implications, but in broad outline it is one we agree with.

5.5 Trees have no legs

Anatol Stefanowitsch also offers an interesting discussion, based on hard data, of the way in which sequences commonly seen by linguists as "ungrammatical" often turn out to be absent from real-life usage not because of grammar, but because they mean things that people don't want to say. Take, as one example, the verb *donate*. It means much the same as *give*, but whereas *give* is a "ditransitive" verb (it can take both direct and indirect objects, as in … *gave them £1000*), *donate* does not seem to take an indirect object (*... donated them £1000*); instead we find … *donated £1000 to them*. According to Stefanowitsch (p. 63), *donate* is a "textbook example" of a verb "whose occurrence with ditransitive complementation has been identified as 'ungrammatical' by traditional acceptability judgments". What is more, this traditional view is supported by corpus data. There are zero instances of *donate* used ditransitively in the hundred million words of the British National Corpus, and Stefanowitsch uses a statistical significance test to show that it is virtually certain that this gap is not due to chance (p less than one in two million). So English must have a grammar rule "Don't use *donate* ditransitively", right?

Wrong. On the internet (which obviously comprises far more than a hundred million words of English, and whose contributors represent a much wider range of usage than the published literature which constitutes the bulk of the BNC), Stefanowitsch finds that there *do* occur sporadic cases of ditransitive *donate* – but for a special reason. Stefanowitsch notes (citing Thompson and Koide 1986) that, for most English-speakers, the meaning of the ditransitive construction is more specialized than the alternative with a preposition (that is, *give X Y* does not mean quite the same as *give Y to X*): ditransitive constructions "impl[y] a close contact between donor and recipient and a strong effect on the latter", while prepositional datives "impl[y] some distance between donor and recipient". Furthermore, although we said just now that *donate* means "much the same as *give*", in fact it is normally used for a specialized type of giving, where the gift is to a public body, and the transfer makes a larger difference to the giver than the receiver. These two points, taken together, imply that the ditransitive construction would not be appropriate with *donate*. But in Stefanowitsch's internet examples of ditransitive *donate*, the verb is used in a subtly different way, e.g.:

(36) *If anyone can donate me a PHP script that can replace […], I will love you forever.*

(37) *A few moments later we found a lovely old lady owning a flower stool[3] to donate us a rose for our list.*

In these cases, there clearly is something like close personal contact between the parties ("love you forever", "lovely old lady"), and the impact of the transfer sounds at least as great on receivers as on donors. For whoever wrote these sentences, *donating* may still be a special kind of *giving*, but (unlike for most English-speakers) the specialness does not relate to impersonality of the recipient. Perhaps *donate* for these writers emphasizes the feature of free will, the fact that there is no social pressure to make the gift.

This is not the currently-standard use of *donate*, which is the use that copy-editors might typically require; hence *donate* does not occur ditransitively in the British National Corpus. But it is no news that vocabulary items gradually evolve their senses as time goes by. There is nothing in the least surprising in the discovery that there are some people out there on the internet for whom *donate* lacks the implication of an impersonal recipient. And if *donate* lacks that implication for you, you will naturally be apt to use it ditransitively on occasion.

The upshot is that what looked to many linguists like a "textbook example" of a negative grammar rule – "Don't use *donate* ditransitively" is better seen as the consequence of a positive rule, "To express a close relationship between the parties and an impact on the recipient, you can use the ditransitive construction". When the meaning of *donate* changes, the constructions in which it appears will change accordingly, without any change in English grammar. We don't need grammar to tell us that people are unlikely to make statements implying that an abstract public organization is an intimate personal contact. There is probably (we haven't checked) no example in the BNC of the noun *tree* as subject of the verb *gallop*, but that isn't because *the tree galloped* … is ungrammatical: it is because trees have no legs.

Stefanowitsch suggests that quite a lot of what linguists take to be "ungrammaticality" turns out, if one pays careful attention to the senses of the words involved, to be wording that people do not produce in practice because it says things that people would not want to say in real life. We agree.

---

3 Perhaps a typing error for *stall*? (This is the internet, after all.)

5.6 Law versus good behaviour

A particularly original response to the "target article" was by Adam Kilgarriff (2007), who believes that it is possible to maintain the idea that certain sequences, such as noun followed by definite article in English, are straightforwardly ungrammatical, and nevertheless to agree with us that partitioning the set of all possible word-sequences into "grammatical" and "ungrammatical" subsets does not make sense.

Kilgarriff discusses an analogy with social life. In any society there will be a difference (perhaps only vaguely understood) between good and bad behaviour, but in a society developed enough to possess the institution of law some kinds of bad behaviour will be formally criminal. Basing himself on this analogy, Kilgarriff urges that:

> Grammaticality is a partial function. There are strings for which grammaticality is a relevant issue – they are either grammatical or ungrammatical. And there are other strings for which it is not an issue. They map neither to "grammatical" nor to "ungrammatical".

There is something we find appealing about Kilgarriff's analogy; but he does not develop it fully enough for us ultimately to know whether or not we agree with him. On p. 93 above we discussed the fact that copy-editors, style manuals, and so forth enforce a certain concept of well-formedness on public written language, but that the rules they apply do not amount to a specification of "all and only" the grammatical sentences of a language. Perhaps Kilgarriff would say that strings which are sufficiently odd or nonstandard that a copy-editor would not let them pass are the analogue of actions which are criminal – but among the other strings, there is still a hard-to-define distinction between sentences which "work" communicatively and those that do not.

But, in the first place, that isn't right, is it? It is not that some word-strings are more satisfying than others, and the very worst ones of all will be blue-pencilled by a copy-editor. In our experience, copy-editors and style manuals impose a *higher* threshold on acceptable structures than is imposed by the test of what works communicatively. For instance, split infinitives in English rarely create difficulties of comprehension, but a style manual might well outlaw them. The linguistic analogues of law enforcement agencies seem to be patrolling the boundary of questionable behaviour, not of actual criminality.

And secondly, what are the strings for which Kilgarriff says that grammaticality "is not an issue"? Clearly he wants to class e.g. *Bread the is on table the* as "ungrammatical"; but among the many strings which contain no oddity as extreme as that, what distinction is he drawing between strings that are actually grammatical and strings for which the grammaticality question does not arise? We see no obvious way to interpret this aspect of Kilgarriff's analogy.

We agree that it makes sense to compare institutions such as copy-editing in the language domain to law in the domain of social activity. But we query whether copy-editors possess a comprehensive enough set of explicit or tacit rules to define a clear partition between sentences that "pass" and sentences that "fail" – surely, copy-editors' decisions necessarily involve a great deal of unformalized discretion. Even if "ungrammatical" were identified with "unacceptable to copy-editors and style manuals" (which is not how theoretical linguists understand the concept), we doubt that it would be a well-defined category.

5.7 Conceptual objections to our thesis

Some critics suggest that possession by speakers of a "mental grammar" generating a grammatical/ungrammatical distinction is something like a conceptual or scientific necessity. Thomas Hoffmann takes issue with our remark on p. 94 above that "relinquishing the hypothetical possibility of defining 'psychologically real' grammars is not really giving much up", arguing (2007: 88) that our road-atlas model for descriptive linguistics is not scientifically adequate. Hoffman writes "As scientists we need to respect our data and the variability they display. But science does not stop at simply documenting data, it aims at explaining them … the source of any variability must be the speakers' mental grammar".

The idea that linguistics must not only "describe" but "explain" is another of the axioms, alongside the reality of the grammatical/ungrammatical contrast, which Chomsky has persuaded the discipline to accept as self-evident truths (the *loci classici* here being Chomsky 1964: 28–30 and 1965: 24–27). But this distinction seems to us much less clear than linguists commonly take it to be – we believe the axiom functions at least in part as a device for inducing linguists to agree that only the generative style of linguistics meets the requirements of a respectable scholarly undertaking, without going to the trouble of arguing the point; and if the suggestion is that the axiom holds for linguistics because it holds for all intellectual disciplines, that is surely false. There is a well-known contrast between subjects like physics, where individual events repeatedly instantiate fixed predictive laws, and subjects like history, which describe unique sequences of events not predictable by general laws.[4] This contrast relates to the

---

4 Obviously, we know that there have been a few philosophers, most notably Karl Marx, who have tried to assimilate history to physics in this respect; but that is a very unusual position, not one that it would be reasonable to take for granted silently, and indeed not one with many supporters in the early 21st century.

distinction labelled in English "science" v. "arts" or "humanities", though that usage is tendentious since the etymology of "science" seems to imply that arts subjects are not concerned with knowledge at all; German offers more neutral terminology in *Naturwissenschaften* v. *Geisteswissenschaften*. But in fact not all "natural sciences" clearly resemble physics more than history. Evolutionary biology is arguably more like history: it deals with unrepeated processes of emergence of unpredictable innovations over time. Philosophers of science recognize it as a large question how, if at all, standard concepts of natural science, developed mainly by reference to physics, apply to biology (Ruse 1973). It is not obvious to us that the study of human language should be expected to yield the kind of predictive laws characteristic of physics, whether the laws relate to individual languages or to human language in general. (This is a point made in response to our ideas by Antti Arppe and Juhani Järvikivi (2007), though they do not draw our conclusion that we shall not discover grammars which predict that some strings of words are unusable.)

Incidentally, while our thesis does imply that the ambitions of linguistics should be scaled down from what generative linguistics suggests, we do not think of that as a "pessimistic" view, as Arppe and Järvikivi repeatedly describe it. We are all, surely, human beings first and scientists a distant second. As human beings the present authors do not relish the idea that our and our fellows' behaviour is constrained by rigid laws akin to those which predict the behaviour of inanimate objects.

As for Hoffman's suggestion that speakers "must" have a "mental grammar" in their heads: this seems a strangely inflexible view of how human language could conceivably work. Even if we limit our attention to highly-formalized theories of language, they do not all make such an assumption. Suppose, for instance, that Rens Bod's "data-oriented parsing" theory were broadly on the right lines (see e.g. Bod and Scha 1996, Bod, Scha, and Sima'an 2003). It is not our concern here whether data-oriented parsing will ultimately prove to be correct or incorrect (we would not presume to predict), but it surely cannot be rejected out of hand as *conceptually* untenable? If not, that is one alternative to generative grammar as a model of human language behaviour, which seems to meet all the requirements for consideration as a serious scientific theory, but which has nothing within it that one could identify as a "mental grammar".

5.8 Do we really mean it?

It is noticeable, among several of the responses to our target article, that our concept of "grammar without grammaticality" is rejected not because it is understood and found wanting for specific reasons, but because the writers do not seem to understand that this is truly the view we want to put forward. We have seen that Geoffrey Pullum treats our concept as a subject for satire. We used the well-worn remark about "no strangers, only friends I haven't met yet" as a concrete analogy in order to try to make our point of view more digestible (p. 64 above). Pullum's response was to introduce his paper with a wisecrack by Barry Humphries about an elderly woman who adopted that attitude to strangers and ended up "in a maximum security twilight home" (Pullum 2007: 33). But compare Detmar Meurers's more sober response to our target article. He takes up our analogy with paths in open grassland (p. 75 above), and argues (Meurers 2007: 50) that a different picture is available:

> language use is more akin to the paths in a mountain region – there still is a wide range of possible paths, but the terrain rules out certain ones for general use; by looking at the topography, one can thus make predictions about where new paths could arise in the future (e.g., alongside a river as opposed to going up the north face of a mountain).

Of course, some kinds of terrain will indeed limit the range of paths that might develop in practice. But we are not claiming that ungrammaticality is a myth because we find the analogy with pathmaking attractive and we have over-looked the possibility of mountains blocking possible routes. Obviously we know that that is a logically-possible model; but we believe it is the wrong model. We explicitly believe that grammar in a natural language is like pathmaking in open prairie, and *not* like pathmaking in a mountainous area.

Jennifer Foster accepts (Foster 2007: 79) that it is unsatisfactory to define ungrammaticality in terms of what "cannot be generated by the grammar rules of the language", since the existence of generative grammar rules is part of what is at issue. But she suggests that the ungrammaticality concept can be opera-tionalized by defining a string of words as ungrammatical if "it contains an error". That gets us no further forward. The only kinds of grammatical oddity that have traditionally been understood as "errors" are, on one hand, the things such as violations of gender or person agreement, which we have conceded might be counted even by ourselves as ungrammatical, and on the other hand socially-deprecated usages, such as double negatives in English. The latter are labelled "errors" not because they systematically fail to occur, but because they *do* occur and some people would prefer them not to. The concept of "grammatical error" which is recognized by the population at large, rather than exclusively by those who have been trained in the doctrines inculcated by university linguistics departments, is a concept that assumes a correlation between erroneous utter-ances and well-formed counterparts. "Hans said *I likes walking* but it should be *I like*." "Don't say *I didn't see nothing*, darling, it's not nice; say *I didn't see anything*." Before the linguistic theorizing of the past half-century, no-one would have said that a sequence like **Furiously sleep ideas green colourless* was "ungrammatical", or represented a "grammar error", because there is no particular utterance of which it is a mistaken version. Rather, people would have called it something such as "an odd thing to say", and would have wondered what the speaker meant. We believe that calling strings like this "ungrammatical" is an idea that conceals rather than clarifies the nature of human languages.

5.9 Grammaticality implied by Universal Grammar

Some linguists believe in ungrammaticality because they simply have not got their minds round the idea that it might not be a reality. But there are other linguists for whom the concept of grammaticality is not an a-priori assumption (and certainly not a generalization based on experience), but rather an implication which they need to believe in, because it follows as a consequence of a more abstract claim about human language to which they are attached. These are linguists who believe in "Universal Grammar" – the idea that there are narrow limits to the structural diversity of human languages, set by our biological makeup, which allegedly equips us with detailed innate knowledge of language structure. In practice those who attempt to put flesh on the bones of the Universal Grammar idea do so mainly by arguing that the grammar of any language learnable and usable by human beings must conform to various constraints, for instance it might have to occupy no rank higher than "indexed grammars" (Gazdar 1988) in the standard hierarchy of grammar- and automaton-types. Linguists who believe in Universal Grammar normally go on to add that other aspects of a language, too, are constrained not to vary outside narrow limits (for instance, we have seen that Jerry Fodor believes that all vocabulary items in any human language are perfectly translatable into a specific innately-fixed "language of thought"). But it is mainly in the area of grammar that substantial attempts have been made to identify specific limits to the diversity of human languages, rather than merely to surmise that limits exist.

Whatever particular constraints are held to be universal, any claim of this sort clearly requires that human languages *have* well-defined grammars. Otherwise, there would be nothing to which the universal constraints could apply (or fail to apply). If an individual language has no fixed rules defining what can be said grammatically in it, as we are arguing, then the Universal Grammar idea becomes not just wrong but meaningless.

The popularity of the Universal Grammar idea has meant that many linguists have taken the grammaticality concept to be a necessary truth: languages *must* have grammars, because otherwise discussion of Universal Grammar could not even get off the ground. The fact that people who discussed grammar before the middle of the twentieth century do not usually seem to have considered grammar in terms of grammaticality would (according to this line of thinking) merely indicate that those people were somewhat naive: they were content to discuss anecdotally issues which in a scientific context ought to be formalized.

Consider, for instance, remarks by Stephen Laurence and Eric Margolis (2001: 231). We saw, on pp. 6–7, that one reason for growing dissatisfaction with what has been the dominant linguistic paradigm is that, to quote David Graddol again, "No one has ever successfully produced a comprehensive and accurate grammar of any language". But Laurence and Margolis see this very fact as an argument for innate grammatical knowledge. They attribute to us the argument that:

> given that linguistics *is* possible (indeed, thriving) and that it is broadly conducted follow-
> ing empiricist strictures, this shows that children could be be empiricist learners after
> all (see, e.g., Sampson [1980b]). [And Laurence and Margolis respond:] The problem with
> this reasoning is that generative linguistics has developed over more than forty years of
> theorizing by a large group of adults with advanced degrees, who have yet to completely
> work out the grammar for even a single natural language. By contrast, language acquisi-
> tion is accomplished by every normal toddler in just a few short years.

For Laurence and Margolis, that last fact demonstrates that the toddler must have built-in unconscious knowledge which is not matched by conscious knowledge available to adult linguists.

Of course, one can quibble with their discussion by debating how far generative linguistics truly is "conducted following empiricist strictures". (This will be a central topic of our chapter 13, and we shall defer until then considering some further target-article responses which relate to linguistic methodology rather than to the concept of grammaticality.) Even if we grant Laurence and Margolis that point, though, their argument only works because they see it as a perfectly uncontroversial assumption that any particular natural language has a specific grammar and that "Children do reliably arrive at the correct grammar for their language" (op. cit.: 221).

We do not believe that languages have "correct grammars" at which a child might or might not arrive. If the reality of language-acquisition is a matter of trying to conform one's own behaviour to the regularities one detects in the speech of others (occasionally extending them in one direction or another), and those others are themselves engaged in the same kind of activity, then the idea that there is a "correct answer" lying behind all these tentative individual models of language simply has no application. So the contrast between empiricist adult linguists, and child mother-tongue learners, disappears.

Surely, if one looks at the chaotic differences among the idiolects of various members of a speech-community (on which cf. Ross 1979, for instance), this latter picture is far truer to life than the picture assumed by Laurence and Margolis?

5.10 The downfall of Universal Grammar

This book is not centrally concerned with the Universal Grammar idea, which indeed has come to occupy a strange status even within the generative-linguistics camp. Belief in structural universals was expressed in extreme form by the linguist Neil Smith in 1999: "A glance at any textbook shows that half a century of research in generative syntax has uncovered innumerable ... examples [of principles of Universal Grammar]" (Smith 1999: 42). But in reality, the literature contains few specific examples of alleged universals, and those claims which do appear do not survive critical examination (see e.g. Sampson 2005: 75ff.).

Recently, generative linguists have been shifting to the other extreme and saying that their theory predicts only that recursive, hierarchical structure occurs in all languages (e.g. "The prevalent view among generativists nowadays is that the only property common ... to human language is recursion ... A real counter-example to generative theory would be a language without hierarchical structure", Faarlund 2010a: 752). Since we have seen (p. 22) that the ubiquity of hierarchical structure is predictable independently of generative linguistics, this appears to drain that theory of content. (Faarlund bases his statement on a 2002 publication whose lead author was the controversial ethologist Marc Hauser but whose co-authors puzzlingly included Noam Chomsky, although the tendency of the article seems to render Chomsky's theories vacuous; see Hauser et al. 2002. In other writing, e.g. Chomsky 2007b, Chomsky does still assert a belief in "Universal Grammar", but described in terms – "CP", "SPEC-T", etc. – too abstract and theory-internal to test against the evidence of real-life languages.) As Ivan Sag says (2010: 495, emphasis in original removed), "accepting with equanimity a progressive reduction of the range of facts that lie within the domain of a scientific theory may be within the mainstream of generative linguistics, [but] it is well outside the mainstream of scientific practice".

(On the bankruptcy of recent versions of generative theory, see e.g. Behme 2013.)

We have argued at length elsewhere that Universal Grammar is a fundamentally wrong-headed idea (Sampson 2005). The arguments which have been used to make it seem a-priori plausible are logically fallacious, and the empirical evidence all points the other way. To date there have been no serious published challenges to the argument of Sampson (2005), and it would be wasteful to repeat that material here. Furthermore, the idea that human beings inherit innate knowledge of language which constrains all human languages to conform to a rigid set of linguistic universals is by now under attack on so many fronts that it may soon be little more than a historical curiosity. It is an idea that has no traction except within university Departments of Linguistics, where belief in it still often ranks as something approaching a professional obligation. When knowledgeable members of other disciplines contemplate the nature of human language, they reject this idea.

Thus, the philosopher Jesse Prinz notes that nativism is still the dominant point of view within the linguistics discipline – "Chomsky's innateness hypothesis – often called linguistic 'nativism' – is widely accepted. If you've ever read anything about linguistics, you've probably read that language is innate" (Prinz 2012: 140), but he also rightly remarks that defence of linguistic nativism is conducted in terms often more reminiscent of wars of religion than of sober scientific debate. The idea that language is acquired without drawing on innate knowledge, through the use of general-purpose learning mechanisms, is "a heretical suggestion ... Debates about the innateness of language are some of the most heated in all of science" (Prinz 2012: 168); but Prinz concludes that the "heresy" is in fact true. "Language is an invention, not an instinct, and it is a conduit for human variation, rather than an inflexible universal" (Prinz 2012: 190). Again, the psychologist Michael Tomasello urges that belief in linguistic nativism has been motivated by failure to appreciate the power of children's general intention-reading and pattern-finding skills, and by a mistaken assumption that a natural language is like a formal language, "a unified set of abstract algebraic rules that are both meaningless themselves and insensitive to the meanings of the elements they algebraically combine" (Tomasello 2003: 5). Tomasello writes (2003: 6–7) that "... the principles and structures whose existence it is difficult to explain without universal grammar ... are theory-internal affairs and simply do not exist in usage-based theories of language – full stop." The physicist Sverker Johansson has carried out a very solid scrutiny of empirical constraints on the range of possible views about the origins of language in the species and the individual, and asserts (Johansson 2005: 243) that "The only thing that can be concluded is that it is not a simple matter of a dedicated 'language organ' with an innate Universal Grammar".

Ten years ago, Penelope Brown (2002: 175) understood Pinker's view of human culture as a set of innate mental modules to be the cognitive orthodoxy: "hard to believe though it may be, this stance is perhaps the mainstream one in cognitive science, taken uncritically from the mainstream linguistics of the past forty years". And, within the linguistic discipline itself, Jesse Prinz is correct to suggest that nativism still dominates. When someone draws public attention to its implausibility, as Prinz has done, even today some true believer is sure to try to slap the heresy down (cf. Wexler 2012).

But by now well-informed discipline insiders, too, are beginning to come forward to argue that the orthodox doctrine cannot be right. N. J. Enfield (2012) summarizes the state of play by writing "When scholars ... have issued challenges to state exactly what is in U[niversal] G[rammar], nobody can provide any specifics." Geoffrey Pullum and Barbara Scholz (2002) combed through the nativist literature and found just four examples of language universals quoted (each of which they regarded as questionable). Steven Pinker and Paul Bloom (1990: 713) claimed to "list some uncontroversial facts" about Universal Grammar, in response to which Thomas Schoenemann (1999: 343) found it "curious that in their paper they did not provide even a single specific formal universal feature found across all languages"; later, Pinker (1998) himself conceded that "U[niversal] G[rammar] has been poorly defended and documented in the linguistics literature". Nicholas Evans and Stephen Levinson (2009) have examined decades of cross-linguistic work on numerous facets of the structures of languages, and they conclude "there are vanishingly few universals of language ... diversity can be found at almost every level of language organization ... The claims of Universal Grammar ... are either empirically false, unfalsifiable, or misleading"; they regard language universals as a "myth". (Cf. also Schoenemann 1999: 325–328.)

Against this background, it might not seem worth wasting many words on the Universal Grammar idea. But it cannot be ignored in connexion with our topic, because while the idea dominated the field it was very successful in creating a mindset that makes it hard for linguists to grasp our thesis that there is no such thing as grammaticality. Because so many linguists did at least until quite recently take the assumption of fixed bounds to language diversity as axiomatic, and because that assumption seems to imply that individual languages are controlled by grammars defining fixed bounds to usage, many linguists (whether or not they now believe in "Universal Grammar") seem to have difficulty getting their minds round the open-ended picture of language that we are defending here and entertaining it as even a hypothetical possibility. It is not that they understand this picture and disagree with it – as we have seen, often they do not understand it in the first place.

Sampson (2005) made, we believe, about as solid a case against the "fixed bounds" axiom as could be made, based on language evidence alone. But it is clear that quite a few linguists feel that, irrespective of particular linguistic facts, there just *must* be fixed bounds to language diversity, because language is an aspect of cognition, and the fact that human beings are finite material organisms seems to guarantee that our cognitive products can vary only within fixed limits.

This idea is not often voiced explicitly, but seems to lurk not far below the surface of many discussions of foundational issues in linguistics. A much earlier attempt to explain its wrongheadedness (Sampson 1979), while well received by philosophers, encountered a shower of uncomprehending objections from linguists. Accordingly, it will be worth closing this chapter by taking a few pages to point out that what many linguists suppose to be axiomatically true in connexion with language directly contradicts a proposition that is seen as equally axiomatic by members of another well-established and successful human science.

5.11 Economic growth and linguistic theory

One social science which is older and practised more widely than linguistics is economics. To date the two subjects have had few points of contact with each other, but they do have in common that they are both highly formalized disciplines – more so, perhaps, than any other *Geisteswissenschaft*. A leading strand in current economic thought runs directly counter to the "fixed bounds" conception that we have been criticizing in linguistics.

Possibly the largest single advance in economic thought in recent decades has been the formulation of "endogenous growth theory" by Paul Romer (e.g. Romer 1990) and others. (An excellent exposition for a non-specialist readership is Warsh (2006); see also Helpman (2004).) Endogenous growth theory claims to solve a longstanding economic paradox. The classical economic principles developed by men such as David Ricardo and Alfred Marshall predict that any society should move towards an economic steady state in which Gross Domestic Product per capita is constant, or even shrinks as increases in population lead to diminishing returns from exploitation of non-labour resources. This contradicts the experience of much of the world over the past two hundred years, during which per-capita GDP has increased dramatically although populations have also risen. For some time economists have understood that the resolution of the paradox must have to do with the creation of new economically-useful ideas, which enable greater value to be extracted from a given range of resources.

Endogenous growth theory incorporates the process of idea creation into the economic machinery; it treats manufacturing, and research to generate ideas which might improve future manufacturing, as alternative uses to which a given set of human and other resources can be put. Considered as economic goods, ideas have some distinctive properties; notably, they are "non-rivalrous": if I give you an apple I can no longer eat it, but I can give you my idea and still exploit that same idea myself. Taking these properties into account, the theorists demonstrate (via algebraic reasoning whose details will be of little interest to linguists) that a society of economically-rational individuals will choose to deploy resources in ways that create sufficient new ideas to cause per-capita Gross Domestic Product to grow at an accelerating rate. This matches observed long-term trends in the advanced countries reasonably well (even if the time when we write happens to be marked by a hiccough in this growth).

One does not have to agree that economic growth is a good thing in order to see endogenous growth theory as a satisfying solution to what was previously a baffling intellectual puzzle. Voters in democratic countries commonly do see growth as good, and evaluate the politicians competing for their votes largely in terms of their ability to deliver growth; and writers such as Ridley (2011) argue passionately that economic growth offers the only realistic solution to a large range of threats facing humanity. But the opposite point of view is also possible. Many people nowadays see the costs of growth, in terms of damage to the environment, as outweighing its benefits. In 2010 John Holdren, director of the White House Office of Science and Technology, advocated a "massive campaign ... [to] de-develop the United States", i.e. to move economic growth into reverse (quoted in Ballasy 2010). This book is not the place to pursue that debate. What no-one will deny is that the phenomenon of economic growth has immense practical significance for human life, for good and/or for ill.

Presenting endogenous growth theory as an innovation which began about 1990 arguably understates the exent to which it amounts to incorporation into mainstream English-speaking economics, and/or independent reinvention, of principles of the "Austrian" school of economics initiated early in the twentieth century by figures such as Ludwig von Mises and Joseph Schumpeter. However, our present aim is not to investigate the history of economic thought but to describe the current state of play. At the beginning of the 21st century, endogenous growth theory is generally accepted as the most persuasive explanation of the phenomenon of economic growth; so much so that it is serving as a basis for policy-making by practising politicians. (Nick Crafts (1996) opened an analysis of the policy implications of the theory by referring to a famous occasion when Gordon Brown, soon to be Chancellor and later Prime Minister in the British government, was lampooned in the press for referring to its abstruse-sounding name in a public speech.) The theory may of course be wrong, but it cannot be ignored as merely an out-of-the-way eccentricity.

Endogenous growth theory makes one assumption which economists see as so uncontroversial that it is often left unstated: the theory takes for granted that the supply of new economically-valuable ideas is unlimited, so that the quantity produced in practice depends only on the quantity of resources devoted to idea-creation. Paul Romer does recognize this as an assumption rather than a truism; in his first paper he argued that rejecting it "would imply that Newton, Darwin, and their contemporaries mined the richest veins of ideas and that scientists now must sift through the tailings and extract ideas from low-grade ore" (Romer 1986: 1020), which he saw as a *reductio ad absurdum*. In his more widely-read 1990 paper, the point is dismissed in less than two lines: "there is no evidence from recent history to support the belief that opportunities for research are diminishing" (Romer 1990: S84). Romer's fellow economists, while often calling other aspects of his work into question, do not seem to have found this assumption problematic. At one point Romer (1994: 16–21) described resistance to the postulate of an unlimited supply of new ideas as a symptom of a widespread but irrational philosophical prejudice, but that prejudice appears not to be influential among the current economics profession.

As we have seen, much linguistic theorizing of the past half-century has been founded on the contrary assumption, that the potential products of human cognition are tightly constrained by our biology. The study of syntax from Chomsky (1956) onwards has by and large taken for granted that humanly-learnable grammars are a narrow subset of the set of recursively enumerable grammars, and much of the effort devoted to the field has aimed to identify the precise boundaries of that subset. In later writing, Chomsky (1981: 11) even claimed that there are probably only finitely many possible human grammars. In the semantic area, we have seen that Jerry Fodor (1975) argued that natural-language vocabularies can be mastered by speakers only because all of them are based on a common, innately-fixed "language of thought" which defines the set of all possible word-meanings, various subsets of which are encoded in the words of individual languages. Steven Pinker's *The Language Instinct* (surely the most widely influential book about linguistics of the last twenty years) has restated these points of view for a new generation (Pinker 1994: see e.g. pp. 106–125, 81–82). Anna Wierzbicka (1996) has attempted to turn Fodor's abstract argument for the existence of a language of thought into a concrete description.

Although some linguists discuss this concept of constraints on cognition purely in connexion with language structure, many others explicitly see language as providing evidence for a much more general picture of the nature of human cognition. Ray Jackendoff (1993: chapter 13) uses Universal Grammar as a precedent to argue for innate cognitive constraints on our ability to recognize music, or to extract meaning from visual stimuli. Pinker (1994: 412–415), citing the anthropologist Donald Brown, argues that innate cognitive constraints impose strikingly similar behavioural conventions and patterns on all human societies. Noam Chomsky has argued (1976: 124–125) that the rapid advances in scientific knowledge and innovations in the arts which have characterized the centuries since the Middle Ages were a temporary phenomenon reflecting a period when human beings were for the first time free to explore novel ideas and had not yet reached the limits of the cognitive possibilities biologically available to our species:

> If cognitive domains are roughly comparable in complexity and potential scope, such limits might be approached at more or less the same time in various domains … It may be that something of the sort has been happening in recent history.

Evidently, for Chomsky, Romer's remark about Newton and Darwin would be not a *reductio ad absurdum* but a plausible description of the current state of the sciences.

We have quoted a handful of linguists, but assumptions akin to those quoted about the supply of novel cognitive constructs being strictly limited are very widely shared by contemporary linguistic theorists. Not all linguists accept these assumptions, and not all economists accept endogenous growth theory, but they are part of the dominant consensus in the respective disciplines.[5]

It is possible that Chomsky is in a minority among linguists in suggesting that the constraints on one important domain of language structures are so very tight as to permit only *finitely many* distinct possibilities. But if other linguists see cognitive constraints as permitting infinitely-numerous, though well-defined, ranges of alternatives, this would not alleviate the incompatibility with the economists' assumption. Economic activities are commonly about optimizing some parameter or parameters, such as profit, market share, work/life balance, or the like. When elements of a solution-space are enumerable, infinite cardinality is usually no hindrance to optimization. (There are infinitely many

---

5 In 2012 Robert Gordon attracted widespread attention with a paper (R. Gordon 2012) arguing that the economic growth which has characterized the West over the past two centuries may be a temporary blip which has now run its course – making a neat parallel within economics to Chomsky's idea quoted in the preceding paragraph. It seems fair to say that Gordon's suggestion is a minority position among economists (for counter-arguments see e.g. *Economist* 2013a).

positive integers, but that creates no special difficulty for a decision about how many people to invite to a party.) Endogenous growth theory depends on the range of future ideas not being identifiable at any particular point in time. It assumes that an economic agent engaged in an optimization exercise will frequently be working with a solution-space which omits numerous possibilities that will not occur to anyone until later, if ever.

Since Romer and his fellow endogenous-growth theorists are concerned with only one category of new ideas, namely economically-valuable ones (as Ridley 2011: 269 paraphrases Romer, "recipes for rearranging atoms in ways that raise living standards"), and this particular category has not to our knowledge been discussed by linguists, it would be logically possible to deny that there is a contradiction. But neither linguists nor economists, surely, would want to suggest that human beings might have two separate faculties for idea-generation, one inexhaustible and specialized for economically-useful ideas, and another drawing on a limited range of ideas relevant to other domains. Much more plausibly, either the economists or the linguists are mistaken in their assumptions about intellectual innovation. Romer's and Chomsky's respective comments about scientific progress, quoted above, make the incompatibility rather explicit.

5.12 Discipline should not contradict discipline

It is perhaps no accident that linguistics is the discipline which poses a challenge to the endogenous growth theorists' assumption, because, apart from economics itself, linguistics may be the only area of social science which is sufficiently formalized to enable the contrary of that assumption to be clearly stated. Here and there one encounters informal hints in other fields of social study, for instance Vladimir Propp's claim that folk tales conform to certain limited patterns. But we know of no field other than linguistics in which it is meaningful and normal to raise questions such as whether a given class of potential cognitive structures is or is not recursively enumerable.

In our experience, few linguists have much interest in economic thought, so we surmise that the above discussion of endogenous growth theory may come as news to many members of the discipline. But the sciences need to be consistent globally, not just within individual disciplines. It is clearly unsatisfactory for two subjects, even if pursued in separate university departments, to continue indefinitely making fundamental assumptions that flatly contradict each other. The contradiction must be resolved, one way or the other, and appealing to first principles cannot resolve it, since first principles have evidently led linguists and economists to conflicting conclusions. If linguists believe that they are correct, and that economists like Paul Romer are mistaken, they would need to provide solid empirical evidence for that. We believe such evidence will not be easy to find.

There is no dispute, of course, that *some* aspects of the cognitive systems encoded in languages are determined by our genetic inheritance. When our work has been criticized, the criticisms have sometimes represented simple misunderstanding. Thus, in the course of an otherwise highly sympathetic discussion, Thomas Schoenemann (1999: 319–320) complains that "Sampson … appears to reject the idea that our semantic world-view has any strong innate components". For Schoenemann it is unreasonable of Jerry Fodor to imagine that even words like *ukulele* correspond to innately-available concepts,[6] but nevertheless "some semantic categories are likely innate at some level" – Schoenemann discusses the example *sweet*.

We thoroughly agree (cf. Sampson 1980a: 39). Our experiences of the outside world are all mediated by our organs of sense, which operate as they do largely because of the structure given them by our genetic endowment, and the impressions delivered to our minds by those organs are one category of thing that our languages encode. The closer an element of language comes to standing directly for a sense-impression, the greater the innate component to its meaning, and *sweet* comes very close. But other words are far less directly linked to sense impressions. *Ukulele* is more distant; *conservative* more distant still. Many of the aspects of thought encoded by grammar are as far removed as any area of language structure from immediate links to sense-data, so grammar is where the nativist story is least plausible of all, to our minds.

5.13 Language is not "special"

If the economists are right about the unbounded nature of intellectual innovation in the field that concerns them, then it would be odd if the intellectual field with which we are centrally concerned were fundamentally different in that respect, unless there was good evidence that language is "special". And there is very little concrete empirical evidence for language diversity being limited by any particular universal constraints. Indeed, those who have argued most influentially for fixed limits to language diversity have quite explicitly not suggested that language is "special" in this respect. They have claimed that all human

---

6 This particular example is quoted by Margolis and Laurence (2012: §5).

intellectual innovation must be bounded in this way, and the reason to cite language as an example is only that this particular human science lends itself more readily than some others to clear formalization of postulated constraints.

If the open-ended concept of intellectual innovation advocated by theorists of economic growth is correct, the natural implications would include not just non-existence of fixed constraints on diversity of languages, which by now is beginning to be widely accepted, but also lack of fixed constraints on what counts as a "grammatical utterance" within an individual language.

That second lack, we believe, remains at the time of writing controversial. It is the point with which our book is centrally concerned.

Chapter 6
Grammatical description meets spontaneous speech

6.1 The primacy of speech

The most biologically-natural form of language is speech. Children become fluent speakers before they learn to read and write, and even in the 21st-century West some adults remain illiterate. It is certain that well-developed spoken languages existed long before any language was reduced to writing, and even today some languages have no written forms, or perhaps possess orthographies which have been created as an academic exercise but play little or no part in the life of the relevant speech community in practice.

Those things being so, it seems particularly desirable to spend some time extending our discussion of limited grammatical precision to spoken language. In the speech domain, the issues we have already looked at do not go away, but further problems arise. On the whole (though there certainly are exceptions, notably J. Miller and Weinert 1998), linguists interested in grammar have tended to work with written material, or with invented examples more similar in style to written language than to spontaneous speech. But that tendency is paradoxical, when one considers how many linguists of the past fifty years have been influenced by the doctrine that grammar is innate in the human mind. If one wants to examine aspects of language that are innate rather than acquired, they are surely more likely to be found in the biologically-natural domain of speech than the relatively artificial domain of writing.

Our own approach to these issues stems from work on extending the SUSANNE treebank-annotation scheme to make it apply in a predictable way to samples of spontaneous spoken English. Some of the annotated samples which emerged from that work have been published, as the CHRISTINE Corpus, and the CHRISTINE documentation file includes many sections defining additions and modifications to the SUSANNE guidelines needed in order to cover spoken English. As in the case of the SUSANNE scheme for written English, the work of developing satisfactory annotation guidelines for speech was a progressive process of proposing tentative rules and "debugging" them through the experience of applying them to particular samples. For spontaneous speech we worked with material from a number of sources of transcribed spoken English; all the material included in the CHRISTINE treebank as published is drawn from the "demographically sampled speech" section of the British National Corpus (which comprises speech of the 1990s produced by a large collection of British speakers balanced in terms of region, age, social class, and sex).[1]

In what follows, we look at some of the difficulties that we encountered in devising modified annotation guidelines which succeed in implementing, for the grammar of spontaneous speech, Jane Edwards's principle that "similar instances [should] be encoded in predictably similar ways".

The problems we encountered are of different kinds: some certainly stem from the nature of spoken language itself, some (such as utterances which transcribers found unclear) perhaps relate more to the research situation than to intrinsic properties of language. But one should not be too quick to set any of these problems aside as merely practical problems of computational data registration, irrelevant to the theme of grammar as a human intellectual capacity. An individual acquiring his mother tongue is himself learning from examples, which presumably he must register and file away mentally in some form in order to build up a body of information about how the language works. That individual too will surely find some heard wording unclear, and will face difficulties comparable to those discussed in 6.9 below. Examining the difficulties in devising a predictable scheme for structural annotation of speech is a good way of identifying and confronting some of the difficulties which face a native speaker seeking to distil a grammar for his mother tongue from exposure to examples.

6.2 An example

Before examining special annotation difficulties, it will be as well first to give the reader an impression of the nature of the material, via an excerpt that involves no special complications. Figure 7 displays the CHRISTINE Corpus analysis of British National Corpus s-unit KSS.04779. (The spoken material in the BNC was divided by the corpus compilers into "s-units" intended to correspond roughly to sentences of written language, though the correspondence is sometimes very loose.)[2]

This s-unit occurred within a speech event recorded in April 1992 in South Shields during conversation at home; the s-unit was uttered by speaker PS6RC,

1 Other speech collections used in our research have included the London–Lund Corpus from the 1960s–70s, and the Reading Emotional Speech Corpus.
2 Here and below, our s-unit numbering relates to the original, 1994 edition of the British National Corpus. Numbering in the year-2000 edition differs slightly, thus example (38) becomes s-unit 04781.

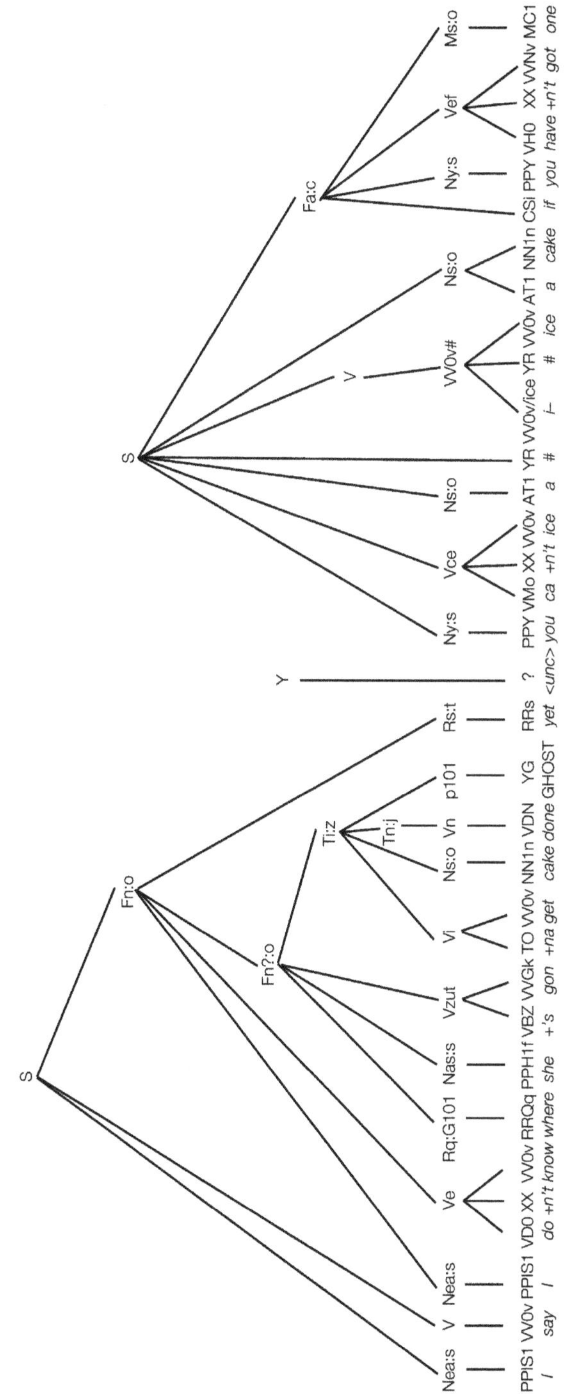

Figure 7: Tree structure of a CHRISTINE speaker turn

female, age 72, dialect Lancashire, occupation Salvation Army, education and social class unspecified. The wording, before analysis, runs:[3]

(38)   *I say I don't know where she's gonna get cake done yet <unclear> you can't ice a i- ice a cake if you haven't got one*

Within the electronic CHRISTINE Corpus the structural analysis is encoded in a one-word-per-line format using labelled bracketing, but for the sake of similarity to conventions commonly used in linguistics, in Figure 7 the CHRISTINE labelled bracketing is replaced by equivalent tree-diagram notation. The item *<unclear>* represents a stretch of speech which the transcriber was unable to make out; the symbol # is used in the analysis of speech repairs, as discussed in 6.4 below.

Above the row of words at the foot of Figure 7, the symbols in the next row up (PPIS1, VV0v, etc.) are wordtags, classifying the words in terms of their grammatical usage. (In Figure 3, p. 32, wordtags were omitted for simplicity, since they were not relevant to the discussion there.) The incomplete word *i-* is tagged VV0v/ice, meaning that it is an uninflected verb capable of being either transitive or intransitive (VV0v) whose form if completed would be *ice*. The tree structure above the wordtags represents the grammar of the speech turn in the same manner as Figure 3 in chapter 2. Thus the turn begins with a main clause having *I* as subject (:s), *say* as verb, and the nominal clause (Fn) *I don't know ... yet* as object (:o). The word *where* has no logical function within the clause where it appears (it is a "guest" tagma, symbolized :G), and it corresponds to a "ghost" Place adjunct (p) within the infinitival clause *−na get cake done*. ("101" is an arbitrarily chosen index number showing which guest corresponds to which ghost.) The symbol Y represents an element whose grammar cannot be identified because of uncertainty about the wording.

There are aspects of this annotation scheme which go beyond what is needed for written prose, notably the use of symbols # and Y. But, once these extra symbols have been defined, nothing in s-unit KSS.04779 makes it problematic to apply them. Now we turn to cases where there are problems.

---

3 The material in our sources uses diverse transcription conventions. For the extracts quoted in this chapter, we use whichever conventions make the prose most easily readable. Thus, the British National Corpus transcriptions include punctuation marks, and we show these although with respect to speech their reality is questionable. Conversely, where London–Lund transcriptions contain pauses, these are provided with indications of pause length, but we eliminate these and show pauses simply as <pause>, since the length indications are not relevant to our discussion and reduce the readability of the transcriptions.

6.3 Wordtagging

One fundamental aspect of grammatical annotation is classifying the grammatical roles of words in context – wordtagging. The original SUSANNE scheme defined an alphabet of over 350 distinct wordtags for written English, most of which are equally applicable to the spoken language though a few have no relevance to speech (for instance, tags for roman numerals, or mathematical operators). Spoken language also, however, makes heavy use of what Anna-Brita Stenström (1990) calls "discourse items", having pragmatic functions with little real parallel in writing: e.g. *well* as an utterance initiator. Discourse items fall into classes which in most cases are about as clearly distinct as the classifications applicable to written words, and the CHRISTINE extension to the SUSANNE scheme provides a set of discourse-item wordtags developed from Stenström's classification. However, where words are ambiguous as between alternative discourse-item classes, the fact that discourse items are not normally syntactically integrated into wider structures means that there is little possibility of finding evidence to resolve the tagging ambiguity.

Thus, three CHRISTINE discourse-item classes are Expletive (e.g. *gosh*), Response (e.g. *ah*), and Imitated Noise (e.g. *glug glug*). Consider the following extracts from a sample in which children are "playing horses", one riding on the other's back:

(39)   speaker PS1DV: . . . *all you can do is <pause> put your belly up and I'll go flying! . . . Go on then, put your belly up!*
       speaker PS1DR: *Gung!*   KPC.00999–1002

(40)   *Chuck a chuck a chuck chuck! Ee ee! Go on then.*   KPC.10977

In the former case, *gung* is neither a standard English expletive, nor an obviously appropriate vocal imitation of anything happening in the horse game. Conversely, in the latter case *ee* could equally well be the standard Northern regional expletive expressing mildly shocked surprise (the speakers were Northerners), or a vocal imitation of a "riding" noise. In many such cases, the analyst is forced by the current scheme to make arbitrary guesses, yet clear cases of the discourse-item classes are too distinct from one another to justify eliminating guesswork by collapsing the classes into one.

Not all spoken words posing tagging problems are discourse items. In:

(41)   *Ah ah! Diddums! Yeah.*   KSU.00396–8

(speaker is a 21-year-old male talking to a 13-year-old boy), any English speaker will recognize the word *diddums* as implying that the speaker regards the hearer as childish, but intuition does not settle how the word should be tagged (noun? if so, proper or common?); and published dictionaries do not help. We have found no principled rule for choosing a predictable analysis in cases like these.

6.4 Speech repairs

Probably the most crucial single area where grammatical analytic standards developed for written language need to be extended to represent the structure of spontaneous spoken utterances is that of speech repairs, where speakers find their utterance unsatisfactory and modify it "on the fly", as they are speaking. The CHRISTINE system for annotating speech repairs draws on work by Wim Levelt and by Peter Howell and Keith Young, which to our knowledge was the most fully-worked-out and empirically-based approach extant when we began working on this topic (see Levelt (1983); P. Howell and Young (1990, 1991)). This approach identified a set of up to nine repair milestones within a repaired utterance, for instance the point at which the speaker's first grammatical plan is abandoned (the "moment of interruption"), and the earlier point marking the beginning of the stretch of wording which will be replaced by new wording after the moment of interruption. However, this approach is not fully workable for many real-life speech repairs. In one respect it is insufficiently informative: the Levelt/Howell and Young notation provides no means of showing how a local sequence containing a repair fits into the wider grammatical architecture of the utterance containing it. In other respects, the notation proves to be excessively rich: it requires speech repairs to conform to a canonical pattern from which, in practice, many repairs deviate.

Accordingly, CHRISTINE uses a simplified version of this notation (Sampson 1995: 448–456), in which the "moment of interruption" in a speech repair is marked (by a "#" sign within the stream of words), but no attempt is made to identify other milestones; and the role of the repaired sequence is identified by making the "#" node a daughter of the lowest labelled node in a constituency tree such that both the material preceding and the material following the # are (partial) attempts to realize that category, and the mother node fits naturally into the surrounding structure. This approach works well for the majority of speech repairs, e.g.:

(42) *That's why I said* [Ti:o *to get ma– ba– # , get you back then*] ... KBJ.00943

(43) *I'll have to* [VV0v# *cha– # change*] *it*   KCA.02828

In (42), *to get ma– ba–* (in which *ma–* and *ba–* are truncated words), and *get you back then*, are successive attempts to produce an infinitival clause (Ti) functioning as object (:o) of *said*. In (43), the node-label VV0v# means "repair structure comprising successive attempts to utter a word tagged VV0v (base form of verb having transitive and intransitive uses)". In Figure 7, the "#" symbol was used at two levels in the same speaker turn: speaker PS6RC makes two attempts to realize a main clause (S), and the second attempt begins with two attempts to pronounce the verb *ice*.

However, although the CHRISTINE speech-repair notation is less informative than the full Levelt/Howell and Young scheme, and seems as simple as is consistent with offering an adequate description of repair structure, applying it consistently is not always straightforward. For one thing, as soon as the annotation scheme includes any system for marking speech repairs, analysts are obliged to decide whether particular stretches of wording are in fact repairs or well-formed constructions, and this is often unclear. In earlier writing (Sampson 1998) we have discussed a variety of indeterminacies that arise. Here we will give one example, repair versus appositional structure, as in:

(44)   *she can't be much cop if she'd open her legs to a first date to a*
        Dutch s– sailor   KSS.05002

– where *to a Dutch s– sailor* might be intended to replace *to a first date* as the true reason for objecting to the girl, but alternatively *to a Dutch s– sailor* could be an appositional phrase giving fuller and better particulars of the nature of her offence. Annotation ought not systematically to require guesswork, but it is hard to see how a neutral notation could be devised that would allow the analyst to suspend judgment on such a fundamental issue as whether a stretch of wording is a repair or a well-formed construction.

6.5 Syntactically Markovian constructions

Even greater problems are posed by a not uncommon type of utterance that might be called "syntactically Markovian", in which each element coheres logically with what immediately precedes but the utterance as a whole would have to be regarded as incoherent, at least by the standards of written prose. The following examples come from the London–Lund Corpus (text numbers are followed by first and last London–Lund "tone-unit" numbers for the respective extracts; the speakers are respectively an undergraduate, age ca 36, describing her interview for an Oxbridge fellowship, and Anthony Wedgwood Benn, MP, on a radio discussion programme):

(45)   *... of course I would be willing to um <pause> come into the common-room <pause> and uh <pause> in fact I would like nothing I would like better*

S.1.3 0901–3

(46)   *and what is happening <pause> in Britain today <pause> is ay– demand for an entirely new foreign policy quite different from the cold war policy <pause> is emerging from the Left*   S.5.5 0539–45

In the former example, *nothing* functions simultaneously as the last uttered word of an intended sequence *I would like nothing better* and the first uttered word of an implied sequence something like *there is nothing I would like better*. In the latter, the long noun-phrase *an entirely new foreign policy quite different from the cold war policy* appears to function both as the complement of the preposition *for*, and as subject of *is emerging*. J. Miller and Reinert (1998: 40) quote further examples; their term is "bi-directional attachment".[4]

Perhaps sequences like these should be thought of as a kind of "repaired speech", but if so they cannot be analysed in terms of the approach described in the previous section: one cannot meaningfully identify a single point where one grammatical plan is abandoned in favour of another. More important, because these structures involve phrases which simultaneously play one grammatical role in the preceding construction and a different role in the following construction, they resist analysis in terms of tree-shaped consituency diagrams (or, equivalently, labelled bracketing of the word-string). In constructing the CHRISTINE Corpus we forced such cases into labelled-bracketing notation as best we could, because that approach to grammar-representation was so fundamental to all the rest of the work that it seemed unthinkable to abandon it for these cases (and even if we had been willing to do so, we could see no specific alternative approach). We were conscious, though, that in doing this we were in fact misrepresenting our data.

For those who take the concept of grammatical description seriously, this situation is almost scandalous. If there is one thing we thought we knew about grammar in human language, it is that it imposes a hierarchical structure on

---

4 While preparing the MS of this book for publication, we noticed for the first time that (at least if one ignores the placement of pauses and considers just the sequence of words), example (46) is open to an alternative, non-Markovian reading, in which the entire clause from *a demand* to *is emerging* functions as complement of *what is happening ... is*. For more than ten years since first working with this example, we had taken for granted that its interpretation is as described above, with the noun phrase headed by *demand* as complement of *is* – and that in itself perhaps establishes that this reading is normal for the spoken language. For (45), and for Miller and Reinert's examples, no alternative to the interpretation discussed appears to be available.

word-sequences: groups of words nested in more inclusive groups of words, dia-grammable as trees branching in one direction. (In 5.10, above, we saw that some members of the generative school are nowadays saying that this is the sole true language universal.) Yet for examples like those quoted, that assumption breaks down.

With respect to spoken English, it is not even clear to us that these cases are properly described as "performance errors". What they are saying seems to us rather clear, and, we suspect, might not seem questionable other than to pro-fessional grammarians or editors, such as ourselves. An editor would change the wording for written publication, certainly; but what gives us the right to see that fact as anything more than a difference between the cultural norms of spoken and written English? Some languages have very large differences between the grammars of their spoken and written forms, but no linguist would treat that as meaning that the spoken languages are "not real languages", or "do not have grammar".

Syntactically Markovian sequences, then, are arguably an extreme illustra-tion of the principle that grammar evolves in unpredictable directions. Someone who tried to specify some kind of range of potential constructions available for languages to adopt would surely not include structures like these in the list; yet we see that in spoken English they occur, and when they occur they work.

6.6 Logical distinctions dependent on the written medium

There are cases where grammatical category distinctions that are highly salient in written English seem much less significant in the spoken language, so that maintaining them in the annotation scheme arguably misrepresents the struc-ture of speech. Perhaps the most important of these is the direct/indirect speech distinction. Written English takes great pains to distinguish clearly between direct speech, involving a commitment to transmit accurately the quoted speaker's exact wording, and indirect speech which preserves only the general sense of the quotation. The SUSANNE annotation scheme uses categories which reflect this distinction. However, the most crucial cues to the distinction are orthographic matters such as inverted commas, which lack spoken counterparts. Sometimes the distinction can be drawn in spoken English by reference to pronouns, verb forms, vocatives, etc.:

(47)   ... *he says he hates drama because the teacher takes no notice, he said one*
       week Stuart was hitting me with a stick and the teacher just said calm down
       you boys ...   KD6.03060

– the underlined *he* (rather than *I*) implies that the complement of *says* is indirect speech; *me* implies that the passage beginning *one week* is a direct quotation, and the imperative form *calm* and vocative *you boys* imply that the teacher is quoted directly. But in practice these cues frequently conflict rather than reinforcing one another:

(48) [reporting speaker's own response to a directly-quoted objection]:
I said <u>well</u> that's <u>his</u> hard luck!   KCT.10673

(49) *well Billy, Billy says <u>well</u> <u>take</u> that and then <u>he</u>'ll come back and then he er gone and pay that*   KCJ.01053–5

In (48), the discourse item *well* and the present tense of *[i]s* after past-tense *said* suggest direct speech, but *his* (which from the context denotes the objector) suggests indirect speech. Likewise in (49), *well* and the imperative *take* imply direct speech, *he'll* rather than *I'll* implies indirect speech. Arguably, imposing a sharp two-way direct v. indirect distinction on speech is a distortion; one might instead feel that speech uses a single construction for reporting others' utterances, though different instances may contain more or fewer indicators of the relative directness of the report. On the other hand, logically speaking the direct v. indirect speech distinction is so fundamental that an analytic scheme which failed to recognize it could seem unacceptable. (The CHRISTINE Corpus does retain the distinction.)

6.7 Nonstandard usage

Real-life British speech contains many differences from standard usage with respect to both individual words and syntactic patterns.

In the case of wordtagging, the SUSANNE rule (Sampson 1995: §3.67) was that words used in ways characteristic of nonstandard dialects are tagged in the same way as the words that would replace them in standard English. This rule was reasonable in the context of written English, where nonstandard forms are a peripheral nuisance, but it quickly became apparent when we worked on spontaneous speech that the rule is quite impractical for analysing speech that contains a high incidence of such forms. For speech annotation we found it necessary to reverse this particular rule; in general, words used in nonstandard grammatical functions are given the same wordtags as those words in their standard uses, though the phrases containing them are tagged in accordance with their grammatical function in context.

This revised rule tends to be unproblematic for pronouns and determiners, thus in:

(50) *it's a bit of fun, it livens up <u>me</u> day*   KP4.03497

(51) *she told me to have <u>them</u> plums*   KCT.10705

the underlined words are wordtagged as object pronouns (rather than as *my, those*), but the phrases *me day* and *them plums* are tagged as noun phrases. It is more difficult to specify a predictable way to apply such a rule in the case of nonstandard uses of strong verb forms, where the word used nonstandardly is head or whole of a tagma which under the SUSANNE rules requires a phrasetag of its own. Standard base forms can be used in past contexts, e.g.:

(52) *a man bought a horse and <u>give</u> it to her, now it's won the race* KCJ.01096–9

and the solution of phrasetagging such an instance as a past-tense verb group (Vd) is put into doubt because frequently nonstandard English omits the auxiliary of the standard perfective construction, suggesting that *give* here might be replacing *given* rather than *gave*; cf.:

(53) *What I <u>done</u>, I taped it back like that*   KCA.02536

(54) *What it is, when you <u>got</u> snooker on and just snooker you're*
       quite <pause> content to watch it …   KCA.02572

These forms will surely sound familiar enough to most British readers, but there has been surprisingly little systematic study of them. Edina Eisikovits ([1987] 1991: 134) has argued in effect that the tense system exemplified in clauses like *What I done* is the same as that of standard English, but that a single form *done* is used for both past tense and past participle in the nonstandard dialect (in the same way that single forms such as *said, allowed* are used for both functions in the standard language, in the case of many other verbs); *I done* here would correspond straightforwardly to standard *I did*. However, this seems to overlook cases like (54) (quite common in our material) where *got* clearly corresponds to standard *have got*, meaning "have", and not to a past tense. Indeed, in chapter 11, below, we shall look at statistical data on verb forms in the CHRISTINE Corpus which suggest to us that a new regional dialect difference is emerging in Britain, in which regions are coming to differ not just in terms of the forms of wording used to realize the various elements of a shared system of tense/ aspect contrasts, but the system itself is coming to differ between regions.

It is quite impractical for annotation to be based on fully adequate grammatical analyses of each nonstandard dialect in its own terms. There are no rigid boundaries between one regional dialect and another, or between a regional dialect and the national standard language; few regional speakers, surely, will lack considerable experience of Standard English. Yet it is not easy to specify consistent rules for annotating nonstandard uses as deviations from the known, standard dialect. The CHRISTINE scheme attempts to introduce predictability into the analysis of cases such as those above by recognizing an extra nonstandard-English "tense" realized as past participle not preceded by auxiliary, and by ruling (as an exception to the general rule quoted earlier) that any verb form used in a nonstandard structure with past reference will be classified as a past participle (so that *give* in the KCJ example above is wordtagged as a nonstandard equivalent of *given*). This approach does work well for many cases, but it remains to be seen whether it will deal satisfactorily with all the usages that arise.

Turning from verb morphology to the level of syntax: an example of a nonstandard construction requiring adaptation of the written-English annotation scheme would be relative clauses containing both relative pronoun and undeleted relativized noun phrase, unknown in standard English but usual in various nonstandard dialects, e.g.:

(55) ... *bloody Colin who, he borrowed his computer that time, remember?*

KD6.03075

Here the approach adopted by the CHRISTINE scheme is to treat the relativized noun phrase (*he*) as appositional to the relative pronoun. For the case quoted, this works; but it would not work if a case were encountered where the relativized element is not the subject of the relative clause.

Examples like this raise the question what it means to specify consistent grammatical annotation standards applicable to a spectrum of different dialects, rather than to a single homogeneous dialect. Written English usually conforms more or less closely to the norms of the national standard language, so that grammatical dialect variation is marginal and annotation standards can afford to ignore it. In the context of speech, it cannot be ignored, but the exercise of specifying annotation standards for unpredictably varying structures seems conceptually confused.

6.8 Dialect difference versus performance error

Special problems arise in deciding whether a turn of phrase should be annotated as normal with respect to the speaker's nonstandard dialect, or as representing standard usage but with words elided as a performance error. Speakers do often omit necessary words, e.g.:

(56)   *There's one thing I don't like <pause> and that's having my photo taken.*
      And it will be hard when we <u>have to photos</u>.   KD2.03102–3

– it seems safe to assume that the speaker intended something like *have to provide photos*. One might take it that a similar process explains the underlined words in:

(57)   *oh she was shouting at him at dinner time <shift shouting> Steven <shift>*
      oh god dinner time she was <u>shouting him</u>.   KD6.03154

where *at* is missing; but this is cast in doubt when other speakers, in separate samples, are found to have produced:

(58)   *go in the sitting room until I <u>shout you</u> for tea*   KPC.00332

(59)   *The spelling mistakes only occurred when <pause> I <u>was shouted</u>.*
      KD2.02798

– this may add up to sufficient evidence for taking *shout* to have a regular transitive use in nonstandard English.

This problem is particularly common at the ends of utterances, where the utterance might be interpreted as broken off before it was grammatically complete (indicated in the SUSANNE scheme by a "#" terminal node as last daughter of the root node), but might alternatively be an intentional nonstandard elision. In:

(60)   *That's right, she said Margaret never goes, I said well we never*
      go for lunch out, we hardly ever really   KE2.08744

the words *we hardly ever really* would not occur in standard English without some verb (if only a placeholding *do*), so the sequence would most plausibly be taken as a broken-off utterance of some clause such as *we hardly ever really go out to eat at all*; but it is not difficult to imagine that the speaker's dialect might allow *we hardly ever really* for standard *we hardly ever do really*, in which case it would be misleading to include the "#" sign.

It seems inconceivable that a detailed annotation scheme could fail to distinguish difference of dialect from performance error; indeed, a scheme which ignored this distinction might seem offensive. But analysts will often in practice have no basis for applying the distinction to particular examples.

6.9 Transcription inadequacies

One cannot expect every word of a sample of spontaneous speech recorded in field conditions to be accurately transcribable from the recordings. Our work relies on transcriptions provided by other researchers, which contain many passages marked as "unclear"; the same would undoubtedly be true if we had chosen to gather our own material. A structural annotation system needs to be capable of assigning an analysis to a passage containing unclear segments; to discard any utterance or sentence containing a single unclear word would require throwing away too many data, and would undesirably bias the retained collection of samples towards utterances that were spoken carefully and may therefore share some special structural properties. Those are considerations for the computational linguist; but thinking about the individual acquiring his mother tongue through exposure to examples, he too must surely encounter patches of speech where words are unidentifiable, and must somehow register those utterances mentally along with the fully-clear utterances – it is implausible that the learner would wholly ignore an utterance if it contains even the briefest unclear stretch.

The SUSANNE scheme uses the symbol Y to label nodes dominating stretches of wholly unclear speech, or tagmas which cannot be assigned a grammatical category because they contain unclear subsegments that make the categorization doubtful.[5]

This system is unproblematic, so long as the unclear material in fact consists of one or more complete grammatical constituents. Often, however, this is not so; e.g.:

(61)   *Oh we didn't <unclear> to drink yourselves.*   KCT.10833

Here it seems sure that the unclear stretch contained multiple words, beginning with one or more words that complete the verb group (V) initiated by *didn't*; and the relationship of the words *to drink yourselves* to the main clause could be quite different, depending what the unclear words were. For instance, if the

---

5 The only Y node in Figure 7 was a root node, because the sequences both preceding and following it appeared to be complete main clauses; but often a Y node will occur in the middle of a tree, because the overall structure of an utterance is clear but some constituent within it is not. Thus, the speaker turn immediately following that displayed in Figure 7 begins:

have you seen <unclear> Mum

where the unclear material is tagged Y:o (direct object) as daughter of an S? (interrogative main clause).

unclear words were *give you anything*, then *to drink* would be a modifying tagma within a noun phrase headed by *anything*; on the other hand, if the unclear stretch were *expect you*, then *to drink* would be the head of an object complement clause. Ideally, a grammatical annotation scheme would permit all the clear grammar to be indicated, but allow the analyst to avoid implying any decision about unresolvable issues such as these.

Given that clear grammar is represented in terms of labelled bracketing, however, it is very difficult to find usable notational conventions that avoid commitment about the structures to which unclear wording contributes. Our best attempt at defining notational conventions for this area is a set of rules which prescribe, among other things, that the Y node dominating an inaudible stretch is attached to the lowest node that clearly dominates at least the first inaudible word, and that clear wording following an inaudible stretch is attached to the Y node above that stretch if the clear wording could be part of some unknown grammatical constituent that is initiated within the inaudible stretch (even if it could equally well not be).

These conventions are reasonably successful at enabling analysts to produce annotations in a predictably consistent way; but they have the disadvantage that many structures produced are undoubtedly different from the grammatical structures of the wording actually uttered. For instance, in the example above, the Y above the unclear stretch is made a daughter of the V dominating *didn't*, because that word will have been followed by an unclear main verb; and *to drink yourselves* is placed under the Y node, because any plausible interpretation of the unclarity would make the latter words part of a tagma initiated within the unclear stretch. Yet there is no way that *to drink yourselves* could really be part of a verb group beginning with *didn't*.

Provided that researchers who work with our data bear in mind that a tree structure which includes a Y node makes only limited claims about the actual structure produced by the speaker, these conventions are not misleading. But at the same time they are not very satisfying.

6.10 Dropping the paradigm

In annotating written English, where one is drawing on an analytic tradition evolved over centuries, it seems on the whole to be true that most annotation decisions have definite answers; where some particular example is vague between two categories, these tend to be subcategories of a single higher-level category, so a neutral fallback annotation is available. (Most English noun phrases are either marked as singular or marked as plural, and the odd exceptional case such as *the fish* can at least be classified as a noun phrase, unmarked for number.)

One way of summarizing many of the problems outlined in this chapter is to say that, in annotating speech, whose special structural features have had little influence on the analytic tradition, ambiguities of classification constantly arise that cut across traditional category schemes. In consequence, not only is it often difficult to choose a notation which attributes specific properties to an example; unlike with written language, it is also often very difficult to define fallback notations which enable the annotator to avoid attributing properties for which there is no evidence, while allowing what can safely be said to be expressed.

For many readers, problems facing computational linguists who set out to construct treebanks are not problems with which they will wish to concern themselves. But the point about annotation becoming specially problematic for a genre of language that lacks the long history of philological scrutiny which written English possesses is a point about language as an aspect of human behaviour. The linguistics of recent decades has tended to think of utterances as having clearcut grammatical structures, even if there are theoretical debates about the identity of those structures. However, this impression of definiteness comes not from the nature of language itself, but from the existence of a well-worked-out tradition of grammatical description, which provides readymade decisions about structure for certain aspects of language, and which encourages people influenced by the tradition to overlook aspects of language for which it does not have readymade answers.

As a simple example, it is obvious that generative linguists' use of the category "VP", that is the decision to treat subject–verb–object sentences as bipartite rather than tripartite structures (p. 32 above), stems from the role of the concepts "subject" and "predicate" in Aristotelian and mediaeval logic. It may be that some theoretical linguists have arguments for a bipartite analysis which are independent of that tradition, but even if so, most linguists who routinely begin sketching grammars of English by writing S → NP VP, VP → V NP (rather than S → NP V NP) are not familiar with those arguments.

When we look at spontaneous speech, we are looking at a language genre for which there is little tradition of philological description – until the advent of sound-recording technology it was not possible to check systematically how people really speak. And, sure enough, when spontaneous speech contains phenomena that are not simply identical to the structures of writing, so that philological tradition gives us no readymade answers about how to analyse them, we often find ourselves at a loss to propose reasonable analyses. The philological tradition is a Kuhnian paradigm which encourages linguists to confine their thinking about grammar to a bounded domain, within which questions have reasonably set answers, and which pushes awkward phenomena to the outside of linguists' field of vision. Corpus-based computational linguistics is a good way of freeing oneself from these intellectual blinkers and exposing oneself to the true messy anarchy of language.

As we have already seen, when we do that, even written English turns out to be far less well-defined than the paradigm led us to imagine. Spoken English emphatically underlines the point.

Chapter 7
Demographic correlates of speech complexity

7.1 Speech in the British National Corpus

Some utterances are structurally more complex than others. Undoubtedly all of us who speak English use a mixture of less complex and more complex utterances, depending on the communicative needs of the moment. But it may be that individuals differ in their average utterance complexity; and it may be that such linguistic differences between individuals correlate with demographic properties of the individuals, such as sex, age, or social class. Research we carried out on the structural properties of spontaneous speech samples in the British National Corpus has indeed uncovered such correlations, and the results we found tend to offer further support to the "open-ended" picture of grammatical competence put forward in this book.

The idea of correlations between grammatical complexity and demographic characteristics of speakers is not new in Britain. In the 1960s and 1970s, Basil Bernstein (e.g. Bernstein 1971) attracted considerable attention with a claim that there exist distinct English "speech-codes", a *restricted code* and an *elaborated code*, characteristic of the working class and the middle class respectively. However, working at a time before good data resources were available, Bernstein necessarily based this argument on limited and rather artificial evidence; whether for that reason or because of changing political fashion, it seems fair to say that Bernstein's claim is not treated as gospel nowadays.[1]

The completion in 1995 of the British National Corpus has created new possibilities of studying such questions objectively. The British National Corpus provides a comprehensive sampling of the English language as used in the UK in recent years. Within its speech section, material totalling about four million words is "demographically sampled": individuals selected by demographic techniques to constitute a fair cross-section of the population, in terms of region, class, age, and sex, recorded the speech events they happened to take part in during days that included working days and weekends. The speech section of the British National Corpus, though it has a number of flaws to be discussed below, is by far the most representative sampling of English speech that yet

---

1 Ulrich Ammon's conclusion in a 1994 encyclopaedia article on Bernstein's theory was that it "deserves to be formulated and tested more rigorously than has been done so far" (Ammon 1994).

exists for any English-speaking country. Our CHRISTINE Corpus comprises structural annotations of a subset of this material. The research findings discussed below were derived from a pre-release version of the CHRISTINE Corpus, comprising annotations of 37 extracts each about 2000 words long.[2]

For a sentence to be "simple" or "complex" in traditional grammatical parlance refers to whether or not it contains subordinate clause(s); and the incidence of subordinate clauses intuitively seems an appropriate, quantifiable property of utterances for use as an index of speech complexity. English uses many types of subordinate clause to achieve greater logical precision than can easily be expressed without them. Relative clauses identify entities by reference to logically complex properties (compare e.g. *the man who came to dinner on Tuesday* with *that old man*); nominal clauses allow explicit propositions to play roles within higher-level propositions (*I know that she mistrusts Julian* v. *I know it*); adverbial clauses express logically complex propositional modifiers (*I shall do it when my daughter gets here* v. *I shall do it soon*); and so on. Of course, subordinate clauses can be used to hedge or add vagueness to what would otherwise be a blunt, clear proposition (*I shall come if nothing arises to prevent me*); but hedging is itself a sophisticated communicative strategy which skilled speakers sometimes need to deploy in order to achieve their purposes successfully. Generative linguists frequently point to grammatical recursion as a central feature distinguishing human languages from the finite signalling systems used by some other species, and clause subordination is the most salient source of recursion in English grammar. There may be other indices of structural complexity that one could choose to measure, but incidence of subordinate clauses is at least one very obvious choice.

Grammatical complexity in this sense was in fact one of the linguistic features on which Basil Bernstein mainly based his theory of sociolinguistic codes (Bernstein 1971: chapters 5–6). But Bernstein's data on this feature, though quantitative rather than merely impressionistic, were drawn entirely from one small experiment in which ten middle-class and fourteen working-class schoolboys between 15 and 18 years of age were asked to produce wording to suit an artificial experimental task. Since better data were not available forty years ago,

---

2 The files used were CHRISTINE texts T01 to T40, omitting T03, T06, and T12 (which were not available at the time the research reported here was carried out). The CHRISTINE Corpus as subsequently released in August 1999 incorporates a number of additional corrections (of the kinds discussed in the documentation files) to British National Corpus data on issues such as assignment of individual speech-turns to particular dialogue participants, or social-class categorization of individual speakers; this means that some of the figures reported below would be slightly different, if recalculated from the August 1999 release, but it is unlikely that the differences would be great enough to modify the conclusions drawn here.

it is no criticism of Bernstein to point out that his findings were far from representative of natural usage in the population as a whole, and that factors such as prior familiarity with the experimental task could have been as relevant as social class in creating the statistically significant differences which Bernstein found in the language of his two groups. (Bernstein drew his subjects from just two schools, and found it necessary to train the working-class group to carry out the speaking task he set, because it was unfamiliar to them, whereas the middle-class group were used to doing similar tasks.)

The British National Corpus gives us the possibility of looking at how a true cross-section of the national population use English spontaneously, in furthering the everyday purposes of their lives. Also, it allows us to look at demographic factors other than social class. We shall see that class is not the factor associated with the most interesting effects in the analysis discussed in the following pages.

7.2 Measuring speech complexity

In examining incidence of grammatical complexity in various speakers' usage, it is clearly important to measure complexity in a way that depends wholly or mainly on aspects of the analytic scheme which are reliable and uncontroversial. This means that the measurement should not refer to sentence units; when one transcribes recordings of spontaneous speech into ordinary orthographic form, there are frequent problems about placement of sentence boundaries (cf. J. Miller and Reinert 1998: 30–45). (For instance, it is often unclear whether successive main clauses should be seen as co-ordinated into a single compound sentence, or as separate sentences. The word *and* is not decisive; in speech it is sometimes omitted from clear cases of co-ordination, and often occurs as the first word of a speaker's turn.) The present research treats degree of embedding as a property of individual words. Each word is given a score representing the number of nodes in the CHRISTINE lineage of that word (the path from the word to the root of its parse-tree) which are labelled with clause categories.[3] Each speaker is then assigned an "embedding index" representing the mean degree of embedding of the various words uttered by the speaker in the sample analysed.

---

3 In the technical terms of the SUSANNE annotation scheme (Sampson 1995: §4.41), a node-label is reckoned as a clause label if it begins with one of the capital letters S F T W A Z L (not immediately followed by another capital).

"Words" for this purpose are those alphabetic sequences treated as word units by the rules of our annotation scheme. Enclitics such as the -*ll* of *he'll* or the -*n't of won't* are treated as separate words, but the punctuation marks used by the British National Corpus transcribers are ignored, as are "stage directions" such as indications of laughter or coughing, and "ghost" elements inserted by the annotator to mark the logical positions of shifted or deleted elements. Grammatical idioms (Sampson 1995: §3.55) such as *up to date*, which are parsed as single words though written with spaces, are counted as one word each; and when a dysfluent speaker makes successive attempts to utter the same word, the sequence is counted as a single word.[4]

As an illustration, consider two extracts from a conversation within CHRISTINE text T11, which was recorded at Llanbradach, Glamorganshire, in January 1992. The utterances, T11.02616 and T11.02623–7, with their CHRISTINE parse-trees are shown in Figure 8. (The speakers are discussing a black tie which they lend between families to attend funerals.)

In Figure 8, clausetag labels are surrounded by a dotted border. By the rules of the annotation scheme, the "discourse item" *well* and the vocative *Mrs* in T11.02616 lie outside the main clause (S), hence these words are at embedding depth zero; each word within the main clause is at depth 1. The exclamation mark inserted by the British National Corpus transcribers is not counted as a word and hence not scored. The embedding index for this utterance would be $4 \div 6 = 0 \cdot 67$. (In the text as a whole, this particular speaker produces many other utterances; her overall index is $1 \cdot 092$.) In T11.02623–7, the first main clause contains a relative clause (Fr) modifying *time*, and the second main clause has a co-ordinated main clause. The words of the relative clause score 2 each (1 for the Fr node, 1 for the S node), but those of the second main clause score only 1 each (whether they are within the "subordinate conjunct" or not – see note 4). The ghost element t147, showing that the relativized item is a Time adjunct, is ignored for depth-scoring; the repetition *I # I* (where the symbol # indicates the start of a repeated attempt to realize the same unit) is counted as a single scorable word. The mean index for this utterance is $21 \div 17 = 1 \cdot 24$.

---

4 Co-ordinate structures are treated in a special way. The SUSANNE scheme annotates co-ordinations in a non-standard (though convenient) manner (Sampson 1995: 310ff.): second and subsequent conjuncts within a co-ordination are treated as constituents subordinate to the first conjunct, thus a unit *X and Y* is given the structure [*X* [*and Y*]]. Since embedding-counts for present purposes ought not to depend on a contentious feature of the annotation scheme, the count is incremented by one, not by two, for cases where a clause node occurs as a "subordinate conjunct" below a higher clause node. (In terms of the SUSANNE scheme, when the label of a node on the path between word and root is a clausetag by the definition above, and includes one of the symbols + – @, the node immediately above it on the path is ignored for purposes of the depth count.)

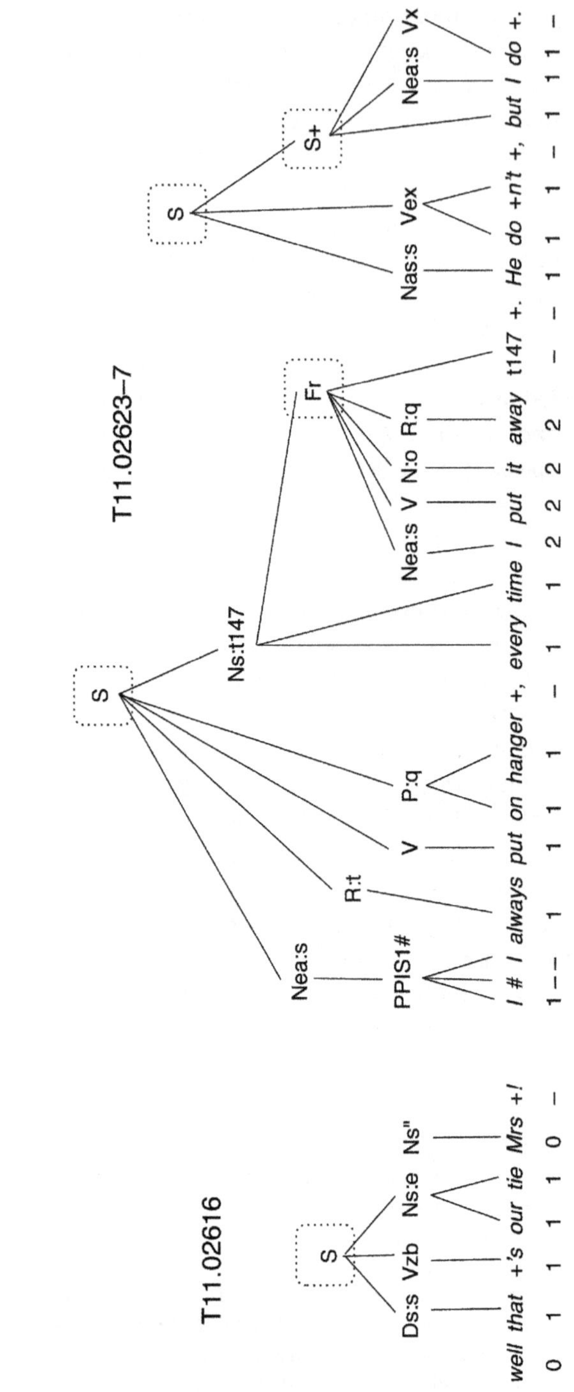

Figure 8: Embedding scores of words in a CHRISTINE extract

This method of scoring speech complexity gives relatively small numerical differences for intuitively large complexity differences. A clause at any particular depth of embedding requires clauses at all lesser depths of embedding to act as grammatical contexts for it, so increasing the depth of the most deeply embedded clause in a sentence will not increase the mean index for the sentence proportionately. But the scoring method has the advantage of being robust with respect to those aspects of the annotation scheme which are most open to disagreement. If one scored speakers by reference, say, to mean number of subordinate clauses per sentence, large and unresolvable debates would arise about whether *well* in T11.02616 ought or ought not to be counted as a "separate sentence" from what follows. For the scoring system chosen, it makes no difference.

7.3 Classifying the speakers

Leaving aside utterances which the British National Corpus transcribers were unable to assign to identified speakers, the material to hand represents 133 speakers who produced varying amounts of verbiage, ranging from 1,981 words for speaker Diane127 down to two words for speaker Jill044. (To preserve speaker anonymity, the names included in CHRISTINE speaker identifiers are not the speakers' real names, e.g. the speaker identified in CHRISTINE as Diane127 is not a Diane in real life.) If very few words are recorded for a particular individual (perhaps an eloquent speaker who just happens to be represented in the sample only by a brief greeting, say), there is no possibility for that individual's embedding index to be high. It was desirable, therefore, to exclude low-wordage speakers; in order to decide a threshold, we divided the speakers into groups whose wordage was similar, and checked the group means of their members' embedding indices. Above sixteen words, there was no tendency for lower-wordage speakers to have lower embedding indices. Accordingly we excluded only the thirteen speakers who each produced sixteen words or fewer from the analyses that follow.

The remaining 120 speakers are represented by a total of 64,726 words, mean 539·4 words per speaker. The grand mean of the 120 speakers' embedding indices is 1·169. All but two of the individual means fall within the range 0·66 to 1·71; the outliers are 1·980 for speaker Jill136, a female lecturer (age unknown), and 0·146 for speaker Scott125, a one-year-old boy.

The British National Corpus includes demographic information for each of these speakers. In principle, for each speaker the corpus aims to record sex, age, regional accent/dialect, occupation, social class in terms of the Registrar-General's classification based on occupation (Office of Population Censuses and Surveys 1991),[5] and relationship to the other participants in the conversation. However (understandably, given the large size of the corpus), this information is often far from perfect. For some speakers some categories of information are missing; in other cases the information given is clearly erroneous. For instance, speaker Gillian091 is specified as a doctor by occupation and as belonging to social class DE (partly skilled or unskilled); these descriptions are incompatible.

The British National Corpus demographic information might be described as detailed but unreliable, whereas for present purposes we want information that is coarse but reliable. Thus, the corpus classifies dialects within England in terms of a system derived from (though not quite identical to) that of Trudgill (1990: 65), who divides England into sixteen linguistic regions. For present purposes, sixteen regions for England (together with categories for the other UK nations) is too refined a classification. Many regions are unrepresented or represented by very few speakers in the sample; and it is hard to believe that there might be a consistent difference in speech complexity between Humberside and Central Northern England, say, though it is perhaps not inconceivable that there could be differences between Northern and Southern England, or between Northern England and Scotland with its separate education system.

Because the CHRISTINE Corpus contains only a small subset of the full British National Corpus, and research such as that presented here needs only a coarse demographic classification, we were able to some extent to correct the information in the corpus, in consultation with its compilers and from internal evidence. (Details on the correction process are given in the CHRISTINE documentation file – see the Preface.) Sex and age information was assumed to be correct. Speakers were assigned to regions primarily on the basis of the place where the conversation was recorded, except for rare cases where this datum was incompatible with a speaker's British National Corpus dialect code and there was internal evidence that the latter was correct. British National Corpus social class codes were adjusted in terms of information about occupation or spouse's occupation, since this relatively specific information is more likely to be accurate (thus speaker Gillian091, as a doctor, had her code changed from DE to AB). Even with these adjustments, social class is unquestionably the variable for which the information is least satisfactory, and 33 speakers remained uncategorized for social class.

The research reported here used a five-way regional classification:

---

5 This was later superseded by a revised social classification scheme; but the 1991 scheme was the one current during the years when the British National Corpus material was compiled.

Southern England
Northern England
Wales
Scotland
Northern Ireland[6]

The Southern/Northern England boundary corresponds to the principal dialect boundary identified by Trudgill (1990: 63), so that most of what is ordinarily called the Midlands is included in "Northern England".[7] The research used a four-way social classification derived from the Registrar-General's scheme:

AB professional, managerial, and technical
C1 skilled non-manual
C2 skilled manual
DE partly skilled and unskilled

There are further sources of inaccuracy in the British National Corpus. The tapes were transcribed by clerical workers under time pressure; sometimes they misheard or misunderstood a speaker's words. (This is indisputable in a case where a speaker reads from the Bible and the transcribed words can be compared with the original, but it is morally certain in some other cases where the transcribed words make no sense but phonetically very similar wording would make good sense, e.g. *unless you've low and detest children* at T29.09621 must surely stand for *unless you loathe and detest children*.) Furthermore some speaker turns are assigned to the wrong speaker, as revealed for instance when a speaker appears to address himself by name. In the CHRISTINE Corpus, such errors are corrected so far as is possible from internal evidence (with logs of the changes made to the original data); undoubtedly there remain cases where corrections should have been made but have not been.

This may seem to add up to a rather unsatisfactory situation. But the incidence of error should not be exaggerated; in transcriptions of almost 65,000 words by 120 speakers we believe the erroneous data are few relative to what is correct, and in any case we had no alternative data source that was better or, indeed, nearly as good.

---

6 Strictly, this category should be labelled simply "Ireland"; as well as material recorded within Northern Ireland, the data include utterances by one Irish speaker living in England, who may have come from the Republic.

7 This five-way regional classification is a simplification of the CHRISTINE Corpus regional classification: "Southern England" in the research of this chapter subsumes the CHRISTINE "South East" and "South West" regions, and "Northern England" here subsumes CHRISTINE "Northern England" and "Midlands" regions.

Perhaps more important, although there are errors in the data, they should be errors of a "fail-safe" type. The purpose of the present chapter is to look for significant correlations between embedding indices and demographic variables, and sporadic errors are likely to make such correlations harder to find: it would be a strange coincidence if errors conspired to create significant correlations where none exist in reality. So it seems worth proceeding despite the imperfections of the data.

7.4 Demographics and complexity indices compared

We searched for correlations with each of the four demographic variables (region, sex, class, age) by grouping the individual speaker indices into categories for the relevant variable (omitting speakers for whom the relevant data were missing), and applying a statistical test to check whether any differences found among the embedding-index distributions for the different categories were significant. The test statistic we used was the F statistic (e.g. Mendenhall 1967: chapter 12). This is suitable for comparing variance among more than two categories, and takes into account the different numbers of individual datapoints in different categories. (This last point is important. For some of the demographic variables examined, the data contain very different numbers of speakers in different categories. As one would expect from the respective populations, for instance, our data contain far fewer speakers from Northern Ireland than from Southern England.)

The "region" variable makes a good initial illustration of the analytic method. For the five regions distinguished, Table 4 shows the means of the embedding indices for speakers from that region, their standard deviations, and the number of speakers from each region. The last column totals 119, because no regional information was available for one of the 120 speakers in the data. (As one would expect with a random sample, speaker numbers are not precisely proportional to regional populations; by chance Scotland is noticeably under-represented in our material.)

Table 4: Mean embedding indices by region

Region	Mean	s.d.	N
Southern England	1·182	0·232	50
Northern England	1·173	0·252	49
Wales	1·120	0·207	8
Scotland	1·261	0·224	4
Northern Ireland	1·105	0·124	8

On the basis of the means alone, one would say that Scots' English is slightly more grammatically complex, and the English of Northern Ireland slightly less, than average. But the F statistic computed from these data is 0.415, which corresponds to a significance level of $p = 0.798$. In other words, supposing that there is in reality no difference between the regions of Britain with respect to the grammatical complexity of speech, then the probability of finding at least this degree of difference among the sample distributions, merely as a consequence of chance fluctuations, is almost four in five. It is much more likely than not that chance would throw up at least this much difference between the categories. So – what will probably surprise few readers – we conclude that there is no evidence for regional complexity differences. In this particular data-set, the Scots happened to score the highest average, but in a fresh sampling it is just as likely that any of the other regions would come out ahead.

Similarly, contrary to what Bernstein might lead us to expect, the CHRISTINE data fail to support a correlation between speech complexity and social class. The data are shown in Table 5. (In this case the speaker numbers total only 87, because – as we have seen – 33 speakers are unclassified for social class.)

Table 5: Mean embedding indices by social class

Social class	Mean	s.d.	N
AB	1·158	0·326	25
C1	1·168	0·178	9
C2	1·257	0·227	20
DE	1·142	0·136	33

The F statistic is 1.065, giving $p = 0.368$. This probability is lower than in the case of the region variable, but is still greater than one in three. A difference in group sample distributions with a probability of more than one in three of occurring by chance would not be seen as evidence of a genuine difference among the group populations.

That does not, of course, mean that our data prove that there is no link between social class and speech complexity. It merely means that our data do not show that there is such a link. It is perfectly possible that Bernstein's theory might be broadly correct, yet the effect fails to show up in the CHRISTINE data. There are many reasons why that might be so; perhaps the most obvious is that, as we have seen, social class is the least reliably recorded demographic variable. If these data were more complete and accurate, it could be that the figures would yield a correlation supporting the "restricted v. elaborated code" idea. But the data we actually have tell us nothing of the sort.

For the sex variable, the results are more interesting; see Table 6 (three speakers' sex unknown). Here, $F = 4 \cdot 052$, giving $p = 0 \cdot 0465$. Conventionally, a probability of less than one in twenty is taken as good reason to think that a statistical phenomenon is real rather than a random effect. It seems that, systematically, British females may on average produce slightly more complex utterances than British males. (However, we shall see below that this inference is not straightforward.)

Table 6: Mean embedding indices by sex

Sex	Mean	s.d.	N
male	1·126	0·263	55
female	1·213	0·202	62

Overwhelmingly the most significant finding relates to the age variable, where we grouped the speakers into categories using the six age bands of the British National Corpus coding. (For most speakers, the British National Corpus gives exact age in years, but it also assigns broader age-band codes.) The figures are given in table 7 (six speakers' ages are unknown). The F statistic from these figures is $5 \cdot 493$, giving $p = 0 \cdot 000152$.

In other words, there is a less than one in 5,000 probability that these different means have arisen by chance in samples drawn from a population that is homogeneous with respect to grammatical complexity.

Table 7: Mean embedding indices by age

Age band	Mean	s.d.	N
up to 15 years	0·941	0·251	18
16–24	1·169	0·188	18
25–34	1·171	0·169	27
35–44	1·226	0·186	12
45–59	1·225	0·219	20
60 and above	1·257	0·194	19

Of course, there is nothing surprising in finding a correlation between age and speech complexity in a set of speakers which includes children as young as one and two years old. The largest gap between means of adjacent age bands is between the two youngest bands – although the means continue to rise, more slowly, in the higher age bands (except for the near-identical means for the 35–44 and 45–59 bands). It might be that these figures represent a growth of speech complexity from zero at birth to a value characteristic of mature speakers, followed by a series of figures representing random fluctuations round a constant mean in adults of all ages. But there is an alternative interpretation.

Before turning to that, since it is at least clear that children's speech is on average markedly less complex than adults', it seemed worth repeating the F statistic calculation for the other variables, omitting speakers in the youngest age band. This is a crude way of attempting to eliminate variation due to age from the figures for variation with other variables; but, since the precise nature of the variation due to age is unclear and, as we shall show below, contentious, it is probably the best that can be done in practice.

Table 8: Mean adult embedding indices by sex

Sex	Mean	s.d.	N
male	1·189	0·220	44
female	1·234	0·197	55

For the region variable, after eliminating under-16 speakers it remains true that there are no significant differences; the five regional means change marginally (we do not show the modified figures here), but the F statistic $0·643$ corresponds to $p = 0·633$. For the sex variable, the significant difference noted above melts away (Table 8). Here, $F = 1·130$, $p = 0·29$. A difference with an almost three in ten probability of arising by chance would not normally be seen as significant. It seems that the appearance of a significant difference between the sexes in connexion with Table 6 earlier may have stemmed from the accident that the sample includes more male than female children.

Table 9: Mean adult embedding indices by age

Social class	Mean	s.d.	N
AB	1·247	0·267	18
C1	1·168	0·178	9
C2	1·300	0·196	18
DE	1·152	0·135	31

On the other hand, with under-16s excluded, the distribution of embedding indices across social classes almost attains significance at the $p < 0·05$ level (Table 9). For Table 9, $F = 2·475$, $p = 0·068$. The figure $0·068$ is a little larger, but only a little larger, than the threshold $0·05$ which is conventionally seen as the point where one ceases to dismiss observed differences as chance fluctuations and begins to believe that they represent real differences between the populations. However, the direction of the differences is very different from what either Bernstein or common sense would predict: anyone who believes in complexity differences between the speech of different social classes would surely expect the relationship to be AB > C1 > C2 > DE – not C2 > AB > C1 > DE. It is difficult to know what, if anything, to make of this finding. We may remind ourselves, again, that social class is the variable for which the data are least reliable.

7.5 "Critical period" or lifelong learning?

So far, in sum, we seem to have established that children's speech is on average less complex than adults', which is to be expected, and that no demographic variable other than age shows reliable correlations with speech complexity. But let us look at the age variable in more detail. It is this variable which will prove to be relevant to the theme of the present book.

Those linguists who believe in an innate Universal Grammar hold that there is a "critical period" for first-language-acquisition: human beings have an innately programmed "language-acquisition device" governed by a biological clock which causes them to be receptive language-learners for a number of years during childhood, but which then switches off so that any language-learning that takes place in later years is a relatively halting, unnatural process, controlled by general psychological problem-solving mechanisms rather than by an efficient special-purpose language-acquisition device. This is supposed to explain why people who learn a second language after early childhood, for instance as a secondary-school subject, typically master it very indifferently (while a child exposed to two languages in early years, for instance as a member of an expatriate family, may grow up bilingual), and also why "wild children" who for some reason are isolated from all language experience during the childhood years (such as the well known, tragic case of "Genie", Curtiss 1977) are allegedly never able to make up for lost time if society first discovers them and attempts to help them learn to speak after their "critical period" has expired.

This idea was introduced into the mainstream of thinking about language by Eric Lenneberg (1967); for a more recent exposition, see for instance Pinker (1995: 37–38, 290–296). At present, the majority of linguists probably adhere to the "critical period" picture of the language-acquisition process.

According to this picture, human lives (unless cut short prematurely) are divided into two sharply different parts with respect to language: an early period when the human is a language-learner, and a later period when he or she has ceased to be a learner and has become a mature language user. As Noam Chomsky puts it (1976: 119), the child attains "a 'steady state' ... not changing in significant respects from that point on". If one asks when the steady state is reached, Lenneberg (1967) gives the age of twelve (in diagrams on his pp. 159–167) or "about thirteen" (p. 153); in several passages, rather than quoting an age in years, he links the switching-off of the language-acquisition device to puberty.[8]

This picture of an individual's linguistic ability as developing on a rapidly rising trend for ten to thirteen years and then levelling out for the remainder of life is sharply at variance with views held by eminent linguists of earlier decades. According to Leonard Bloomfield (1933: 46):

> there is no hour or day when we can say that a person has finished learning to speak, but, rather, to the end of his life, the speaker keeps on doing the very things which make up infantile language-learning.

Fifty years earlier, W.D. Whitney wrote (1885: 25):

> We realize better in the case of a second or "foreign", than in that of a first or "native" language, that the process of acquisition is a never-ending one; but it is not more true of the one than of the other.

These writers saw the trend of linguistic ability as continuing upwards throughout life, with no sudden flattening out. Clearly, our picture of linguistic competence as an open-ended matter of learning to use more and more constructions, with no particular set limit on the range of constructions to be acquired or invented, suggests that Bloomfield and Whitney are right about this, and the "steady state" idea is wrong.

Learning to use grammatical subordination devices is one important part of learning to use one's mother tongue, so the CHRISTINE data might help to choose between these alternative conceptions of language-learning. Do they show a change from growth to steady state at puberty?

Figure 9 displays graphically the means of Table 7 above, but with the "up to fifteen" age band divided into four narrower bands. For the age band 9–12 there is a complication: one twelve-year-old speaker, Marco129, has an extremely low embedding index (0·663 – lower than the index of any other speaker in the data except for Scott125, a one-year-old); because numbers of speakers in these narrow bands are small, a single outlier has a large impact on the overall average. The cross in the 9–12 column of Figure 9 gives the mean including

---

8 For completeness it should be mentioned that Lenneberg's diagrams suggest that a linguistic biography has three parts, not just two, because they show language-acquisition as beginning at two years of age. More recent writers have paid less attention to the idea that language-acquisition has a well defined beginning than that it has a well defined endpoint.

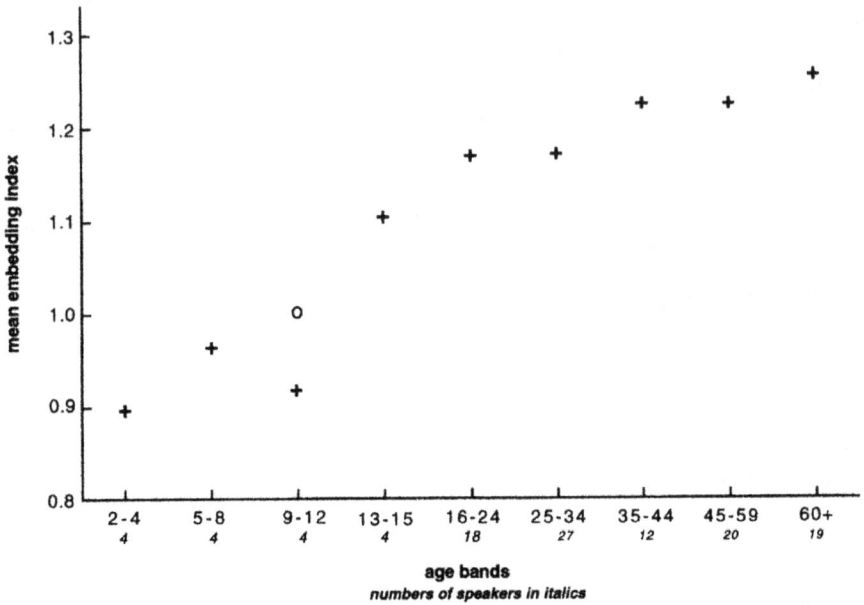

Figure 9: Embedding indices plotted against age

Marco129; the circle gives the mean omitting Marco129. (This could be appropriate, if Marco129 were in some way abnormal. We have no real information about that, but this speaker's CHRISTINE identifier uses the name "Marco" to reflect the fact that his true name sounds foreign; put together with the fact that the relevant conversation was recorded in London, this suggests a fair possibility that Marco129 may be a non-native speaker.[9])

To the eye, Figure 9 looks more like a graph of "lifelong learning" than of childhood learning followed by a steady state. Note that – even with the version of the graph that excludes Marco129 – the largest single jump between adjacent age bands is from the 9–12 to the 13–15 band: that is immediately *after* the steady state has allegedly been reached. (With Marco129 included, this jump would be far larger.)

One would like objective, statistical confirmation of this appearance of lifelong growth in speech complexity. Inferences drawn from Figure 9 might be challenged as misleading, for instance because the graph ignores the fact that

---

9 *The Times* of 22 January 2000 reported research by Philip Baker and John Eversley showing that London had become the world's most linguistically diverse city, with only two-thirds of schoolchildren speaking English at home.

the early age bands are narrower than the later ones. (It is widely regarded as a truism that learning, of all kinds, is a more concentrated, rapid activity in childhood than in maturity, so arguably it is quite appropriate for age bands of a few years in childhood to be represented on a par with bands of a decade or more of adult life; but the impression produced by a display like Figure 9 is so heavily dependent on a variety of graphic imponderables that inferences from it cannot be regarded as reliable.)

Accordingly we examined the correlation between embedding index and age in years (ignoring age bands) among those individual speakers who, in terms of their age, should have passed the putative "critical period" for language-acquisition. The question now is: how probable is it that the appearance of upward trend in the distribution of mature individuals' embedding-index/age values would occur as a chance fluctuation in a sample, if mean embedding index in the population from which the sample was drawn is invariant with age?

The first decision here is what age to use as a fair cut-off to exclude speakers who might still be within their alleged "critical period". We have seen that, writing in the 1960s, Eric Lenneberg identified the end of the critical period variously as twelve or thirteen years, or as puberty. Age of puberty has been dropping in subsequent decades; figures we were given in the late 1990s for age at onset of puberty in Britain are:[10]

males: average, 11·5 years; range including 2·5 s.d.s, 9–14 years

females: average, 10·5 years; range including 2·5 s.d.s, 8–13 years

If Lenneberg counted individuals of thirteen years and above as beyond the critical period in 1967, we shall surely be safe in using that age as the cut-off for speakers represented in the British National Corpus, whose speech was gathered in the early 1990s; accordingly we examined the data for speakers aged thirteen or over (there were 100 such speakers in the data).

The line of best fit to this sample of 100 embedding-index/age points has intercept 1·125, slope 0·00191, that is a gentle upward trend in embedding index with increasing age. (There is of course much variance round the line of best fit; $s=0·193$.) In order to test the null hypothesis that the line of best fit to the population from which the sample is drawn has zero slope, we computed the Student's t statistic (e.g. Mendenhall 1967: 232–233); $t = 1·813$. This comfortably exceeds the critical value for the $p < 0·05$ significance level (though it does not attain the $p < 0·025$ level).

---

10 We are indebted for these data to Dr G.H. Stafford of the Conquest Hospital, Hastings.

In other words, these figures give us grounds for saying that (while the evidence is not overwhelming) increase in average grammatical complexity of speech appears to be a phenomenon that does *not* terminate at puberty, but continues throughout life. As Figure 9 suggests, not only do people around twenty produce more grammatical complexity than people in their early teens, but over-sixties produce more complexity than people in their fifties and below.

Supporters of the "critical period" picture of language-acquisition, if they did not simply dismiss these figures as a statistical fluke (the only answer to which would be to gather more material and hope for higher significance levels), might respond by saying that their concept of a language-acquisition device which switches off at puberty does not imply that grammatical complexity ceases to grow after the switch-off. It is true that average grammatical complexity of utterances is not a property which has featured very heavily in the "critical period" literature, so far as we know. Proponents of that concept tend to focus more on individual linguistic constructions than on statistics of usage of an overall grammatical system. But learning the individual constructions of one's mother tongue, and learning to make fuller use of the system of constructions one has encountered to date, are both part of what most people would understand by "language-acquisition".

If we doubt whether findings of lifelong growth in complexity of usage are relevant to the "critical period" hypothesis, we should consider how believers in the critical period would have responded to the opposite finding. If Figure 9, rather than displaying a continuing upward trend, had shown an upward slope to the age of puberty, followed by a horizontal trend from puberty to the end of adult life, it will be clear to anyone familiar with the "critical period" debate that this would have been seized on as confirmation of the theory. It is always open to proponents of a scientific theory to respond to adverse evidence by reinterpreting the theory so that it makes no prediction about just those points where negative evidence has emerged. The penalty is that this procedure converts true science into pseudoscience – the evolving theory becomes what Imre Lakatos (e.g. 1970: 118) called a "degenerating problemshift", which reacts to cumulations of new evidence not by increasing its empirical scope but by defensively shutting itself off from possibilities of refutation. To take the concept of an age-bounded innate "language-acquisition device" seriously as a scientific hypothesis should require one to admit the findings discussed here as at least *prima facie* counter-evidence.

If acquiring a language meant acquiring each of a fixed, finite list of grammatical rules, then at some point in life the job would be done and it would be reasonable to think of the speaker after that point as having entered a "steady state". The "lifelong learning" scenario suggested by the data presented here harmonizes much better with our picture of a language as having grammar but no grammaticality.

7.6 Individual advance or collective retreat?

These findings are of interest from other perspectives too. There is social and educational significance in the discovery that people seemingly advance in terms of the structural, logical richness of their spontaneous speech habits as they progress from youth through middle age towards old age.

It is important, therefore, to note that there is an alternative possible interpretation of the upward slope of Figure 9. In fairness we must point out that our data do not at present allow us to determine which interpretation is correct.

The data give us a snapshot of the usage of people of different ages at a single period, the early 1990s. We have been assuming so far that data gathered in the same way several decades earlier or later would show an essentially similar picture; but it might not. Possibly, what the figures are telling us is that people who were born about 1930, and hence were in their sixties when their speech was collected for the British National Corpus, have *throughout their adult lives* spoken in a grammatically more complex manner, on average, than (say) people who were born about 1970, who were in their twenties when the corpus was compiled.[11] Changing patterns of schooling, and/or cultural shifts from written to visual media, might conceivably have led to this sort of change in speech styles.

To us it seems more plausible that the upward trend of Figure 9 represents a lifelong-learning effect which is repeated generation after generation, than that it represents a historical change in the nature of British speech. But many others to whom we have presented the data have found the second interpretation more plausible. At present, there is no way to know which is right. That would require a comparable body of data, gathered at a period at least some decades earlier or later than the British National Corpus. It is too late now to regret that no "fair cross-section" of British speech was sampled earlier than the 1990s. (Such earlier speech corpora as do exist are too unrepresentative, socially and otherwise, to offer a meaningful comparison.)

---

11 This alternative would be no more compatible than the original interpretation, so far as we can see, with the "critical period" theory; genetically determined linguistic behaviour should be constant across the generations.

In years to come, if anyone is willing to devote the considerable resources of effort and expense needed to compile a newer equivalent of the demographic-speech section of the British National Corpus and to analyse its grammar, we may find out whether Britons are individually growing subtler, or collectively growing cruder, in the structure of their speech. Until then, we can only wait and wonder.

Chapter 8
The structure of children's writing

8.1 Moving from spoken to adult written norms

Most English children arrive at school speaking English fluently. If all goes well they complete compulsory schooling, a decade or so later, as skilled users of the written language. Written and spoken structural norms differ in a number of ways. The compilation of structurally annotated electronic corpora of spoken and written English is starting to open up new possibilities of studying the trajectory taken in moving from one stage to the other. This chapter represents a first attempt to extract findings shedding light on the process of writing-skills acquisition from our CHRISTINE and LUCY corpora.

8.2 The language samples

For the purposes of this analysis, the annotated language samples to hand at the time when the research was done are divided into three groups, which we shall refer to as "speech", "published writing", and "child writing".

The "speech" samples consist of 39 of the 40 files in our CHRISTINE Corpus, i.e. extracts taken from random points in the demographically-sampled speech section of the British National Corpus.[1] It thus represents the usage of a cross section of the UK population in the 1990s, balanced in terms of age, sex, region, and social class, in the speech events of their everyday lives – overwhelmingly, informal conversation with family, colleagues, and acquaintances.

The 31 "published writing" samples come from our LUCY corpus, which was not yet complete at the time when the investigation reported here was carried out; they represent a section of the LUCY corpus consisting of passages drawn from random points in British National Corpus written-language files that were themselves taken from sources which are published, and which contain a low incidence of linguistic errors or features that would be regarded as solecisms by professional editors. It includes extracts from sources as diverse as novels, industry house organs, social science textbooks, computer magazines, etc. The "published writing" can thus be seen collectively as in some sense representative of the target towards which writing-skills education is directed.

---

1 Of the forty text files in CHRISTINE, file T40 was omitted from this study because of a format error which interfered with the statistics extraction software.

The "child writing" is taken from material published by a research project sponsored by the Nuffield Foundation in the 1960s. Researchers visited a number of schools in London, Kent, Sussex, and Yorkshire collecting various kinds of data on pupils' use of oral and written language. (The schools included state primary and grammar schools, one secondary modern, and one then-novel comprehensive school; their locations appear to have been suburban and semi-rural rather than either "inner-city" or fully rural.) For the exercise relevant here, the researchers invited children aged from nine to twelve in 1964–1965 to write essays on a choice of open-ended topics (e.g. "My hobby", "Our last holiday") which were transcribed into typescript and published as Handscombe (1967a, 1967b). The present study uses 67 of these, comprising roughly equal quantities of wording from ages 9, 10, 11, and 12 and from the two sexes.

A very rough indication of the wordage in the three samples is:

speech	80,000
child writing	12,500
published writing	63,500

Exact figures are difficult to specify because (particularly in the case of spontaneous speech) there are real questions about how words should be counted. These figures, and the data used for the following statistical analyses, exclude written material identified as "headings" rather than continuous text. The statistical analyses of grammatical tree structures also ignore root nodes (representing written paragraphs or oral speaker-turns) and all words immediately dominated by them, which means for instance that spoken "discourse items" such as *well* or *yes* are ignored when they are not included within a larger grammatical construction.

The speech sample includes speech by both adults and children; the age range is from one to 84 years. For present research purposes, all this material is treated as a single sample. The analyses below also treat the Nuffield material as a single sample; in the present investigation we did not attempt to study development over the nine- to twelve-year-old age range.

8.3 The suitability of the child-writing sample

Being almost forty years old, our sample of child writing might be seen as rather dated, but in one way its age is a positive advantage for comparison with the BNC published-writing data: children aged from nine to twelve in the mid-1960s are centrally placed within the generation span likely to have been composing published writing in the 1990s, when our published-writing sample was produced. The fact that the child writing sample is somewhat biased towards children who overcame the eleven-plus hurdle also presumably makes them a better-than-random match to the class of adults whose writing gets into print.

We know that incidence of different grammatical constructions in children's writing is heavily influenced by the overall nature of a particular writing task (Perera 1984: 239) – and the same is obviously true of adult prose, for instance one will not find interrogatives in a weather forecast. So the fit between the Nuffield material and the BNC published writing might be criticized because the prose genres are different. That is unavoidable: children do not write social-science textbooks, and the middle-aged do not normally write little narratives about their last holiday. But the two written data-sets are a good match in that they both represent what people are capable of writing spontaneously at the respective stages in life. A common problem with corpora of children's or young people's writing is that the writing tasks are unnatural and the prose style derivative. We have found when trying to use first-year undergraduates' coursework to sample young adults' writing, for instance, that its verbal texture commonly seems to have more to do with the nature of the set books prescribed by lecturers than with the students' spontaneous usage – not in the sense that the students are plagiarizing the books word for word, but they very often seem to interpret the coursework task as requiring a sort of stylistic pastiche which one can guess to be quite different from anything they would write spontaneously. The Nuffield project was very successful in getting away from this kind of problem, by providing a wide choice of general topics known to be attractive to children at the respective ages, and by making it obvious to the children that this was a voluntary activity separate from the school curriculum, in which their performance would not be graded. The resulting corpus (which is far larger than the the the child-writing section of our LUCY corpus) gives every appearance of being the spontaneous, unaided output of children of different levels of skill. (We have often been surprised that greater use has not been made of it since its original publication.)

8.4 Writing "wordier" than speech

An initial expectation is that words in published writing are likely to be organized into more elaborate constructions, on average, than words in spontaneous speech. Converting this intuitive idea into a precise, quantifiable concept is not as straightforward as it may sound. Linguists oriented to written language research might think in terms of "greater average sentence length", but that concept is not usable in connexion with spontaneous speech: spoken utterances are not divided unambiguously into "sentences" (J. Miller and Weinert: chapter 2), and in general the area nearest the roots of parse-trees is where the annotation tends to be most debatable.

What we have done as an attempt to get round that problem is to look at the mean length in words of *all grammatical constructions*, averaging over not just the most inclusive tagmas, such as sentences, but their constituents, and the constituents of their constituents, and so on down to include each nonterminal node that dominates more than one word. The figures are:

speech	4·62
child writing	7·68
published writing	9·45

If one accepts this as a reasonable way to measure "wordiness", then we can say that the average construction in published writing is indeed about twice as long as the average spoken construction; and the average construction in child writing is intermediate in length – in terms of these figures one might say that the children have moved a little more than halfway from spoken to written norms.

(There is undoubtedly something odd about averaging over a set of elements, some of which are parts of other elements in the set. We used this method of measuring "wordiness" because no better method occurred to us, but nothing in later sections of this chapter depends on it.)

One incidental point about the above figures is that the speech data contain a structural feature that is completely absent from writing: speech repairs, where the speaker embarks on a construction, breaks off, and starts again using the same or different words, e.g. *Has he # has he gone Rovers?* In our annotation scheme *all* the words in a speech repair like this are ultimately dominated by a single nonterminal node (see 6.4 above), so those nodes will dominate relatively long sequences of words; yet, despite the fact that repair structures are frequent in spontaneous speech and are edited out of writing, we see that speech still comes out on average with relatively short tagmas.

8.5 Width v. depth in parse-trees

If we forget about the details of particular grammatical constructions and think just about the abstract geometry of parse-trees, there are fundamentally two ways in which average construction length can differ. Branching can be wide, or it can be deep.

By wide branching we mean that individual tagmas can have many immediate constituents (daughter nodes): for instance *a man* is a noun phrase with two daughters (the two words), whereas *a funny little man who made us laugh* is in terms of our scheme a noun phrase with five daughters (the first four words, and the relative clause *who made us laugh*) – J. Miller and Weinert (1998: 135–143) claim that "wide" noun phrases such as the latter example are common in writing and rare or absent in spontaneous speech.

By deep branching we mean the extent to which structures exploit the recursive properties of grammar, to produce long chains of branches between words and root nodes.[2] A tree in which branching is "deep" in this sense will dominate many words even if each nonterminal node has just two daughters.

Width and depth are not mutually exclusive, and one might expect both to contribute to the difference in "wordiness" between the genres. In our data that turns out not to be so. Average number of ICs per construction are as follows:

speech	2·860
child writing	2·860
published writing	2·759

It must surely be just a coincidence that the first two numbers agree to four significant figures, but nevertheless (contrary to what is suggested by the Miller and Weinert passage cited above) our three genres are evidently all very similar in terms of node "width".

(These averages cover only nodes which do have at least two daughters. Our annotation scheme recognizes some "unary branching" nodes – for instance, in *she was feeling depressed*, we count *she* as a noun phrase consisting of just a pronoun, and *depressed* as a past participle clause consisting just of a verb group consisting just of a past participle. Here and in other statistics quoted below, single-daughter tagmas are omitted from the averages, because their status seems much more theory-dependent and debatable than that of multi-daughter tagmas. If unary branching nodes are included in the calculations of

---

2 An earlier study (Sampson 1997) used the term "depth" in a different sense, inspired by the work of Victor Yngve (e.g. 1961), to refer to the extent to which parse-trees contain left-branching structures. (The left-branchingness measure of that study, applied to the present data, gives mean figures which are similar for all three genres.) "Depth" in the present chapter refers to distance between leaf and root nodes, and not to a measure of asymmetry between left and right branching.

average width, then there are differences, but quite small differences, between the genres:

speech	1·98
child writing	2·16
published writing	2·25

This might correspond for instance to speech using more pronouns while writing uses more explicit referring expressions.)

When we look at depth, the picture changes. As in chapter 7, we examine average depth of words not in terms of raw numbers of branches between word and root node, but specifically in terms of how many of the nodes dominating a word are labelled with clause categories, that is how deeply embedded the words are in terms of subordinate clauses. Again, this makes the numbers less theory-dependent. For instance, for those linguists who believe in "VP" units, objects would have more branches above them than subjects, whereas our annotation scheme treats subjects and objects as sister nodes; on the other hand, linguists are in much more agreement about where to recognize subordinate clauses.

Mean word depths are:

speech	1·365
child writing	1·401
published writing	1·857

These means may not look very different, but (as we saw on p. 141) that is a consequence of the way depth is calculated. Differences in average depth figures will always seem small relative to the corresponding structural differences in sentence complexity. But the differences between these means are statistically extremely robust. Even in the case of child writing v. speech, a one-tailed t-test gave a significance statistic far larger than the critical value for the $p < 0·0001$ threshold, which was the largest critical value we found in the literature (and for the two other pairwise comparisons the significance statistics are massively larger still).

This is not to say that the whole of the large difference in mean depth between speech and published writing is necessarily attributable to the difference in linguistic mode. The speech sample represents the full age range in society, while published writers are likely to be older than the average of the population as a whole; in chapter 7 we found that mean depth of grammatical structures increases with age throughout life, so the authors of the published prose may be people whose *speech* structures are more complex than average. But mean depth in middle-aged speakers' oral output is only about five per cent greater than the mean for all utterances in the speech sample, whereas the published-writing v. speech differential shown above is about seven times that.[3] (The smallness of these age-related differences in speech structure made it seem reasonable to treat our full set of annotated speech samples collectively as representing the spoken language in which children are already fluent when they begin schooling; if we had used only speech by children as the basis for comparison with child writing, the quantity of available material might not have been enough to yield statistically-reliable findings.)

8.6 Interim summary

Summing up what we have found so far, then: it seems that constructions are on average wordier in writing than in speech, that this difference relates entirely to depth of branching, i.e. grammatical recursion, rather than to node width, and that the child writing is in this respect intermediate between spontaneous speech and published writing.

It might sound as though we are taking wordiness to be desirable in its own right. Of course we agree that simple written style is good style, and it is a pity for written prose to abandon the pithy, punchy structure of speech where it does not need to. But often it does need to. Subordinate clauses have work to do, and if there are more of them in published writing than in spontaneous speech that is, surely, mainly because writing is used to express ideas that are logically subtler than those expressed in social chat. There may have been periods in the past when writers deliberately and pompously made their sentence structures more ramified and verbose than was necessary to get their messages across; we do not believe this has much to do with the structural differences between writing and speech in the British National Corpus. But if we are pressed on this issue, our fall-back position would be that published writing in some sense represents the end point of the process which children acquiring literacy skills

---

3 The depth figures in chapter 7 are not directly comparable with those shown here; in that study we averaged over all words, including discourse items not contained in clauses (which were assigned depth zero) – this was a suitable approach for research which compared the oral output of different speakers, but becomes less appropriate when speech is compared with writing.

are in fact embarked on, whether we think it is the ideal end point or not; so it is surely interesting to look at the trajectory which children who begin as illiterate but fluent speakers take to reach that end point.

8.7 Phrase and clause categories

Let us look at the grammatical differences between the genres in more detail. Presumably differences in depth of recursion are likely to correlate with differential usage of particular grammatical constructions that allow recursion. Our annotation scheme categorizes tagmas other than main clauses, at the coarsest level, into eight types of phrase and fifteen types of subordinate clause. (There are many refined subcategories, but we shall not look at those here; and we shall not look at the frequency of main clauses, which are necessarily a higher proportion of all tagmas in a genre which has less recursion. Also: in the speech data a small proportion of parse tree nodes are explicitly labelled as unclassifiable, usually because of inaudible wording; these nodes are ignored in the statistics below.)

You can get recursive structure in English without subordinate clauses, for instance through nesting of noun phrases and prepositional phrases in a structure like:

(62)   [*the key* [*in* [*the top drawer* [*of* [*the cabinet* [*by* [*the fridge*]]]]]]]

– but the measure of recursion used in the figures earlier in this chapter counted only recursion involving clause subordination, and our guess is that it is differential use of clause subordination which is mainly or exclusively responsible for the greater "wordiness" of published writing than spontaneous speech.[4]

Before giving quantitative breakdowns of the use of particular grammatical categories, we should explain one special point about the figures for child writing. This material naturally sometimes contains grammatical errors; our annotation scheme has developed a system for recording such deviations together with the target structures apparently being aimed at, which goes beyond the notation

---

4 We have not checked whether the wordiness differential might be partly attributable to phrase within phrase recursion of the kind just illustrated – it is not entirely clear how, formally, one should tease apart the contributions of different types of recursion; but, impressionistically, noun phrase within prepositional phrase within noun phrase structures seem very common in the speech data.

of Sampson (1995) (which was developed for edited prose in which grammatical errors are less frequent). The statistics quoted in the present paper count "target" constructions; when these are not correctly realized, the statistics take no account of that failure. There are many ways in which one could analyse the child-writing material statistically, but this is both the simplest and arguably the most suitable initial approach; we know that learners must sometimes make mistakes when they try to do difficult things, and surely it is more interesting to monitor what they attempt, than to monitor the essentially accidental shapes of their failures.

(We would add that in any case for the 9–12-year-olds' writing examined in this paper, this choice probably has little impact on the statistics presented. The area in which our project found really tangled deviant structures was the undergraduate coursework mentioned earlier, where the nature of the task seemed to push the writers towards prose that is logically more complex than they would produce spontaneously. That material has not been examined in the present study.)

8.8 Use of phrase categories

Taking phrase categories first: for each of the eight grammatical categories and for each pair of the three genres we applied the chi-squared test (with Yates's correction for continuity) to a two by two contingency table with the columns representing the two genres, and rows representing instances of that category versus instances of all other grammatical categories. In the table below, figures represent percentages of all tagmas counted in the relevant sample which are instances of the category shown. Asterisks mark significant differences between the two figures on either side,[5] using the following codes:

*	$p < 0.05$
**	$p < 0.01$
***	$p < 0.001$
–	not significant

---

5 More strictly, between the raw figures from which those percentages are calculated. The chi-squared test does not apply to percentages.

In all eight cases, the differences between speech and published-writing figures are significant at the $p < 0 \cdot 001$ level.[6]

Table 10: Incidence of phrase categories in different genres

	speech		child writing		published writing
noun phrase	19·7	***	34·6	–	35·8
verb group	15·8	***	7·44	***	9·52
prepositional phrase	10·7	***	18·0	***	21·7
adjective phrase	1·91	***	2·73	–	2·58
adverb phrase	1·67	–	1·31	–	1·19
number phrase	1·60	**	1·10	***	0·602
determiner phrase	1·30	**	0·777	–	0·824
genitive phrase	0·488	***	0·949	–	1·17

In each case but that of number phrases, the figure for child writing is closer, often much closer, to the published writing than the speech figure. This is true both for categories which are commoner in published writing, such as noun phrase, prepositional phrase, genitive phrase, and in the converse cases, e.g. determiner phrase. Broadly speaking it seems that in the area of phrase grammar these children have proceeded quite a long way along the path of adaptation to the norms of "model" written prose.

It is hardly necessary to add that we fully realize how very broad-brush such an analysis is. Even if "model" writing is characterized by a much higher incidence of noun phrases than speech (which often uses one-word pronouns rather than explicit phrases as subject, object, etc.), obviously the aim of writing-skills education is not anything so crass as "getting the percentage of noun phrases up into the thirties". Writing skills are about using an appropriate construction to express a particular idea in a particular context, not about percentages. But it seems that, systematically, the right construction in written contexts is much

---

6 For detailed definitions of these categories and the subordinate-clause categories discussed below, see Sampson (1995). It is not possible in a brief space to illustrate the full range of constructions covered, but we give one example from the child-writing sample for each category:

noun phrase	*all the first formers*
verb group	*had been*
prepositional phrase	*in the world*
adjective phrase	*very small*
adverb phrase	*as soon as she's used to her toys*
number phrase	*the other two*
determiner phrase	*any of the girls*
genitive phrase	*Mary Todd's*

more often a noun phrase than is the case in speech. From the simple figures alone we cannot tell whether the children's choices of grammatical construction are appropriate even when their frequency matches the published writing frequency; conceivably they could be using as many noun phrases as published writing, but in all the wrong grammatical contexts. That does not seem very likely *a priori*, though (and if it were true, our team's annotation task would surely be far harder than it is). With data sources as rich in detail as these, we have to start somewhere in analysing them, and counting percentages of main grammatical categories seems a reasonable first way into the material.

8.9 Use of subordinate clause categories

For subordinate clauses, the picture is rather different. Of the fifteen types recognized by our scheme, we ignore the rare cases of infinitival relative clauses and *for-to* clauses, neither of which show a frequency as high as $0 \cdot 1$ per cent in any of the three genres. Figures for the other thirteen categories are shown in Table 11.[7]

The most frequent of all subordinate-clause types, the infinitival clause, occurs at essentially the same rate in all three genres. For the other twelve categories, the frequency differences between speech and published writing are significant at the $p < 0 \cdot 001$ level (except *with* clauses, where the significance level is only $p < 0 \cdot 05$).

These twelve categories fall into four groups, depending whether their frequency in speech is greater or less than in published writing (S > P or S < P), and on whether their frequency in child writing is closer to that in speech or to that in published writing (C ≈ S or C ≈ P).

---

7 Again we give a single example from the child writing for each category (wording in brackets is included to show the context, and is not part of the example tagma):

infinitival clause	*to keep her out of trouble*
adverbial clause	*if he had him*
nominal clause	*that it is a Four of Diamonds*
verbless clause	*(they go in to dinner,) then the second bell*
present participle clause	*(by) adding some more to it*
relative clause	*(one pup) who looked just like his mother*
antecedentless relative	*What I like doing*
bare non-finite clause	*(make us) do the right thing*
past participle clause	*(a girl) named Jennifer*
comparative clause	*(as black) as Alan's is fair*
with clause	*(a yellow door ...) with the name wrote on it*
special *as* clause	*(field archers do not use sights) as target archers do*
whiz-deleted relative	*("Amazon Adventure") also by Willard Price*

Table 11: Incidence of subordinate-clause categories in different genres

	speech		child writing		published writing
infinitival clause	3·02	–	2·92	–	3·00
adverbial clause	2·92	–	3·09	***	1·93
nominal clause	2·88	***	1·12	***	2·17
verbless clause	1·07	***	0·207	*	0·400
present participle clause	1·04	–	1·17	***	2·18
relative clause	0·970	***	2·11	–	2·15
antecedentless relative	0·494	*	0·242	–	0·199
bare non-finite clause	0·450	*	0·242	–	0·166
past participle clause	0·310	***	0·863	**	1·30
comparative clause	0·173	–	0·207	–	0·308
with clause	0·107	–	0·104	–	0·166
special *as* clause	0·0595	–	0·0345	**	0·243
whiz-deleted relative	0·0268	*	0·104	–	0·113

$S > P, C \approx P$ group

Nominal clauses, verbless clauses, antecedentless relative clauses, and bare non-finite clauses are less frequent in published writing than speech, and the child-writing figure is closer to published writing; as we might put it, children have successfully learned to ration their use of them.

In the case of verbless clauses, the child-writing figure is actually much lower even than the published-writing figure, which perhaps reflects teachers' injunctions to "write in complete sentences". A similar relationship obtains between the three figures for nominal clauses, which at this point we do not understand – we would not have guessed beforehand that this category was commoner in speech than writing. (Possibly one explanation might be the frequency, in speech, of introductory hedging phrases like *I think* ... or *you know* ...?, where the material following *think* or *know* will be analysed as a nominal clause object of the respective verb – we have not looked into this.)

Antecedentless relative clauses, and bare non-finite clauses, do feel like relatively "intimate" constructions – the latter because their use is restricted mainly to the verb *make* meaning "force" and to verbs of perception, and the former because formal prose tends to favour explicit antecedents (think of the way that stuffy writing uses *that which* in contexts where *what* would be far more idiomatic); so the differences between the three genres are unsurprising.

$S > P, C \approx S$ group

Adverbial clauses are commoner in speech than in published writing, and the child-writing figure is about the same as the speech figure.

S < P, C ≈ S group

Present participle clauses, comparative clauses, *with* clauses, and special *as* clauses are more frequent in published writing than in speech, and the child-writing figure remains closer to the speech figure.

S < P, C ≈ P group

Finally, there are relative clauses (with explicit antecedents), whiz-deleted relative clauses, and past participle clauses.[8] These are constructions used more frequently in published writing than in speech; and the frequencies in the child writing are closer to the former than to the latter. (In the case of past participle clauses, the child writing frequency is admittedly not far from the mid-point between the other two genres.)

These three categories are also, logically speaking, varieties of the same construction, in which a nominal element is postmodified by a clause in which the nominal plays a grammatical role. A past participle clause is, or at least can be, a whiz-deleted relative clause based on a passive construction, where what is left after the relative pronoun and *BE* are suppressed begins with a past participle. In our scheme, the category "past participle clause" also covers tagmas which are similar in their internal structure but occur in functions other than noun postmodifiers, e.g. (*to hear the winner's name*) *called out*; but most past participle clauses in the child-writing sample are cases functioning as reduced relatives. (The great majority of these are clauses based on the participles *called* or *named*, e.g. (*a road*) *called the Ring*, (*a girl*) *named Jennifer*.)

Summing up, then: if we think of children's acquisition of writing skills as, in part, the replacement of the grammatical habits of conversational speech with the norms of adult writing, it seems that, at the stage represented by our child writing data, the children have already achieved much of this adaptation with respect to phrasal constructions (whether this means using more of one type or fewer of another type); but less adaptation has occurred with respect to clause constructions. For a number of types of clause, the children's written usage remains closer to spoken norms (C ≈ S). For various clause-types which are used less in published writing than in speech (S > P), the children have learned to reduce their usage. But the only clause categories used more in published writing than in speech and where the child writing has risen close to the published norms (S < P, C ≈ P) are various kinds of (full or reduced) relative clauses.[9]

---

8 For "whiz-deleted relative clause", see note 8, p. 43.
9 It is interesting to compare these findings with those of Perera (1984), an excellent book which is the only previous substantial study of the grammar of child writing known to us,

8.10 The complexity of the relative construction

It seems easily understandable that children will take longer to adapt to adult norms (where these involve increased rather than decreased use) in the case of subordinate clauses, which are complex structures, that in the case of phrases. We find it more surprising that adaptation occurs sooner with relative clauses than other kinds of subordinate clause. This surely cannot be because relative clauses are structurally simpler; considered as abstract formal structures, relative clauses seem strikingly more complicated than some other subordinate clause types.

Assuming that declarative main clauses can be seen as basic, producing a relative clause involves modifying that basic structure by deleting some element which may be related only remotely to the main verb of the declarative structure (for instance it may be a subordinate constituent of an immediate constituent of the structure), yielding a word-sequence that would be bizarre in isolation. In some cases an appropriate relative pronoun is used, and if the relativized item is object of a preposition then the preposition may be shifted ("Pied-Piped") to precede the relative pronoun. Cases with zero relative pronoun are formally simpler, but are arguably no simpler to master, since the logical relationship between clause and antecedent is inexplicit and may be very diverse.

Adverbial clauses or nominal clauses, by contrast, are constructed simply by prefixing a subordinating conjunction to a declarative structure; in the case of nominal clauses, although they may be signalled by the conjunction *that*, not even this is necessary. Admittedly, these two categories are S > P cases (their formal simplicity may perhaps be relevant to their high speech frequency), so there is no issue about how children develop the skill of using them in writing. But, among S < P categories, present participle clauses, for instance, are surely no more formally complex than relative clauses – one might well see them as less complex – yet their child-writing frequency is little different from their speech frequency. It is not easy to understand why relative clauses should lead present participle clauses so strikingly in the degree to which child writers increase their use of them towards adult written norms.

---

though written slightly too early to exploit the possibilities now opened up by computer manipulation of machine-readable annotated corpora. Perera's table 19, p. 232, does not match our finding of child writing assimilating to adult norms earlier with respect to use of relative clauses than other subordinate clause types (though she does note that relative clauses *increase in frequency more rapidly* during the school years than other clause types, p. 234). Exact comparisons between Perera's and our findings are difficult, for one thing because her statistics relate to children's speech and children's writing but do not give comparative figures for adult writing.

8.11 Simple v. complex relatives

It is true that some relative clauses are simpler than others. A subject relative (a relative clause in which the relativized item is clause subject) has the same shape as a declarative clause, with a *wh-* pronoun in place of the subject, and since the logical and surface position of the relative pronoun is immediately adjacent to the antecedent it is straightforward to interpret. Likewise a relative in which the relativized item is the whole of an adjunct of the clause (e.g. *(every time) we hit a wave*, where the relativized item is a Time adjunct of *hit*) has the same shape as a declarative (there is no obvious gap, because adjuncts are optional extras), and the logical relationship between relative clause and antecedent is usually clear because the antecedent is a general noun like *time* or *place*. If relative clauses are more profuse in child writing than the complexity of the construction would lead one to expect, one might guess that this is because children confine themselves to the simplest types of relative, so that for them the construction is not a complex one. Children's written English might occupy an earlier point on the Keenan–Comrie relativization hierarchy (Keenan and Comrie 1977) than adult written English.

From a limited sampling it appears that this is not so. It would be tedious to check all the relative clauses in our data manually, so we checked forty "full" relative clauses (i.e. not whiz-deleted relatives or past participle clauses) from each of the speech, child writing, and published writing samples.[10] We classified the 120 relative clauses according to whether the relativized element is:

A, subject of the relative clause: *(the Christmas story,) which took place many years ago*

B, an entire adjunct of the relative clause: *(every time) we hit a wave*

C, object or complement of the relative clause: *(a small animal) they catch*

D, a constituent of a phrase constituent of the relative clause: *(the person) to whom it points*

---

10 For speech we took all the full relative clauses (omitting one case whose type could not be determined because it was broken off before completion) in CHRISTINE files T07, T14, T21, T28, T35, and the first five from T20. For child writing we took the first twenty relative clauses in both the 9–10-year-old and the 11–12-year-old files, which were not in a systematic sequence – the forty cases were produced by nine 9-year-olds, seven 11-year-olds, and one 12-year-old. For published writing we took the first twenty cases from a passage of *Independent* sports reporting (part of BNC file A4B) and from an extract from a book on provision of legal services in Britain (part of BNC file GVH).

E, a constituent of a phrase constituent of a phrase constituent of the relative clause: *(some flowers [...]) that I do not know the name of*

F, a constituent of a subordinate clause constituent of the relative clause: *(I am in K. [House],) which I naturally think is the best*

G, a constituent of a phrase constituent of a subordinate clause constituent of the relative clause: *(a village dance) which the headmistress has forbidden any of the girls to go to*

(Examples in italics are quoted from the child-writing sample in each case.)

Intuitively, the sequence A to G roughly corresponds to complexity of relative clause types, so if it were true that relative clauses in children's writing were simpler than in adult writing, one would expect the breakdown to show higher figures for child writing than for published writing in rows A and B, with the child-writing figures declining to zero in lower rows.[11]

It is true that the simpler relative structures are more frequent than the more complex structures in all three genres, but in other respects the figures by no means conform to that prediction; see Table 12.[12] The proportion of A- and B-type relatives is actually considerably *higher* in the published writing than either the child-writing or speech sample. These samples are admittedly small and possibly unrepresentative, but if the frequency of relative clauses in child writing were explainable in terms of children using simple versions of the construction, one might expect this to be visible even in small samples.

---

11 At one point (1998: 109), Miller and Weinert claim in effect that the standard English relative clause construction occurs in spontaneous speech only in patterns A to C. They note the existence of an alternative construction which occurs only in speech, and is more transparent because the relativized item is represented by a pronoun in its logical position, as in *the book that I found these words on its pages*; Miller and Weinert say that the relativized item can play far more diverse roles in this latter construction. However, Miller and Weinert's claim about the spoken use of the standard construction seems to be contradicted by examples they quote at other points (e.g. *the shop I bought it in*, their p. 106 – and see our data in Table 12). The alternative construction involving a "shadow pronoun" does occur in our CHRISTINE speech data, though impressionistically it is far rarer than standard relative clauses, and so far as we have noticed it does not occur at all in the child-writing data.

12 The bracketed figure in row D of Table 12 corresponds to the fact that the one 9-year-old type D relative clause in the sample is deviant: *(there are many others* [scil. *birds*]*) in which I often read about.* The bracketed figure in row F relates to the spoken example *(all) she's supposed to do now*, which by the rules of our scheme is analysed as having the relativized item as object of an infinitival clause subject of *supposed*. One might well prefer to see *BE supposed to* as a quasi-modal construction, in which case the F figure under "speech" would reduce from 2 to 1 and the C figure would increase from 13 to 14.

Table 12: Incidence of relative-clause types in different genres

	speech	child writing	published writing
A	16	18	25
B	7	7	5
C	13	7	1
D	2	(4)	5
E	–	2	3
F	(2)	1	1
G	–	1	–

The figures seem to imply that the relative clause construction used in the child-writing sample is the full adult relative-clause construction; and, hence, that complexity of different constructions is not a reliable predictor of the extent to which the constructions will be deployed in child writing.

8.12 Unanswered questions

If children make heavy written use of relative clauses earlier than some simpler constructions, one would like to know what it is about relative clauses that permits or encourages this. Are relative clauses for some reason more useful, in the kinds of written communication represented in the Nuffield material, than some other subordinate-clause types which are needed for adults' more diverse communicative goals? Is it that relative clauses, though formally complex, represent a more straightforward development from simpler and earlier written usage than some other constructions? In the next chapter we attempt to address this question.

Chapter 9
Child writing and discourse organization

9.1 A fixed grammatical programme?

In this chapter we look further at the question which we raised and left un-answered at the end of chapter 8. Since it seems uncontroversial to say that relative-clause formation is one of the more complex processes provided by the grammar of English, how comes it that in their spontaneous writing style children seem to move towards the norms of skilled adult writing sooner with respect to use of relative clauses than in the case of other, inherently simpler grammatical constructions?

On the face of it, the findings of chapter 8 might seem adverse for the concept of language put forward in this book. If numerous English-speaking children all resemble one another in mastering a particular complicated piece of grammar earlier than other, simpler pieces, does that not suggest that their language-skills acquisition is governed by some fixed programme which causes various areas of grammar to unfold in a set order? – and would that not in turn imply that the general grammatical architecture of language is laid down in a child's mind in advance, presumably coded in his genetic inheritance, rather than grammatical constructions being freely invented and spreading from individual to individual through imitation alone?

It might seem so. But in this chapter we shall see that the facts about relative clauses in children's writing are not so simple. The patterns are less unified than was apparent in chapter 8: the relative frequencies of subordinate clauses, measured as their proportions to all constituents, vary as a function of clause type. Moreover, the children's usage is not necessarily intermediate; it may match the statistical properties of speech in some respects while fitting the adult model of writing in others.

9.2 New information about a previously identified object

There are various possible reasons for differences between spoken and written genres. The simplest explanation is that, in speech, people prefer to avoid relative clause construction, which is computationally "costly" given the non-canonical mapping pattern from semantic representation to syntax. In that case we expect a high probability of "simpler" constructions fulfilling the function of relative clauses, i.e., the function of introducing additional information about a previously identified or type-referenced entity or event. The commonest such constructions are perhaps prepositional phrases modifying noun phrases, as in (63) below, main clauses with an anaphoric pronoun, as in (64), and appositional noun phrases, as in (65). Each of these express the same information that could be expressed by a relative clause, as in (66) or (67).

(63) *Alex saw a wooden statue in Leuven with mirrors for its eyes.*

(64) *Alex saw a wooden statue in Leuven. It had mirrors for its eyes.*

(65) *The wooden statue, the work of several artists, was decorated with mirrors.*

(66) *Alex saw a wooden statue in Leuven which had mirrors for its eyes.*

(67) *The wooden statue, which was the work of several artists, was decorated with mirrors.*

Another possible reason, though, why one might observe statistical differences between genres is that discourse-pragmatic or sociolinguistic factors cause there to be fewer contexts in conversation where a relative clause could occur. The quantitative analysis of chapter 8 measured frequency relative to the total number of syntactic units in each sample of text rather than in absolute terms, but it did not take contextual information into account. What is more, the findings of chapter 8 did contain a hint that this issue might be worth looking at: the proportion of lexical noun phrases was significantly greater in writing than in speech. Since relative clauses are typically nominal modifiers, there may indeed be fewer contexts in conversation which are conducive to relative clause construction.

Conversely, when comparing the probabilities of relative clauses in published prose and in schoolchildren's compositions, similar frequency figures do not necessarily mean that the children use syntactic devices in introducing additional information in the same way as adults. We could find that, for stylistic reasons, child writing contains a higher proportion of contexts where relative clauses might be an appropriate option.

9.3 The new study: data and methods of analysis

To study these possibilities, we further analysed a subset of the material used in chapter 8: the full corpus of children's writing used there, and (in order to keep our workload within bounds) similarly-sized randomly chosen subsets, about 12,000 words each, of the published-writing and the speech material (the latter being produced by speakers of all ages, but mostly adults). Other than the invented examples (63–67) above, all numbered examples in this chapter will be taken from the child-writing corpus.

The relevant sets of sentences/utterances were selected and categorized by hand taking wider contextual information into account. Relevant linguistic contexts, which we shall call *conducive*, are those where a certain entity has roles in two distinct, adjacent propositions (events or state descriptions), and one of those propositions could be encoded as a relative clause without loss of information. (We emphasize that the criterion for a context to be conducive is that a relative clause be a grammatical option, regardless of whether it would be considered stylistically appropriate or not. This approach was used to minimize subjectivity in making decisions.)

The following examples illustrate conducive and non-conducive contexts:

Conducive contexts

(68)   *We have a shoot,[1] it has a metal lid to stop it from smelling.*
       (… which has a metal lid …)

(69)   *Two years ago there was a swimming pool built in C, there I went three times*
       a week. (… where I went …)

(70)   *Daddy bought me a new bike. I have still got that bike now.*
       (… which I have still got …)

(71)   *In the evening we went to a place called Yarmouth.*
       (… which is called Yarmouth.)

(72)   *We were staying at Port St Mary, which I like very much.*

Non-conducive contexts

(73)   *We could see the back of the houses because behind them there were only*
       fields. (… because behind which …)*

(74)   *When I had done the bacon, it was all burnt. (≠ When I had done the bacon,*
       which was all burnt.)

(75)   *We went back into the hotel for dinner. We had a lovely dinner.*
       (… which we had (a) lovely (of).)*

---

1 Clearly a spelling error for the homophone *chute*.

(76)   *What shall I do with the circle? Ah, move it to the corner.*
       (≠ ... *which I move to the corner.*)

Only those conducive contexts were included in the analysis where the propositions are encoded as full or reduced clauses; that is, prepositional phrases and appositional noun phrases were not analysed. The clauses encoding the second of each pair of propositions were classified as main clauses, past- or present-participle clauses, or relative clauses.

In what follows, 9.4 looks at the frequencies of conducive contexts in the three types of text, and the overall proportions of the different clause types. We examine the syntactic properties of the contexts, and their effects on the probability of selecting relative clauses as opposed to main clauses, in 9.5. Finally, in 9.6 we ask what can be deduced from the mistakes children make with the relative clause construction.

9.4 Context frequency

As already said, it is a reasonable hypothesis that informal conversation, published writing, and child writing are organized in different ways, leading to significant differences in the frequencies of those linguistic contexts which are conducive to relative-clause construction. Figure 10 suggests that this hypothesis is correct. In similarly-sized samples, speech contains 110 conducive contexts, while the corresponding figures are 241 for published writing and 319 for children's compositions. Looking at the proportions of relative clauses and participle clauses to all clause types in the three types of text reveals that they are least likely to be selected in speech (40 per cent). This figure is somewhat higher for children's writing (51 per cent), and considerably higher for published writing (73 per cent). The two kinds of subordinate clause are represented with approximately equal proportions across the three datasets: relative clauses make up 75 per cent of subordinate clauses in speech and published writing, and 73 per cent of subordinate clauses in children's writing.

It now seems that while linguistic contexts conducive to relative clause construction are significantly less frequent in informal speech than in writing, speakers indeed disprefer relative clauses in favour of main clauses with anaphoric reference. We also find that children are less likely to produce relative clauses in their writing than adults, when context frequency is taken into account.

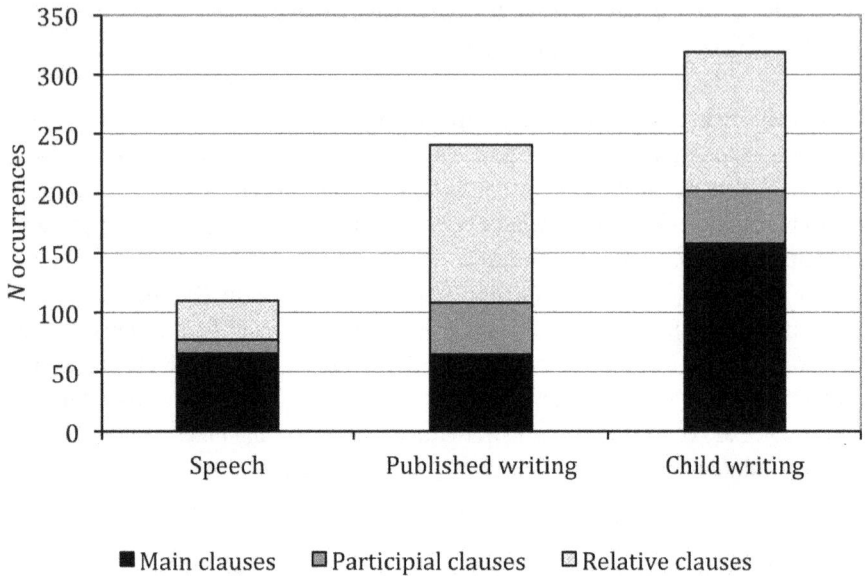

Figure 10: Frequencies of clause types in conducive contexts, by genre

9.5 Syntactic patterns

A further interesting question is whether the differences between speech, published writing, and children's writing are located in specific types of context or are evenly distributed. In order to try to answer that, we classified the contexts according to the syntactic properties of the phrases referring to the common participant in the two propositions (events or state descriptions). In what follows we shall call the noun phrase or clause occurring in the earlier proposition the *antecedent*, and the overt or covert noun phrase coindexed with the antecedent in the later proposition the *anaphor*.

In constructing relative clauses the complexity of the process of mapping the elements of the semantic representation onto syntax may in part be determined by the grammatical function of the extracted phrase. A number of studies have observed that, in oral comprehension tasks, young children perform significantly better with subject relative clauses than with object relative clauses (see e.g. de Villiers et al. 1979, Goodluck and Tavakolian 1982). Subject relative clauses, as in (77) below, in some sense involve less planning than object (78) or prepositional-complement (79) relatives, since the relativizer occurs in clause initial position, which is the canonical position of the subject. Adjunct relative clauses (80) can also be considered simpler, as adjuncts may occur clause initially.

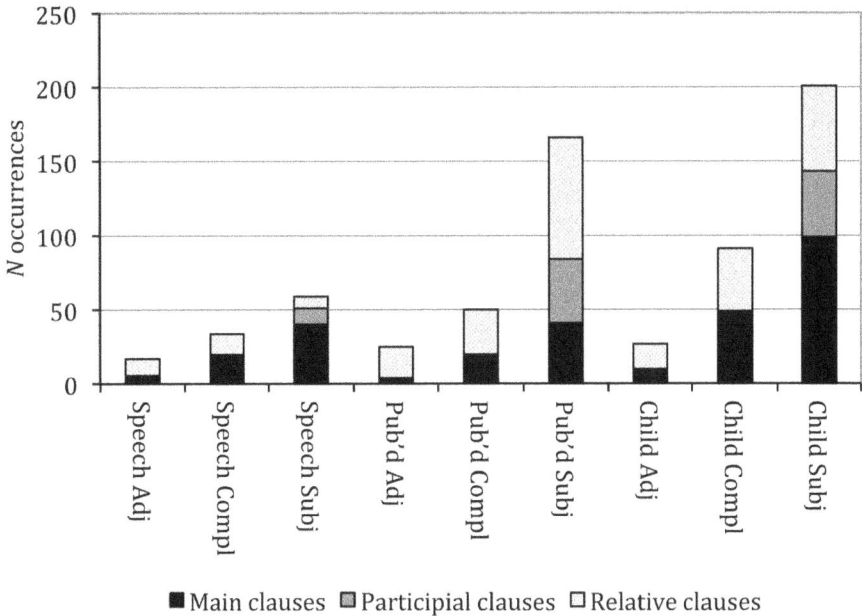

Figure 11: Frequencies of clause types by clause-function of anaphor and by genre

(77) *She gave me a model of a scarab beetle, which lives in those parts.*

(78) *I keep an album of the stories that I write.*

(79) *We have also got some flowers that I do not know the name of.*

(80) *The wood owl only likes to live in places where there are a lot of trees.*

If speakers and child writers are indeed motivated by simplicity of computation in selecting from alternative structures, we would expect a higher proportion of relative clauses in contexts where the anaphor is a subject or adjunct than in contexts where it is a complement. We would further expect this difference not to appear, or to appear to a lesser extent, in published writing. Figure 11 breaks the data down according to the grammatical function of the anaphor within its clause. Three categories are distinguished: subjects, complements (direct objects and complements of prepositions), and adjuncts. For all three data types, subject anaphora is the most frequent grammatical function, which is expected on the assumption that the referent of the anaphor tends to be given information and therefore the topic of the clause.

We also see a clear pattern in the frequency of relative/participial clauses in terms of the function of the anaphor. For published writing and child writing, the proportion of relative/participial clauses is highest where the anaphor is an adjunct (84 per cent and 63 per cent respectively), lowest where the anaphor is a complement (60 per cent and 46 per cent), with subject contexts in between (75 per cent and 51 per cent). The difference between subject and complement anaphor contexts is, however, considerably smaller in the children's compositions than in adult writing. In conversation we also find the highest proportion of relative/participial clauses in adjunct anaphor contexts (65 per cent), but the order of complement and subject contexts is reversed. Contrary to the predictions of the simplicity hypothesis, the frequency of relative/participial clauses is lowest in subject anaphor contexts (32 per cent).

A further basis for classifying anaphora is by the grammatical role of the anaphor within its phrase – that is, whether the anaphor expression is: the whole or head of the argument/adjunct phrase; a possessive modifier; or the complement of a preposition. The three cases are illustrated in examples (81–83):

(81)   *The horse that I rode was called Ladybird.*

(82)   *The book was all about a girl whose real name is Miranda Prinkle.*

(83)   *It is my brother that I get my sports talents from.*

In the first case relativization involves extraction of a phrase as a whole, which may be considered simpler than the other two sentence types, where the internal structure of the anaphor phrase needs to be modified. Figure 12 shows the percentages of relative clauses, participial clauses, and main clauses in NP head, possessive modifier, and prepositional complement anaphor environments. Although numbers are low in possessive and prepositional-complement contexts (respectively 17 and 66 in total), the results indicate that in all three text types relativization is most likely to occur in contexts where the anaphor is a full argument/adjunct phrase. While these findings confirm the intuition that it is simpler to manipulate an argument/adjunct phrase as a whole than to extract only parts of it, they do not support the hypothesis that differences between child and adult writers are greater in more complex contexts than in simpler contexts.

The final classification criterion we shall consider is the position of the antecedent in its clause. Two types of context may be distinguished: those where the antecedent occurs in clause-final position, and those where it is followed by a predicate or one or more complements and/or adjuncts. When the antecedent is in non-final position, a subordinate clause modifier will need to be either inserted clause-medially or separated from its head noun, as shown in examples

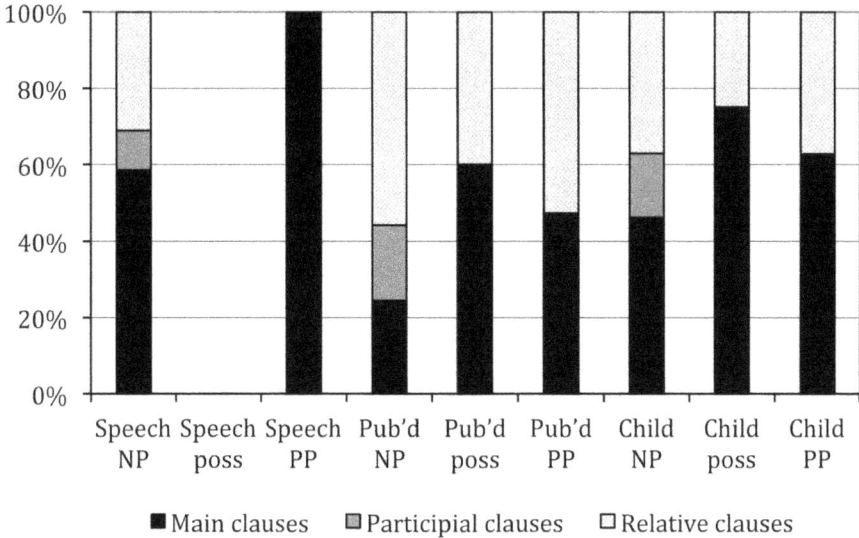

Figure 12: Frequencies of clause types by phrase-function of anaphor and by genre

(84–85). It is, again, a reasonable assumption that relative clauses are less readily constructed in this context than in instances where the antecedent is in clause-final position and neither centre embedding nor discontinuous constituents result.

(84) *My mum's friend, who lives over the road, has a yellow labrador.*

(85) *There is a small brook here too which provides quite a bit of fun.*

The proportions of relative clauses, participle clauses and main clauses with clause final and clause initial/medial antecedents are shown in Figure 13. As expected, antecedents which are in final position in their clause are more likely than non-final antecedents to be modified by a relative/participial clause, in both published writing and child writing. The difference is somewhat greater in the children's compositions (22 percentage points) than in the published texts (13 percentage points). In the speech data, however, the position of the antecedent seems to have no effect on the likelihood of relativization.

9.6 Mistakes with relative clauses

The analyses above show that the probability of relative clause construction is reduced in writing when it would force (a) the extraction of an expression from

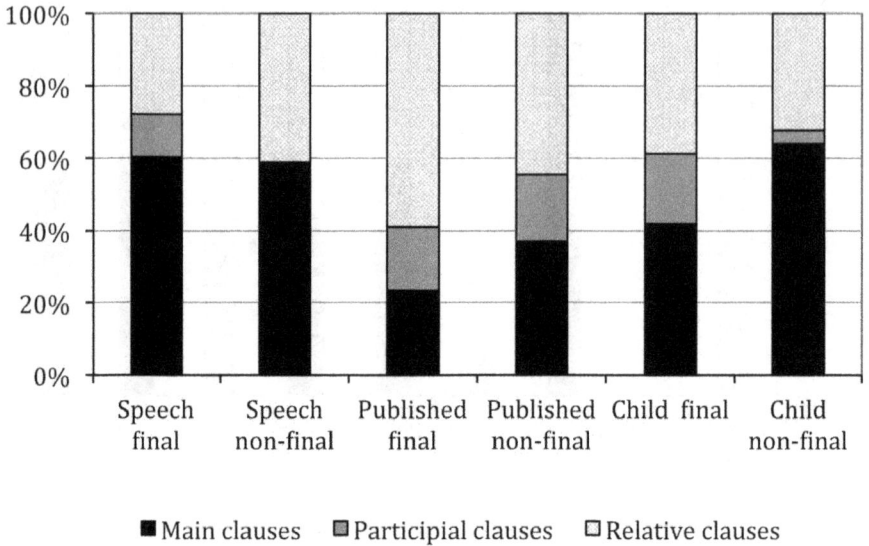

■ Main clauses   ▥ Participial clauses   ☐ Relative clauses

Figure 13: Frequencies of clause types by antecedent position and by genre

within a phrase, or (b) the insertion of a clause between arguments or between an argument and a predicate. It is not surprising, then, that grammatical errors involving relative clauses occur in these and only these contexts. The overall error rates are negligibly low: five per cent of relative clauses in the children's prose, and just a single possible example (to be discussed below) in adult writing. No ungrammatical relative clauses were found in the speech data.

(We take it that, whether or not the concept of "ungrammaticality" applies to adults' usage, it is uncontroversial that pre-teen children should be seen as trying and sometimes failing to conform their written language to norms of grammaticality, though some linguists prefer to use the term "non-target-like" for child writing which deviates from adult grammatical norms.)

Considering different contexts separately, in the children's compositions we find two erroneous sentences in category (a) above, which constitute a 12 per cent error rate in that category. One of the sentences involves double prepositional marking, while the preposition is omitted in the other:

(86) ... *there are many others in which I often read about.*

(87) ... *there is a passage which there are stairs.*

Errors in sentences with centre-embedded relative clauses make up 11 per cent of contexts where the antecedent is in non-final position in its clause in children's writing. There are four non-target-like sentences in this category, as follows:

(88) *Philip is keen on fishing and swimming, Martin on gardening and Alan,* *[whose hobby, [which you can hardly call a hobby], is being a monkey].*

(89) *So he told her that a dream [he read about once about a man [who had a* *dream and told the other man he would not go sailing with him because his* *dream told him he would drown]].*

(90) *That dream [that Chanticleer] came true.*

(91) *Some of the teachers [that came with us] they helped me to.*

In (88) and (89) we find multiple relative clauses the first of which modify the subjects. In both sentences the relative clauses are complete but the predi-cate of the subject of the higher clause has been omitted. In (88) the phrase *is being a monkey* seems to be the predicate of *whose hobby*, and *Alan* is left as a "hanging" subject. Similarly, in (89) the complement clause whose subject is the first mention of *a dream* is left unfinished.

The other two errors occur in less complex sentences. In (90) the verb of the centre-embedded relative clause is omitted, and in (91) the child has inserted a resumptive pronoun after the embedded relative clause. (The use of resumptive pronouns in child speech was discussed by Pérez-Leroux (1995), although that author finds them to occur in relative clauses rather than in main clauses.)

The single arguably "ungrammatical" example in the sample of published writing also involves centre embedding:

(92) *... his favourite aunt (called by her clergyman father in remembrance of the* *line in Acts [where [when "Peter knocked at the door of the gate], a damsel* *came to hearken, [named Rhoda]]") ...*

For us, (92) is incomplete until the name *Rhoda* is inserted after *called* in the first line (either as the immediately-following word, or postponed to a later point): *call* in the relevant sense needs both an object and a complement. But although this could be an error by the writer, it might alternatively be an example of how speakers unpredictably extend the grammatical possibilities of their language: if this writer uses *called* in the same way that we use *named*, then for him the com-plement would be an optional element, naturally omitted here since the name is about to be supplied in the Biblical quotation. (And even if, for the writer, (92) was an error which he would have corrected if he had caught it, how is a reader to know that (92) is not a good sentence suitable to treat as a precedent?)

9.7 The upshot of the analysis

We can sum up the findings of the analysis as follows:

- There are differences in the frequencies of contexts conducive to relative clause/participle clause construction in the three text types. Conducive contexts are most frequent in children's writing, and least frequent in informal conversation.
- The probabilities of selecting relative clauses/participle clauses in conducive contexts also vary across text types. They are most likely to be selected by adult writers, and least likely to be selected by speakers.
- The likelihood of relative clause construction is increased in all three text types when the anaphor is an adjunct of the relative clause, and reduced in all three text types when it would involve extraction of an element from within a phrase.
- The position of the antecedent has a strong effect on clause type selection in the two written text types, but not in speech. Clause final antecedents are more likely to be modified by relative clauses/participial clauses than non-final antecedents.
- Syntactic errors are rare. They occur in those contexts where we find the lowest proportions of relative clauses and participial clauses.

Table 13 summarizes the effects of context types on relative clause selection. The figures represent the result of dividing the proportion of relative clauses and participial clauses in speech (first row) or in child writing (second row) by the corresponding proportion in published writing, counting separately clauses in adjunct anaphor contexts, possessive-modifier and prepositional-complement contexts, and in sentences where the antecedent is in non-final position; the rightmost column shows the ratios for all contexts taken together.

Table 13: Effects of context type on relative-clause selection

	adjunct anaphor	poss/PP compl anaphor	non-final antecedent	all contexts
Speech	0·77	0	0·52	0·55
Child writing	0·75	0·68	0·57	0·70

As we can see, the degree of differences between the three text types is not entirely consistent across various syntactic contexts. Over all contexts, the likelihood of selecting relative clauses/participial clauses in speech is 55 per cent of the corresponding probability in published writing. This figure is somewhat greater in adjunct anaphor contexts, and considerably lower in possessive and prepositional complement anaphor contexts. These results indicate that the facilitating effect of the former and the limiting effect of the latter are stronger in speech than in adult writing. The pattern is different when we compare child writing with published texts. Over all contexts, the proportion of relative clauses/participle clauses in the children's compositions is 70 per cent of the corresponding proportion in adult writing. This figure is not very different in adjunct anaphor or possessive- and prepositional-complement anaphor contexts. It is, however, slightly lower in contexts where the antecedent is in non-final position in its clause, suggesting that children are more reluctant to produce centre-embedded subordinate clauses than adults.

The general conclusion that can be drawn from the analysis is that the stage of child writing represented in the study cannot be considered syntactically intermediate between informal speech and adult writing. Although certain kinds of simplicity considerations were found to bear on relative clause construction, no specific syntactic phenomena were identified whose simple presence or absence in children's grammatical competence could account for the observed differences between children's writing, published prose and spoken language. The data of chapter 8 do not imply any innate programme under which grammar unfolds in a child's mind in a fixed sequence. They are simply a consequence of the fact that written prose, including children's writing, contains a higher frequency of contexts where a relative clause could be useful than spoken language contains. And this in turn is surely just a consequence of the different ranges of jobs that written communications and face-to-face conversation perform for language users.

In this case, we encountered data that seemed *prima facie* to point towards "innate grammatical knowledge" – but when we looked harder, that conclusion melted away. We chose to look harder, because we felt sceptical about the nativist conclusion. Many present-day linguists are all too ready to believe in arguments for innate grammar. It is worth asking how many of the pieces of evidence they quote might melt away similarly, if one looked at them harder and with a larger dose of healthy academic scepticism.

Chapter 10
Simple grammars and new grammars

10.1 Pidgins and creoles

In chapter 1, we set out to undermine the plausibility of the idea that languages are all cut to a common, universal logical pattern, by quoting two languages, Riau Indonesian and Old Chinese, whose structures are or were largely devoid of the logical machinery which is central to European languages.

There is one class of languages for which it is almost uncontroversial, even among believers in Universal Grammar, to say that they often lack structural mechanisms which one might otherwise be tempted to see as universal: namely the class of pidgins and creoles. A "pidgin" is a form of speech created when groups of speakers of separate languages come into contact, through trade or colonization, and need to bodge up some makeshift system of communication for limited purposes which neither group will use among themselves as a general-purpose language. In some cases, what began as pidgins later become the native languages of subsequent generations of speakers, and a language which has emerged from that transition is called a "creole". Pidgins and creoles will draw on one or both of the languages whose contact spawned them for their vocabulary, stock of phonemes, and so forth, but they will typically ignore many or most of the structural niceties that those languages may contain – for instance, if the language from which the vocabulary is mostly taken has irregular verbs, they are likely to be regularized in the pidgin and later creole. *I am, you are, he is* might in a pidgin (assuming that it uses a verb "be" at all) become *I be, you be, he be*.

A language could be completely regular in its inflexion system while nevertheless containing all the logical apparatus of Latin or a modern European language. The artificial language Esperanto, for instance, was deliberately designed to resemble European natural languages in terms of the logical machinery its structure makes available, while eliminating all the irregularities that act as obstacles to acquiring these as second languages. But it is generally agreed that pidgins certainly, and probably creoles also, not only lack the useless irregularities found in many old-established languages but also tend to be relatively simple in terms of the abstract categories and relations they encode in their grammars. And this should not be surprising: pidgins and creoles are new languages, with at most a few centuries of history behind them (whereas other natural languages all emerge from a process of evolution that extends back far beyond the beginnings of the human historical record), and we expect systems that evolve naturally to start simple and become gradually more complex.

There has been considerable debate about the structural relationship between creoles and pidgins. Some linguists argue that acquisition as a mother tongue (that is, turning into a creole) corresponds to a step-change in structural complexity, so that creoles are internally more like "old" languages than like pidgins. However, a leading authority on the topic, John McWhorter, has argued that "The world's simplest grammars are creole grammars" (McWhorter 2001a). This claim has been vigorously rebutted by Michel DeGraff (2001), but DeGraff's response seems based more on political sympathy for the often downtrodden groups who use creole languages than on judicious scholarly assessment of the evidence – this is unfortunately an area of linguistics which has become very "ideological". For our present purposes it is not crucial to try to discern where the truth lies in that debate.

What matters here is that McWhorter's claim about creoles is stronger than "if a language is a creole then it is simple" (our paraphrase). He argues that the conditional is actually a biconditional, so that if a language is simple it must be a creole (or a pidgin).

This amounts to making a claim about the biographies of languages which is rather comparable to the claim made by generative linguists about the biographies of individual speakers (though McWhorter does not draw the parallel). Generativists recognize that children start speaking their mother tongue in simple forms and gradually develop more complexity, but we have seen that ever since Lenneberg (1967) they have argued that this process terminates at a "critical period" some time about the age of puberty, after which for the rest of a speaker's life he or she is linguistically in a "steady state" during which essentially no further structural learning of the mother tongue occurs. We on the other hand hold with Leonard Bloomfield that "there is no hour or day when we can say that a person has finished learning to speak" (cf. p. 149 above). Mother-tongue learning may slow as individuals age, as other kinds of learning surely do, but it never abruptly halts. With respect to the lives of languages, McWhorter is saying that a new language starts simple when it is created as a pidgin and remains relatively simple while it is historically recognizable as a creole, but it eventually passes a threshold at which it becomes a "regular language" (his term) and is from then on permanently more complex than any creole. (The analogy with the generativists' "critical period" is not perfect: if it were, a language that had made the transition into "regular language" status would cease changing structurally altogether – of course McWhorter does not make that claim, which would be obviously quite untrue.) McWhorter, so far as we can see, recognizes that "regular languages" change, and differ from one another, in terms of structural complexity as in other respects. But he believes there is some kind of complexity threshold, below which are only pidgins and creoles and above which all languages with long histories are located.

We, on the other hand, see development of novel logical or abstract categories, and loss of existing categories, as normal aspects of the life of all human languages, however old-established, and we see no reason to expect all languages with long histories to contain any particular minimum of structural complexity (even supposing that we had a way of measuring this).[1] Because of the particular intellectual interests of the thinkers of ancient Greece, which have heavily informed all subsequent European education systems, European languages might be described as having specialized in encoding logic; and the political and cultural dominance of Europe over the past two to three hundred years has led the languages of other continents often to be heavily remodelled on European patterns. But European-style grammar is not actually necessary for the operation of complex advanced societies. David Gil (2009: 30–31) argues that the structurally-vague type of language exemplified by his Riau Indonesian examples

> is enough to run a country of some two hundred million people and, by extension, most contemporary human activity throughout the world.... it is sufficient to support most daily activities throughout one of the world's largest countries, from the giant metropolis that is Jakarta to the most far-flung of island provinces ...

> Admittedly, there are contexts, mostly of a more formal and official nature, where the colloquial language is inappropriate, and instead the somewhat more complex standard language is used. ... [However, in many cases at least, this] is motivated not by any functional gain in expressive power but by social conventions. For example, the president addressing the nation on television could easily get his message across in colloquial Jakarta Indonesian, but to do so would result in loss of face, thereby endangering his elevated standing.... even if there do exist some contexts where the greater grammatical complexity of the standard language really plays a necessary communicative role (something that is not at all obvious), such contexts are marginal and few in number ...

Thus, while we are happy to concede to McWhorter that "if creole then simple" (and we are inclined to believe that he has made his case there), we are not willing to concede that "if simple then creole". It is important for our general view of the nature of human language that languages like Old Chinese or Riau Indonesian, as described in chapter 1, are not "special cases", peculiarly structurally undeveloped because of newness. There is no good reason not to see them as just two among the broad spectrum of structurally-different old-established natural languages.

---

1 This book has been much more concerned with creation of new grammatical/logical categories than with loss of existing ones, but (as we shall see in chapter 11) the latter happens also.

10.2 Old Chinese as a counterexample

In response to Gil's discussion of Malay/Indonesian, McWhorter (2001b: 405–408) has in fact argued that Malay/Indonesian as a whole should be classified as a creole. He discusses historical considerations which, he claims, make this proposition plausible. We find that surprising, but we are not qualified to debate the history of Malay/Indonesian with McWhorter.

What we can do is discuss, in more detail than in chapter 1, the case of Old Chinese. We shall show that this language had all the features seen by Gil as refuting "Eurocentric" beliefs about language universals and by McWhorter as distinctive of creoles, though it was certainly not a creole.

We have been using the term "Old Chinese" in the broad sense of e.g. Axel Schuessler (2007: 1), to cover the stage of the Chinese language which lasted from the beginnings of Chinese writing, ca 1250 BC, to about the second century of our era. (This is obviously a very long period to identify as "one stage" of a language, and some Sinologists divide the history more narrowly – see e.g. Norman 1988: 23.) Old Chinese is ancestral to all present-day Chinese "dialects" or "languages", such as Mandarin, Cantonese, Hakka, etc., and many characteristics which made Old Chinese structurally simple are inherited by modern varieties of Chinese. However, Old Chinese is a clearer case: partly because it differs from all modern Chinese varieties with respect to one specific feature, tone, that McWhorter sees as important in this context, and partly because recent varieties of Chinese have tended to embody rather more explicit structural apparatus than their ancestor – possibly in part as a consequence of the increasing complexity of Chinese civilization, but over the last 150 years certainly also as a consequence of the influence of European languages.

The example we discussed in chapter 1 was taken from the Confucian *Analects*, dating from the middle of the Old Chinese period. In what follows we shall look at a series of rather older examples, drawn from one of the earliest works of Chinese literature, the *Book of Odes* (or *Classic of Songs*), an anthology of poems or songs believed to date between the tenth and seventh centuries BC.

Note that we take our examples from this source because one of us happens to be particularly familiar with it (Sampson 2006), but the unfamiliar features discussed below do not represent some special "poetic" use of language (we could have used prose from the same period) – they are just the way this language is (or rather was).

10.3 Old Chinese not a creole

We begin by making the point that Old Chinese has never to our knowledge been taken to be a creole, and there seems to be no reason whatever for supposing that it was one. It is a member of the Sino-Tibetan language family (on which see Thurgood and LaPolla 2003), and its predominantly monosyllabic, isolating character is shared with other members of that family (hence cannot have resulted from a creolization event). So far as we know, creoles are usually or always created by members of a subordinate ethnic group in contact with a more powerful group who speak a different language; but the speakers of Old Chinese were by far the most culturally advanced group in the East Asia of their time – historically, other East Asian nations borrowed the elements of their cultures from the Chinese, far more than the other way round. No language is ever wholly cut off from the influence of neighbouring languages, but Old Chinese gives the impression of being as "pure" in that respect as any language we know. The most obvious non-Chinese element in premodern Chinese is the subset of vocabulary consisting of polysyllabic foreign loan words, such as *luòtuo* "camel";[2] but according to Pulleyblank (1995: 9) no clear cases of such loans are found before the Han dynasty – i.e. at the very end of the Old Chinese period. (On contacts between Chinese and other languages see Norman 1988: 16–22. The extremely low incidence of loanwords even in modern Chinese is quantified by Tadmor (2009).)

Thus there is no evidence that Old Chinese was anything other than a "regular language", descended by normal processes of language change from an unwritten Proto-Sino-Tibetan ancestor. We shall show that it had the hallmarks which McWhorter sees as typifying creoles. But if one were led by that to postulate some hypothetical creolization episode in Chinese prehistory, this would turn "if simple then creole" into a circular truism, rather than an interesting empirical claim. Experts on early Chinese history would, we believe, be incredulous if it were suggested that Old Chinese was acquired "more often by adults outside of a school setting than by children" (the feature which McWhorter identifies (2001b: 408) as crucial for the empirical status of his claim).

10.4 Examples of structural vagueness

We move on now to examine the specific properties which Gil sees as refuting Eurocentric assumptions about language universals and McWhorter sees as distinctively creole, and how far Old Chinese shares those properties.

---

2 Here and below we represent Chinese words via the *pinyin* transliteration of their modern Mandarin pronunciations. The Old Chinese pronunciations were very different; where they are relevant, they will be shown in Baxter's (1992) reconstruction.

The overall picture Gil gives of Riau Indonesian is one of a language where the logic of utterances is strikingly vague and/or ambiguous, relative to any European language. This has long been recognized as a characteristic of Malay in general, in writings about language stemming from outside the world of modern academic linguistics. For instance, a Malay self-instruction manual (M.B. Lewis 1947) comments:

> Malay is a flexible, eel-like language (p. xii)
>
> [a word] which, in the list below, is given an adjectival meaning ..., will sometimes be found as a noun ... at other times it will be a verb. Moreover, when it is a verb it may correspond to any of the verb forms found in the paradigm of e.g. a French verb; it is singular or plural, it is past, present or future, it is active or passive, according to the context (p. 51)
>
> Subordinating Conjunctions are less common in Malay than in English.... A speaker will usually balance a pair of short simple sentences, and expect his hearer to infer the relationship between them (pp. 134–135)

To show how similar Old Chinese is in these respects, we begin by quoting a few sample lines from various poems in the *Book of Odes*. We have chosen lines which support our point, but such lines do not need to be searched for; they are entirely typical, even though there are also lines which would illustrate the point less vividly.

For each example we show:
- the Chinese original in *pinyin* transliteration, followed in brackets by the number of the Ode from which the line is taken.
- word-by-word English glosses of the Chinese words, with obliques showing where the Chinese word is ambiguous between more specific English translations. (Where a Chinese graph is ambiguous between semantically-unrelated homophones, we gloss only the meaning relevant to the given context, provided it is clear which this is. Stops link multiple English words used to express a single meaning.)
- Bernhard Karlgren's (1950) translation of the line, accompanied in some cases by our own explanatory material in square brackets. Karlgren's book gives scholarly renderings which aim to make the original meaning clear rather than to achieve poetic effects in English.

(93) *guī yàn Wèi hóu* (Ode 54)
      return.home condole Wei marquis

      "I went home to condole with the prince of Wei"

(94) *fěi wǒ sī cún* (Ode 93)

not I/me/my think dwell.on/be.among

"[these girls:] they are not those in whom my thoughts rest [I love another]"

(95) *zhōng fēng qiě bào* (Ode 30)

everlasting/indeed wind and violent/sudden.rain

[An opening, scene-setting line:] "There is wind indeed and violent weather"

(96) *jià yú yǔ xíng* (Ode 88)

yoke I/me together.with go

[asking her menfolk to arrange a marriage:] "let yoke the carriage for me to go with him"

(97) *yǒng shǐ fú gù* (Ode 56)

eternal swear will.not/cannot announce

[a woman is having a secret affair with an important man:] "forever, he swears, he will not tell (of our love)"

(98) *nǚ yuē guān hū, shì yuē jì jū* (Ode 95)

girl open.inverted.commas look Q, gentleman open.inverted.commas perfect.particle final.particle

"a girl says: 'have you been and looked?' The knight says: 'I have'"

10.5 Lack of word classes

A central feature of Gil's contrast between Riau Indonesian and the "Euro-centric" model of language is that the former has no distinctions among open word classes – the categories noun, verb, adjective are not differentiated, there is simply one general "open" class of words. This is true of Old Chinese. Some words have meanings which map more naturally into English words of one part of speech than others: the first word of (93), *guī* "to return, go back where one belongs", is most likely in any context to be rendered by an English verb. But many words stand for concepts which in English are associated equally closely with more than one part of speech, and in those cases one will not normally be able to say that one translation is more correct than another.

In (94), *sī* is glossed "think" in Karlgren's dictionary of Old Chinese (1957) but is translated by him in this passage as "thoughts"; either part of speech would do equally well to render the Chinese (an alternative translation might be "they are not those I think about and dwell on"). In (95), *bào* is glossed by Karl-gren (1957) as either "violent", an adjective, or "sudden rain", a noun phrase (these are not accidental homophones, a sudden cloudburst is seen as "violent" weather). In another context, *bào* would more naturally be translated by the noun "violence"; for instance, in the line *zhì yú bào yǐ* "arrive at *bào* oh" in Ode 58, where a wronged wife is complaining about her husband, the prepositional nature of *yú* "at" makes a nominal translation of *bào* more natural – Karlgren's version is "I have (come to:) met with maltreatment". For that matter, only the fact that the English noun "wind" has no closely-related verb inhibits one from translating *bào* in (95) as a verb; if one accepts "blow" as an adequate verbal equivalent to "wind", then a rendering such as "Everlastingly it blows and storms" would be equally justifiable grammatically.[3]

10.6 Logical indeterminacy

The two features of Riau Indonesian which Gil (2005) sees as most extremely different from European languages are "indeterminacy of thematic roles", and "indetermina[cy] with respect to ontological types": that is, the language is commonly inexplicit both about case relationships (elements are not clearly identified as agent, patient, benefactive, etc. with respect to actions mentioned) and about the logical status of propositions – the same utterance can be vague as between describing an action, ascribing a property to a thing, asserting the existence of a thing with a certain property, and so forth.

The same is true of Old Chinese. In (93), neither the quoted line itself nor neighbouring lines mention, via a pronoun or otherwise, the person who is returning home and planning to condole; and this is usual – probably more often than not, when an Old Chinese word is used in a verbal sense it lacks an explicit subject. Likewise, the relationship between "return home" and "condole" is not spelled out. Karlgren translates it as "to", i.e. "in order to", which is appropriate because, as we learn from a later passage, the poet was prevented from reaching home; if we did not know that, "I went home and condoled ..." would be an equally justifiable translation.

---

3 The choice between the glosses "everlasting" and "indeed" for *zhōng* is a case where one Chinese graph stands for apparently unrelated homophones and the context does not clearly disambiguate; Karlgren chooses the translation "indeed", we would have thought "everlasting" slightly more plausible. "Everlasting" versus "everlastingly", on the other hand, is a purely English distinction with no parallel in Old Chinese.

In (93), the poem as a whole allows us to infer that the agent of *guī* and *yàn*, "return home" and "condole", must be the poet. But such things are not always clear. In (97), Karlgren chooses to translate on the assumption that the man is promising to the woman poet that he will not kiss and tell ("he swears that he will not ..."); but one could equally well take the wording the other way round ("I swear that I will not ..."). The man might be thought to have more to lose from publicity; elsewhere the poem suggests that the woman is unmarried (there was little or no social stigma attached to fornication at this period – Maspero 1955: 98–100). It is routine for such issues to be left vague in Old Chinese.

Even when an overt pronoun occurs, its "thematic role" is frequently debatable. In (96), Karlgren translates the first-person *yú* as agent of *xíng* "go", and treats *jià* "yoke" as having an object understood ("yoke the carriage"). But on the face of it, since the speaker is begging her family elders to marry her off to the man under discussion, one might equally take *yú* as object of *jià*: "yoke me (to him) ...". Perhaps it could be argued that this is too metaphorical a use of *jià* "yoke" to be plausible in this language; but nothing in the *grammar* of the line forbids that interpretation.

Example (98) reports an entire question-and-answer exchange containing only a single content word, *guān* "look". The man's answer literally says that somebody has done something, but who and what are left wholly inexplicit.

As for "ontological types": example (95), for instance, is very comparable to the examples (his examples 9–12) which Gil (2005) offers to illustrate this kind of indeterminacy, where a linguistic form is interpretable interchangeably as asserting the existence of things ("there is wind and violent weather"), occurrence of processes ("it eternally blows and storms"), ascription of a property ("everlasting are the wind and cloudbursts"), etc. Or again, Karlgren translates (94) as negating an equation ("they are not those who ..."), but another translator might treat it as negating an action ("it is not that my thoughts are dwelling on them"). We have already seen that, out of context, (93) might be understood as asserting either a single action ("I am returning in order to ...") or two separate actions ("I returned, and I condoled ..."); a similar remark could be made about (96).

Let us repeat that there is nothing unusual or unrepresentative about the handful of examples we have used to illustrate the structural nature of Old Chinese. This language regularly departs from the Eurocentric model in very much the same ways that Gil says Riau Indonesian departs from it. What is more, whereas Riau Indonesian is a "basilectal", colloquial variety of a language which has an "acrolectal" official variety that is more explicit in various respects, there is no reason to think that Old Chinese as recorded in the documents that have come down to us existed alongside a language-variety which was more explicit but went unrecorded. Old Chinese as illustrated here appears to have been the standard language of an early stage of what is now the world's oldest and most populous civilization.

10.7 McWhorter's diagnostics

John McWhorter (1998: 792–799; 2001a: 126 n. 1) gives diagnostics for classifying a language as creole. According to McWhorter, all *and only* languages which emerged historically through the creolization process have all three of the following properties:
- no inflexional affixation
- no lexical or grammatical tone
- no semantically-unpredictable derivation

The first of these properties in particular relates to the distinctive features Gil ascribes to Riau Indonesian, since languages which make thematic roles and ontological types explicit commonly use inflexion for the purpose. It is because McWhorter believes that Riau Indonesian has all three of these diagnostic properties that he wants to classify Malay as a creole.

10.8 No tone in Old Chinese

We shall first dispose of the point about tone. It seems surprising to find tone included in McWhorter's list alongside the other two properties. In the first place, tone is a purely phonological rather than grammatical feature. (Some tone languages use tone distinctions to express grammatical categories, but other tone languages do not – Chinese tone contrasts serve only, like contrasts among consonants and among vowels, to keep items of vocabulary apart.) And secondly, even if one is interested in language complexity in general rather than specifically in grammatical complexity, while it is easy to see languages as simpler if they lack inflexion and semantically-unpredictable derivation, it is not obvious (to us at least) that tone makes a language complex. One might regard a language with a lexical contrast between two or three tones, and a very restricted inventory of segmental phonemes, as just as simple as a non-tone language with a richer range of consonants, vowels, and diphthongs. McWhorter is aware that Chinese has some of the characteristics he ascribes to creoles; it is possible that his diagnostic list includes tone specifically in order to exclude Chinese from the class of creole languages.

If so, this does not succeed for Old Chinese. All modern Chinese dialects are tonal, but it has been recognized for some time that Chinese tones developed within the historical period. Old Chinese was not a tone language. (The tone contrasts reflect earlier contrasts among consonants; for instance, Mandarin tone 1 versus tone 2 reflects an earlier contrast between voiceless and voiced initial consonants, and tone 4 commonly reflects a lost final -s.)

10.9 No inflexion in Old Chinese

Old Chinese wholly lacks inflexional affixation; it is commonly seen as an extreme case of the "isolating" or "analytic" language type. The only serious challenge to this generalization that we are aware of is that it has sometimes been suggested that the language had a contrast between nominative and oblique cases in pronouns, because (taking first-person pronouns as an example) the forms *wú* and *wǒ*, whose Old Chinese pronunciations are reconstructed by Baxter (1992) as *nga* and *ngajʔ*, are typically found in subject and non-subject contexts respectively. But it is, we believe, now generally agreed that this is not a case of true grammatical inflexion, but of phonetically reduced versus full forms, somewhat akin to French *me* versus *moi* (Pulleyblank 1995: 76–77); non-subject pronouns tend to occur in positions where phonetic reduction is less likely, but there are cases where *nga* means "me" rather than "I".

10.10 Derivational morphology in Old Chinese

The one of McWhorter's creole diagnostics which might exclude Old Chinese is the third, lack of semantically-unpredictable derivation. Most Old Chinese words were simple roots, but it is clear that there was some derivational affixation. For instance, there was a suffix -s which in some cases had a verbalizing and in other cases a nominalizing force; examples (quoting reconstructed Old Chinese forms, with modern Mandarin reflexes in brackets) are:

ak "bad", *aks* "to hate" (*è, wù*)

lak "to measure", *laks* "a measure, degree" (*duó, dù*)

And there was a prefix which Baxter reconstructs as [ɦ] (a voiced h) that sometimes converted transitive into intransitive senses:

kens "see", *ɦkens* "appear" (*jiàn, xiàn*)

Although the full facts about Old Chinese derivational morphology are far from clear, there is little doubt that the meanings of derived forms were sometimes not wholly predictable from the meaning of the roots and the nature of the affix (one might have expected a verbalizing suffix added to a root for "bad, wicked" to give the sense "behave wickedly", or perhaps "make bad, spoil", rather than "hate").[4]

If creoles never have any semantically-unpredictable derivation at all, then we must accept that Old Chinese is different in kind from creoles. But McWhorter argues that Riau Indonesian should be regarded as a creole; that seems to imply that he cannot be committed to the strong claim that creoles entirely lack semantically-unpredictable derivation, because Riau Indonesian does appear to have some.

Here the present authors are hampered by having limited knowledge of Malay, and no personal knowledge of Riau dialect. But we have some acquaintance with the former; and Gil's own examples permit deductions about Riau Indonesian.

General Malay certainly has semantically-unpredictable derivational affixes, such as *ber-*, *ter-*, *-kan*, *-i*. But use of these is often associated with high ("acrolectal") style rather than the basilectal Riau dialect Gil discusses. In Gil's own example (Gil 2001: (23–24)) of the difference between how Malay students translate English formally, and how Malay is actually used in everyday life, the acrolectal translation of English "That match was great!" involves Malay *permainan*, in which affixes *per-* and *-an* are added to the root *main* "play", while the basilectal version uses the unaffixed root.

Nevertheless, even basilectal Riau Indonesian does seem to contain some semantically-unpredictable derivation. For instance, Malay has the words *gigi* "tooth" and *gigit* "bite": both forms evidently occur in Riau Indonesian (see Gil 1994: (4), (14)). And again, Malay has a word *mainan* "toy" derived from the root *main* "play" just mentioned; we have seen that Riau Indonesian uses *main*, and elsewhere (1994: (25)) Gil quotes a use of *mainan*. We do not know enough about Malay to say what the broader derivation patterns are which these individual cases exemplify (we do not know, for instance, whether there are other cases where adding *-t* to a word for a body-part gives a word for an action characteristic of that body-part); but it seems undeniable that these are cases of derivational morphology (they are treated as such by an online dictionary we have

---

4 One Sinologist, Laurent Sagart (1999), believes that the derivational morphology of Old Chinese was far richer than suggested here, holding that any consonant cluster is evidence of derivational complexity. However, we are not convinced by Sagart's arguments. He urges that his claim that roots contained only single consonants is a strong hypothesis which in terms of Popperian scientific method should be believed unless it can be refuted, but this seems unsound: it is not clear what kinds of evidence would be accepted by Sagart as a refutation.

consulted), and it would be hard to deny also that derivational processes which use affixation to give "bite" from "tooth", or "toy" from "play", must contain an element of semantic unpredictability. Actions performed by the teeth include chewing and gnashing as well as biting; in colloquial English, teeth are sometimes called "gnashers", but "biters" always refers colloquially to animals or misbehaving children, not specifically to teeth.

On Gil's evidence, Riau Indonesian does contain *some* semantically-unpredictable derivation. So, if McWhorter classifies this language as a creole, he must accept that that classification is compatible with a limited amount of such derivation. In a corpus of Old Chinese similar in size to the small collection of Riau Indonesian examples we have seen in Gil's writings, it is very doubtful whether there would be more evidence than this of semantically-unpredictable derivation in Chinese. Impressionistically, we would guess that there might probably be even less evidence, and there could easily be none at all. The case for seeing Old Chinese as typologically creole-like seems fully as strong as the case for seeing Riau Indonesian as creole-like.

10.11 An accident of history

There is a further point here. Even if our treatment has understated the incidence of semantically-unpredictable derivational morphology in Old Chinese, a time came in the history of Chinese when that morphology was no longer visible; in Old Chinese the derivation of *ɦkens* "appear" from *kens* "see" was transparent, but in modern Mandarin the historical relationship between their reflexes *xiàn* and *jiàn* is entirely opaque. (It is not regularly the case that *x*-words are related to *j*- words.) By some point after the Old Chinese period, *xiàn* was for all practical purposes just another simple root word.

It would be very difficult to say just when that change was complete, and whether it happened before or after Chinese began to develop tones; but these two processes seem quite unconnected with one another. McWhorter seems to require that tones must have arisen before relationships of the *kens/ɦkens* type became opaque – because, if it happened the other way round, the intervening language-stage would have all three properties which McWhorter claims to co-occur only in creoles. But even if the Chinese language developments did as a matter of fact occur in the order McWhorter requires, as they may well have, it is very hard to see why they *had* to occur in that order. Surely there can be nothing in the nature of human language which would have prevented a language like Old Chinese losing transparent relationships of the *kens/ɦkens* type and only afterwards going on to evolve tones – since there is no apparent way in which one of these features impinges on the other. So even if Chinese never did fully exemplify all three of McWhorter's diagnostics, another non-creole language could do so.

10.12 "Hidden" versus "overt" structure

One interesting point of view contrary to ours has been argued by Walter Bisang (2009). As we saw in chapter 1, Bisang notes that a number of languages of "East and mainland Southeast Asia", including Old Chinese, characteristically contain little explicit marking of grammatical categories such as European languages commonly require to be marked.[5] But he holds that it is a mistake to infer from this that the categories are not as real for speakers of those languages as they are for Europeans. These languages may contain logical complexity similar to that of European languages, but rather than "overt complexity" it is "hidden complexity":

> the absence of the overt marking of a grammatical category or of a construction-indicating marker does not imply that the speaker may not want to express it – he may simply have omitted it due to its retrievability from context (Bisang 2009: 35)

Bisang gives several examples, from modern Southeast Asian languages and from "Late Archaic Chinese", the language of the Chinese philosophical canon (including the *Analects*), ca 500 BC,[6] of how logical categories or relationships which are often left unexpressed can on occasion be explicitly marked. For instance, a conditional relationship between two states of affairs which English would typically express as "If *A*, (then) *B*" will in Late Archaic Chinese often be expressed simply as the juxtaposition of two clauses, "*A, B*"; but alternatively it was possible to include *rú* or *ruò* for "if" and/or *zé* for "then".

Our difficulty with this is that we do not understand how to tell the difference between: on one hand, language-users habitually having a category in their mind, wanting to express it, and omitting to do so; and on the other hand simply not having the category in their mind. If a language-user has a category in his mind, wants to express it, and has a verbal means of doing so, then surely he will express it? If one assumes that the Riau Indonesian speakers described by David Gil have in their minds the panoply of logical distinctions expressed by

---

5 Perhaps surprisingly, Bisang's definition of the class of "East and mainland Southeast Asian languages" excludes Malay/Indonesian.

6 Like some other Sinologists, Bisang uses "Archaic Chinese" for what we have been calling "Old Chinese".

the alternative translations offered on pp. 10–11 for *ayam makan*, "chicken eat", and that they simply choose to allow their specific meaning on a particular occasion to be inferred by the hearer from context, then that assumption appears merely to beg the question with which the present book is concerned. We would take it that what speakers overtly say is normally a good guide to what they have in mind to communicate (leaving aside irrelevances such as situations where a speaker intends to deceive). We do not understand on what grounds someone would argue against that, unless they take it as axiomatic that all languages express the same universal structures of thought.

Granted that, as Bisang says, the Late Archaic Chinese of e.g. the Confucian *Analects* did sometimes deploy overt markers to express logical categories or relations which often go unexpressed in contexts where a European language would require them to be expressed, the fact remains that it made strikingly little use of such markers relative to European languages (cf. our discussion of the *Analects* extract on p. 14), and the early history of written Chinese shows a development from a language-stage where they were used even less. William Boltz (1999: 89) describes the Chinese of 1200–1000 BC as

> Grammatically ... far less characterized by overtly analyzable syntactic constructions ... than standard Classical Chinese [i.e. Bisang's Late Archaic Chinese] ... and has far fewer grammatical particles ... Much grammatical structure is apparently indicated by no more than juxtaposition of the words involved, and grammatical relation seems therefore to be implicit rather than explicit, at least from the perspective of later stages of the language.

We would argue that (as Boltz's wording seems to suggest) the grammatical relations in question might exist, even implicitly, only "from the perspective of later stages of the language", just as the difference between alternative interpretations of Riau Indonesian *ayam makan*, "chicken eat", exists implicitly only from a Eurocentric perspective. For the Riau speakers, and for many Old Chinese speakers, the grammatical relationships which we insist on imposing on the utterances may not have had any reality at all. Where we see ambiguity, the reality may be vagueness.

The fact that overt markers of some grammatical category crop up sporadically at a period when they were commonly omitted does not, to our mind, refute this point of view. When members of a society create a fundamental new intellectual category that did not previously exist in that society, we would surely expect the adoption of this novelty to proceed gradually, diffusing over a long period from the original inventors, who were perhaps engaged in cognitive activities for which the category was specially useful (Bisang's Late Archaic Chinese examples are mostly taken from philosophical writing), to other individuals and perhaps eventually to the entire population. There is no reason to assume that even those who originated the category will always use it in their subsequent thinking and expression. On the contrary, it would be if the innovation, once made, were immediately taken up consistently by everyone that one might suspect it of corresponding to some category already present in everyone's mind and merely waiting for someone to coin an overt means of expressing it.

10.13 Deutscher on Akkadian

We are not knowledgeable enough about early Chinese epigraphy to say whether there is evidence for a stage when expressions for (e.g.) the if–then relationship were totally absent. But, if the record is not clear in this case, it is very clear in a comparable case from the opposite end of the Asian continent. Guy Deutscher (2000) has described how the history of Babylonian Akkadian shows a development from a stage, early in the second millennium BC, when the language had no means of expressing finite complement clauses (that is, clauses functioning nominally, such as the clause which functions as direct object of *told* in the English sentence *I told Judy that the power was off*), to a later stage in the middle to late second millennium BC when finite complement clauses were regularly used.

One commentator (Faarlund 2010b) has misunderstood this point, arguing that " 'absence of evidence' is not 'evidence of absence'" (implying that early Akkadian might have had complement clauses which simply happened not to show up in the evidence that has come down to us). But Deutscher gives us evidence of absence, not merely absence of evidence: he shows in detail how a mechanism for expressing finite complements was evolved by pressing into service a form which had previously been used for a different function – a process that would have served no purpose, if a mechanism for expressing finite complements had already existed in the language. (Faarlund does not appear to have read Deutscher's book himself; his comment quotes a brief second-hand reference to its contents. So far as we know, no-one who has read Deutscher has challenged his interpretation of the Akkadian data.) Deutscher argues (2000: chapter 11) that the new grammatical mechanism was created as a response to new communicative pressures in Babylonian society.

10.14 Diverse paths of evolution

When the idea of "universal grammar" first became a recognized point of view in the discipline of linguistics, more than forty years ago, sceptics often complained that proponents of the idea seemed to argue for the existence of language universals while quoting data drawn almost exclusively from English. That criticism ceased to be fair some time ago now; the literature of generative linguistics these days does draw on material from a wide range of languages. But it is still true today that generativists' data is overwhelmingly taken from present-day languages, and among those from languages which either belong to Western societies or have been heavily exposed to Western cultural influences. (A generative paper on Malay, for instance, would be much more likely to use the acrolectal variety, standard Malay, than a basilectal variety such as Riau Indonesian.)

Of course, these are the languages for which data are most accessible; but there is little recognition among believers in language universals that this strategy fails to give a fair sampling of the range of linguistic possibilities open to mankind. We have been surprised, for instance, to see how little attention has been paid to Deutscher's 2000 book, from a leading academic publisher, which appears to offer solid evidence against a key assumption of nativist linguistics. (We are not aware that any journal has reviewed it.)

If we can directly watch a logical construction being evolved *ex nihilo* in the Babylonian case, then it seems unreasonable to doubt that similar things were happening, with respect to other grammatical categories, in the Chinese and Malay/Indonesian cases, even if in the latter cases the historical record is perhaps not full enough to show a stage where some category was unquestionably entirely absent.

Structural simplicity does not imply a history of creolization. European languages are rich in logical apparatus because that happened, historically, to be a road those languages travelled down. It is not a natural, inevitable consequence of the fact that they are old (as all languages other than pidgins and creoles are).

Chapter 11
The case of the vanishing perfect

11.1 Losses as well as gains

Our discussion in this book of grammatical constructions as cultural inventions, rather than items fixed in human minds by genetic inheritance, coupled with the uncontroversial fact that (pidgins and creoles aside) natural languages all have very long histories, might suggest that every language ought to display a very rich panoply of constructions, contrary to what we saw in chapter 10. That might follow, if constructions, once invented, were never abandoned. But languages can lose existing constructions as well as gaining new ones.

This would be a banal thing to say, if it referred merely to cases where a language abandons one particular mechanism for expressing some intellectual category or relationship which continues to be expressible by other mechanism(s). Spoken French has given up the use of the simple past tense (e.g. *je vins* for "I came" nowadays occurs exclusively in writing, and one might foresee that it will eventually be dropped even there), but that does not affect the range of conceptual distinctions expressed by French grammar, since the *passé composé* (*je suis venu*) is a tense in everyday spoken use which (to our knowledge) does the same semantic job. However, one might imagine that once a language has created a means of encoding some new conceptual distinction, it would not give that distinction up. Vocabulary items frequently drop out of use, often because the things they refer to have disappeared (*cuirass*, for a piece of armour consisting of linked breastplate and backplate, must be close to extinct in spoken English), but grammar is not like that: the concepts encoded by grammatical forms and constructions are normally quite abstract, so that one would not expect them to become less communicatively valuable because of changes in a society.

Nevertheless, languages can lose as well as gain means of expressing grammatically-encoded conceptual distinctions. Perhaps some readers will feel that even this is a statement of the obvious. But, for believers in Universal Grammar, it surely raises a problem: if the range of possible meanings is given to us all in advance, and a language has developed a means of expressing some element of that range, why would it cease to do so?

Consequently it seems worthwhile to look in detail at a case of such loss occurring in present-day English.

As is invariably the case when one looks at empirical data from real-life language, the issue we are centrally concerned with is embedded in a mass of complications that are only tangentially related to it. But, since we are discussing present-day English, we hope that many readers will find some of those complications interesting for their own sake, and will hence be willing to follow our story through to its conclusion.

11.2 The Perfect aspect and spontaneous speech

The area of grammar we shall look at relates to the Perfect aspect: the verb qualifier exemplified in e.g. *I have seen your sister*. In standard English this is a usual form of words with a clear sense, sharply distinct from past-tense *I saw your sister*: the latter is a statement about an event which occurred at a particular past time, the former is a statement about the present and identifies a state I am now in as a consequence of an event which occurred at some unspecified past time. (For detailed analyses of the meanings of the two constructions see e.g. Elsness 1997; Quirk et al. 1985: 189–197.) Apart from the Perfect, English appears to have no alternative grammatical means of expressing the concept it encodes. One might suggest that Perfect aspect could be replaced by an adverb, e.g. *I saw your sister already*. But that carries extra meaning: *already* implies something like "one would not have expected that to happen so soon".

We studied the incidence of the English Perfect as part of a corpus-based examination of the overall system of English verb qualifiers in spoken usage. By "verb qualifiers" we mean what is sometimes called the "tense/aspect" system; but the same system also includes the modal verbs, which would not normally be included under either "tense" or "aspect". Thus it is convenient to use "verb qualifiers" as a term embracing tense, aspect, and modality markers. We were particularly interested in looking at differences between real-life usage in spontaneous speech, and standard usage as described in numerous textbooks and usage manuals.

For this purpose we used our CHRISTINE Corpus. To recap, CHRISTINE comprises 40 extracts, grammatically annotated in accordance with the detailed and comprehensive scheme of Sampson (1995), drawn from random points in randomly-selected files from the (unannotated) "demographically-sampled" speech section of the British National Corpus. It thus represents the spontaneous, conversational usage of a cross-section of the United Kingdom population, balanced in terms of age, sex, social class, and region, during the early 1990s. CHRISTINE contains about 80,500 "full words" of speech (not counting distorted words, hesitation phenomena, etc.) uttered by 147 identified speakers together with a number of unidentified speakers.

Since it was completed in 1995 the British National Corpus has been criticized with respect to the reliability of its demographic classification of speakers (cf. 7.3 above). But considerable effort was devoted, during compilation of the CHRISTINE Corpus, to correcting these data, in consultation with the BNC team and from internal evidence. The CHRISTINE classifications are accounted for in detail in the various documentation files which form part of the resource. Unquestionably, even these corrected data are less "clean" than one might ideally like; but no alternative source of evidence on present-day British speech comes close to the BNC in representativeness. Any errors in classification of individual speakers are likely to be random and hence are likely to blur statistically-significant correlations that may exist in the "true" data; therefore, if correlations are found in the data we have, they should be genuine.

The present study depends heavily on the regional classification of speakers. As we saw in 7.3 above, CHRISTINE uses a simpler system of regional classification than the BNC, dividing the United Kingdom into just seven regions: SE England, SW England, Midlands, Northern England, Wales, Scotland, and Northern Ireland. This makes the classification more reliable, because the inconsistencies of the BNC system relate largely to subdivisions of these broad regions. The four English regions correspond to the second level from the root in Trudgill's hierarchical classification of modern dialects (1990: p. 65, Fig. 3.1). The Northern England/Midlands boundary runs north of Merseyside, south of Yorkshire, and through the north of Lincolnshire. The southern boundary of the Midlands runs south of Shrewsbury and Birmingham and north-eastwards to the Wash. The SE/SW boundary runs between Northampton and Oxford and southwestwards to Bournemouth.

This chapter uses the CHRISTINE data to study nonstandard spoken usage with respect to the English system of verb qualifiers.

11.3 The standard system and nonstandard alternatives

For standard English we assume a verb qualifier system which can be expressed by the following formula (adapted from Chomsky 1957: 39):

(Past) (Negative) (Modal) (Perfect) (Progressive) (Passive) Main-verb

Any verb group (sequence of zero or more auxiliaries and a main verb) in a finite clause can be treated as realizing a set of markers qualifying the main verb, each of which is optional and which occur in the order given. (Here and below, forms in capitals represent lexemes, for instance *DO* stands for *do, does, did*, etc.) The logical markers are realized morphologically as follows:

Past is realized as the past tense form of the next verb

Negative is realized as *-n't* or *not* suffixed to the next auxiliary verb, or to *DO* if no auxiliary follows

Modal is realized as one of the verbs *CAN, WILL*, etc.

Perfect is realized as *HAVE* with the past participle form of the next verb

Progressive is realized as *BE* with the present participle form of the next verb

Passive is realized as *BE* with the past participle form of the next verb

Thus in theory a verb group might contain all six markers, e.g. *couldn't have been being eaten*. In practice no CHRISTINE verb group has more than four markers, e.g. *that he wouldn't have said* this T10.00976: Past Negative Modal Perfect.

We shall use terms such as "Past", "Negative Progressive", to describe verb groups (e.g. *ate, isn't eating*) containing just the markers named and no others. We shall use e.g. "Past-marked" to describe verb groups which contain a particular marker irrespective of whether it also contains others.[1] This article does not consider verb inflexion for subject agreement, although CHRISTINE data show plenty of nonstandard phenomena in this area.[2]

It has often been noted (e.g. V. Edwards 1993) that nonstandard dialects show many differences from standard English in the forms used for past tenses and past participles of individual verbs. Dialect usage frequently has the same form for past tense and past participle of an irregular verb which has distinct forms in the standard language (e.g. *drove* for both parts of *DRIVE, done* for both parts of *DO*). The form used for these two parts is sometimes identical to the base form, e.g. *run*, and sometimes different from any standard form, e.g. *seed* as past tense/participle of *SEE*.

One author who has examined such phenomena in detail, Edina Eisikovits (1987), discusses them on the assumption that the *system* of the nonstandard dialect she describes is the same as the standard system, and the differences relate only to the forms used to realize particular elements of the system; cf. 6.7 above. (Eisikovits describes the English of inner-city Sydney; but, as Trudgill

---

1 Some grammarians would describe a verb group which is both Past-marked and Perfect-marked as "pluperfect", but this term might better be reserved for languages like Latin which contain special pluperfect paradigms.

2 A further feature which might be included in the verb qualifier system is contrastive *DO*, as in *does eat* v. *eats*. This study has nothing to say about it.

and Chambers (1991: 52) rightly say, many of her findings apply to other English dialects.) A point which makes this assumption seem problematic, with respect to the CHRISTINE material, is that by far the commonest nonstandard verb use there is *got* without an auxiliary replacing standard *HAVE got* in the meanings "possess" or "must", e.g. *you got a nice case* T11.02751, *all you got +ta do is ...* T03.00943. The form *got* in isolation can of course be either past tense or past participle in standard English (and Eisikovits does not discuss it); but *got* = "possess"/"must" can only be a past participle in the standard language, and has to occur within a Perfect construction (although the usual meaning of the Perfect does not apply to this special idiom).

It seems possible that sometimes nonstandard dialects might use the same form for past tense and past participle because their verb qualifier system makes no distinction between Past and Perfect, and therefore has little use for separate past-tense and past-participle forms even in those verbs for which the standard language offers separate forms. That is to say: a speaker who produces forms like *they done it* might (as Eisikovits assumes) be using a dialect which contains the same contrast as standard *they did it* v. *they've done it*, but which expresses the contrast as *they done it* v. *they've done it*; an alternative hypothesis, though, is that the speaker's dialect contains no such contrast – *they done it* is this speaker's equivalent of both standard *they did it* and standard *they've done it*.

11.4 Verb qualifiers in CHRISTINE

In the present study we investigate this issue by examining those CHRISTINE verb groups which occur in finite clauses, where neither the verb group itself nor the clause is a second or subsequent conjunct (in which case its constituency might be affected by Co-ordination Reduction). We excluded cases which formed part of tag questions, cases where the verb group is split into two parts by Subject-Auxiliary Inversion (for instance in questions), "semi-auxiliaries" (Quirk et al. 1985: §3.47) such as *it +'s going to be well less than a minute* T25.00177, and cases where the main verb is "understood", e.g. *I have to plug in earphones – no you don't* T30.00684. Thus the cases retained for study should be ones in which all verb qualifiers are available to the speaker and explicit for the researcher. There are 9,430 such verb groups in the data.

The proportions of these tagmas which include the various markers (or category of markers in the Modal case, which covers each of a range of modal verbs with different meanings) are shown in Table 14.

Table 14: Verb qualifier frequencies

Past	25.8%
Negative	12.4%
Modal	12.5%
Perfect	7.9%
Progressive	5.7%
Passive	0.9%

The incidence of various combinations of markers is very broadly in line with the figures predicted if these proportions are treated as probability estimates. For instance, the incidence of Past Negative Progressive forms that would be predicted from these figures is:

$$9430 \times 0 \cdot 258 \times 0 \cdot 124 \times 0 \cdot 057 \times (1 - 0 \cdot 125) \times (1 - 0 \cdot 079) \times (1 - 0 \cdot 009) = 13 \cdot 9$$

– the figure observed is 9, not hugely lower. The most noticeable deviations are that combinations including both Past and Modal marking, and combinations including both Negative and Modal marking, are more frequent than expected. The former case is not surprising, since forms like *could*, *would*, have important uses other than as the past tense of *can*, *will*. Why Negative Modal combinations should be specially frequent is less obvious; but it is noteworthy that English morphology recognizes close links between these markers via special forms such as *won't*, *shan't*. (Tottie 1991: 38 quotes a finding by Svensson that negatives and modals tend to co-occur in Swedish.)

It does not appear that there is any systematic tendency to avoid verb groups with large numbers of markings. If no verb group with more than four markers occurs in our data, this is easily explained by the fact that the expected incidence of the most-probable five-marker combination would be far below 1 (in fact $0 \cdot 17$).

Notice that the Passive marker, which is the other verb qualifier apart from Perfect that involves past participle forms, is extremely infrequent – for many speakers there is no evidence in our data that the standard Passive construction is used at all.[3] This is of course no surprise: linguists often describe the Passive construction as characteristic of formal style, suggesting that it is not likely to occur much in spontaneous speech. If a speaker's verb qualifier system were to lack the Passive term, this would be one factor reducing the value of a morphological constrast between past participle and past tense.

---

3 We have not investigated the use of "catenative" *GET*, which can be used to express an alternative construction with passive meaning.

11.5 Past and Perfect

It is well known that there is a difference between the standard English verb qualifier system and the dialect of at least one region: the standard Perfect construction is little used in Irish English. John Harris (1991: 205; and see p. 201ff.) describes this dialect as "lack[ing] a fully grammaticalized perfect form" and using a range of constructions not found in standard English to express perfective meanings (e.g. *she's her course finished, he's after doing ...*). This is sometimes explained as an inheritance from a Gaelic substrate, although Harris argues that it is more likely to reflect development from an earlier state of English, with the modern Perfect construction being a relatively recent innovation in standard English (Visser 1973: 2042–2043).

The ten Irish speakers represented in CHRISTINE bear this out. They do produce some standard Perfect forms, and this is not surprising: probably most Irish speakers, and certainly all those represented in CHRISTINE, are exposed to a greater or lesser extent to the British standard language. But the Irish speakers between them uttered only 26 Perfect-marked forms in 545 verb groups. This proportion of 4·8 per cent of verb groups Perfect-marked is the lowest figure for any region in the CHRISTINE data.

On the other hand, it has not been reported previously, to our knowledge, that regional differences with respect to the incidence of Perfect constructions occur within Great Britain, where the special Irish perfective constructions discussed by Harris are not used. But the CHRISTINE data show large differences. The figures are given in Table 2, including the Irish figures just quoted, and the corresponding figures for Past marking, for the sake of comparison. (Again the utterances of some speakers are omitted because their regional classification is unknown, or in two cases because they are classified as non-native-speakers.) Numbers of speakers for each region are given in brackets after the region name; numbers of marked verb groups are given as absolute counts and as proportions of all verb groups.

Table 15: Perfect and Past marking by region

	All verb groups	Perfect-marked	Past-marked
SE England (22)	1379	74 (5.4%)	344 (24.9%)
SW England (22)	1163	77 (6.6%)	333 (28.6%)
Midlands (22)	1117	95 (8.5%)	273 (24.4%)
N England (38)	2339	221 (9.4%)	660 (28.2%)
Wales (12)	593	73 (12.3%)	165 (27.8%)
Scotland (6)	420	42 (10.0%)	97 (23.1%)
N Ireland (10)	545	26 (4.8%)	133 (24.4%)

("Perfect-marked" here, and below, includes cases of the nonstandard forms *ain't* or *in't* + past participle, as well as standard *HAVE* + past participle. The data include three cases of Perfect-marking with *ain't/in't* for SW England and one each for SE England, Northern England, and Wales, with none for other regions.)

The figures for Southern England (that is, SE England and SW England together) are only marginally higher than those for Irish English, which we have seen described as lacking a Perfect construction. Leaving aside Irish English, this large difference between Southern England and the rest of Great Britain is statistically very robust indeed. A count of 151 Perfect-marked out of 2,542 verb groups for Southern England, versus 431 out of 4,469 for the rest of Britain, gives a X^2 figure of 28·72 (using the formula incorporating correction for continuity given e.g. by Siegel and Castellan 1988: 116, Eq 6.3), corresponding to $p < 0.000004$.

Since British speakers, even more than Irish speakers, are all exposed to the British standard language, which does include the Perfect construction, the relatively low incidence of this construction among Southern English speakers suggests variation between two competing verb qualifier systems: the standard system which includes the Perfect, and a nonstandard regional system which lacks it.

Among the 106 regionally-identified CHRISTINE speakers who each produced at least ten verb groups, there were fourteen speakers who produced no Perfect-marked forms at all. All but three of these had the regional classification "SE England" (four speakers), "SW England" (four speakers), or "Northern Ireland" (three speakers).[4] The three other speakers who produced no Perfect-marked forms in ten or more verb groups all have the classification "Midlands", which is geographically the transitional area between Southern England and the rest of Britain.[5]

In passing it is worth noting that the figures show no tendency for regions which use less Perfect marking to use more Past marking in compensation. It may be misleading to think of Past and Perfect constructions as alternative ways of expressing similar ideas.

---

[4] The individuals concerned are: (SE England) Anthony065, Ernest068, Benjamin083, Flissy117; (SW England) Darren011, Madge017, Norah022, Dean057; (Northern Ireland) Jane093, Melvin095, Mark111.

[5] These are: Celine026, who lives in Nottingham; and Solange046 and Geoff048, work colleagues in a Birmingham press agency, who are assigned a code defined as "Midlands" in BNC — though this is one of the BNC codes which does not relate clearly to the Trudgill dialect classification.

11.6 *got* for *HAVE got*

If Southern English (and Irish) speakers systematically tend not to utter Perfect forms, one might expect that *got* without auxiliary, as an alternative to standard *HAVE got* in the sense "possess" or "must", would also be characteristic of these regions. The figures of Table 16 confirm this. (Although column 2 of Table 16 includes only *got* in the senses "possess" or "must", column 3 includes all cases of *HAVE got*, a few of which may occur in the sense "have obtained"; our anno-tation system does not permit cases of the latter type to be distinguished, but inspection of a sample revealed no such cases and they are likely to be very few if they occur at all. As before, *HAVE* here covers the nonstandard forms *ain't/in't*.)

Table 16: *got* for standard *HAVE got* by region

	got = possess/must	**HAVE** *got*	col 2 / (cols 2 + 3)
SE England	7	24	22.6%
SW England	24	29	45.3%
Midlands	5	38	11.6%
Northern England	7	76	8.4%
Wales	8	29	21.6%
Scotland	1	13	7.1%
Northern Ireland	4	10	28.6%

Column 4 shows, for each region, the *got* = possess/must figure as a propor-tion of the total for this and the *HAVE got* figure. We see that the proportion of cases lacking the auxiliary is higher for Ireland and Southern England than for other regions. In this case, the figures for the three former regions are widely different from one another, and the SE England figure is only marginally higher than the highest rest-of-Britain figure, namely that for Wales. Nevertheless, if again we set aside the Irish data, and within Britain compare the Southern England totals of 31 *got* v. 53 *HAVE got* with the rest-of-Britain totals of 21 v. 156, the X^2 statistic (calculated as before) is $20 \cdot 8$, $p < 0 \cdot 0002$.

11.7 Casual subject-auxiliary omission

At these significance levels, we are clearly dealing with a genuine regional difference of usage within Great Britain. Statistics alone cannot show that the difference relates to the verb qualifier system, if there is any other structural phenomenon which might explain the figures. The only alternative that occurs to us is the rule whereby a subject and any clitic attached to it can be omitted in casual speech: people say things like *saw them catch him up* T25.00167 for *I saw them catch him up*, or *taken my Sundays away in April* T22.01282 for *they've taken my Sundays away in April*. For most verbs, the standard past tense and past participle forms are identical, so a clause intended by the speaker as a Perfect form with subject and *HAVE* "understood" in this way can be indistinguishable from a Past form and may be registered as such in the CHRISTINE Corpus.

This might explain the regional differences reported above, if "casual subject/ auxiliary omission" were more frequent in the relevant regions. However, the data suggest that it is not. We checked the proportion of all verb groups in our data which are the first constituent of a non-co-ordinate declarative main clause. This will not catch every case of casual subject/auxiliary omission, because for instance a clause in which the omission occurs may begin with an adverbial – *I've just come back* may be reduced to *just come back*. But, if the Perfect data were to be explained away in terms of different rates of casual subject/auxiliary omission, one would expect that difference to be reflected in rates of verb-group-initial declarative clauses. Instead, the proportion of verb groups in our data which occur in this configuration is 2·9 per cent for Southern England and 3·2 per cent for the rest of Britain – a small difference, in the wrong direction. The proportions for the seven separate regions in fact vary in a random-looking way within a narrow band.[6] We infer that there is no systematic regional difference in casual subject/auxiliary omission; in the absence of other possible explanations for the figures, we conclude that the Perfect aspect is genuinely marginal in Southern English vernacular.

11.8 Modals + *of*

If this conclusion is correct, it may explain another puzzling phenomenon: the nonstandard use of *of* after modals in writing. The BNC speech transcriptions include many cases where Modal Perfect forms are written with *of* rather than *have*, e.g. *could of been*. In America, at least, this seems to be an orthographic deviation of long standing; Booth Tarkington's 1914 novel *Penrod* used it in representing the speech of a boy uninterested in schooling ("*'Cause if they had they'd of give you a good name!*", Tarkington 1914: 193). It is very familiar in present-day British undergraduate prose. Either spelling would normally correspond to the same pronunciation [əv], with an obscure vowel, so we had taken

---

6 The figures in ascending order are: Northern Ireland 2·2%, Midlands 2·4%, SE England 2·5%, Scotland 2·9%, SW England 3·3%, Northern England 3·6%.

the *of* spelling to represent a simple orthographic confusion. The BNC transcribers, who produced the corpus by listening to sound recordings and taking
them down in writing, made many spelling mistakes; our policy on the CHRISTINE
project was to standardize their spellings, except where these reflected nonstandard spoken-language structure (e.g. *nowt* for *nothing*). We took this to imply
that cases like *could of* should be corrected to *could've*; but two researchers
with whom we discussed the issue on separate occasions felt that this was inappropriate – one, with a language-teaching background, protested vigorously
that *could of* should be retained because, for the speakers, the word "really is"
of rather than *have*.

As a practical issue about policy for the CHRISTINE Corpus this point was
difficult to act on, because we had no way of knowing whether any particular
case of *of* for standard *have* represented the speaker's or the transcriber's model
of English. But the fact that qualified observers believe that some English speakers
have such a model, and the pervasiveness of this particular "spelling mistake",
are problematic from the perspective of the standard qualifier system. The
patterning of that system would seem to make it obvious that [əv] in this context
represents *have*: *he could've eaten*, including Past and Modal markers, alternates
with *he's eaten*, without them – [z] in the latter phrase certainly has nothing to
do with *of*; and no-one, surely, would utter a question form like *Of you seen it?*
for standard *Have you seen it?*, where pronunciation would distinguish *of* from
have.

On the other hand, if a sizeable group of speakers do not have the Perfect
term in their verb qualifier system, then it is perhaps understandable that they
will reanalyse sequences such as *could've*, uttered by speakers who do use the
Perfect construction, as *could of* and write it accordingly.

This explanation for the *could of* spelling would predict that this spelling
deviation should be commoner in Southern England than in the rest of Britain.
The only relevant data we know of is a report by Cheshire and Edwards (1993)
on the results of a survey in which teachers and pupils in a sample of schools
throughout Great Britain responded jointly to a questionnaire on local grammatical usage. Question 196 related to *of* after modals; the questionnaire example
was *You should of left half an hour ago!*[7] Writing from a British perspective, Cheshire and Edwards argue that this is a feature which "may well be of

---

7 Cheshire and Edwards write, p. 66, as if this *of* is sometimes actually pronounced with a full
vowel, [ɔv]. Cheshire and Edwards's methodology in the publication cited could not have
shown this, but others have told us anecdotally that they have heard it.

relatively recent origin".[8] Unfortunately, the survey findings are not very conclusive for our purposes, because *should of* was reported from almost all schools throughout Britain. Nevertheless, the minority of schools which did not report *should of* were disproportionately located outside Southern England, as predicted. Of 57 schools outside Southern England, six (10·5 per cent) did not report *should of* (in Oldham, Warrington, Rotherham, Scunthorpe, Nottingham, and Derbyshire); of 22 schools within Southern England, only one (4·5 per cent, in Oxford) did not do so. However, this difference is not statistically significant.

11.9 Nonstandard verb forms

There remains the issue which initially triggered this investigation: verb forms occurring without a preceding auxiliary which are either standard past participles rather than past tenses, or are standard base (present-tense) forms being used in clearly "past" contexts.

Our data contain a number of such cases, although taking all such verbs together the phenomenon is less frequent than the use of *got* without auxiliary for standard *HAVE got*. Counting cases is not straightforward, because of several interfering factors. Among the possible cases uttered by regionally-classified speakers, we excluded cases where the verb group was not preceded by a subject, because these may have been (and in many instances probably were) the result of casual subject-auxiliary omission rather than nonstandard inflexion; likewise we excluded the question *you ever seen that?* T27.03792. When Catherine059 interrupts herself, talking about the *telly that Tom give us # that give us* T13.01084, we counted one instance rather than two of *give* with past meaning. In the case of speech repairs such as *cos er gone in # it's gone in this week* T13.01006 or *but I thought it was just wo # you know just been left somewhere* T05.01168, we do not count the underlined groups at all, since it seems likely that the speaker is correcting the omission or "understanding" the omitted auxiliary as having been uttered before the point of interruption. A particularly problematic case occurs in text T09, where Beatrice039 says at three widely-separated points during a game of Cluedo *I know who done it*. On the face of it these are cases of *done* for standard *did*; but in the specific context of murder

---

8 However, since writing the first draft of this paper we have encountered a British example from a printed source not very much younger than the Booth Tarkington example quoted above. In her 1939 mystery *Murder is Easy*, Agatha Christie's educated amateur detective suggests to a country bumpkin that perhaps someone pushed the victim off a bridge. The bumpkin agrees *They might of*, and the detective continues *He might have made a few enemies* (Christie 1939: 125). Agatha Christie had a firmly Southern English background.

mysteries the phrase *who done it* has become an idiom of the standard language, written as one word *whodunit* or *whodunnit* – Beatrice039's *done*'s should perhaps be excluded for that reason.

With these provisos, the cases in our data, with numbers of examples, are:

come	18
done	13 (10 without the "Cluedo" cases)
give	3
gone	1
seen	1
shown	1
sung	1

(In the last case, Lass (1994) shows that the use of *sung* as past tense of *sing* has a long history. But we find nothing in his paper to suggest that the other forms in this list occurred as past-tense forms in dialects which existed before the emergence of a standard language.)

The totals by region are:

SE England	4
SW England	8
Midlands	6 (3 without the "Cluedo" cases)
Northern England	14
Wales	6
Scotland	0
Ireland	0

Our hypothesis at the beginning of this chapter was that confusions between past tense and past participle forms might arise as a consequence of speakers making no Past/Perfect distinction in their verbal system, so that the morphological distinction between past tense and past participle forms of the standard language appeared to be meaningless variation. However, that hypothesis implies that these confusions should correlate with absence of Perfect marking. Our data do not show that. Twelve nonstandard forms in 2,542 verb groups is 0·47 per cent for Southern England; even without the "Cluedo" cases, 23 in 4,469 is 0·51 per cent for the rest of Britain. The region for which Perfect is most clearly marginal, Ireland, shows no examples of nonstandard past forms.

The most judicious conclusion might be that there is truth in *both* the alternative ideas about nonstandard verb usage. The figures do seem to demonstrate that Southern England resembles Ireland in making limited use of Perfect marking as a logical category; and this would explain *got* replacing standard *HAVE got*. At the same time, it is probably true, as Eisikovits suggests, that nonstandard uses of *come*, *done*, and *give*, at least, are often merely equivalents of *came*, *did*, *gave*, representing the Past term of a system that does not differ from standard English in its logic.[9]

11.10 A possible explanation

A further question, if the concept of a Southern English vernacular lacking Perfect aspect is correct, is about the historical process which has created this situation.

We shall not enquire further into the factors behind the low incidence of Perfect aspect in Irish English; we are not qualified, and the CHRISTINE data would not be suitable, to take that question further than has been done by John Harris, quoted in 11.4 above. But the finding of a regional difference within Great Britain is new, and Harris's discussion does not bear on it.

Regional dialects sometimes preserve old structural properties which have been lost from the modern standard language, but this usually applies to individual regions distant from the centre of national life. It would be surprising to find that a historical development such as the introduction of the Perfect construction had occurred in standard English and in the vernacular speech of all regions *other* than Southern England. Besides, if that were true, GRS as a Southern Englishman[10] might expect to recognize this nonstandard usage pattern. In fact, the people among whom GRS grew up seemed, so far as he can tell, to use the Perfect routinely in casual conversation in the ways specified in descriptions of the standard written language. It is more likely, surely, that within Great Britain loss of the Perfect is a recent change which began in Southern England and has not yet spread to more peripheral regions, or to the standard (and which GRS was born too early to participate in).

---

9 Of the four one-off cases in our data, *seen* and *sung* were from Southern English speakers, so could be explained in either way; *gone* and *shown* were from Midlands speakers, but two isolated examples seem as likely to represent "performance errors" as systematic nonstandard usage patterns.

10 Born in 1944, parents Londoners, lived for about his first four years in North London and for the rest of his childhood near Bristol; never lived and very rarely travelled in Britain outside Southern England before age thirty.

We believe it may not be too strong a conclusion to infer that, for the spontaneous spoken English of Southern England, the Perfect aspect is dying, and will probably be dead once those who are now the younger generation become the older generation.[11]

It is well known that colloquial American English often uses the Past where British English (and the written American English standard) uses the Perfect (see e.g. Vanneck 1958, Elsness 1997). This is particularly striking where the clause contains a time adverb incompatible with the (British) sense of the simple past construction, e.g. *Did he do it yet?*, where *yet*, meaning "at any time prior to now", conflicts to British ears with the Past marking, meaning "at the particular time to which we were referring".[12] There are other cases (such as *I'm tired – I had a long day*, quoted by Quirk et al. 1985: §4.22 n. [a]) where the American Past construction could occur in British English, but the American use seems to be intended in a sense which British English expresses via the Perfect. Presumably there must be many occasions when British hearers fail to realize that an American Past construction is not intended to mean what the same construction would mean in standard British English.[13]

Elsness (1997) shows clearly that the Perfect construction is less frequent (and the Past construction more frequent) in American than in British written

---

11 This development seems to be peculiar to (some dialects of) English. Bowie et al. (2012: sec. 1.1) note that in other European languages which historically had a Past v. Perfect contrast, it is the Past which tends to be displaced by the Perfect.

12 Opinions differ (e.g. Vanneck 1958: 241, Visser 1973: §806) about whether this distinctively American use of the Past is more likely to represent influence from the English of Irish or Continental European immigrants, or to be a survival from the Early Modern English of the original settlers. Our late American colleague Larry Trask told us that the usage is deprecated by American editors; but it certainly is often seen nowadays in published American writing.

13 So far as we know, the CHRISTINE Corpus does not contain examples comparable to *Did he do it yet?*, including an adverbial element which would require Perfect marking in standard British usage. However, Lorenz (2001) has found five such cases in the full ten-million-word (demographic and context-governed) BNC speech section, and in using grep to locate his examples we have found a sixth. Quoting BNC filename and s-unit number, these are:

We'd always get one, we never lost one yet. H5H.00668, recorded 1987, Suffolk Sound Archive recording of memories of working at Ipswich docks in the 1920s-30s, speaker male, 77, retired.

Since when did they ever? KC4.00734, recorded 1991, conversation at home in Croydon, Surrey, speaker details unknown.

She said to me ehm, didn't count those, didn't give a re {pause} refund on those cigarettes yet, I said no. KDY.01678, recorded 1993, conversation in Croydon, Surrey, speaker female, 66, retired, social class C1.

Did she decide what she's doing with her money yet? KE3.05858, recorded 1991, conversation at home of BNC respondent's aunt, speaker female, 59, shop assistant.

English (though he shows, e.g. 1997: 358, that even in the latter the incidence of the Perfect construction has declined over the past two hundred years).[14] When we were carrying out the present study, spoken American English had not yet been equipped with research resources comparable to the CHRISTINE Corpus, which might have allowed us to discover whether there are American speakers who lack the Perfect construction in spontaneous speech altogether. If the Perfect were more or less marginal for some American speakers, then the findings for British usage discussed above might be another example of American influence on British English. In that case, a pattern of strong American influence on Southern English speakers, less in the Midlands and Northern England, and less still in Wales and Scotland, might perhaps be explained by suggesting that a stronger sense of local identity in regions distant from the metropolis makes speakers more resistant to American linguistic influence (cf. Labov 1963).

Finally: if the Perfect is disappearing from the spontaneous speech of Southern Englishmen and women, one would expect sooner or later to find this reflected in careful written prose. As we were completing the research reported here, we encountered the first example that we have seen. The national press on 11 December 2000 carried an advertisement by the Benefits Agency of the UK Department of Social Security, headed *Calling people 60 or over – keeping warm this winter just got easier!* Although it would be unremarkable in American

---

I never lost mine yet. KP4.01651, recorded 1993, conversation in a London park, speaker details unknown but he/she is joking as an equal with the BNC respondent who is female, 15, student, social class AB.

Did you put my red light up yet? KP5.03037, recorded 1993, conversation over a meal at an Indian restaurant in Twickenham, Middlesex, speaker female, 20, student, social class C1.

All six cases were recorded in SE or SW England, and, where the BNC file headers specify dialect details for the speakers, these match recording locations. According to the BNC user's manual, 45·61 per cent of total spoken BNC wording was recorded in the "South". How "South" in that context relates to the 20-way BNC regional classification of speakers, and hence to SE/SW England in the sense used in this chapter, is far from clear; but, if all the recording locations listed above fall within the region to which the 45·61 per cent figure applies, then the probability of getting this sample distribution, on the null hypothesis that such constructions are not correlated with region in the utterance population, would be less than one in a hundred.

14 Another, briefer recent discussion of grammatical change in Britain suggests that the opposite trend has been observable recently: Hughes and Trudgill (1996: 10–11) report a growing incidence of utterances like *And Roberts has played for us last season*, where the Perfect construction would traditionally be incompatible with the adverbial *last season*. We do not recognize this usage from our own experience, but, if there are now speakers for whom the Perfect is a feature only of the prestige dialect, absent in their own vernacular, one might expect forms like this to occur as hypercorrections. Vanneck (1958: 24) describes similar forms occurring as occasional hypercorrections in written American English.

English, this use of a Past form with *just* in the sense "just now" is clearly deviant with respect to standard British English: the word *just* implies reference to a current state of affairs, whereas Past tense implies reference to a past event. Such a construction would (we believe) never have been seen in print much before the date of this example. (Since the intended readers belonged to the older generation throughout the country, many of them may have been mildly puzzled by it.)

11.11 If one feature can go, what cannot?

Some readers might respond to the above by feeling that, for those concerned with the English language for its own sake, the findings could have some interest; but with respect to the overall thesis of the present book, they amount to rather little. The distinctive semantic category expressed by Perfect aspect (for those of us who use it) is certainly not one of the most crucial semantic features of the English language. Is it surprising if such a small-scale feature, which according to our own account (see the Visser reference on p. 207 above) first arose in the language only recently, should drop out again?

Perhaps the example would be more satisfying if it related to some more crucial semantic category, say the definite/indefinite contrast encoded by *a*/*the*, or the contrast between singular and plural in nouns. Catching a change to the logical structure of a language "on the wing" is an infrequent enough occurrence that one has to take whatever example one can get, and this is the one we encountered. But it seems to us that the important issue is that such changes do occur, whether small or large. Doubtless loss of a semantic distinction on the scale of definite v. indefinite, or singular v. plural, would be a much rarer event in the life of languages, so that it is no surprise that we have not observed one. But we see no reason to take it as axiomatic that such large-scale losses never occur. The resulting languages would not be "unnatural". Latin, despite its rich system of grammatical markers, does not encode the definite/indefinite contrast (at least, we see no way that it could be said to do so). Although we know of no Indo-European language which lacks the singular/plural contrast, plenty of other languages do (in modern Chinese the distinction is marked only with nouns or pronouns denoting people).

Languages, and the logical or semantic concepts which they express, are cultural creations. As with other cultural institutions, languages can become more complex as new features are thought up and succeed in diffusing among the community, and can become less complex as particular features fall into disuse and drop away. There is no underlying universal system dictating their logical or semantic architecture.

Chapter 12
Testing a metric for parse accuracy

12.1 The need for a metric

Chapter 2 discussed the problem of quantifying the degree of resemblance between separate analyses of a given stretch of wording. We mentioned in 2.4 that the metric we use, the *leaf-ancestor* metric, is not the one standardly used in our discipline but, we believe, is considerably superior to the standard metric. In that chapter, the purpose for which we needed a tree-comparison metric was investigation of how far a set of parsing guidelines succeeded in predicting a unique analysis for a given language sample, so that separate human analysts dealing with the same samples would be constrained to come up with the same analyses.

Within computational linguistics, this type of metric is more commonly used for a different purpose. One of the central tasks in human language technology, required for many practical applications of natural language processing, is *automatic parsing*: development of software that takes in chunks of prose and outputs correct grammatical analyses of that prose. Many research teams worldwide (including, in the past, our own group) are active in creating and improving automatic parsing systems, and this kind of work requires a means of measuring success. The typical situation is that one has a set of language samples and a set of analyses of those samples which are deemed to be correct (*gold-standard* analyses), and one wants to quantify how closely the output of an automatic system, run over the samples, matches the gold-standard targets.

The metric which has come into widespread use for this purpose is the Grammar Evaluation Interest Group (GEIG) metric (see e.g. Black et al. 1991), which has been seen internationally as standard thanks to its use in the "Parseval" series of competitions between automatic-parsing systems. We have argued (Sampson 2000b) that the leaf-ancestor (LA) metric is superior to GEIG, and the present chapter presents the results of an experiment comparing the performance of the two metrics on a sample of automatic-parser output.

Choice between parse-evaluation metrics might seem a topic excessively distant from discussion of the concept of grammaticality, with which this book is centrally concerned. The relevance is that the experiment to be described makes a clear, neatly self-contained illustration of the extent to which the conceptual claims of our book emerge from a background of hard-nosed, careful objective research. Our linguistics, we would like to claim, is not mere armchair theorizing. (Furthermore, the fact that a technique which has been widely taken for granted in the field can fairly easily be shown to be inadequate might perhaps suggest that, just because most linguists take the grammaticality concept for granted, there is no need to assume that they are right to do so.)

12.2 Alternative metrics

The essence of the problem with which this chapter is concerned is how best to quantify the degree of similarity between alternative tree structures over the same sequence of words. The widely-used GEIG or Parseval metric responds to this problem by counting the numbers of tagmas (multi-word grammatical units) identifed by both trees, or by only one of them.

From our point of view, this approach lays excessive weight on locating the exact boundaries of constructions.

As originally defined by Black et al. and as it is often applied, the GEIG metric takes no account of node labels at all: it *only* considers the location of brackets. And in consequence, this metric includes no concept of approximate correctness in identifying tagmas: a pair of brackets either enclose a sequence of words (or other terminal elements) exactly corresponding to a sequence bracketed off in the gold-standard parse, or not. More recently (Magerman 1995, Collins 1997) a refined variant of the GEIG metric has been used which does check label identity as well as wordspan identity in matching tagmas between gold-standard and candidate parses. Nowadays, this variant of the GEIG metric is frequently used in preference to the original, label-free variant; but we shall argue that even this variant is substantially inferior to the LA metric. We shall refer to the Black et al. (1991) and Collins (1997) variants of the GEIG metric as GEIG/unlabelled and GEIG/labelled respectively.

We think of "parsing" as determining what kind of larger elements are constituted by the small elements of a string that are open to direct observation. Identifying the exact boundaries of the larger elements is a part, but only one part, of that task. If, for instance, in the gold standard, words 5 to 14 are identified as a noun phrase, then a candidate parse which identifies a noun phrase as beginning at word 5 but ending at word 13, or word 15, should in our view be given substantial though not full credit; under the GEIG metric it is given no credit. The LA metric quantifies accuracy of parsing in this sense.

Our research group is far from alone in finding the GEIG metric unsatisfactory. Srinivas Bangalore et al. (1998) say that "it is unclear as to how the score on [the GEIG] metric relates to success in parsing". Sandra Kübler and Heike Telljohann (2002) comment "it is well known that [the GEIG/Parseval] measures do not give an accurate picture of the quality of the parser's output". Cf. also Manning and Schütze (1999: 434–437).

Incidentally, we believe that the LA metric was the earliest parse-assessment metric in the field, having been used, and briefly described in print, in the 1980s (Sampson, Haigh, and Atwell 1989: 278), though it was later eclipsed by the influential Parseval programme.

One strategy that has recently been adopted by a number of researchers who are dissatisfied with the Parseval approach to parse evaluation has been to use dependency rather than phrase-structure grammar formalisms. In principle, the LA metric can be applied equally well to dependency or to phrase-structure trees (Sampson 2000b: 62–64). However, the advantages of LA assessment are clearer and more striking in connexion with phrase-structure trees, and in what follows we shall consider only this type of grammar formalism. Briscoe, Carroll, et al. (2002) propose a metric that counts the individual semantic relations encoded in a dependency structure, rather than what they call "more arbitrary details of tree topology". That approach may be very suitable, for researchers who are committed to using grammar formalisms of the specific type required for it to be applicable. Our approach by contrast is to use a measure which applies equally well to a wide range of formalisms, but which assesses success and failure in a way that matches intuitive judgements of good or bad parsing better than the metric which has been standardly used until now.

12.3 The essence of leaf-ancestor assessment

The LA metric evaluates the parsing of an individual terminal element in terms of the similarity of the lineages of that element in candidate and gold-standard parse trees (see 2.4 above for the term "lineage"). The LA value for the parsing of an entire sentence or other many-word unit is simply the average of the values for the individual words. Apart from (we claim) yielding figures for parsing accuracy of complete sentences which succeed better than the GEIG metric in quantifying our intuitions about parse accuracy, the LA metric has the further practical virtue of identifying the location of parsing errors in a straightforward way.

We illustrate the general concept of LA assessment using one of the shortest sentences in our experimental data-set. (The nature of that data-set, and the gold-standard parsing scheme, will be discussed below.) The sentence runs: *two tax revision bills were passed*. (Certain typographic details, including capitalization, inverted commas, and sentence-final punctuation marks, have been eliminated from the examples.) The gold-standard analysis, and the candidate analysis produced by an automatic parser, are respectively:

(99G)   [S [N1 *two* [N1 *tax revision*] *bills*] *were passed*]

(99C)   [S [NP *two tax revision bills*] *were passed*]

(Here and below, "*n*G" and "*n*C" label gold-standard and candidate analyses for an example *n*.)

The automatic parser has failed to identify *tax revision* as a unit within the tagma headed by *bills*, and it has labelled that tagma NP rather than N1. Lineages for these tree structures are as follows, where for each terminal element the gold-standard lineage is shown to the left and the candidate lineage to the right of the colon, and within each of the paired lineages the Leaf end is to the Left and the Root end to the Right:

two   N1 [S : NP [S

tax   [N1 N1 S : NP S

revision N1] N1 S : NP S

bills   N1] S : NP] S

were   S : S

passed S] : S]

The only aspect of the relationship between this notation and the tree structures which is not self-explanatory is the inclusion of boundary markers (left and right square brackets) in many of the lineages. The reason for including these is that, without them, a set of lineages would not always uniquely determine a tree structure; for instance the structures "[P [Q *a b*] [Q *c*]]" and "[P [Q *a b c*]]" would not be distinguishable, since the lineage for each terminal element in both cases would consist of the sequence Q P. A set of lineages uniquely determines the tree structure from which it is derived, if boundary markers are inserted by the following rules. (These rules, although intuitive enough once grasped, are unfortunately rather cumbersome to express in words.)

(i) A left-boundary marker is inserted in the lineage of a terminal element immediately before the label of the highest nonterminal beginning with that element, if there is such a nonterminal. Thus, in the gold-standard analysis for the example, *two* begins the entire sentence, so the left-boundary marker is placed in the lineage before S; *tax* begins the lower N1 tagma but is not initial in the higher N1 tagma which dominates it, so the left-boundary marker is placed before the lower N1 in the lineage; *revision* is not the first word of any tagma, so no left-boundary marker is included in its lineage.

(ii) Conversely, a right-boundary marker is inserted in the lineage of a terminal element immediately after the label of the highest nonterminal ending with that element, if there is such a nonterminal. Thus *bills* is the last word of the higher N1 tagma in the gold-standard analysis (but is not rightmost within the S tagma which dominates that N1), so a right-boundary marker is placed after N1 in the lineage; *were* is neither the first nor the last word of any tagma, so no boundary marker occurs in its lineage.

So, in the example above, the LA metric equates the accuracy with which the word *two* has been parsed with the degree of similarity between the two strings NP [S and N1 [S, it equates the parse-accuracy for *tax* with the degree of similarity between NP S and [N1 N1 S, and so forth; for the last two words the lineages are identical, so the metric says that they have been parsed perfectly. We postpone discussion of our method for calculating string similarity until after we have discussed our experimental material.

12.4 The experimental material

Our experiment used a set of sentences from genre sections A and G of the SUSANNE Treebank analysed by an automatic parser developed at the Universities of Cambridge and Sussex by Ted Briscoe and John Carroll (Carroll and Briscoe 1996); of those sentences for which the parser was able to produce a structure, a set of 500 was randomly chosen. For the purposes of illustrating the performance of the LA metric and comparing it with the GEIG metric, we wanted material parsed by a system that used a simple parsing scheme with a smallish vocabulary of nonterminal labels, and which made plenty of mistakes in applying the scheme to real-life data. There is no suggestion that the parses in our experimental data-set represent the present-day "state of the art" for automatic parsing; they certainly do not, but for current purposes that is a good thing. A state-of-the-art parser might make only small errors of a few kinds, and these might happen not to differentiate the performance of alternative parse-accuracy metrics very clearly. In order to discover which metric does best across the board at punishing bad mistakes heavily and small mistakes lightly, we need parser output containing a wide variety of errors of different degrees of gravity.

Likewise the use of SUSANNE as a source of experimental material may offer a better test than the obvious alternative, the Pennsylvania *Wall Street Journal* treebank, whose language samples are more homogeneous; Briscoe and Carroll (2002: 1500), quoting Bangalore (2000), suggest that that is so. We would not want to place much emphasis on this point: our test material was less diverse than the full SUSANNE treebank, and the small differences between the SUSANNE and *Wall Street Journal* figures in Bangalore's table 7 (op. cit.: 134) might equally well be explained by the fact that his system was trained on *Wall Street Journal* material. But we agree with the general principle, expressed satirically by "Swift Redux" (2001 – not a pseudonym for either of ourselves), that it is unwise for the discipline to allow itself to depend too exclusively on research using material from a single newspaper.

The parsing scheme which the automatic parser was intended to apply used seven nonterminal labels, which we gloss with our own rather than Briscoe and Carroll's labels:

S   finite clause

VP   nonfinite clause

NP   noun phrase containing specifier

N1   noun phrase without specifier (generative linguists' "N-bar")

PP   prepositional phrase

AP   adjectival or adverbial phrase

T   "textual constituent", defined by Briscoe and Carroll as a tagma enclosing "a sequence of sub-constituents whose relationship is syntactically indeterminate due to the presence of intervening, delimiting punctuation"

The use of these seven categories is defined in greater detail in documentation supplied to us, but for present purposes it is unnecessary to burden the reader with this material. The automatic-parser output occasionally included node-labels not on the above list (e.g. V, N2), but these were always regarded by the developers of the parser as mistakes.

Briscoe and Carroll's original data included GEIG/unlabelled precision and recall scores for each automatic parse, assessed against the SUSANNE bracketing as gold standard. For the purposes of this experiment, the Evalb program (Sekine and Collins 1997) was used to produce GEIG/labelled precision and recall figures for the same data. In order to be able to compare our LA scores with single GEIG/labelled and GEIG/unlabelled scores for each sentence, we converted pairs of precision (P) and recall (R) figures to F-scores (van Rijsbergen 1979) by the formula, $F = 2PR/(P + R)$, there being no reason to include a weighting factor to make precision accuracy count more than recall accuracy or *vice versa*.

We constructed a set of gold-standard trees that could be compared with the trees output by the automatic parser, by manually adding labels from the seven-element Briscoe and Carroll label vocabulary to the SUSANNE bracketing, in conformity with the documentation on that seven-element vocabulary. Because the parsing scheme which the automatic parser was intended to apply was very different from the SUSANNE scheme, to a degree this was an artificial exercise. In some cases, none of the seven labels was genuinely suitable for a particular SUSANNE tagma; but one of them was assigned anyway, and such assignments were made as consistently as possible across the 500-sentence data-set. The admitted artificiality of this procedure did not seem unduly harmful, in the context of an investigation into the performance of a metric (as opposed to an investigation into the substantive problem of automatic parsing).

12.5 Calculation of lineage similarity

Leaf-ancestor assessment depends on quantifying the similarity between pairs of strings of node-labels. The standard metric for string similarity is Levenshtein distance (Levenshtein 1966), also called edit distance. The Levenshtein distance between two strings is the minimum cost for a set of insert, delete, and replace operations to transform one string into the other, where each individual operation has a cost of one. For instance, the Levenshtein distance between A B C B D and A D C B is two: the latter string can obtained from the former by replacing the second character with D and deleting the last character. If len(s) is the length of a string s, and Lv(s, t) is the Levenshtein distance between strings s and t, then a simple way of defining the similarity between candidate and gold-standard lineages c, g for a given terminal element would be to calculate it as

$$1 - \text{Lv}(c, g)/(\text{len}(c) + \text{len}(g))$$

which for any c, g must fall on the interval (0, 1). The accuracy of a candidate parse would be defined as the mean similarities of the lineage-pairs for the various words or other terminal elements of the string.

For our purposes this is a little too simple, because it does not allow for the fact that some labelling errors are more serious than others. For most schemes of natural-language parsing in practice, node labels will not be single letters but symbols with internal complexity; we want to be able to distinguish between cases where a label is entirely wrong, and cases where the candidate label is close to the gold-standard label although not identical to it. Furthermore, it has often been put to us that the seriousness of a mislabelling may sometimes be application-dependent (cf. Sampson 2000b: 64–65). We allow for this by specifying that any particular application of LA assessment will involve defining a function from all possible pairs of node labels into the interval (0, 2); in assessing parse accuracy as above, simple Levenshtein distance is replaced by a modified calculation in which the cost of deletions and insertions remains one, but the cost of replacing one by another of a pair of node labels is determined by the function just described. The intuition here is that if two grammatical categories are entirely dissimilar, then for a parser to mistake one for the other amounts to two separate errors of failing to recognize the existence of a tagma of one kind, and falsely positing the existence of another type of tagma (a delete and an insert) – hence the cost should be two; but if the categories are more or less similar, then the lineages should be treated as less far apart. (Using this modification of Levenshtein distance, it remains true that the distance between two lineages must always fall on the interval (0, 1).)

In the case of Parseval-type competitions where the chief consideration is that rival systems should be judged on an equal footing, it may be appropriate to use the simplest version of LA assessment, in which replacement of any node label by any distinct label always costs two (labels are treated either as correct or as entirely wrong). But there is more to automatic parsing than competitions between rival systems. In a situation where parsing is applied to a practical task, it may be preferable to use a string-distance measure in which the costs of various label replacements are more differentiated.

The present experiment exemplifies this possibility by setting the cost of replacing a symbol by an unrelated symbol at 2, but the cost of a replacement where both symbols share the same first character at $0 \cdot 5$; thus partial credit is given for mistaking, say, a noun phrase for an N-bar, which is surely a lesser error than mistaking it for a subordinate clause. We are not suggesting that this particular cost function is likely to be ideal in practice, but it offers a clear, simple illustration of the possibility of partial credit for partly-correct labelling.

Applied to our short example sentence, the LA metric as defined above gives the scores for successive terminal elements shown in the left-hand column below:

$0 \cdot 917$ *two*   N1 [S : NP [S

$0 \cdot 583$ *tax*   [N1 N1 S : NP S

$0 \cdot 583$ *revision* N1] N1 S : NP S

$0 \cdot 917$ *bills*   N1] S : NP] S

$1 \cdot 000$ *were*   S : S

$1 \cdot 000$ *passed* S] : S]

To illustrate the calculation for the word *revision*: replacing either one of the N1 symbols by NP costs 0.5; deletion of the boundary symbol and the other N1 symbol each cost 1; $1 - (0 \cdot 5 + 1 + 1)/(4 + 2) = 0 \cdot 583$.

The average for the whole sentence is $0 \cdot 833$. For comparison, the GEIG/ unlabelled and GEIG/labelled F-scores are $0 \cdot 800$ and $0 \cdot 400$.

12.6 Are the metrics equivalent?

The figure for the LA metric just quoted happens to be very similar to one of the two GEIG figures. An obvious initial question about the performance of the metrics over the data-set as a whole is whether, although the metrics are calculated differently, they perhaps turn out to impose much the same ranking on the candidate parses.

To this the answer is a clear no. Figures 14 and 15 compare the scores of the 500 parses on the LA metric with their scores on the GEIG/unlabelled and GEIG/

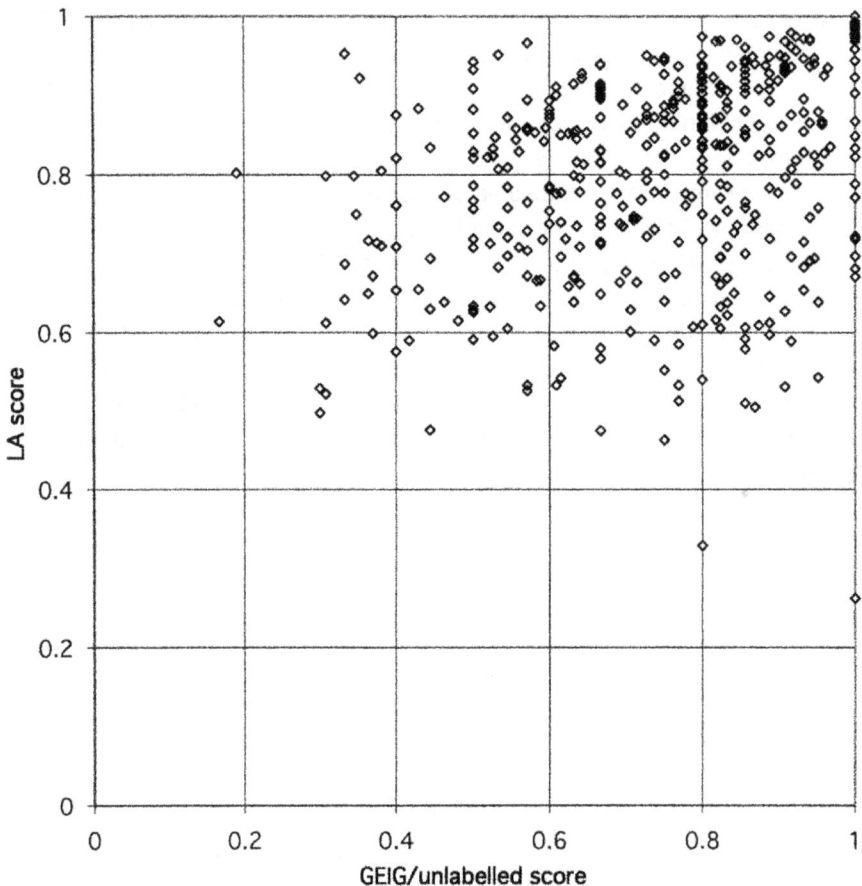

Figure 14: GEIG/unlabelled v. LA parse scores

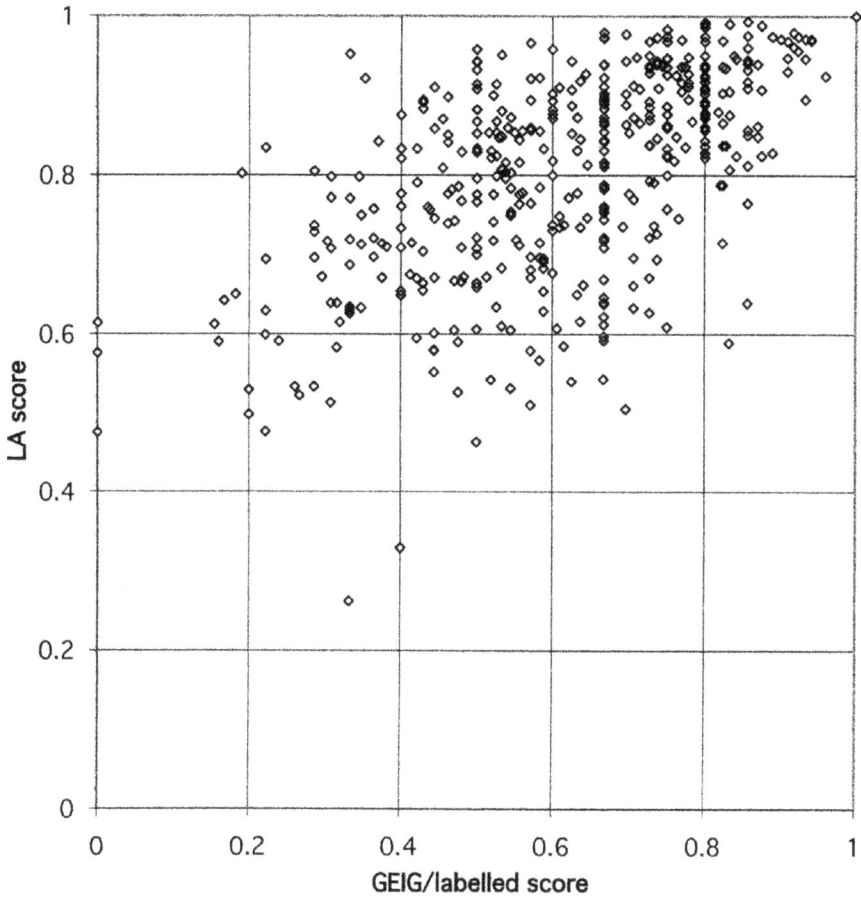

Figure 15: GEIG/labelled v. LA parse scores

labelled metrics respectively. In Figure 14, little or no correlation is visible between scores on the two metrics. (We find this surprising. If two alternative methods for measuring the same property yield uncorrelated results, one might have supposed that at least one of the methods could never be taken seriously at all.) Figure 15 does display a degree of clustering round a lower-left to upper-right axis, as expected, but the correlation is clearly quite weak.

An extreme case of contrasting scores is (100), which corresponds to the most "north-westerly" point in Figures 14 and 15:

(100G) [S *it is not* [NP *a mess* [S *you can make sense of*]]] G12:0520.27

(100C) [S *it is not* [NP *a mess* [S *you can make sense*]] *of*] (0·333, 0·333, 0·952)

(Here and below, gold-standard analyses are followed by the SUSANNE location code of the first word – omitting the last three characters, this is the same as the Brown Corpus text and line number. The location for example (99) was A02:0790.51. Candidate parses are followed in brackets by their GEIG/unlabelled, GEIG/labelled, and LA scores, in that order.)

The LA and GEIG numerical scores for (100) are very different; but more important than the raw scores are the rankings assigned by the respective metrics, relative to the range of 500 examples. For both GEIG/labelled and GEIG/unlabelled, the parse of (100) is in the tenth (i.e. the lowest) decile; for LA, it is in the second decile. (The "nth decile", for any of the metrics, refers to the set of examples occuping ranks $50(n-1)+1$ to $50n$, when the 500 candidate parses are ordered from best to worst in terms of score on that metric; for instance the second decile is the set of examples ranked 51 to 100. Where a group of examples share identical scores on a metric, for purposes of dividing the examples into deciles an arbitrary order was imposed on members of the group.)

The difference between the low GEIG scores and the high LA score for example (100) is a classic illustration of one of the standard objections to the GEIG metric. The parser has correctly discovered that the sentence consists of an S within NP within S structure, and almost every word has been given its proper place within that structure; just one word has been attached at the wrong level, but because this leads to the right-hand boundary of two of the three tagmas being slightly misplaced, the GEIG score is very low. We believe that most linguists' intuitive assessment of example (100) would treat it as a largely-correct parse with one smallish mistake, not as one of the worst parses in the data-set – that is, the intuition would agree much better with the LA metric than with the GEIG metrics in this case.

An extreme case in the opposite direction (LA score lower than GEIG score) is (101), corresponding to the most "south-easterly" point in Figure 14:

(101G) [S *yes,* [S *for they deal* [PP *with distress*]]] G12:1340.42

(101C) [T *yes,* [PP *for they deal* [PP *with distress*]]] (1·0, 0·333, 0·262)

The GEIG/unlabelled metric gives 101C a perfect mark – all brackets are in the right place; but its LA score is very low, because two of the three tagmas are wrongly labelled. One might of course debate about whether, in terms of the Briscoe/Carroll labelling scheme, the root tagma *should* be labelled S rather than T, but that is not to the point here. The relevant point is that, *if* the target is the gold-standard parse shown, then a metric which gives a poor score to 3C is performing better than a metric which gives it a perfect score.

For example (101), GEIG/labelled performs much better than GEIG/unlabelled. Where parsing errors relate wholly or mainly to labelling rather than to structure, that will be so. But we have seen in the case of (100), and shall see again, that there are other kinds of parsing error where GEIG/labelled is no more, or little more, satisfactory than GEIG/unlabelled.

12.7 Performance systematically compared

In order systematically to contrast the performance of the metrics, we need to focus on examples for which the ranking of the candidate parse is very different under the different metrics, which implies checking cases whose parses are among the lowest-ranked by one of the metrics. It would be little use to check the highest-ranked parses by either metric. Many candidates are given perfect marks by the LA metric, because they are completely accurate, in which case they will also receive perfect GEIG marks. (In both Figures 14 and 15, the data point at $(1 \cdot 0, 1 \cdot 0)$ represents 63 of the 500 examples.) Some candidates receive perfect GEIG/unlabelled marks but lower LA (and GEIG/labelled) marks, however this merely reflects the fact that GEIG/unlabelled ignores labelling errors.

We have checked how many examples from the lowest GEIG/unlabelled and GEIG/labelled deciles fall into the various LA deciles, and how many examples from the lowest LA decile fall into the various GEIG/unlabelled and GEIG/labelled deciles. The results are shown in Table 17.

The examples of particular interest are those counted in the higher rows of these four tables, which are assessed very differently by the alternative metrics. The GEIG/unlabelled and GEIG/labelled 10th-decile, LA 2nd-decile example is (100), already discussed above. The GEIG/labelled 10th-decile, LA 3rd-decile example (and this is also one of the GEIG/unlabelled 10th-decile, LA 3rd-decile examples) is (102):

Table 17: Ranking on either metric of parses ranked lowest by the other metric

LA deciles for GEIG/unlabelled 10th decile:

1st	0
2nd	1
3rd	3
4th	2
5th	2
6th	4
7th	8
8th	7
9th	11
10th	12

LA deciles for GEIG/labelled 10th decile:

1st	0
2nd	1
3rd	1
4th	0
5th	0
6th	1
7th	7
8th	8
9th	13
10th	19

GEIG/unlabelled deciles for LA 10th decile:

1st	1
2nd	0
3rd	4
4th	9
5th	3
6th	8
7th	4
8th	5
9th	4
10th	12

GEIG/labelled deciles for LA 10th decile:

1st	0
2nd	0
3rd	1
4th	1
5th	3
6th	8
7th	5
8th	5
9th	8
10th	19

(102G) [S *then he began* [VP *to speak* [PP *about* [NP *the tension* [PP *in art*]
[PP *between* [NP *the mess* [N1 *and form*]]]]]]]] G12:0610.27

(102C) [S *then he began* [VP *to speak* [PP *about* [NP *the tension*]] [PP *in* [N1 *art*
[PP *between* [NP *the mess*]] [N1 *and form*]]]]]] (0 · 353, 0 · 353, 0 · 921)

The two further GEIG/unlabelled 10th-decile, LA 3rd-decile cases are:

(103G) [S *Alusik then moved Cooke across* [PP *with* [NP *a line drive* [PP *to left*]]]]
A13:0150.30

(103C) [S *Alusik then moved Cooke across* [PP *with* [NP *a line drive*]] [PP *to left*]]
(0 · 500, 0 · 500, 0 · 942)

(104G) [S [NP *their heads*] *were* [PP *in* [NP *the air*]] *sniffing*] G04:0030.18

(104C) [S [NP *their heads*] *were* [PP *in* [NP *the air sniffing*]]] (0 · 500, 0 · 500,
0 · 932)

Examples (103) and (104) are essentially similar to (100) above, since all three concern errors about the level at which a sentence-final element should be attached. The LA scores are marginally lower than for (100), because the misattached elements comprise a higher proportion of total words in the respective examples. In (103) a two-word phrase rather than a single word is misattached, and in (104) the misattached element is a single word but the sentence as a whole is only seven words long while example (100) contains ten words. Intuitively it is surely appropriate for a misattachment error involving a higher proportion of total words to be given a lower mark, but for these candidates nevertheless to be treated as largely correct. (Notice that the candidate parse for (103) verges on being a plausible alternative interpretation of the sentence, i.e. not mistaken at all. It is only the absence of *the* before *left* which, to a human analyst, makes it rather certain that our gold-standard parse is the structure corresponding to the writer's intended meaning.)

The candidate parse for (102) contains a greater variety of errors, and we would not claim that in this case it is so intuitively clear that the candidate should be ranked among the above-average parses. Notice, though, that although several words and tagmas have been misattached, nothing has been identified as a quite different kind of tagma from what it really is (as *for they deal with distress* in (101) above was identified as a prepositional phrase rather than subordinate clause). Therefore our intuitions do not clearly suggest that the candidate should be ranked as worse than average, either; our intuitions are rather indecisive in this case. In other cases, where we have clear intuitions, the LA ranking agrees with them much better than the GEIG ranking.

Turning to cases where LA gives a much lower ranking than GEIG: the most extreme case is (101), already discussed. The LA 10th-decile, GEIG/labelled 3rd decile case (which is also one of the GEIG/unlabelled 3rd-decile cases) is (105):

(105G) [S [NP *its ribs*] *showed*, [S *it was* [NP *a yellow nondescript color*]], [S *it suffered* [PP *from* [NP *a variety* [PP *of sores*]]]], [S *hair had scabbed* [PP *off* [NP *its body*]] [PP *in patches*]]] G04:1030.15

(105C) [T [S [NP *its ribs*] *showed*], [S *it was* [NP *a yellow nondescript color*]], [S *it suffered* [PP *from* [NP *a variety* [PP *of sores*]]]], [S *hair had scabbed off* [NP *its body*] [PP *in patches*]]] (0·917, 0·833, 0·589)

There are large conflicts between candidate and gold-structure parses here: the candidate treats the successive clauses as sisters below a T node, whereas under the SUSANNE analytic scheme the gold-standard treats the second and subsequent clauses as subordinate to the first, with no T node above it; and the candidate fails to recognize *off* as introducing a PP. The presence v. absence of the T node, because it occurs at the very top of the tree, affects the lineages of all words and hence has a particularly large impact on LA score. (Sampson 2000b: 66 discussed the fact that the LA metric penalizes mistakes more heavily if they occur higher in a tree, because mistakes high in a tree affect the lineages of many words. This might be seen as an undesirable bias; on the other hand, one commentator has suggested to us that this feature of the LA metric is a positive virtue, because parse errors higher in trees tend to have more severe practical consequences for natural language processing applications.)

The three other LA 10th-decile, GEIG/unlabelled 3rd-decile cases are:

(106G) [S [S *when* [NP *the crowd*] *was asked* [S *whether it wanted* [VP *to wait* [NP *one more term*] [VP *to make* [NP *the race*]]]]], *it voted no* – [S *and there were* [NP *no dissents*]]] A01:0980.06

(106C) [T [S [PP *when* [NP *the crowd*] *was asked* [PP *whether it wanted* [VP *to wait* [NP *one more term*] [VP *to make* [NP *the race*]]]]], *it voted no*] – [S *and there were* [NP *no dissents*]]] (0·952, 0·667, 0·543)

(107G) [S [S *we wo +n't know* [NP *the full amount*] [S *until we get* [NP *a full report*]]], *Wagner said*] A09:0520.12

(107C) [T [S *we wo +n't know* [NP *the full amount*] [PP *until we get* [NP *a full report*]]], [S *Wagner said*]] (0·909, 0·545, 0·531)

(108G)   [S [S [NP *her husband*] *was lying* [PP *on* [NP *the kitchen floor*]]], *police said*] A19:1270.48

(108C)   [T [S [NP *her husband*] *was lying* [PP *on* [NP *the kitchen floor*]]], [S *police said*]] (0·909, 0·727, 0·627)

Each of these involves the same problems as (105) of presence v. absence of a root T node and co-ordinate v. subordinate relationships between successive clauses. Example (106) includes further large discrepancies: *when* and *whether* are both treated as initiating prepositional phrases rather than clauses, though neither word has a prepositional use (in terms of the traditional part-of-speech classification as represented in published dictionaries – this may be another case where the candidate parse is correct in terms of special assumptions about linguistic theory incorporated in the software which produced it, but the relevant point for us is that *if* 106G is the gold standard then 106C is badly wrong). Example (107) has a similar error involving *until* (this is more understandable, since *until* can be a preposition). Intuitively, to the present authors, the LA metric seems correct in characterizing (106) and (107) as two of the cases where the candidate parse deviates furthest from the gold standard, rather than as two of the best parses. The case of (108) is admittedly less clearcut.

Some readers may find this section unduly concerned with analysts' intuitions as opposed to objective facts. But, if the question is which of two metrics better quantifies parsing success, the only basis for comparison is people's intuitive concept of what ought to count as good or bad parsing. Both metrics give perfect scores to perfect matches between candidate and gold-standard structure; which departures from perfect matching ought to be penalized heavily can only be decided in terms of "educated intuition", that is intuition supported by knowledge and discussion of the issues. It would not be appropriate to lend such intuitions the appearance of objectivity and theory-independence by "counting votes" from a large number of subjects. (Since the GEIG metric is widely known, raw numbers from an exercise like that could have as much to do with the extent to which individual informants were aware of that metric as with pre-theoretical responses to parse errors.) Deciding such an issue in terms of averaged subject responses would be as inappropriate as choosing between alternative scientific theories by democratic voting. Rather, the discussion should proceed as we have conducted it here, by appealing to readers' and writers' individual intuitions with discussion of particular examples.

12.8 Local error information

Different accuracy rankings assigned to complete parses are not the only reason for preferring the LA to the GEIG metric. Another important difference is the ability of the LA metric to give detailed information about the location and nature of parse errors.

Consider, for instance, example (109), whose gold-standard and candidate analyses are:

(109G) [S *however*, [NP *the jury*] *said* [S *it believes* [S [NP *these two offices*] *should be combined* [VP *to achieve* [N1 *greater efficiency*] [S *and reduce* [NP *the cost* [PP *of administration*]]]]]]]] A01:0210.15

(109C) [S *however*, [NP *the jury*] *said* [S *it believes* [NP *these two*] [S *offices should be combined* [VP *to* [VP *achieve* [N1 *greater efficiency*] [VP *and reduce* [NP *the cost* [PP *of administration*]]]]]]]] (0·762, 0·667, 0·889)

The score of 0·889 assigned by the LA metric to this candidate analysis, like any LA score, is the mean of scores for the individual words. For this example, those are as shown in Table 18.

The display shows that, according to the LA metric, the early part of the sentence is parsed perfectly, and that the worst-parsed part is *these two offices*. That seems exactly right; in the correct analysis, these three words are a NP, subject of the clause which forms the object of *believe*, but the automatic parser has interpreted *believe* as a ditransitive verb with *these two* as indirect object, and has treated *offices* as grammatically unrelated to *these two*. Intuitively, these are gross mistakes. The next stretch of erroneous parsing is from *achieve* to the end, where each word's mark is pulled down by the error of taking *achieve* to open a subordinate VP within the VP initiated by the preceding *to*. Relative to the SUSANNE scheme used here as gold standard, this also seems a bad error. It is an understandable consequence of the fact that the Briscoe/Carroll automatic parser was based on a parsing scheme that made different theoretical assumptions about grammar, but in the present target scheme no English construction ought to be analysed as "[VP *to* [VP...".

We would not pretend that our intuitions are so refined that they positively justify a score for *reduce* which is marginally lower than those for the surrounding words, or positively justify the small difference between 0·727 as the lowest score in the second bad stretch and 0·667 in the earlier stretch; the present authors' intuitions are vaguer than that. But notice that, as it stands, the GEIG metric offers no comparable technique for identifying the locations of bad parsing performance within parsed units; it deals in global scores, not local scores.

Table 18: Leaf-ancestor scores for individual words in a parse tree

1.000	*however*	[S : [S
1.000	,	S : S
1.000	*the*	[NP S : [NP S
1.000	*jury*	NP] S : NP] S
1.000	*said*	S : S
1.000	*it*	[S S : [S S
1.000	*believes*	S S : S S
0.667	*these*	NP [S S S : [NP S S
0.750	*two*	NP S S S : NP] S S
0.667	*offices*	NP] S S S : [S S S
1.000	*should*	S S S : S S S
1.000	*be*	S S S : S S S
1.000	*combined*	S S S : S S S
1.000	*to*	[VP S S S : [VP S S S
0.800	*achieve*	VP S S S : [VP VP S S S
0.923	*greater*	[N1 VP S S S : [N1 VP VP S S S
0.923	*efficiency*	N1] VP S S S : N1] VP VP S S S
0.769	*and*	[S VP S S S : [VP VP VP S S S
0.727	*reduce*	S VP S S S : VP VP VP S S S
0.800	*the*	[NP S VP S S S : [NP VP VP VP S S S
0.769	*cost*	NP S VP S S S : NP VP VP VP S S S
0.824	*of*	[PP NP S VP S S S : [PP NP VP VP VP S S S
0.824	*administration*	PP NP S VP S S S] : PP NP VP VP VP S S S]

True, one can envisage ways in which the GEIG metric might be developed to yield similar data; it remains to be seen how well that would work. (Likewise, the GEIG/labelled metric could be further developed to incorporate the LA concept of partial matching between label pairs. On the other hand, there is no way that GEIG could be adapted to avoid the unsatisfactory performance exemplified by (100) above.)

Using the LA metric, researchers developing an automatic parser in a situation where large quantities of gold-standard analyses are available for testing should easily be able to identify configurations (e.g. particular grammatical words, or particular structures) which are regularly associated with low scores, in order to focus parser development on areas where further work is most needed. If the parsing scheme used a larger variety of nonterminal labels, one would expect that individual nonterminals might regularly be associated with low scores, though with the very austere nonterminal vocabulary of the Briscoe/Carroll scheme that is perhaps less likely to be so. Even with a small-vocabulary scheme like this, though, one might expect to find generalizations such as "when a subordinate S begins with a multi-word NP, the parser tends to fail". Note that we are not saying that this is a true generalization about the particular automatic parser used to generate the data under discussion; one such mistake occurs in the example above, but we do not know whether this is a frequent error or a one-off. Any automatic parser is likely to make errors in *some* recurring patterns, though; the LA metric is potentially an efficient tool for identifying these, whatever they happen to be.

12.9 Authority is fallible

From these results, we would argue that the leaf-ancestor metric comes much closer than the GEIG metric to operationalizing our intuitive concepts of accurate and inaccurate parsing.

Someone looking for reasons to reject the LA metric might complain, correctly, that the algorithm for calculating it is much more computation-intensive than that for the GEIG metric. But intensive computation is not a problem in modern circumstances.

More important: there is no virtue in a metric that is easy to calculate, if it measures the wrong thing.

The GEIG metric has been widely accepted by the computational-linguistics community for the same reason that the grammaticality concept has been accepted by linguists more generally: it has appeared to have authority behind it. In the case of the Parseval competitions, the authority was in a sense real: teams who wanted to take part in the series had to accept its success metric. But that did not make it a good metric.

In the case of grammaticality, any appearance of authority is spurious. This idea belongs to abstract linguistic theory, and in such purely intellectual domains there is (or should be) no "you have to accept ...". Compared to members of some older-established academic disciplines, linguists perhaps tend too readily to believe "all the books these days say *X*, so *X* must be right". All the books can be wrong. In connection with grammaticality many linguistics books, we believe, are wrong.

Chapter 13
Linguistics empirical and unempirical

13.1 What went wrong?

This book has been arguing that, over the past half-century, many linguists have been taking for granted a fundamentally misleading conception of the nature of grammatical structure. Since we are saying that the facts run counter to that conception, an obvious question is: how can so many linguists have got thing so wrong? Do they not look at the facts?

There are a range of factors relevant to the "what went wrong" question, some of which are sociological rather than strictly intellectual (cf. Sampson 2005: 189–193). But an important part of the answer is that, indeed, the linguists in question have often not been looking at the facts. Part of their intellectual mind-set has been a belief that linguistics is not and has no good reason to be an empirical subject.

13.2 Two kinds of empiricism

In embarking on a discussion of empiricism in linguistics we need to begin by making the point that there are two facets to the scientific concept of empiricism, which the literature of linguistics does not always distinguish. Clearly, "empiricism" is always about laying emphasis on the role of experience of the external world in the growth of knowledge. (The word derives from Greek *empeiria*, experience.) But, on one hand, the principle holds that anyone, as a child beginning to learn while still too young to understand verbal teaching, *does* as a matter of fact gain knowledge mainly by distilling it from sense-data, rather than by extracting knowledge from mental mechanisms that are built-in at birth (perhaps coded in the child's DNA). On the other hand, the empiricist principle urges that those whose social role is to generate new knowledge (e.g. scholars, scientists) *ought* to make their discourses accountable chiefly to inter-personally-observable data, rather than treating great names of the past as authoritative or relying on aprioristic argument and speculation.

These two aspects of empiricism, which we might respectively call *descriptive empiricism* and *normative empiricism*, are clearly interrelated; but they are in principle quite separable. For instance, whether or not it is likely in practice, logically it is entirely conceivable that psychologists, studying the behaviour of infants using standard scientific techniques of observation, hypothesis-testing, etc., might discover that children gain significant swathes of factual knowledge without any exposure to relevant experience (or teaching), purely as a consequence of the operation of innate cognitive equipment. If that were to happen, empiricism in the normative sense would have undermined descriptive empiricism.

Before we examine the relevance of these ideas to linguistics, we should briefly look at the alternatives to them. To many people, empiricism (whether normative or descriptive) sounds like "plain common sense", so that it is not obvious why it needs a long name ending in –ism. And, at least in the English-speaking world at most times after the Middle Ages, empiricism has indeed been the dominant intellectual attitude. But it is not the only possible attitude, and at other times and places it has not always held sway.

Arguments for and against empiricism, like many philosophical controversies, go back to the ancient Greeks. But, in the modern period, descriptive empiricism was contradicted most notably by the French philosopher René Descartes (1596–1650), who held that although a small child cannot in a straightforward sense be said to "know" many things that an experienced adult knows, nevertheless knowledge is already present within the infant, much as it is present in the adult while he is asleep. What we think of as "learning" by the child does not involve acquiring novel concepts, but merely (according to Descartes) discovering the truth or falsity of propositions built out of ideas that were implanted in the child's mind before birth, though they were initially dormant. Recent linguists have used the term "tacit knowledge" for this dormant knowledge which a person possesses without being conscious of it.

Descartes illustrated the concept of "innate ideas" using highly abstract examples, such as the idea of God or the geometrical idea of a triangle – it is relatively plausible to suggest that these cases are independent of physical experience. But he claimed that his principle applies much more widely: "all [propositions] are innate in us" (Descartes 1641: 418, our translation). This rejection of descriptive empiricism is called either *rationalism* or *nativism*. (The logic of these names is that knowledge stems not from experience but from the faculty of reason, Latin *ratio*, and that knowledge is "native", i.e. inborn, in us rather than acquired after birth.) The foundational text of modern empiricism, *An Essay Concerning Human Understanding* by John Locke (1632–1704), is believed probably to have been consciously intended as a reply to Descartes.

In the case of normative empiricism one cannot point to an influential individual, comparable to Descartes, who has systematically opposed it in modern times. Rather, the hallmark of the intellectual life of the modern period, from the seventeenth century onwards, has largely been a general acceptance of normative empiricism. In the Middle Ages, although some thinkers operated empirically, others were more interested in deducing theories about matters of fact from aprioristic principles, or in "arguments from authority" – deciding how the world must be by working out what would be most compatible with pronouncements by some great name of antiquity.[1]

13.3 Universal Grammar versus empiricism

Until the 1960s, linguists took empiricism for granted. Infants were seen as acquiring their first language by listening to the speech of their elders and imitating it (descriptive empiricism), and linguists were expected to pursue their researches by observing speakers' behaviour and using it to test the validity of linguistic theories (normative empiricism). However, Noam Chomsky disagreed with empiricist assumptions, and succeeded for many years in carrying much of the discipline with him. Chomsky's anti-empirical linguistic stance is better called "nativist" than "rationalist": he stresses the claim that much of language structure is innate in the human mind, without linking that claim to the particular mental faculty of reason. Chomsky's linguistic nativism was briefly adumbrated in his 1964 book *Current Issues in Linguistic Theory*, and was developed at length in later writings.

Chomsky's linguistics contradicts descriptive empiricism by claiming that the child's ability to master its mother tongue depends chiefly on much of the structure of language being encoded in our genetic inheritance, as our bodily structure uncontroversially is – this "innate knowledge of language" needs only the trigger of exposure to speech in order to be aroused and applied by the growing child, and the only specific features of the mother tongue which have to be learned from experience are those details which differentiate one language from another. (Chomsky, perhaps remarkably, holds that these features are fairly trivial as compared to the properties which are common to all human languages.)

Chomsky also rejects normative empiricism as a recipe for doing linguistic research. There is obviously a difference between linguistics and sciences such as, say, meteorology, or marine biology: a student of the latter is considering things which lie entirely outside himself, but an English-speaking linguist describing some aspect of the English language is discussing, among other things, features of his own cognitive functioning. This is uncontroversial; but it leads Chomsky to hold that grammatical description need not be based on objective evidence, because a native speaker can look inside his own mind and extract reliable "intuitions" about what he can and cannot say.

---

1 Arguably the extent to which leading mediaeval thinkers embraced the principle of argument from authority has been considerably exaggerated (see e.g. Hannan 2009: 216–219).

Chomsky's rejection of descriptive empiricism was revived and reinforced a generation later by Steven Pinker in his book *The Language Instinct* (1995), which made linguistic nativism accessible to an audience far wider than Chomsky's readership. Although both Chomsky and Pinker base their arguments for innate knowledge mainly on facts about language and language-acquisition, for both of them language is merely an aspect of cognition where the evidence for innateness happens to be specially clear. They believe that in other areas of cognition also, the contents of our minds are largely what our genetic endowment makes them.

This turning away from descriptive empiricism became noticeable in a variety of human sciences towards the end of the twentieth century, and was recognized (e.g. by Donald Broadbent, 1973: 189) as stemming from the influence of Chomsky's linguistics. (Many strands of late-twentieth-century academic discourse turned away from normative empiricism also, though there the influence of linguistics was probably not significant.) For Maurice Gross, reflecting on the failure of attempts to produce successful generative grammars as discussed on pp. 6–7 above, linguists' belief in rationalist psychology is seen as a response to that failure:

> G[enerative] G[rammar] could have been demonstrated to be a descriptive method far superior to all previous traditional and structural attempts. But the insistence on an experimental paradigm which depends entirely on introspection to provide the linguistic examples ... has caused the field to evolve toward some surprising philosophical speculations. Work based on sentences demonstrably acceptable to all but a few speakers ... has almost entirely vanished. Academic discussions on forms of Universal Grammar have appeared instead. (Gross 1979: 861)

Which way the cause-and-effect relationships run between rationalist belief in Universal Grammar, rejection of normative empiricism, and failure of attempts to produce adequate generative grammars, no doubt varies among various individual linguists and groups of linguists; we suspect that, for many, it may have been a prior acceptance of the Universal Grammar concept which encouraged rejection of empiricist methodology in linguistics and discouraged serious work attempting to construct concrete generative grammars answerable to real-life data. But we can agree at least that these logically-independent positions have tended in practice to reinforce one another, so that if we want to understand how an unrealistic picture of language structure has taken such hold of the discipline, it will be worth looking at the extent to which the discipline has rejected empirical methods.

13.4 Arguments against empiricism

A point worth stressing before we look further at empiricism in linguistics is that the general philosophical issue is a less-or-more rather than all-or-nothing question. Thinking of descriptive empiricism, it is obvious that the newborn child brings something important of its own to the process of gaining knowledge: a stick or stone will never know anything, no matter what external stimuli impinge on it. Conversely, not all knowledge can possibly be innate – neither of us could have known when we were born, even "tacitly", that the British or Hungarian prime ministers in 2013 would be respectively David Cameron or Viktor Orbán. Similarly for normative empiricism, while the modern scientific method expects hypotheses to be tested against objective experience, it accepts that as candidates for testing they emerge in a fairly mysterious way from the scientist's mind. And conversely, even a highly aprioristic mediaeval thinker would undoubtedly have conceded some relevance of experience to knowledge. So, when we describe someone as an empiricist (or as opposed to empiricism), what we mean is that he sees the role of experience as in some respects greater (or less) than it is deemed to be by the current consensus, or by some particular comparison group.

In those terms, Chomsky unquestionably ranks as an anti-empiricist. Although standard scientific method accepts that hypotheses depend on individual scientists' intuition, it vehemently opposes the idea that they can be relied on as veridical (as Chomsky believes in the case of native speakers' intuitions about their language). In the case of descriptive empiricism, probably no-one for centuries before Chomsky believed that children inherit knowledge of detailed language structure in the way he claims.

Since Chomsky was the first to argue against empiricism in linguistics, and other linguistic nativists have essentially developed Chomsky's thought rather than taking opposition to empiricism in additional directions, it is inevitable that an account of empiricism in recent linguistics must largely be about reactions to Chomsky's ideas.

There have been many such reactions. On the normative issue, it was argued from an early stage that introspective judgements are not a reliable guide to the way a language is spoken. People's intuitions about a given construction are often vague or contradictory, and sometimes a speaker is plain wrong about his own usage. (Remember the discussion of Philadelphian "positive *anymore*", p. 80 above.)

As for descriptive empiricism, the nativists' arguments against this are many and various (so that space does not permit a comprehensive discussion). But, for instance, we have seen that belief in innate knowledge of language is based in part on a claim that all human languages share extensive common features – *language universals* – which can only be explained as the consequence of a shared genetic inheritance. However, the strength of that argument clearly depends on how extensive the language universals are, and we saw in chapter 5 that it is questionable whether there really are any.

Another consideration which has impressed many readers as evidence against descriptive empiricism is the Genie case. "Genie" was a girl born to insane parents in California, who reared her as if she were an animal, with no exposure to speech or most other normal human experiences, until at age 13 the authorities discovered and released her, and attempted to rehabilitate her. In the years immediately following her release, Genie did not become a normally-competent speaker of English, though she acquired some language ability; nativists have claimed that this lack of success was because Genie first encountered language only after the biologically-fixed age at which a child's innate knowledge is available to be aroused. However, the linguist who originally investigated and documented this harrowing case, Susan Curtiss, at the time saw Genie as evidence against, not for, linguistic nativism (Curtiss 1977: 208–209). In later years Curtiss appears to have become converted to the nativist position, and took to writing about Genie as if the case contradicted descriptive empiricism; but, as Peter Jones (1995) points out, it is not clear what justified that *volte-face* – it cannot have been fresh evidence about Genie's development, because there was no new evidence. (To safeguard Genie's welfare the authorities forbade further scientific study.)

One reason why attacks on descriptive empiricism seemed persuasive to some in the late twentieth century was that certain empiricists had developed the principle in an extreme and strange direction. The behaviourist school of psychology founded by J. B. Watson (1878–1958) argued, in essence, that because scientific method required psychological theory to be based on observations of stimuli impinging on people and on their behaviour, rather than on subjective introspection about what might be going on within the mind, therefore patterns of linkage between stimuli and behavioural responses are all there is – "mind" is a layman's fallacy. This conflates normative with descriptive empiricism, and seems no more sensible than saying, because I can only see the keystrokes that users enter into a computer and the output appearing on screen or from the printer, that therefore the computer has no internal workings – concepts like "compiler" or "half-adder" are naive fictions. One of the earliest writings that brought Chomsky to public attention was a slashing review in 1959 of a behaviourist account of language (Skinner 1957). If empiricism were identified with behaviourism it would certainly be natural for linguists to reject empiricism. However, behaviourism is a crude distortion of empiricism rather than a typical version of it. Locke would have given behaviourism short shrift.

13.5 How empirical should linguistics be?

Let us be clear about how far we believe linguistics *should* be empirical. We wrote, above, about linguistic statements being accountable to interpersonally-observable evidence whenever in principle they can be; but not all aspects of linguistics can be empirical.

In the first place, in linguistics as in other sciences, analysis of methodological or mathematical underpinnings will not normally consist of testable statements about observations. But also, unlike physics, linguistics straddles the humanities/science borderline, and because of this borderline status there are valid areas of linguistics where empirical scientific method does not apply. Literary stylistics might be one example, and word semantics another (on the latter case, see Sampson (2001: chapter 11)).

On the other hand, in the study of syntax, in particular, it is perfectly possible to take a statement that sentence *A* is grammatical and sentence *B* is ungrammatical as a prediction that someone observing naturally-occurring language behaviour might hear an utterance of *A* but will not hear an utterance of *B* – so that an observation of *B* would call for the grammar to be reformulated (unless the observation can be explained away by some special factor, for instance a linguistics lecturer quoting an example of ungrammaticality). We know that people can alternatively interpret these statements as meaning something like "As a speaker I find that sentence *A* gives me a feeling of rightness, while *B* gives me a feeling of oddity or wrongness"; and many linguists have quite explicitly placed that kind of interpretation on statements about grammaticality, so that the statements cannot in principle be refuted by observation. Nothing we observe can show that you do not have the feeling you say you have. We are assuming that, in the large areas of linguistics for which rival interpretations like these are available, people who care about advancing human knowledge should choose the former interpretation, not the latter. In the next section we shall consider just how badly things can go wrong, if that normative assumption is rejected.

13.6 How intuition has led linguists astray

One consequence of the availability of computing technology is that nativist beliefs which for years were accepted because they sounded plausible are now being objectively tested, and often refuted. In chapter 4 (p. 81) we looked at a straightforward case (the case relating to prefixed verbs, such as *overindulge* or *reaffirm*). Now, let us turn to a subtler case.

The nativist doctrine of *poverty of the stimulus* asserts that children regularly acquire grammar rules for which the speech they hear includes no evidence. This is the central argument that is claimed to establish the reality of innate knowledge of language. Nativist linguists' standard example relates to the rule for forming yes/no questions in English, which is done by modifying the verb of the corresponding statement (either moving it to the front, or adding an auxiliary verb and moving that to the front). The issue for which the average child's evidence is allegedly deficient concerns which verb is affected, if a question contains subordinate as well as main clauses. How does the child discover that the rule is "structure-dependent", that is, that the verb to be marked as interrogative is identified by its position within the grammatical tree structure (the verb of the main clause), rather than by its sequential position – how does the child know that the rule is not, say, "make the *first* verb interrogative"?

This could well be the single most frequently-considered grammatical phenomenon in all of modern theoretical linguistics. Geoffrey Pullum and Barbara Scholz (2002: 39) cite eight places where it is discussed by Noam Chomsky, at dates ranging from 1965 to 1988, and they give a (non-exhaustive) list of eight examples of other linguists who have discussed it in publications at different dates in the 1990s. Discussion has continued in the new century.

In order to establish empirically that the English question rule is "structure-dependent" (as it in fact is), a child would need to hear a particular type of question uttered. The linguists quoted by Pullum and Scholz define the relevant structure as a yes/no question corresponding to a statement in which there is a subordinate clause preceding the verb of the main clause. An example would be the question *Since we're here, can we get some coffee?*, corresponding to the statement *Since we're here, we can get some coffee* – the *Since* clause precedes the main verb *can*. Hearing such a question, from a mature speaker, shows that the rule cannot be "make the first verb interrogative" (because that rule would give the odd-sounding *Are since we here, we can get some coffee?*). But linguist after linguist had claimed that questions of the relevant type are vanishingly rare – without checking the data of real-life usage. According to Noam Chomsky, that question-type "rarely arise[s] ... you can go over a vast amount of data of experience without ever finding such a case" (Piattelli-Palmarini 1980: 114–115); the belief that each child encounters relevant evidence "strains credulity" (Chomsky 1976: 213).

One may wonder at the confident tone of these assertions (Pullum and Scholz express scepticism), but when they were made, in the 1970s, they would probably have been difficult or impossible for a sceptic to test. However, in 1995 the British National Corpus was published, containing among other material some four million transcribed words of casual, spontaneous speech by a cross-section of the British population; and this turns out to include plenty of relevant examples. Using the British National Corpus, Sampson (2002) calculated that an average rate at which one will hear the forms at issue must be at least once every few days. In this and other ways, empirical linguistic research is suggesting that the language data available to a child are far less "impoverished" than nativists have supposed.[2]

Indeed, the facts that emerged from the British National Corpus were subtler and more interesting than explained so far. Nativist linguists defined the class of questions which they alleged to be rare in the way we have defined it above, and the logic of their argument for innate knowledge of grammar depended on all questions of that class being vanishingly rare. However, the particular instances they quoted were always drawn from one special case of that class, where the subordinate clause preceding the main verb is part of the subject – for instance *Will those who are coming raise their hands?* (corresponding to the statement *Those who are coming will raise their hands*, in which the relative clause *who are coming* modifies *Those*). They never discussed cases like *Since we're here, can we get some coffee?* (where the subordinate clause functions as an adjunct to the main clause rather than as part of its subject), though this type of structure equally fits the generativists' definition of the allegedly rare class of questions, and serves equally well to establish that the question-forming rule is structure-dependent. It turned out that, in spontaneous spoken English, questions of the special kind are indeed systematically absent – although they are common in written English, and questions belonging to the wider class defined by generative linguists, but not to this narrower class, are common even in spontaneous speech. (Sampson 2005: 83–87 offers explanations for the non-occurrence of the special-case questions in spontaneous speech, by reference to considerations having nothing to do with innate knowledge.)

In other words, on a grammaticality issue which lies at the heart of a leading attempt to make language shed light on human nature, the nativist linguists shared one intuition – the relevant questions are all vanishingly rare – while we, and Pullum and Scholz, shared a different intuition – all these questions

---

2 Incidentally, there is more than one reason to think that children would not need exposure to these forms (or innate knowledge, either) in order to master the correct version of the question-forming rule: see Sampson (2005: 88, 141–158), and J. Lewis and Elman (2001), quoted by Scholz and Pullum (2006). But that is a side issue here; what matters in the present context is that, if children did need to hear the forms, they will hear plenty of them.

are perfectly normal; and empirical evidence showed that we were *all* quite wrong.[3]

(If these are the facts of usage, for us there is no separate issue to be addressed about whether either or both types of question are "grammatical". What Chomsky's, or Pullum's, position on that would be is for them rather than us to say.)

In view of cases like this, or the case about prefixed verbs discussed in chapter 4, it is not clear to us how anyone can suppose that intuition is a reliable source of data for linguistics (or any other science).

13.7 Were our intuitions correct after all?

We should in fairness add that, in his response to our "target article" discussed in chapter 5, Geoffrey Pullum has claimed (2007: 44–45) that we are wrong to say that the "special case" questions, such as *Will those who are coming raise their hands?*, never occur in spontaneous speech. Pullum quotes three instances he has encountered, one in a passage of dialogue quoted in a *Wall Street Journal* story, and two in extempore talk on the BBC World Service.

We are not sure how robust the *Wall Street Journal* example is: while journalists on responsible newspapers are careful not to distort the sense of what is said orally by interviewees, it is normal for them to tidy up dysfluencies and the like, in ways that do not affect the content of what is said but might make a large difference from the point of view of a grammar theorist. However, we

---

3 Cedric Boeckx (2006a: 25–26) is aware that we have refuted the earlier claim that questions of the relevant type fail to occur in a typical child's experience; he shifts the argument by claiming that they do not occur *often enough* to allow the child to infer the rule. We do not understand, in the first place, why a child should need a *lot* of examples. (We know that reorganization of a child's lexical knowledge can be triggered by hearing a single example (G. Miller and Gildea [1987] 1991: 151) – why should it be so very different for grammar?) More important, Boeckx's claim that the relevant question types are very rare in the CHILDES Corpus of child speech appears, arbitrarily, to count only the "special case" questions referred to above. Although Boeckx cites us, he ignores our finding that the wider class of relevant questions are actually quite common in the kind of conversational speech which children hear. Yet, as we had pointed out, any of these examples suffice to establish the structure-dependence of the question rule. It sometimes seems as though generative linguists are so sure that their intuitions about language are reliable that they are unable to hear counter-evidence. In his discussion of the question-formation rule, Boeckx asserts bluntly that "nobody makes mistakes like [**Is Mary will believe that Frank here?*]" Yet in our own discussions of this issue, including the book cited by Boeckx (Sampson 2005: 87), we have repeatedly given a verbatim quotation, complete with date and place, of an adult English native speaker making just such a mistake.

must clearly accept the BBC World Service examples as verbatim transcriptions by Pullum.

The conclusion we drew from our British National Corpus findings (Sampson 2005: 79–88) was that written and spontaneous spoken English differ systematically in their toleration of "special case" questions (and that this fact underlies the erroneous belief of many generative linguists that they never occur at all). We are not sure that this conclusion is incompatible with Pullum's observation of between one and three spoken examples. We are not familiar with languages that are well known for having systematic grammatical differences between spoken and written registers (Czech and Arabic are sometimes cited as examples), but we surmise that characteristically-written constructions might occasionally show up in speech, though far less frequently than they do in writing. (Do French speakers not occasionally use the *passé simple* rather than the *passé composé*, if only to paraphrase written prose orally?)

However, if the truth is that "special case" questions are reasonably frequent even in spontaneous spoken English, and our British National Corpus search missed them because of some technical oversight (which could easily have happened), then we would have been wrong to say that our own prior intuitions had been mistaken on this particular point, but all the more correct about the wrongness of nativist linguists' intuitions. (And our refutation of the nativist argument for innate linguistic knowledge would be stronger, also.)

Whether or not our intuitions happened to be correct in this case, though, we do not believe that our own or any other speakers' intuitions about grammar are reliable enough to treat as scientific data.

That does not mean, certainly, that introspection has no place in linguistics. Our opponents sometimes urge, as if it were an argument against linguists who think as we do, that even the most well-established and respectable sciences make heavy use of intuition. Of course that is true: just heaping up more and more observations will never, in itself, yield a theory to account for the observations, in any domain. But, as Patrick Hanks has recently put it, with admirable incisiveness (Hanks 2013: 20):

> There is a huge difference between consulting one's intutions to *explain* data and consulting one's intutions to *invent* data. Every scientist engages in introspection to explain data. No reputable scientist (outside linguistics) invents data in order to explain it. It used to be thought that linguistics is special – that an exception could be made in the case of linguistics – but comparing the examples invented by linguists with the actual usage found in corpora shows that this is not justifiable.

13.8 Can intuitions be empirical?

One possible response to what we have said in the preceding sections would be to suggest that we have overstated the extent to which the generative approach to linguistics is in fact non-empirical. A number of respondents to our "target article" took that line. They did not deny that generative linguistics bases itself on intuitive data, but they argued that linguists have become more sophisticated than they used to be about resolving the tension between empirical method, and use of speaker intuitions as data. For instance, several respondents independently drew attention to Carson Schütze's book *The Empirical Basis of Linguistics* (Schütze 1996), seen by Kepser and Reis (2005: 2) as an "important turning point" for the discipline in this respect.

This is really a separate issue from the central topic of this book, i.e. the question whether grammaticality is a meaningful concept for human language; so we set it aside in our "replies to critics" chapter (chapter 5). But, in our experience, discussions of the validity of the "grammaticality" concept very regularly seem to morph into discussions of whether intuitions can be treated as empirical data. Our 2007 target article was intended to be about the former issue, but many of those who responded insisted on discussing mainly the latter issue. So we must inevitably address the latter issue in the present book, and this is the appropriate place to do that.

We agree that Schütze's book was an interesting one, which took seriously questions about the evidential basis of generative linguistics that had scarcely been considered earlier. It was a step in the right direction – but only a step. It certainly did not amount to a demonstration that generative linguistics as standardly practised is an empirical science (which it is not).

At one point (1996: 48–52), Schütze discussed the psychologist Wilhelm Wundt's use of introspective techniques,[4] which Schütze saw as methodologically unacceptable, but Schütze then argued that generative linguists' use of speakers' "intuitions" is not a form of "introspection". After reading this passage several times, when Schütze's book appeared and again since, we cannot understand it. "Intuition" (as that word is used in generative linguistics) and "introspection" seem to be just two names for the same thing, and that thing is a phenomenon that is essentially private rather than intersubjective.

Of course, people's *reports* of their linguistic intuitions or introspections are themselves interpersonally observable data, and it would be possible to construct empirical descriptions of those reports; Schütze (1996: 4) notes that many

---

4 We understand that there is debate about how far it is fair to describe Wundt's psychology as "introspectionist"; we are not qualified to take part in that debate, which is a side issue in the present context.

writers have suggested that that is in effect what generative linguists do, though they claim to be doing something else. The writers Schütze refers to are correct, in our view.

A defender of the use of intuitive data might say: suppose we find some set of techniques for gathering and systematizing speakers' grammaticality judgements that is shown experimentally to make predictions about usage which coincide perfectly, within the limits of experiment, with what speakers are observed to utter and not to utter in spontaneous conversation – would an empirical scientist still be obliged to avoid drawing on the intuitive data in constructing language descriptions? No, in those hypothetical circumstances it would clearly be sensible for the empirical scientist to draw on intuitions as a convenient short-cut towards formulating adequate language descriptions.

But notice, in the first place, that the experimental findings would have to overcome quite a high hurdle before this became appropriate. The first objection that sceptics tend to make to data about speaker intuitions is that they seem chaotic, or even contradictory (in so far as it is meaningful to think of one person's private feeling as "contradicting" someone else's private feeling). So it might seem that the problem with intuitive data would be solved if we could find techniques for eliciting consistent, systematic intuitions; and defenders of intuition-based linguistics often claim nowadays that such techniques are available, citing publications such as Cowart (1997), Kepser and Reis (2005), and other items listed by Arppe and Järvikivi (2007: 103) to show that grammaticality judgements are open to empirical study, exhibit stability rather than unsystematic fluctuation, and so forth.

But (as already said in chapter 4), the fact that sophisticated techniques may succeed in identifying systematic patterns of intuition underlying apparent chaos is not in itself an adequate reason for treating the systematic patterns as a reliable guide to the true structure of the speakers' language. Factors which cause a person's linguistic intuitions to fail to reflect his language behaviour may themselves be systematic – they often are. For instance, many people's intuitions about "their language" are heavily though unconsciously influenced by the properties actually possessed by another dialect, or even a separate language, which happens to have higher prestige. At a period when the study of Latin was a core element of British education, many English speakers sincerely believed that their use of English had various properties which no form of English actually possesses, but Latin does possess.

So, before it became reasonable for empirical scientists to use intuitive linguistic data as short-cuts, they would need to establish that these data could not merely be systematized but that this could be done in a way that reflected the speakers' own usage rather than any interfering factors – this would be difficult to achieve. Extraneous factors may influence different individuals in the same way. In his response to the "target article", Thomas Hoffmann misses this point, writing "if it can be shown that judgments elicited via carefully constructed experiments are in fact intra- and inter-subject consistent ... then it is much more plausible to assume that this is due to speakers sharing aspects of their mental grammars (Hoffmann 2007: 92). And Schütze came close to embracing the same fallacy when he wrote (1996: 77) "empirical facts are useful (and interesting) if they are systematic, because they must tell us something about the minds of the subjects who produce them."

Moreover, even if the hurdle could be surmounted, the empirical linguist would need to remain alert to the possibility that the experimentally-established match between systematically-elicited intuitions and observed usage might break down in circumstances that the original experiments did not control for (one can never control for *everything*). Perhaps the intuitions can be shown to coincide with real usage across the range of normal circumstances in university research, but it might later turn out, say, that in some commercial environment, where speakers are routinely subject to pressures not commonly found in academic settings, their reported intuitions would turn out to diverge from their actual usage – if so, the empirical scientist must forget the intuitions and base his description on observed usage. In the long run, it might be simpler to use observable data from the start.

Judgements about language, and language itself, are unquestionably related topics, but the relationship is complicated and not well understood. It is certainly not direct.

Our "target article" said that if we have a language-description based on empirical data, then an intuition-based description would be redundant. Thomas Hoffmann (2007: 93) objects that when two people witness a crime, the police do not take just one of their statements. That is a false analogy: the two witnesses are logically equivalent in status. A better analogy is that, if we have used a ruler to measure the precise length of a line, we shall not be interested in asking a person to estimate its length by eye.

Readers should bear in mind that these are not just fine-drawn philosophical considerations which the practical working generative linguist can afford to ignore. We have looked at specific, concrete examples of erroneous theoretical conclusions which have been held widely, and which depend for their plausibility on the assumption that speakers', or linguists', intuitions are veridical. These included an issue which is crucial to what is claimed as the leading "discovery" of generative linguistics (the idea that language structure is largely innate in our species).

13.9 Is our characterization of generative linguistics misleading?

We have argued, contrary to some of the respondents to the "target article", that it is not clear that a version of linguistics which makes heavy use of intuitive data *could* be an empirical science. But the further point is that, whether or not writers such as Schütze have succeeded in showing that such a version of linguistics could in principle be empirical, generative linguistics in practice is not empirical. Arppe and Järvikivi (2007: 104) say that it is a "mischarac-terization" to describe generative linguistics as "inherently an intuition-based scientific enterprise"; but the description is accurate. Of course, in a worldwide activity as loosely organized as academic research, one will always be able to find isolated exceptions to any generalization – and one cannot specify a rigid partitioning of a subject into separate schools, enabling one to describe *A* as a "true generative linguist" while *B*, who writes in a more empirical style, is, say, a "cognitive linguist rather than a generative linguist". Such categories are always blurry at the edges. But the generative paradigm which has dominated linguis-tics for half a century has been overwhelmingly intuition-based.

Notice that the very earliest of the publications which Thomas Hoffmann, and Arppe and Järvikivi, list as identifying ways in which empirical method might be reconciled with intuitive data are Schütze (1996) and Ellen Bard et al. (1996). By 1996, generative linguistics had been the dominant paradigm in the subject for a full generation. (When *Syntactic Structures* (Chomsky 1957) appeared, the average linguist probably saw it as a possibly interesting but idiosyncratic approach to the subject, but eight years later it seems fair to say that *Aspects of the Theory of Syntax* (Chomsky 1965) was accepted as the manifesto of the new mainstream way of doing linguistics.) During those three decades, very few generative linguists cared twopence about empiricist objec-tions to the use of intuitive data. Nelson Francis's Brown Corpus was available from 1964 on, but for decades little use was made of it. In a famous conversation of the early 1960s, R.B. Lees told Francis that compiling the Brown Corpus was "a complete waste of . . . time" because as a native speaker "in ten minutes you can produce more illustrations of any point in English grammar than you will find in many millions of words of random text" (quoted by Biber and Finegan 1991: 204).

And even if the challenging, experimental-psychology-inspired protocols for systematizing data elicitation that writers such as Schütze have begun to recom-mend could be accepted as removing the methodological objections to using introspective data, is there any realistic likelihood that linguists loyal to the Chomskyan, generative approach would decide in large numbers to adopt them? That is hard to believe. Kepser and Reis may see Schütze's book as an "important turning point", but although the book won respect, and may well have helped to encourage the flourishing of corpus-based research which began at about that time, it did not seem to lead to much change in the way that generative linguists use intuitive data. Tom Wasow and Jernnifer Arnold (2005), also cited approvingly by Arppe and Järvikivi, do not think it did:

> the findings of the experimentalists in linguistics very rarely play a role in the work of generative grammarians. Rather, theory development tends to follow its own course, tested only by the unreliable and sometimes malleable intuitions of the theorists themselves.

If a discipline has relied on unreliable data for several decades, it is not enough to adopt a superior methodology for future research. One has to accept that the findings from the period are suspect, so that a great deal of existing work needs to be redone.

Linguistics will not move forward healthily until the generative approach is bypassed, with its remaining practitioners retiring from academic life and new recruits to the discipline ignoring its ethos, assumptions, and alleged results. But happily, that does now seem to be happening. In the remainder of this chapter, we look at evidence that recent linguistics has been reverting to the methodological norms of empirical science.

13.10 New possibilities

The computer has made a large concrete difference to the outlook for empiricist linguistics: the availability of computers has enlarged the range of issues which can be empirically checked. In the 1950s, linguistics focused mainly on phonology, which typically involves a few dozen phonemes combining in limited ways, so one could expect to encounter all possibilities within a reasonable time. When attention shifted in the late 1960s to syntax, where many thousands of words can be assembled into effectively innumerable combinations, it was less practical to check whether particular sequences occur simply by listening out for them. As a result, basing syntactic theory on native-speaker introspection was appealing. However, electronic corpora – large samples of real-life language usage – are now commonplace, and these can quickly be searched to answer questions which would take too long to resolve by manual methods.

The present co-authors have spent much of their careers working with language corpora, so we are very conscious of the practical possibilities and virtues of this research style. We wanted to discover how far linguistics as a whole has embraced the logic of empiricism. In our formative years in the discipline, there is no doubt that the linguists seen by the public as representatives of the field were overwhelmingly the breed described by Maurice Gross (p. 240) as happy to rely on subjective judgements of introspection. We had the impression that things have begun to change; but, while such a change might be detectable to discipline insiders, the outside world is as yet barely aware of it. How far has the change really proceeded? The remainder of this chapter sets out to discover the answer to that question.

13.11 The Hirschberg survey of computational linguistics

To check how far the discipline has actually moved, we carried out a publication survey. Shortly after we first looked at this (for the present book we have brought the survey up to date), we discovered that for our own special subfield of computational linguistics or natural language processing (these alternative phrases are used essentially for the same area of research, by people whose wider subject affiliation is to linguistics or to computing respectively) this kind of survey had already been done, by Julia Hirschberg (1998). Her talk has not been published, but salient points are repeated in various publications by others, for instance Cardie and Mooney (1999). As stated by Cardie and Mooney, Hirschfeld's findings were striking (see Figure 16):

> a full 63.5% of the papers in the Proceedings of the Annual Meeting of the Association for Computational Linguistics and 47.4% of the papers in the journal *Computational Linguistics* concerned corpus-based research in 1997. For comparison, 1983 was the last year in which there were no such papers and the percentages in 1990 were still only 12.8% and 15.4%.

The flat section at the left-hand side of Figure 16 possibly misrepresents Hirschberg: the words "1983 was the last year" seems to imply other zero years before 1983, but these may perhaps have been interspersed with years that did see a few corpus-based papers published. Nevertheless the broad picture is clear, and it matches our anecdotal impressions very well. In 2004 GRS and Diana McCarthy edited an anthology of leading contributions to corpus linguistics, arranged by date, and (even though very few of the selections in Sampson and McCarthy (2004) were drawn from the sources used by Hirschberg, as it happens) this showed a pattern, not anticipated when we embarked on that editorial task, of a sparse trickle of corpus-based work up to 1990, and then a sudden explosion. Lillian Lee's comment (Lee 2000: 177) on the same findings was "Nowadays, the revolution has become the establishment".

But that was computational linguistics, which could well be a special case. Many researchers contributing to Association of Computational Linguistics meetings or to the journal *Computational Linguistics* work in computer science rather

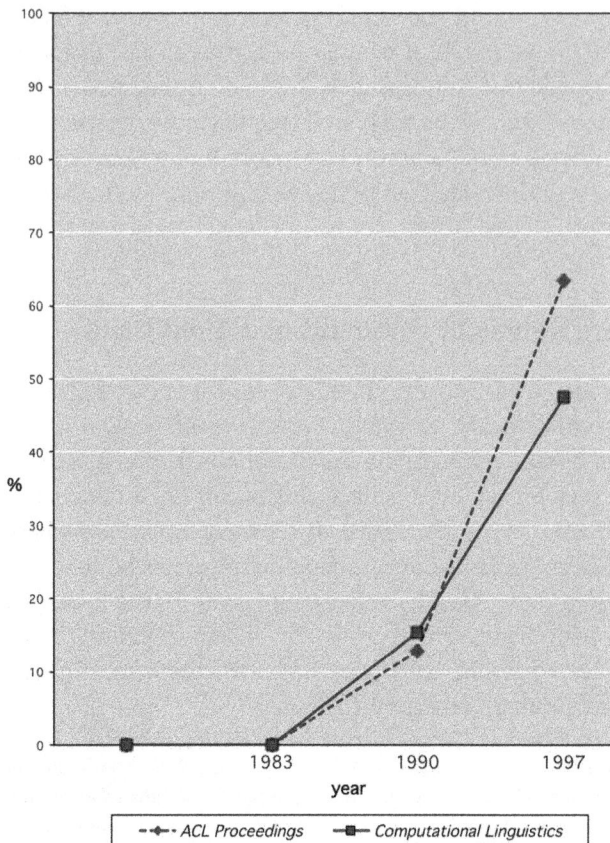

Figure 16: Corpus-based computational linguistics papers (after Hirschberg 1998)

than linguistics departments, and these have a very different "culture" of methodological assumptions. For one thing, computer scientists, even if they work on
natural language processing, are not much influenced by linguistic discussion
of "competence versus performance". If researchers come to natural language
from a computing rather than linguistic background, they may never have
encountered these concepts. Even if they are aware of them, the ethos of computer science encourages a focus on practical systems that have or lead to
potential applications in real-life circumstances, rather than on abstract theoretical study of human psychological mechanisms. Much research on natural
language processing is best classified as engineering. We wanted to look at how
things have moved in general linguistics as a pure science.

13.12 The literature sample

We therefore carried out a literature survey comparable to Julia Hirschberg's, but with a longer time depth, on the journal *Language*, which is generally recognized as the world's leading linguistics journal (see e.g. Zwaan and Nederhof 1990: 554), and which has long aimed to publish the best in the field as a whole, irrespective of particular theoretical orientations (cf. Joseph 2002: 615–616). Although *Language* belongs to an American learned society, its authors include plenty of non-American scholars.[5]

We examined the 1950 volume of *Language*, to establish a baseline well before the emergence of the concepts of linguistic competence and of native-speaker intuition as a possible basis for linguistic research, and then two out of every five volumes from 1960 up to 2011.[6] For statistical purposes we considered only articles in the normal sense, excluding reviews and review articles, "Editor's Department" pieces, and items such as reader's letters, "notes", and "miscellanea", which have been included in *Language* at different periods.

13.13 Evidence-based, intuition-based, or neutral

We assigned papers in the sampled volumes to three categories: evidence-based, intuition-based, and "not applicable" or neutral.

Papers were assigned to the neutral category for several different reasons. The question we are interested in is how far linguists have felt it appropriate to cite the authority of interpersonally-observable data rather than relying on introspection in order to support claims that might be challenged by other scholars. We have seen that some valid topics in linguistics do not purport to be empirically testable, for instance a discussion of methodology is likely to consist essentially of recommendations about how linguists ought to proceed, which cannot be "confirmed" or "falsified" by any particular factual observations.

5 An initial plan to get fuller international coverage by additionally using the British *Journal of Linguistics* had to be given up, because this journal was founded much more recently than *Language* and had very small numbers of papers in early volumes, which would have made statistics difficult to interpret.
6 Up to 1992 we took years ending in 0, 2, 5, and 7. Because some quarterly issues of the 1995 volume happened to be unavailable to us, we took four issues from the two years 1995 and 1996, and thereafter took years ending in 1, 3, 6, and 8. The earlier version of this study published in 2005 (see Acknowledgements) proved on rechecking to contain minor clerical errors in the calculations for years 1960, 1962, and 1965, which are now corrected.

That then would be one kind of paper classified as neutral; but that was not the commonest case. A different kind of case would be a paper on a topic in the history of linguistics, which is certainly empirical in the sense that linguist *A* either did or did not advance particular views in a book published at a particular date, and if anyone disputes it one can go to the library to check: but nobody suggests that native-speaker intuitions cover facts like that, so again we assigned papers on history of linguistics to the neutral category.

Apart from cases like these, though, there are also large areas of linguistic data which are in principle entirely testable, and which do relate to the kinds of issue that speakers may have introspective beliefs about, but for which one would not expect the most empirically-minded linguist to cite observational evidence, because one would not expect others to challenge those data. Suppose for instance that the data for a research paper include the genders of a range of common French nouns. It would be possible for the article to include citations of real-life utterances in which the relevant nouns are used in their respective genders, but no author would trouble to do this, because if anyone thinks the genders may be wrong it is so easy to look the words up in a dictionary.

The principle here was classically stated by Karl Popper (1968: 111):

> Science does not rest upon solid bedrock.... It is like a building erected on piles. The piles are driven down from above into the swamp, but not down to any natural or "given" base ... We simply stop when we are satisfied that the piles are firm enough to carry the structure, at least for the time being.

Empirical scientific discourse cannot quote ultimate observable authority for every datum it uses, because any premiss no matter how seemingly well-established could in principle be challenged; a scientist takes a view on which of his premisses need explicit empirical support and which can safely be taken for granted. Genders of common French nouns surely fall into the latter group, even for linguists who see the subject as accountable to observation rather than intuition; whereas, for those linguists, the grammatical acceptability of some long and unusual sequence of words is likely to fall into the former group (of data that do need support).

This meant that in doing our literature survey we had to take a view on which papers used premisses for which an empirical linguist would expect evidence to be cited, and which ones used only premisses that empirical linguists were likely to concede without cited evidence: the latter type of paper went into the neutral category, and accounted for the largest part of its contents.

We developed various rules of thumb for making these decisions consistently. For instance, papers dealing with finite linguistic subsystems, particularly phonology or morphology, were normally counted as neutral, and so were articles about Greenbergian word-order universals – word-order is an aspect of syntax, which as a whole is a non-finite system, but choices between SVO, SOV, and VSO, or between noun + adjective and adjective + noun, are finite sub-systems within syntax. Conversely, papers containing examples marked with asterisks or question marks to denote ungrammaticality or doubtful gramma-ticality were normally treated as cases to which the evidence-based versus intuition-based distinction was applicable. These rules of thumb were over-ridable in either direction – a paper which used ungrammaticality asterisks solely to mark things such as gender errors (*le voiture*) would be "neutral", while a paper on the phonology of some little-known language or dialect which did find it appropriate to cite evidence of naturally occurring utterances ob-served at particular times and places would be "evidence-based". Our rules for deciding whether the evidence-based versus intuition-based distinction was or was not applicable to a paper became more elaborate than there is space to go into here, but we must ask the reader to believe that these decisions were made in about as consistent a fashion as was reasonably possible.

13.14 How much evidence counts as "evidence-based"?

For a paper where it seemed that the distinction was applicable, there was a further issue about deciding consistently whether or not the paper should count as evidence-based. We have seen that an empirical scientist is not expected to quote observational evidence for every one of his premises, only for the ones he sees as open to challenge.

Here, our rule of thumb was that a paper which quoted observational support for at least two separate data items counted as evidence-based. The paper might also make numerous other (un)grammaticality claims without quoting evidence, but that could be a reasonable empirical strategy if the author saw those claims as less likely to be challenged. A single citation of evidence in a paper other-wised based on introspection was discounted, as when Maria-Luisa Rivero's "Referential properties of Spanish noun phrases", which includes numerous unsupported claims about (un)grammaticality and semantic anomaly of example sentences which are often long enough to spill over two lines, quotes one exam-ple from Cervantes in a footnote (Rivero 1975: 36 n. 7). There are many reasons why a linguist who sees intuition as authoritative might nevertheless choose to include a single authentic example in his paper, for instance as a rhetorical strategy to capture the reader's interest. If an author cites real-life evidence twice or more, we took this as a significant indication of a propensity to treat observation as the ultimate authority.

The threshold of two is of course arbitrary. Sometimes it forced us to count as evidence-based some paper which, overall, seemed to belong much better in the intuition-based category. Geoffrey Pullum and Deirdre Wilson's 48-page "Autonomous syntax and the analysis of auxiliaries" (1977) makes numerous unsupported and sometimes, as we saw it, quite debatable grammaticality claims (for instance it is not obvious to us that one cannot reduce *I had my servant bring in my bags* to *I'd my servant bring in my bags*, or that there is a difference in grammaticality between *Sam was being examined by a psychiatrist, and Bill was too*, and *Sam was being examined by a psychiatrist, and Bill was being too*); but then their last two examples, numbered (70) and (71), are respectively a sentence taken by Madeline Ehrman (1966: 71) from the Brown Corpus, and another sentence given them by Andrew Radford who heard it on a BBC current-affairs programme. So Pullum and Wilson (1977) had to go into the evidence-based category. Rather than using an absolute threshold figure, it might ideally have been preferable to set the threshold at some proportion of all data items quoted, but that would have required a great deal of complicated counting which would have been very hard to carry out in a consistent manner, even if we had had enough time. The division between evidence-based and intuition-based papers clearly had to rely on something solider than our subjective impressions; probably any objective criterion we could have chosen would have yielded odd decisions in some individual cases. What matters is that we used the same fixed criterion across all years.

Notice on the other hand that where observable evidence was cited, we made no distinction between cases where this was drawn from a standard corpus such as Brown or the British National Corpus, and cases where authors quoted other sources, such as overheard conversations or literary works, or for instance instrumental readings in the case of research on phonetic topics. Intersubjectively observable evidence is evidence, wherever it is found. Corpus linguists compile and work with standard corpora because they are specially convenient data sources, but there is no reason to suggest that evidence has to occur in a recognized corpus to count as evidence. In the earlier part of the period examined, authors commonly quoted literary examples and rarely or never quoted from electronic corpora, because they were familiar with the former and had no access to the latter. Until quite recently, very few people had access to representative, documented recordings of spontaneous spoken language, so it would be unreasonable to reject an observation of an overheard remark just because it is difficult for a sceptical reader to cross-check it. Such a datum was potentially intersubjectively observable; the difficulty of checking in practice just means that spontaneous spoken language was a difficult topic for empirical research until recently – which is true.

13.15 Explicit authenticity claims

A special classification problem arose with the very many cases, for instance in papers on exotic languages, where an author cited examples from earlier publications without saying whether the source publications quoted the examples from observed usage or made them up. Sometimes it is easy to guess from the nature of the examples that some were authentic and others invented. Thus, N. Evans, Brown, and Corbett (2002: 126) quote a passage in the Australian language Kunwinjku whose translation begins "The red color in the crocodile is the blood from Likanaya". Not only do they not explicitly assert that this was a real-life utterance but they do not even (so far as we can see) explain the abbreviation they give for their source; however we surmise that the example is a genuine extract from something like a native folktale, because it does not sound constructed. Conversely, when David Basilico (1996: 509) quotes from Molly Diesling a German subordinate clause *daß Otto Bücher über Wombats immer liest*, "that Otto always reads books about wombats", we feel convinced that Diesling made it up. Often, though, quoted examples could have been either authentic or invented, and chasing up all the cited publications would have taken far more time than we had available.

However, this is less of a problem than it seems, if we consider that the issue we are fundamentally concerned with is whether authors treat observation rather than introspection as the source of scientific authority. An author who assumes that observation is what matters and who quotes authentic data from an earlier publication will surely not fail to make clear that it is indeed cited as authentic, in an intellectual environment where many other linguists are using invented examples. If an author cites such data without making an explicit authenticity claim, that seems to imply that he does not see the fact of their being real-life data as specially significant. For instance, Donald Winford's paper on Caribbean English Creole syntax (Winford 1985) quotes many examples from previous researchers which to us seem to have the ring of authenticity, for instance *ah me fi aks dem if dem neva gi im no nurishment* (translated as "I was supposed to ask them if they ever gave him any nourishment"), or *mi no iebl unu tieraof mi kluoz* ("I can't risk the chance of you tearing off my clothes"); but Winford never actually asserts that these are taken from real-life usage, and he says that many other examples "are based on my own intuitions as a native speaker of Trinidadian Creole", which makes it clear that observed occurrence in natural usage is not a crucial issue for Winford.

So there was no reason for us to chase up earlier publications when classifying a paper as based on evidence or intuition. What mattered was whether the paper we were classifying itself made an authenticity claim, not whether the data were or were not in fact authentic.

Needless to say, there were plenty of marginal cases where it was hard to decide whether an authenticity claim was explicit, but again we developed rules of thumb to make such decisions consistent rather than subjective. For instance, where linguists quoted American Indian examples from transcriptions of naturally-occurring speech, it seemed that they commonly used the term "texts" to describe these records, whereas field notes of examples elicited from informants were not called texts; so we treated the term "text" in such cases as an explicit authenticity claim. (Examples produced by asking an informant "Can you say so-and-so in your language?", inviting a grammaticality judgement on an invented example, or "How do you say such-and-such in your language?", inviting a translation, are no less intuition-based than data constructed by the linguist for his own language: they merely treat the informant's intuition rather than the linguist's as the source of authority.)

13.16 Raw and smoothed counts

Figure 17 shows the year by year results of imposing this three-way classification on *Language* papers from the sample years. Each bar represents 100 per cent of that year's papers, within which the white section stands for evidence-based cases, the dotted section represents entirely intuition-based cases, and the black section represents neutral cases. Because we tried to define "not applicable" in such a way that it would include papers based on empirical premises which are too well-established to be worth challenging, it follows that the dotted sections of the bars should include papers quoting unsupported premises that many linguists might see as questionable – and they certainly do. To us it was quite surprising to find Geoffrey Huck and Younghee Na (1990) claiming without evidence that *To whom did Mary give a pie during yesterday's recess of BILLY's* is good English but that *What did Tom speak to Ann yesterday about?* is bad English, or to encounter unsupported claims by Samuel Bayer (1996) that one cannot say *I made John above suspicion* but it is all right to say *That Himmler appointed Heydrich and the implications thereof frightened many observers.* However, querying other linguists' intuitions is easy sport, and we shall not indulge it further.

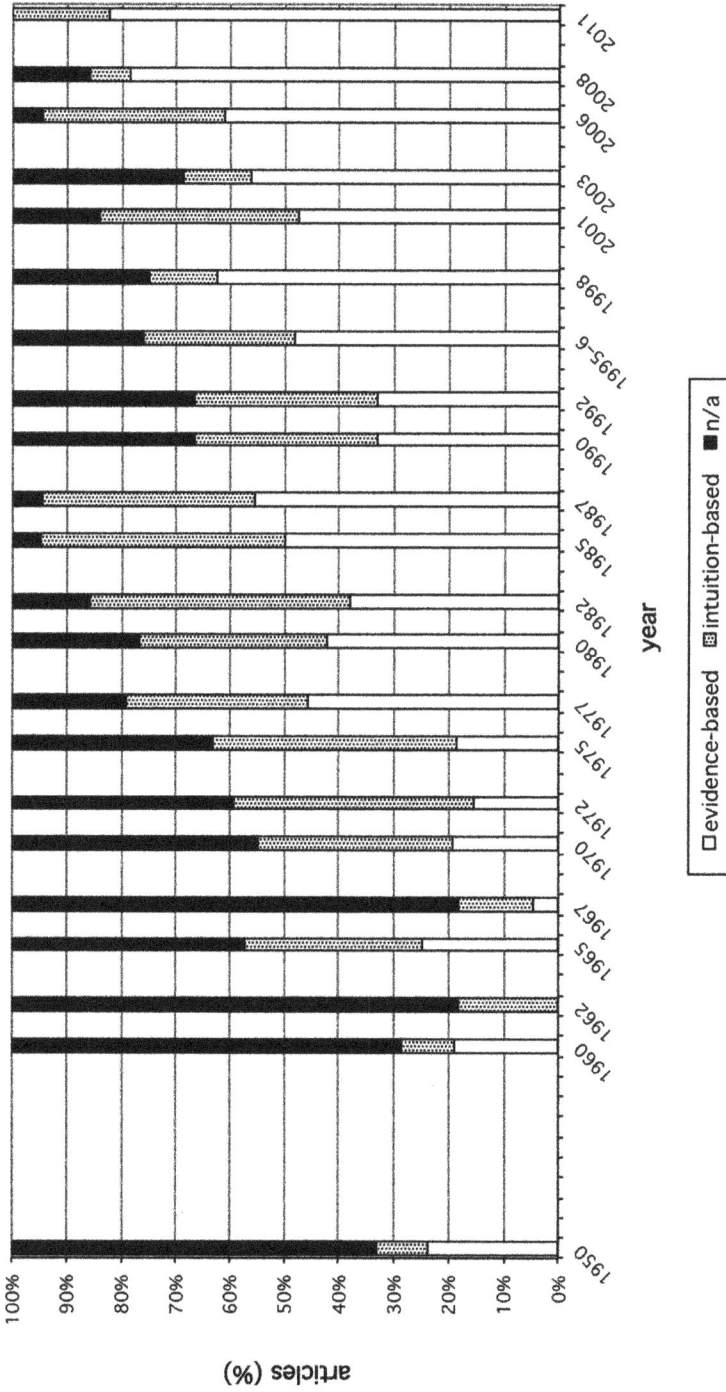

Figure 17: Raw 3-way classification of *Language* articles

The raw quantities displayed in Figure 17 are not particularly easy to interpret. Perhaps the most noticeable feature is the way that the neutral category accounts for a specially large proportion of the early samples. One way of interpreting that might be that when synchronic linguistics got under way in the twentieth century, research focused initially on "low-hanging fruit", areas where the basic data could simply be checked in standard textbooks, and the linguist's task was only to organize the data into enlightening patterns. It is well-known that (as mentioned in 13.10) research on the finite areas of phonology and morphology was in vogue in the 1950s and early 1960s, whereas syntactic research came to the fore in the later 1960s and beyond. Phonological and morphological research continues today, of course, but nowadays it is more likely to involve considerations of experimental data or other data that require effort to acquire.

Although we have explained that topics relating to finite systems were normally classified as neutral, a preponderance of these topics in the earlier years surveyed does have relevance for the question how far linguists were empirically-minded. Gathering observational data on non-finite systems like syntax was relatively difficult before computers and computer corpora became routinely available to linguists, which did not really happen until the 1980s. If a linguist is empirically-minded and cannot easily get hold of syntactic data, he will naturally be drawn to work on areas like phonology where data availability is not usually a difficulty. So the large amount of black towards the left-hand side of Figure 17 is one indirect indication that linguistics at that period tended to make empirical assumptions, and the fact that the black is greatly reduced long before the 1980s correlates with the fact that linguists came to believe that unavailability of observational data was no barrier to syntactic resarch.

The central facts, though, are represented more clearly in Figure 18, which is based on the same numerical counts as Figure 17 but reworks the display in two ways. In the first place, Figure 18 excludes the neutral papers: for each sample year the bar represents the number of evidence-based papers as a percentage of the total of evidence-based and intuition-based papers. Secondly, except for the 1950 figure which is separated from the others by a large gap in time, the individual year figures are smoothed by averaging with neighbouring figures, which is an accepted statistical technique for revealing underlying trends in an irregular series. The observation-based and intuition-based percentages for each sample year were averaged with the next earlier and later sample years (and the percentages for the first and last years of the series were smoothed by half-weighting the figures for the sole adjacent years when averaging).

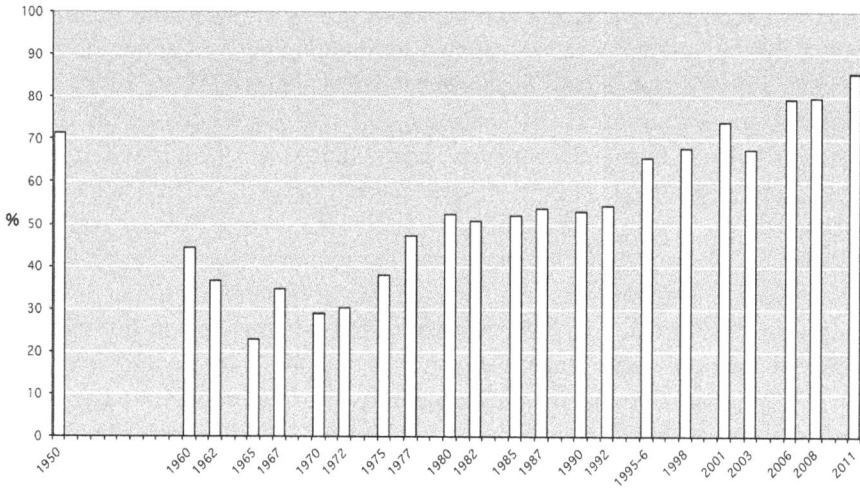

Figure 18: Evidence-based as % of non-neutral *Language* articles (smoothed)

13.17 The match between statistics and history

The main features of Figure 18 square well with our impressions of the develop-ment of linguistics over sixty years. In the first place, the 1950 figure, before the emergence of generative linguistics, shows a high proportion of observation-based papers. This was the period when Charles Fries was working on *The Structure of English* (Fries 1952) – surely entitled to be seen as the first major milestone in corpus-based linguistic science.

In fact the 1950 figure deserves detailed analysis, because it was a prob-lematic year to assess and we could have chosen an even higher observation-based figure without distorting the facts. One item that we counted as intuition-based, William E. Welmers's "Notes on two languages in the Senufo group", was published in two parts in separate journal issues – if we had treated them as two distinct papers, the bar for 1950 in Figure 18 would be lowered from 71 per cent to 63 per cent, but it seemed that inclusion of the two parts was a single editorial decision and the separate parts applied identical methodologies to two related languages, so it would be statistically misleading to count them twice. However, Welmers's descriptions were mainly concerned with phonol-ogical and morphological levels of the languages described; we counted the material as intuition-based only because it included some quite brief and

limited discussion of syntax which appeared to rely on elicitation from informants. And the other item we counted as intuition-based, Charles Hockett's
famous paper "Peiping morphophonemics", had an even better claim to be
classified as neutral: as its title suggests, it is not about syntax at all, but it
happens to begin by quoting some specimen Chinese sentences that have every
appearance of authenticity but for which Hockett made no explicit authenticity
claim, which would have been fairly irrelevant to his purpose. We wanted to play
absolutely fair, so we put this paper into the intuition-based category. On the
other hand, the papers we have counted as observation-based, for instance
Henry and Renée Kahane's "The position of the actor expression in colloquial
Mexican Spanish", and Simon Belasco's "Variations in color and length of
French [a]: a spectrographic study", are very clearly observation-based: they
deal centrally with non-finite systems and refer to abundant authentic data of
various categories. It would not be hard to argue that the 1950 bar in Figure 18
ought to be raised from 71 per cent to 100 per cent.

By the early 1960s, Figure 18 shows a falling trend; this was the time of R.B.
Lees's scathing remarks about the Brown Corpus project quoted on p. 251 above.
The lowest proportions of evidence-based papers occur in the years round 1965–
1970, which GRS remembers as the high-water period of linguistic rejection of
empiricism. After the early 1970s, the slope rises again.[7]

Skimming through these old volumes of *Language* we encountered sporadic
comments which showed the authors as having been well aware of these changing trends at the time. For instance, Charles Hockett in his Linguistic Society of
America presidential address (Hockett 1965) includes spirited comments on the
"group of Young Turks, armed with a vitally important idea and with enormous
arrogance, [who were] winning converts and making enemies as much through
charisma as by reasonable persuasion" – later in the paper Hockett names
names; while by 1975 Matthew Chen and Bill Wang argue that "it is perhaps
time for a return to an enlightened empiricism", and David S. Rood (1975: 336)
comments:

---

7 The original version of the research presented in this chapter, published in 2005, examined
the period up to 2002. At that time, in order to check that the trends appearing in the earlier
version of Figure 18 were real rather than chance fluctuations, we applied the runs test described
e.g. in Siegel and Castellan (1988: 58–64) to a sequence showing, for each of the 22 sample
years examined at that time, whether the ratio of unsmoothed counts of evidence-based to
intuition-based papers in that year was greater or less than the mean of the 22 ratios. (We
used the runs test as a one-tailed test, since we were interested only in whether runs are
specially few, not whether they are specially numerous.) The observed figure of seven runs
was significant at the ·05 level according to the criterion given by Rohlf and Sokal (1981: table
28): the variation was unlikely to be random. We have not repeated the test for the new, larger
data-set, where the trend is much clearer to the naked eye.

No serious linguist questions the importance of theory or of the search for true universals … But certainly one of the reasons for, and one of the results of, a return to data-oriented sessions at the L[inguistic] S[ociety of] A[merica] … is a recognition by most linguists that neither of these activities is valid or useful apart from consideration of what real languages do.

13.18 A rearguard action?

On the other hand, another feature of Figure 18 which we find striking is how gentle the upward rise is. Compare this slope with the cliff rearing up after 1990 in Figure 18, based on Julia Hirschberg's survey of corpus linguistics. True, linguists might observe that the computing world is notorious for chasing after whatever fashion happens to be flavour of the month, be it sensible or foolish; they might pride themselves that the more gradual shift of Figure 18 is a sign of greater maturity in linguistics. Others might hold, though, that maturity lies in fully embracing the long-established disciplines of empirical science.

Since it is computer corpora which have made it easy for syntactic research to move on from intuitive to evidence-based techniques, it is natural that computational linguistics has run ahead of general linguistics in shifting away from the anti-empiricism of the 1960s towards more scientifically respectable methods. And even if linguists had become thoroughly empirically minded, doubtless the bars of Figure 18 would still not consistently reach quite up to the 100 per cent mark. The complexities of classifying papers in these terms are so great that we are sure even in that situation a proportion of worthwhile papers would still fall into the "intuition-based" category. However, we are not sure that the numerical trend of Figure 18 implies a thoroughgoing change of mind among influential members of the discipline. Indeed, when this research was first undertaken, examining data only up to the year 2002, the numerical trend appeared to go into reverse in the mid-1990s: after a fairly steady rise from 1970 to 1996, the trend proceeded to fall at a similar rate for a few years about the turn of the century.[8] It seemed that opponents of empirical methods may have been mounting a somewhat successful rearguard action against

---

8 The right-hand side of Figure 18 here is not directly comparable with the corresponding Figure in the 2005 version of our survey: recent years were sampled on a changed basis, in order to make the treatment of the entire period since 1960 consistent, and also some years used on both occasions were re-examined for the present analysis. These points, and the smoothing which has applied to different sets of years in the new sampling, explain how the downturn from 1996 to 2002 which was very noticeable in the earlier data has become invisible in the data displayed here.

them. Anecdotal evidence supporting that would include remarks by Thomas Nunnally in his review of Rosamund Moon's corpus-based investigation of English fixed expressions, already cited in chapter 4:

> it is intuition that signals ill-formedness, not frequency of formations per million words ... [Moon's] shortchanging of native speaker understanding as evidence until a massive corpus can locate, say, five examples is worrying (Nunnally 2002: 177)

This review was the first occasion we are aware of when the corpus-based approach was explicitly attacked as positively undesirable, rather than just bypassed by generative linguists as uninteresting. But it was not the last: in 2003 Frederick Newmeyer used his Linguistic Society of America presidential address to argue against "usage-based" linguistics, urging that "There is no way that one can draw conclusions about the grammar of an individual from usage facts about communities" (Newmeyer 2003: 696).

Although there had been changes over thirty years, the virtues of empirical scientific method evidently remained less thoroughly accepted in linguistics than in other scientific disciplines.

13.19 Empiricism reasserted

However, as the 21st century proceeded, this trend-reversal turned out to be a blip. In Figure 18 we see that the rising trend is not perfectly steady (with such a complex issue, relating to a discipline on the borders of science and humanities, one could hardly expect it to be), but after smoothing it is clear that the overall rise has continued ever since the low of forty-odd years ago, without a reversal, so that the empiricism counts recently have reliably exceeded even the high figure for 1950. And again this trend was noticed by observers of the field. For instance in 2008 Brian Joseph, then editor of *Language*, wrote:

> research papers are more experimentally based now than ever before ... Also, they are more corpus-based ... referees increasingly are demanding such multiple sources of data from authors who fail to offer them ... this trend toward "cleaner" and more "natural(istic)" data is all to the good of the field (Joseph 2008: 687)

Notice that this very quotation argues against a sceptical objection that basing a survey of this kind on the contents of one journal merely demonstrates the partisan biases of that particular journal. We used *Language* alone because, with limited time available, that seemed to be the only practical way forward. But it is clear from Joseph's comments that the increase in empiricism in the material he printed reflected preferences of the authors and of the wide range of referees used by *Language*, rather than being imposed by editorial prejudice.

Our conclusion, then, is that (always assuming that the journal *Language* is adequately representative – and we believe it is), the unscientific trend which allowed numerous linguists to believe that language worked the way they wanted it to work is now rather definitely a thing of the past, among academic professionals.

That last qualification is important. Changes of mind on the part of an academic discipline take time to filter out to the wider audience of educated general readers (or even to members of neighbouring disciplines), so we believe that plenty of members of the public who take an interest in ideas about language are still heavily influenced by unempirical approaches and their "findings". In this case the general time-lag which applies to all new intellectual trends is reinforced by a powerful special factor: speculative, intuition-based theorizing makes for easier reading than discussion based on detailed empirical data. The latter will inevitably involve numerous complications and qualifications which matter, but which are tedious for non-specialists to wade through (whereas linguists who rely on intuition are free to paint their pictures in broad and simple strokes). Writings addressed by empirical linguists to wider audiences can only do so much to shield readers from those complexities, if they aim to be true to the underlying realities. On student courses, where it is not over-cynical to suggest that most hearers are far more interested in acquiring just enough knowledge to get their degree than in chasing the truth down crooked byways, the speculative style of linguistics certainly goes down far better than the empirical style. (Claude Hagège noted as long ago as 1976 how language-teachers who study some linguistics as part of their professional training find the genre of linguistics criticized here relatively accessible and hence appealing – Hagège (1976: 17 note 1); and in practice language-teachers form a chief avenue via which academic linguists' ideas about language disseminate into the wider world.)

So it is comprehensible if the general public understanding of language and its nature continues to be distorted by the unempirical style of research which came into vogue in the 1960s. But the implication of this chapter is that things are not always going to be like that. A current of opinion that is created by a novel academic trend cannot survive indefinitely unless it receives ongoing support from the survival of that trend, and unempirical linguistics is not surviving. Max Planck is one of many who have pointed out that a new scientific truth does not win acceptance by convincing opponents, but by the fact that the opponents eventually die and a new generation grows up familiar with it

(Planck 1949: 33–34). At present, unempirical linguistics is still being written and read. But it is safe to say that this is a temporary state of affairs.

We conclude, then, that the unscientific trend which, forty years ago, allowed numerous linguists to believe that language worked the way they wanted it to work, irrespective of any concrete evidence, is now rather definitely a thing of the past among academic professionals. No doubt for some time to come there will remain holdouts putting forward arguments for the value of linguistic research based exclusively on introspection, akin to the remarks quoted on p. 266 above, but history is evidently not on their side. For young entrants to the profession, a commitment to the intuition-based techniques that were recently so fashionable looks as though it could be a career-limiting move.

And we believe that "grammaticality" is one of the concepts destined to be jettisoned, as the importance of empirical methods comes to be more universally accepted among linguists.

Chapter 14
William Gladstone as linguist

14.1 Ducking an intellectual challenge

Those who resist the idea that separate cultures evolve their languages separately, and independently of any foreordained structural plan, often misunderstand claims about structural contrasts between languages as relating to something other and more superficial than different ways of conceptualizing the world. To many readers, the idea that differences between languages may in some cases correlate with differences in societies' perceptions of the world they inhabit is so alien that they may assume the writer cannot mean what he or she says in so many words, and may impose some less literal but more comfortable interpretation on the writing in question. If this happens much, an important point of view about language and cognition is rejected not because it is examined and found wanting, but because it is not entertained as a candidate for acceptance.

We have seen that many linguists have difficulty with the idea that there are deep differences between the grammars of languages; and our grammar is so fundamental an aspect of our thought-processes that it is perhaps easy to sympathize with those who assume that it must be universal. Meanings of vocabulary items, on the other hand, seem like an aspect of language structure which we know to evolve as history progresses, so one might think that the kind of misunderstanding just described would be less tempting in connexion with word-semantics. But in fact the same kind of rejection through misinterpretation happens there too.

Currently, one example of this has become the centrepiece of what is probably the most widely-read book about language of the 21st century to date. The writer being misinterpreted is the British statesman William Ewart Gladstone (1809–1898), who published a series of studies of the vocabulary of Homeric Greek (that is, the language of the *Iliad* and *Odyssey*), covering words for numbers (Gladstone 1858: vol. 3, pp. 425–456; 1869: 535–539), speed (Gladstone 1879), and in particular colour (Gladstone 1858: vol. 3, pp. 457–499; 1869: 539–541; 1877). In those writings Gladstone argued that Homer's language showed that Greeks of his time perceived or understood these fundamental aspects of reality in ways very different from modern Europeans. (In what follows, references to Gladstone (1858: vol. 3), Gladstone (1869), and Gladstone (1877) will be abbreviated as *SHHA3*, *JM*, and *CS* respectively; and Greek script in quotations will be transliterated.)

Gladstone's writings about Homer's language have received a bad press down the decades. Notably, Gladstone has repeatedly been described as believing that Greeks of the Homeric period were colour-blind: that is, rather than accepting that Gladstone thought members of another culture might mentally categorize the world differently from us, people have supposed that he must have meant that there was something physically different about their eyesight (an idea which was seen as absurd). This misinterpretation has now been used as the central plank of an outstandingly successful new book, Guy Deutscher's *Through the Language Glass* (Deutscher 2011) – a book which in some respects is more sympathetic to Gladstone's views on language than many have been. Deutscher's book is probably the most popular book about language to have appeared so far this century, being bought and read by many people with no special knowledge of linguistics.[1] Thus we must reckon with the fact that Deutscher's interpretations, if they go unchallenged, are destined to become part of received educated belief about human language and cognition. And the issue is important, not just because Deutscher's book is being so widely read, but also because of Gladstone's great eminence. Nobody can be much surprised if some minor academic working in an obscure institution puts forward original ideas which never succeed in receiving the attention they perhaps deserve. But when one of the most internationally eminent men of his time argues, and argues hard and skilfully, for a novel point of view, when his writings are widely noticed, and yet still his distinctive idea gets buried under a heap of misinterpretation, then we are forced to recognize that the weight of inertia which the idea has to overcome before it can be taken seriously is immensely heavy.

Gladstone did not believe that Homer or the Greeks of his day were colour-blind, and his linguistic contributions have been seriously undervalued. Gladstone's discussion of Homer's vocabulary would have been a worthwhile scientific contribution even if it had been made a hundred years later than its actual date; appearing when it did, it was quite remarkable. From a 21st-century vantage-point Gladstone's work did have flaws; but this is forgivable, considering that the same flaws recur in very recent published research on the same topic.

---

1 On 27 Aug 2012 Deutscher's book had the very high amazon.co.uk "Bestseller Rank" 2467. For comparison, Steven Pinker's *The Language Instinct* (which many people might see as the best-known recent popularization of linguistics) ranked lower, at 4315. (Of course Pinker's book may have ranked higher when it was as new as Deutscher's is currently.) All references to Deutscher in this chapter will be to Deutscher (2011).

This chapter will show that Gladstone meant what he said about the Homeric Greeks, and will give detailed justification for a high evaluation of Gladstone's achievement as a social scientist.[2]

It might seem that the topic of the chapter is of purely historical interest. But the tendency to reinterpret claims about cultural differences in ways that turn them into something easier to digest, or even trivialize them, is perennial. It takes a case where historical depth is available to demonstrate how successful that tendency can be at eliminating from consideration even a well-argued, widely publicized point of view put forward by an author of high prestige – and hence to help arm us against the same tendency as it applies to research today.

14.2 What Gladstone didn't say

14.2.1 The colour-blindness misinterpretation

Although the Homeric epics contain what appear to be colour words (some of which became straightforward colour words in later Greek), Gladstone noted that these occurred surprisingly infrequently, even in descriptive passages where one might expect to find colours mentioned (*SHHA3*: 477–483); and, more remarkably, that some of the apparent colour words which do occur are attributed to ranges of things which no present-day European would see as sharing

---

2 Certain related issues will not be covered here. Gladstone wrote not just about Homer's vocabulary but, in his three-volume 1858 work *Studies on Homer and the Homeric Age* and in various later contributions, about many other aspects of the Homeric world, some of which had nothing to do with language (e.g. an attempt to reconstruct the geography of the *Odyssey*, *SHHA3*, 249–365), while others perhaps verged on language but related more to early Greek psychology (e.g. their concept of beauty, *SHHA3*, 397–424; *JM*, 516–519). We shall not touch on these aspects of Gladstone's work. (We feel quite sceptical about the value of Gladstone's attempt to link mythical sections of the *Odyssey* to real locations, but this does not reduce our respect for Gladstone as a linguist.)

Also, there has been longstanding controversy about whether "Homer" was a single individual; and if he was, the legend had it that he was blind (really blind, not colour-blind). It is unnecessary to enter into these issues here. The *Iliad* and *Odyssey* are what they are; they include plenty of visual description, so evidently sighted individual(s) were heavily involved in their composition, whether or not they were edited into final form by one man and whether or not, if so, that man was himself sighted. It is convenient to use "Homer" as shorthand for "whatever Greek or Greeks composed the *Iliad* and *Odyssey*", and "Homeric Greeks" for "Greeks of the period described in those poems, and/or the (perhaps considerably later) period when they were composed"; nothing more specific will be implied by these terms here.

a common colour (*SHHA3*: 461). For instance the adjective *porphyreos*, which in later Greek meant approximately "purple" or "dark red", is applied to the following natural objects: blood, dark cloud, wave of a river when disturbed, wave of the sea, disturbed sea, and rainbow (as well as to things such as garments, which might be of various colours, and metaphorically to bloody death). The cognate verb *porphyrō* is applied to the sea darkening (and to the mind brooding); and the compound adjective *haliporphyros*, "sea-*porphyreos*", is applied to wool.

From a modern European perspective it seems impossible to link the red of blood and the blue or green of the sea as shades of one colour; and since "The art … of dyeing was almost … unknown" to the Homeric Greeks (*SHHA3*: 480), it seems likely that coloured wool was naturally-brown wool, so that again it is paradoxical to find its colour described by a word which compares it to the sea. Yet this is not merely a matter of eccentric usage conventions for a particular word (as the English conventionally use the word "pink" for the scarlet coat of a huntsman, which is by no means pink in the normal use of that word). A stock Homeric epithet for the sea is *oinops* "wine-looking" (in English translations often rendered "wine-dark"); evidently red wine really was seen as sharing an important visual property with blue or green sea.

Gladstone's proposed solution to these paradoxes was that Homer's visual vocabulary referred mainly to contrasts of light versus dark, and only to a minor extent to contrasts of hue (i.e. position in the rainbow spectrum from red to violet): "Homer's perceptions of the prismatic colours, or colours of the rainbow, … were, as a general rule, vague and indeterminate" (*SHHA3*: 483); "Homer seems to have had … principally, a system in lieu of colour, founded upon light and upon darkness" (*SHHA3*: 488); "the Homeric colours are really the modes and forms of light … and … darkness: partially affected perhaps by ideas drawn from the metals, like the ruddiness of copper … and here and there with an inceptive effort, as it were, to get hold of other ideas of colour" (*SHHA3*: 489). Thus *porphyreos* for Homer seemed to Gladstone (*SHHA3*: 486) to mean essentially "dark" rather than referring to any particular hue; on the other hand *xanthos*, for instance, did already for Homer appear to refer to a yellow hue, being applied to human hair and to horses – a head of blond hair and a bay horse are closer in hue than in lightness.

Again and again this idea of Gladstone's has been interpreted as a claim that Homeric Greeks were colour-blind. That interpretation began to be expressed soon after the publication of *CS*, which appeared in a magazine whose readership will have been far wider than that of *Studies on Homer*, at a time when Gladstone had become much more famous than when that book was published. Thus, Grant Allen, objecting in 1879 to Gladstone's theory and the related ideas of the German ophthalmologist and historian of medicine Hugo Magnus (to be discussed further below), asserted that "the main points of their hypothesis" began with "an absolute blindness to colour in the primitive man" (Allen [1879] 1892: 202–203); Allen went on to object, correctly, that the development of a new sense over just three thousand years is unacceptable in terms of biological evolution. An unsigned article in the *British Medical Journal* discussed a Danish paper about colour-blindness published in 1880, saying "The author ... quotes frequently ... from the writings of Holmgren, Gladstone, ... and others, who have investigated it" (*British Medical Journal* 1881). Even the popular press contained attributions of this view to Gladstone; writing in *Popular Science Monthly*, William Eddy (1879) explained that "Mr. Gladstone ... does not maintain that everybody in Homer's time was color-blind. He simply [claims] that, we will say, where one person is color-blind now, nine were color-blind then."

(Not everyone at the time read Gladstone this way. William Pole (1878), who was colour-blind himself, believed that Gladstone *failed* to appreciate that his data on Homer's colour vocabulary suggested colour-blindness.)

In recent times the same interpretation has recurred too frequently for a comprehensive survey. The art historian John Gage (2000: 12) discusses "Gladstone's belief in the colour-blindness of the Ancient Greeks". Barry Cole (2003) states in an optometry textbook that Gladstone "concluded they [the Greeks] had defective colour vision". Jordanna Bailkin (2005) in a paper about the history of labour relations claims that Gladstone "argue[d] that Homer and his contemporaries had been effectively color blind". And now Guy Deutscher tells us that Gladstone "argued that Homer and his contemporaries perceived the world in something closer to black and white than to full Technicolor" (Deutscher: 30; spelling of trade name corrected); "what Gladstone was proposing was nothing less than universal colour blindness among the ancient Greeks" (p. 37).

14.2.2 Correcting the misunderstanding

In fact, Gladstone was not saying that the Homeric Greeks were colour-blind. After asking whether the odd use of colour terms can be explained in terms of the legend of Homer's blindness, Gladstone went on to ask "Are we to suppose a defect in his organization, or in that of his countrymen?"; his answer to both questions was no (*SHHA3*: 483–484). "[We are not] to suppose that ... he bore, in the particular point, a crippled nature; but rather we are to learn that the perceptions so easy and familiar to us are the results of a slow traditionary growth in knowledge and in the training of the human organ" (*SHHA3*: 495–

496). In his 1877 article Gladstone summarized his ideas about Homer's colour sense in a pair of propositions, and immediately added "I rejected the supposition, that this was due to any defect in his individual organisation" (*CS*: 366); by contrast, "Colour-blindness proper ... appears to partake of the nature of organic defect" (*CS*: 367).

In his 1879 paper Gladstone discussed Homer's vocabulary for visible movement, and again noticed a difference from present-day languages in that Homer's vocabulary is rich in words for different types of rapid movement but barren in words for slow movement; "I do not recollect that [Homer] anywhere distinguishes majestic and stately movement from such as is merely slow" (Gladstone 1879: 463). This discussion is explicitly introduced by Gladstone as an extension of his earlier work on Homer's colour vocabulary: "It is a matter of interest to consider as kindred topics the manner in which [Homer] appreciated other visual phenomena, such as those of form and movement" (ibid.). This would make no sense if the material on colour were intended to refer to colour-blindness, because there is no analogous physical condition that prevents a sighted person distinguishing between fast and slow motion. The contrast between a stately progress and a torpid crawl is a conceptual distinction, which depends largely on matters such as the inferred motives or causes of slowness; drawing the distinction does not depend on one's eyesight being free of some innate abnormality. If Gladstone's treatment of motion words is a "kindred topic" to his account of colour vocabulary, the latter cannot be interpreted in terms of colour-blindness.

Nevertheless, colour-blindness is such an obvious way to misunderstand Gladstone's 1858 discussion (as demonstrated by the number of writers who have misunderstood it that way) that one might ask "If indeed Gladstone did not intend to suggest colour-blindness, why did he not say so explicitly?" There is a straightforward answer to that question, which Gladstone alluded to in 1877 (*CS*: 366): when he wrote his 1858 work the colour-blindness phenomenon was not yet widely known. Gladstone wrote "The curious phenomena of colour-blindness had then been very recently set forth by Dr. George Wilson" (he footnotes Wilson 1855). Gladstone did not say in so many words "I failed to explain that I was not referring to colour-blindness, because at the time I had not heard of it" (Gladstone had a politician's instincts, after all), but that is the obvious explanation for his failure to avert the misunderstanding.

Colour blindness was in fact first described in English in 1798, by the chemist John Dalton, who himself had the condition (it was sometimes, though more often in Germany than Britain, called *Daltonism*); but it did not become a widely-known phenomenon until far later. According to Google Ngrams (accessed 19 Jun 2011), the frequency of the bigram *colour blindness* in British sources was essentially zero until about 1850, rose gradually to about four per billion bigrams until about 1890, and then climbed abruptly to a peak of about 13 per billion bigrams, roughly the same frequency as in recent years. There is no reason to expect Gladstone (who was not medically qualified) to have known about colour blindness by the time he was writing a book published in 1858. Even when in 1869 he first (to our knowledge) explicitly referred to the condition (*JM*: 540), his words suggest that he may then have taken colour-blindness to be a consequence of deficient experience rather than a congenital condition. (It is not clear whether Gladstone was making that mistake, but this is much more plausible than the suggestion that he mistakenly supposed Homer's non-modern colour vocabulary to result from a congenital condition.) By 1877, as we saw above, Gladstone did understand that colour-blindness was congenital, and hence that it was not what he was attributing to the Homeric Greeks.

Deutscher (in his chapter 2) points out that a number of German scientists in the 1870s were discussing the issue of colour perception in early Man, and some at least of these Germans did mistakenly believe that the physiology of colour vision had changed over the three thousand years between Homer and themselves. One of this group, Hugo Magnus, who had evidently read *SHHA3*, sent Gladstone a copy of one of his own books in early 1877, after which Gladstone was in friendly correspondence with him and discussed his work favourably in his own article published later in that year. (In 1880 Magnus asked Gladstone if he could help him find a better academic job in Britain, though nothing came of that – see Bellmer 1999: 42.) Deutscher suggests to us (personal communication) that Magnus's writing may have been inconsistent about whether the development of colour vocabulary was a matter of physiological evolution or of cultural development. Elizabeth Bellmer (1999: 30) quotes passages pointing to the former; but there were certainly other passages where Magnus explicitly adopted the latter view. He responded (1877: 3) to the objection that members of primitive cultures are said to have particularly sensitive sight, hearing, etc. with the very relevant point that keen eyesight but failure to recognize colours is akin to having acute hearing but no musical appreciation (the latter being uncontroversially to a large extent a matter of education and experience rather than physiological capacity):

> Ebenso mag das Ohr schon auf unglaublich ferne Strecken hin das geringste Geräusch vernehmen können, und doch fehlt ihm die Fähigkeit, die klangreichen und melodischen Tonfiguren der Musik zu verstehen oder auch nur als solche zu vernehmen.[3]

---

3 Likewise his ear may be able to detect the slightest sound at incredible distances, and yet he lacks the ability to comprehend, or even to perceive as such, the vibrant and melodic sound-motifs of music (our translation).

This is a good analogy for what Gladstone believed about the Homeric colour sense, and Gladstone (*CS*: 368) picked out this analogy of Magnus's for approval.

It is perhaps true that in discussing in a friendly spirit the work of this younger and vastly less eminent writer, Gladstone was insufficiently alive to the risk of endorsing a complex body of ideas that included some which he disagreed with. That is not the same as saying that Gladstone himself argued for or believed in Homeric colour-blindness. He explicitly did not. But by the time Grant Allen said that he did (cf. pp. 272–273), Gladstone was leading what is sometimes described as the world's first modern political campaign (the "Midlothian Campaign"). Doubtless he had more urgent calls on his time than correcting misrepresentations of his beliefs about Homer's vocabulary.

14.2.3 Are biological explanations of colour-vocabulary differences unreasonable?

Writers who took Gladstone to attribute colour-blindness to Homeric Greeks have often not merely rejected that specific hypothesis, but claimed more generally that it is absurd to suppose that any differences between the colour vocabularies of different languages could be caused by differences in the eyesight of different ethnic groups. But that is not at all absurd. Marc Bornstein (1973) surveyed numerous studies demonstrating that the darker-skinned races have pigmentation in the eye which reduces sensitivity to the blue region of the spectrum, and he argued that this was a plausible explanation for the often-noticed fact that languages which possess few colour words tend to lack a word for "blue" in particular. Deutscher treats as untenable the claim by W.H.R. Rivers (1901: 94, quoted by Deutscher, pp. 67–68) that the natives of Murray Island in the Torres Straits have a "certain degree of insensitiveness to blue (and probably green) as compared with ... Europeans"; but although Rivers's experimental techniques may well have been flawed by present-day standards, the researches quoted by Bornstein suggest that his conclusion may nevertheless have been correct. Biological differences between human groups could well be relevant to some cases of differences among colour vocabularies.

However, they were not relevant to Gladstone's ideas about the Homeric colour vocabulary.

14.2.4 Convention and training

A key to Deutscher's misunderstanding of Gladstone (and a key to others' incomprehension when faced with the suggestion that members of alien cultures may perceive the world differently from us) is a passage (p. 55) where he asks, rhetorically, "Are the concepts of colour directly determined by the nature of our anatomy – as Gladstone, Geiger, and Magnus believed – or are they merely cultural conventions?" The word "convention" here makes this a false opposition.

Standardly, a "convention" is a behaviour pattern which participants, if they are reflective, recognize as contingent. If the present co-authors are walking together and we come to a door, GRS (male) opens it and lets AB (female) through before him. Logically that need not be the rule – there could be (we believe there are) cultures in which the man goes first; but GRS long ago adopted the social role of Englishman, so he follows the English rule. The situation which Gladstone was describing is more like the following: if we are with a geologist gazing at a stretch of landscape, he may see a glacial valley, a row of drumlins, or the eroded remains of a volcanic crater. All we see are hills and valleys. That is not because our eyesight is inferior, but it is not a matter of "convention", either. It is not that we have adopted the role of "geological layman" and consequently avoid noticing drumlins or using that word to describe them: we truly cannot recognize them as such, because we have not been trained to do so.

In the case of landforms this is easy to appreciate, since so many of us lack the training. We are all trained to identify and name colours in early childhood, so it is harder to appreciate that this ability is a matter of training, but so it is. As Gladstone summarized his thesis in 1877 (*CS*: 367), "painters know that there is an education of the eye for colour in the individual. The proposition, which I desire to suggest, is that this education subsists also for the race." An experienced painter has a more refined ability to recognize and identify shades of colour than many non-artists, but this is not because there is anything special about the anatomy of the painter's eye: it is uncontroversially the result of "education", or training. Gladstone is saying that that kind of training has occurred in the history of civilizations as well as in the biography of individuals. A painter may have acquired the ability to recognize and identify various precise shades, say gamboge or citrine, which the average layman might lump together simply as "yellow", but this does not imply that the painter's eyesight is physically acuter than the layman's. Gladstone is saying that even the ability to identify yellow and distinguish it from green or red, which in our time and culture is universal, itself had to be learned at an earlier stage in human history, again without that implying any change in the biological apparatus of human vision.

14.2.5 Changing terminology

Gladstone's word "race" in the passage just quoted might suggest to some that he must have been thinking about biological properties rather than cultural developments. But that would be to misinterpret nineteenth-century writing in terms of 21st-century preoccupations. We are familiar, today, with the idea that there is no necessary correlation between cultural inheritance and biological descent, and "race" is used to make explicit a reference to classification in terms of biological descent rather than membership of a particular culture. In the nineteenth century, in many nations the two classification principles coincided much more closely than they do now (large-scale immigration into Britain began only in the mid-twentieth century), and writers were not careful to distinguish the two principles: "race" could refer to what we should call a society or a culture. When Charles Lamb in his *Essays of Elia* wrote "The human species ... is composed of two distinct races, the men who borrow, and the men who lend",[4] or when Benjamin Jowett translated Plato's *Laws*, 3.700d, by writing "after a while there arose a new race of poets ... who made pleasure the only criterion of excellence",[5] they were not implying that these groups formed separate gene pools but only that they were distinguished by characteristic cultural norms. Gladstone knew that there was some ethnic diversity in the ancestry of the Greeks (this was one of his main topics in the first volume of *Studies on Homer*); his phrase "education [of] the race" referred to the development over generations of a particular culture, in this case the culture whose members spoke Greek.

Another potential source of misunderstanding is Gladstone's use of the word "organ", as when he wrote "I conclude, then, that the organ of colour and its impressions were but partially developed among the Greeks of the heroic age" (*SHHA3*: 488). Today, the word "organ" (used for an aspect of human functioning rather than for the musical instrument) certainly tends to suggest a physical element of anatomy, such as eye or heart. But in the nineteenth century, although "organ" could and often did mean that, it could also be used for a mental faculty. In a lecture written in 1836–1837 Sir William Hamilton (1859: 531) wrote "Faith, – Belief, – is the organ by which we apprehend what is beyond our knowledge". This usage was not wholly obsolete more recently; in 1961 Sir Julian Huxley wrote "A religion is an organ of man in society which helps him to cope with the problems of nature and his destiny ... It always involves the sense of sacredness or mystery and of participation in a continuing enterprise ..." (Huxley 1961).

---

4 The collected *Essays of Elia* have been published in numerous editions. The essay "The two races of men" first appeared in the *London Magazine*, December 1820.
5 Jowett (1875: 56). The word "race" here was supplied by Jowett; his translation is fairly free, and there is no corresponding word in the Greek original.

Clearly Hamilton and Huxley were referring to mental software rather than hardware, as we might put it today: faith or belief are not innately fixed aspects of cognition, since what a person believes, or believes in, is heavily affected by his or her upbringing and education; and Huxley's reference to "sense of sacredness or mystery" shows that he is discussing religion not as a social structure but as an aspect of individuals' cognitive functioning, which again depends on upbringing. So Gladstone's use of "organ" in the passage quoted did not imply that an aspect of the Greeks' physical anatomy was "undeveloped". Indeed, in 1877 Gladstone quoted that 1858 passage in the same sentence in which he denied that he was suggesting a "defect" in Homer's organism (*CS*: 366) – showing that by "undeveloped" he meant untrained or uneducated.[6]

14.2.6 Was Gladstone a Lamarckian?

Deutscher reinforces his claim that Gladstone believed in a biological rather than cultural difference between Homer's colour-sense and ours by quoting Gladstone's statement, in the introduction to his discussion of Homer's number words, that "the acquired aptitudes of one generation may become the inherited and inborn aptitudes of another" (*SHHA3*: 426, quoted by Deutscher, p. 54). Deutscher characterizes this as Gladstone "spouting received wisdom" and embracing the Lamarckian rather than Darwinian model of biological evolution.

It is unsurprising that Gladstone was not a Darwinian in 1858, since *The Origin of Species* had not yet been published (whereas Lamarck's *Philosophie zoologique* had appeared in the year of Gladstone's birth). Nevertheless, "spouting received wisdom" does not do justice to Gladstone's position. Gladstone's main point, in the passage quoted, was that a child's learning does not begin with formal schooling but includes a great deal of "insensible training, which begins from the very earliest infancy, and which precedes by a great interval all the systematic, and even all the conscious, processes of education" – no student of linguistics will disagree with that, since mother-tongue acquisition is the most obvious example. Gladstone wanted to say that acquiring what we think of as elementary number and colour concepts are also examples, so that even if it seems to us that we have "always" had these concepts and were never

---

6 The eminent biological statistician Karl Pearson even used "organ" explicitly to mean *any* quantifiable characteristic which might show resemblance or difference between parent and child (see Pearson 1896: 259). We do not suggest that Gladstone was using the word in as general a sense as that, but Pearson's usage underlines the point that there is no reason to interpret nineteenth-century uses of "organ" as referring narrowly to anatomy.

formally taught them, that does not contradict the claim that we acquired them from our early experience while Homeric Greeks did not acquire them from their different early experience. Only as an afterthought to this did Gladstone add "Nor am I for one prepared by any means to deny that there *may* [our emphasis] be" what we would now call a Lamarckian conversion of acquired into genetically transmitted characteristics, and he adds "we *may* [our emphasis] believe that the acquired aptitudes … [and so on as quoted by Deutscher]".

By 1869, when Gladstone had read *Origin of Species* (he read it in December 1859, shortly after it came out, see Bellmer 1999: 29 note 14), he toned this down by omitting "inborn": "the acquired knowledge of one generation becomes in time the inherited aptitude of another" (*JM*: 539). Rewritten that way, the statement was compatible with Darwinism, since "inheritance" can be cultural as well as genetic: a painter's child may inherit awareness of painting techniques through hanging round his father's studio.[7]

Lamarck versus Darwin is really a side-issue, since the more interesting question with respect to differences between cultures is how people's awareness of colours can *change* over history, rather than what mechanism transmits it from generation to generation during periods when it is not changing. Gladstone was always clear that the historical development of colour awareness was a matter of education and experience rather than of biological innovations. But even if it mattered whether or not Gladstone was a Lamarckian, the truth is that he expressed a Lamarckian view only hesitantly, and only at a period when it was the sole concept of evolution on offer.

14.3 Gladstone's positive contributions

We turn now from what Gladstone did not say to what he did say. What are the positive aspects of his writings which entitle him, in our view, to a high place in the history of the social sciences?

We see at least four:

---

7 Elizabeth Bellmer (1999: 32) seems to suggest that since Gladstone in 1877 had read Darwin he ought to have treated the development of colour-vocabulary as a Darwinian process: "He did not address the absence of Darwin's theory from Magnus's paper, nor did he really discuss it at any depth in his own. Inadvisedly, perhaps, since one hardly expects any work of evolutionary import written in 1877 to give Darwinism only passing mention, or to ascribe only non-Darwinian mechanisms to a process of change over time." Surely, if Gladstone believed (correctly) that the development of colour vocabularies since Homer was a non-Darwinian process, that was a very appropriate way for him to write?

(1) the idea that chaotic-seeming structure in a "primitive language" represents system of its own rather than mere failure to achieve the kind of system found in recent European languages;

(2) the idea that differences between languages may not be merely alternative methods of encoding a common world of experience but may correlate with different ways of experiencing or understanding the world;

(3) the idea that properties which an exotic language groups together as jointly contributing to the meaning of a vocabulary item are not necessarily sets of properties which familiar languages encourage us to see as linked;

(4) the idea that abstract structural features of a language may correlate with language-external features of the culture which uses the language, to the point that linguistics might succeed in being a predictive science.

All four of these ideas have been seen as significant intellectual achievements of the past hundred years; each was anticipated by Gladstone in the nineteenth century. We now discuss them in turn.

14.3.1 "Primitive languages" have system of their own

This, surely, is the central insight of modern linguistics as it has developed over the past century, and the point which gives that subject its chief claim on the attention of the educated public at large.

An assumption which has been (and probably still is) widely held outside the academic community is that European languages of the historical period approximate in their structures to a unique ideal system for articulating thought, and if languages of non-Western cultures resist analysis in terms of familiar European grammatical categories, that must be because those languages are just defective. (A variant of this idea, advocated for instance by August Schleicher (1848) and underpinned by the philosophy of Hegel, was that the classical European languages approximated to the structural ideal and modern languages have been decaying from that ideal.)

It was against this intellectual background that the linguistics pioneer Franz Boas strove to show that, with respect both to phonology and to grammar, various American Indian languages were structurally very different from European languages but equally or even more subtle in their own ways. English grammar requires certain logical categories, e.g. singular versus plural, to be expressed but allows others to be left vague; some American Indian languages require precision about categories that would commonly be ignored in English, as illustrated by Boas's 1911 Kwakiutl example (p. 18 above). For comparable remarks about American Indian versus European sound systems, see Boas ([1911] 1966: 12–14). A decade later, Edward Sapir wrote:

> One may argue as to whether a particular tribe engages in activities that are worthy of the name of religion or of art, but we know of no people that is not possessed of a fully developed language.... Many primitive languages have a formal richness, a latent luxuriousness of expression, that eclipses anything known to the languages of modern civilization (Sapir [1921] 1963: 22, and see also pp. 123–124).

When Boas and Sapir were writing, "linguistics" was scarcely established as a subject in its own right. As the twentieth century proceeded, the growing community of professional linguists came to take these ideas for granted, but they certainly were not equally axiomatic outside that narrow academic community. The *Guinness Book of Records* has for many decades aimed to provide a popular compendium of sober factual information about the world's biggest, smallest, fastest, etc. in all areas of science and human life. Its 1956 edition (Guinness Superlatives 1956) had an entry for "most primitive language", the answer being the Australian language "Arunta" (now called Aranda), which is "grammatically primitive" and in which "Words are indeterminate in meaning and form". A 21st-century publication might be less forthright, if only out of political caution, but the axiom that, with respect to language structure, unfamiliar implies unsystematic is surely not yet dead.

When we consider how badly Boas's and Sapir's points needed making in the twentieth century, we might expect that it would have been virtually inevitable for Gladstone in the 1850s to take the apparently chaotic application of colour terms by Homer as representing real chaos in the vocabulary of a preclassical society. It would have been very easy for Gladstone to conclude, in the words of the *Guinness Book*, that Homer's colour words were "indeterminate in meaning". Instead, Gladstone argued that they represented a system whose basis contrasted with that of modern European colour vocabularies. Our modern colour words are based mainly on place in the wavelength spectrum – what Gladstone called "prismatic colours"; Homer on the other hand had "principally, a system in lieu of colour, founded upon light and upon darkness" (*SHHA3*: 488); "the Homeric colours are really the modes and forms of light, and of ... darkness ... the quantity of light, not decomposed [i.e. regardless of wavelengths included in it], which falls upon [an] object, and ... the mode of its incidence" (*SHHA3*: 489).

To see what Gladstone meant by "modes and forms of light", consider his discussion (*SHHA3*: 473) of the words *aithōn* (derived from *aithō* "to kindle") and its compound *aithops* ("*aithōn*-looking"). Homer applies these words to:

horses; iron; a lion; copper utensils; a bull; an eagle; wine; copper; and smoke.[8]
Gladstone asks "In what manner are we to find a common thread upon which
to hang the colours of iron, copper, horses, [etc.]? We must here again adopt
the vague word 'dark' ... But as the idea of *aithō* includes flame struggling
with smoke, so there may be a flash of light upon the dark object." In English,
Gladstone suggests, to indicate a low position on the light-to-dark dimension we
have only the vague term "dark", while Homer had separate words for different
kinds of "dark": *aithōn* was something like "dark with gleams of light" (in the
case of the animals, the gleams perhaps came from eyes and/or teeth), whereas
for instance *porphyreos* denoted "dark" without any implication of gleams of
light, as in the case of blood or dark cloud; and Gladstone quotes other Homeric
words too for which English provides only the translation "dark".

It might fairly be objected that Gladstone did not succeed in articulating
the system he discerned in Homer's vocabulary to any degree of detail. He was
hampered in trying to do this by limited understanding of the physics of light
and colour. But this shortcoming is very forgivable, when we consider that (as
we shall show below) much more recent scholarly writing on the same topic
suffers from the same limitations, with less excuse in terms of the general state
of scientific knowledge.

Physically, to define the colour of a surface requires specifying points on a
number of dimensions or scales. Three important dimensions are *hue* (place in
the spectrum of wavelengths from red to violet), *lightness* (from white through
pale and dark tones of any hue to black), and *saturation*: what in layman's terms
might be called the "richness" of a colour – the extent to which it departs from
a grey of the same degree of lightness.[9] The human eye can perceive greater
saturation at some points on the two-dimensional hue/lightness surface than at
others: an intense scarlet is much more vivid than the most intense possible pale
blue-green, for instance. George Collier (1973) showed that the "focal colours"
which Brent Berlin and Paul Kay found to recur as denotata of basic colour terms
in diverse modern languages coincide almost perfectly with the hue/lightness
points where the eye can perceive most saturation.

Hue, lightness, and saturation do not exhaust the dimensions of colour
perception. For instance the difference between "gold" and "yellow" has to do

---

8 Gladstone also linked *aithōn* and *aithops* with *Aithiops* for a dark-skinned African; but the
stem here seems to have meant literally "burnt", Africans being taken by the Greeks as heavily
suntanned, rather than being a colour word.

9 The dimension of "lightness" is sometimes alternatively called "brightness" in the literature;
but that is potentially confusing, because in everyday English *bright red* (e.g.) is more likely to
mean "highly saturated red" than "light red".

not with those dimensions but with a contrast between shiny and matte. Jaap Van Brakel (1992: note 21), referring to a monograph (Beck 1972) on the psychology of colour perception, lists as further dimensions:

> size, shape, location, fluctuation (flicker, sparkle, glitter), texture, transparency, lustre (glossiness), glow, fluorescence, metallic appearance (iridescence), insistence, pronouncedness, and possibly more.

Gladstone clearly recognized the dimensions of hue and lightness, and phrases such as "modes and forms of light" show that he had some awareness that there was more to it than just those two dimensions; but he had no clear grasp of further dimensions. There was certainly no explicit concept in Gladstone's writings corresponding to saturation, and this may well have prevented him going further than he did to articulate Homer's system of colour words. Looking at Gladstone's account of Homer's uses of *porphyreos*, it seems possible that what this term actually meant was something like "dark but high on the saturation scale (irrespective of place on the hue dimension)". The colour of blood is a vivid (high-saturation) red; a wave of the sea shows a high-saturation blue-green (whereas a flat sea shows largely reflected sunlight rather than high-saturation colour). In the modern world we are surrounded by highly-saturated samples of many contrasting hues, so it might be odd to have a term that meant merely "highly saturated, irrespective of hue". But in Homer's low-tech world highly saturated colour will have been rare. Look at a rural landscape today, and the few vivid splashes of colour, if there are any, will often coincide with artificial objects: say, a scarlet postbox, or a yellow warning sign; fields and woods are much more subdued in colour. Homer's world had no postboxes or warning signs. High saturation, irrespective of hue, may have been remarkable enough to call for its own descriptive term. "Dark but highly saturated" could have been the property which motivated *oinops*, "wine-looking", as an epithet for the sea.

We do not claim certainty about our gloss for *porphyreos*. (We suspect the data are not sufficient to permit a full, reliable reconstruction of Homer's colour vocabulary.) But the gloss is at least plausible, and it illustrates the way in which Gladstone's success in linguistic reconstruction was limited by his limited understanding of the scientific facts: if our gloss is correct, it is unlikely that Gladstone could have formulated it.[10]

---

10 Our hypothesis about *porphyreos* could not be right if Gladstone were justified in claiming that Homer applied the word to "The grey and leaden colour of a dark cloud when about to burst in storm" (*SHHA3*, 462): leaden grey is an entirely unsaturated colour. But Gladstone appears to be thinking here of *Iliad* xvii.551, which contains no mention of "lead(en)". British

From the perspective of 150 years later we might see Gladstone's "two-dimensional" concept of colour as naïve. But academics in recent decades have been no less naïve.

Many students in the 1950s and 1960s came to linguistics via H.A. Gleason's *Introduction to Descriptive Linguistics*. Gleason's initial example ([1955] 1969: 4–6) of structural differences between languages related to the non-equivalence of colour terms between languages of diverse cultures. Where English has six basic terms for different hues, two African languages, Shona and Bassa, were described as having respectively three and two. Gleason's exposition is based on a model of colour which was not two-dimensional but one-dimensional: hue was the only dimension considered.

One-dimensional models of colour have a respectable scientific ancestry. John Beare (1906: 69) notes that Aristotle held such a view, and that it survived as late as Goethe's early-nineteenth-century *Farbenlehre*.[11] However, by the 1950s a one-dimensional model could hardly be taken seriously.

It may be that Gleason did not take it seriously: it is reasonable to simplify complicated things in an introductory student textbook. But if we examine Berlin and Kay's *Basic Color Terms* (1969), written as a research monograph rather than an undergraduate textbook, we find that Berlin and Kay are still using a model based on just two dimensions, i.e. no more sophisticated than Gladstone. Berlin and Kay investigated colour vocabularies by asking language informants to define their colour terms with respect to a standard set of colour samples (the Munsell set, Nickerson 1940). The Munsell set consists of 1600 samples ("chips") representing points spaced at psychologically-equal intervals through the three-dimensional space defined by the hue, lightness, and saturation scales. But Berlin and Kay did not use the 1600-sample set; they worked just with the 320 samples of maximum saturation for each hue/brightness combination, plus the ten samples of zero saturation. In other words, except for words corresponding to English *black*, *white*, and *grey*, Berlin and Kay simply assumed that contrasts among colour terms in the languages they studied would not relate to differences on the saturation dimension (or on any other dimensions apart from hue and lightness). Furthermore Berlin and Kay were not idiosyncratic in studying colour vocabulary this way; Robert MacLaury (1992: 138)

---

stormclouds are leaden grey, but those of southerly latitudes are sometimes described in English as "coppery". The Wikipedia article on "Clouds" (accessed 3 March 2011) describes the "blood-red" appearance of "large, mature thunderheads" near sunrise or sunset. Homer may have meant that the cloud was dark and had as much colour in it as clouds ever do.

11 Beare bases his account of Aristotle's colour theory on Carl Prantl (1849). If we understand Prantl (pp. 116–119) correctly, Aristotle saw colours as arranged in a sequence white–yellow–red–violet–green–blue–black.

points out that ethnographers since Eric Lenneberg and John Roberts's 1956 book *The Language of Experience* have consistently used this restricted version of the Munsell system – though the availability of the full system implies that recent ethnographers, unlike Gladstone, knew that they were choosing to ignore at least the dimension of saturation. (Van Brakel 1993: 112 has suggested that this methodology may eliminate as many as "95 per cent of the world's colour words" from consideration.)

Clearly, if recent scholars knowingly adopt an impoverished model of colour, we cannot criticize Gladstone for adopting the same model without knowing that it was over-simple. Not long ago Robert MacLaury published a "target article" (MacLaury 1992) which attracted considerable discussion, arguing that an evolution from vision vocabulary based on the lightness dimension to one based on hue can regularly be observed as cultures develop in technological sophistication. Well over a century earlier, Gladstone had argued for just such a transition as the Greeks emerged from their dark age.[12]

14.3.2 The Sapir–Whorf hypothesis

The idea that exotic languages are systematic in their own way may be the aspect of linguistics which most deserves the public's consideration; but the area of the subject which has actually attracted most attention from laymen is probably the so-called Sapir–Whorf hypothesis, which is the topic of Guy Deutscher's 2011 book. As Edward Sapir (1929: 209) expressed this idea: "the 'real world' is to a large extent unconsciously built up on the language habits of the group. . . . The worlds in which different societies live are distinct worlds, not merely the same world with different labels attached." People are understandably fascinated by the idea that our perception of basic, abstract features of the world we inhabit may differ radically in ways that relate to the structure of our native language.

Most 21st-century academics probably dissent from the Sapir–Whorf hypothesis in the strong form in which Sapir and Benjamin Lee Whorf propounded it. This is partly because Whorf's analyses of the language and world-view of

---

12 To a reader who persists in believing that Gladstone was discussing colour-blindness, we would comment: clearly MacLaury at the end of the twentieth century did not suppose that members of technologically simple societies are colour-blind. MacLaury has put forward a coherent hypothesis about cultural development of sensitivity to colours; what could we reasonably expect Gladstone to have said that he did not say, if he were aiming to advocate the same hypothesis which MacLaury certainly does advocate?

the Hopi tribe of Arizona, which made that strong hypothesis seem plausible, are now known to have been based on very limited acquaintance with Hopi, and Whorf's large claims about Hopi being a "timeless language" (Whorf [1940] 1956: 216) have been contradicted by independent evidence (Malotki 1983, discussed by Deutscher, p. 143). But it is also because the hypothesis seemed to ascribe to language too much control over individuals' minds. Sapir wrote (1931) about the "tyrannical hold" of grammar over our interpretation of experience, and (in the 1929 passage excerpted above) about people being "very much at the mercy" of their language. But we know that people can and sometimes do learn to see the world in radically new ways, and their native language does not prohibit that. The German language served successfully to express mediaeval and then Newtonian concepts of physics, but it did not hinder Albert Einstein from replacing these with a very different model of space, time, and other fundamentals.

Nevertheless, one can reject the idea that language constrains original thinking, and yet accept the possibility that societies may differ in their usual ways of perceiving the world, and that those differences may sometimes be reflected in the structures of their respective languages. Language will not prevent our ideas changing, but if they do change and the change pervades our society then it might trigger corresponding changes in our language.

In this weaker form the Sapir–Whorf hypothesis (if we can still call it that) remains an idea of great public interest. We have already seen in 14.2.1 how Gladstone used the case of colour to argue for this idea. The appearance of surfaces is one fairly fundamental aspect of perception: Gladstone argued that the Homeric Greeks categorized them in terms of light and dark but were only beginning to learn to categorize them also in terms of hue, which to us is so basic a feature of vision that we can scarcely imagine ignoring it. By claiming that Gladstone believed in Homeric colour blindness, Deutscher makes it appear that no-one before Sapir and Whorf imagined that language differences might reflect socially-determined differences in perception. In reality, Gladstone proposed such a correlation in a subtler form than Sapir and Whorf; Gladstone did not suggest that the Greek language prevented its speakers learning to develop a hue-based colour system – he knew that, in due course, they did so.

Deutscher does not discuss what Gladstone wrote about Homer's arithmetic concepts, but this was even more telling. Gladstone gave a long, detailed argument to support the claim that Homer's "mind never had before it any of those processes, simple as they are to all who are familiar with them, of multiplication, subtraction, or division" (*SHHA3*: 438). Homer "has not even the words necessary to enable him to say, 'This house is five times as large as that.' If he had the idea to express, he would say, Five houses, each as large as that, would hardly be equal to this" (*SHHA3*: 430).

Arithmetical operations are as abstract and fundamental an aspect of our world-view as there could be, so if Gladstone was right to infer from the numerous passages he cites that Homer had no concept of them, this is very striking support for the Sapir–Whorf hypothesis – in its reasonable, weaker version (later Greek-speakers certainly learned about multiplication, etc.). How far one can make inferences from a language to the arithmetical concepts of its speakers is a matter of intense controversy among anthropological linguists today (see e.g. P. Gordon 2004; Frank, Everett, et al. 2008).

We know of no-one other than Gladstone who so clearly and carefully anticipated this important intellectual issue.

14.3.3 Natural families of properties

The categories encoded by vocabulary items of a natural language will commonly not be single, simple physical properties but families of properties which for speakers of the language are somehow related. William Labov (1973) showed how the meaning of English *cup* involved separate properties such as a particular width-to-height ratio, possession of a handle, use for liquid rather than solid food, and others, which jointly differentiates this word from similar words such as *beaker* or *bowl*.

Because modern technology gives us the ability to endow manufactured objects with surfaces of any visual appearance we choose, it seems to us natural for words describing the quality of light reflected by surfaces to combine various of the "colour" properties already discussed, such as hue, lightness, and so forth, but unnatural for them to combine some of those properties with properties unrelated to light quality. There is nothing surprising about the English adjective *navy*, which combines a "blue" value on the hue dimension with a "dark" value on the lightness dimension, but we would not expect to find a word combining the properties blue and heavy, say – what has weight got to do with colour?

Which properties relate closely enough to one another to be linked verbally in this way is a culture-dependent issue, however. Harold Conklin (1955) showed that colour terms in the Philippine language Hanunóo combine light-quality properties with non-visual properties such as wet or fresh versus dry/withered. In terms of hue and lightness, *rara?* and *latuy* denote red and light green respectively; but a "shiny, wet, brown-colored section of newly-cut bamboo" is called *latuy* rather than *rara?*: the brown hue is closer to red than to light green (or to the focus of other Hanunóo colour terms), but the fact that the bamboo is fresh and wet rather than old and dessicated outweighs its hue in determining the applicable "colour" word. For Hanunóo culture, wet/dry and hue are related properties: very often (though not in this particular case), vegetable materials are green when fresh and change hue towards the red end of the spectrum when they wither. And this correlation is important in practice, because people need to distinguish foodstuffs that are good to eat from those that are stale.

Conklin's analysis of Hanunóo colour terms had great impact. The Harold Conklin page on the Minnesota State University "EMuseum" website[13] treats his four-page "Hanunóo color categories' paper as so important that it is the only Conklin publication to be individually identified; it is described as a pioneering exercise in helping "anthropologists to see how people in different cultures conceptualize their world in their own ways". The classic status of the paper was confirmed by inclusion in Dell Hymes's standard anthology *Language in Culture and Society* (Hymes 1964). By now, it is well established that words of non-Western cultures whose senses include colour as one aspect may combine this with diverse other properties, including even properties such as nice/nasty or traditional/modern. (See references by Van Brakel 1992: 169, 172; MacLaury 1992: note 69.) But when Conklin published it, this idea seemed new.

It seemed new; but it wasn't. What Conklin said about Hanunóo *latuy* was said a century earlier by Gladstone about Homer's word *chlōros*. *Chlōros* is the only word in Homer that could be a candidate for the meaning "green", and (according to Liddell and Scott 1855) it derives from *chloē*, "the first light green shoot of plants in spring", which makes "light green" a plausible translation.[14] Sometimes Homer uses *chlōros* in contexts where that translation makes sense, e.g. *chlōras rhōpas* for (presumably leafy) brushwood gathered to create a makeshift bed (*Odyssey* xvi.47) or *rhopalon … chlōron elaïneon* for a freshly-cut olive branch (*Odyssey* ix.319–320). But he also applies *chlōros* to honey, whose hue we would describe as yellow rather than green; and in other cases again the word seems to mean simply "pale", applied to a face pale with fear, or by extension to fear itself – that metaphorical usage accounts for the majority of occurrences of *chlōros* in Homer. (In English, of course, we do sometimes describe a frightened person as "going green".) Gladstone's conclusion (*SHHA3*: 468) is that visual appearance is only one aspect of the meaning of Homer's *chlōros*: "the governing idea is not the greenness, but the newness"; "Next to paleness, [*chlōros*] serves chiefly for freshness, i.e. as opposed to what is stale or withered: a singular combination with the former sense". The combination is "singular", or in modern English strange, because we would not want to combine a property

---

13 <www.mnsu.edu/emuseum/cultural/anthropology/Conklin.html>, accessed 3 March 2011.
14 J. P. Mallory and D. Q. Adams (1997: s.v. "yellow") appear to reject this etymology; we are not qualified to resolve the disagreement.

of light-quality with properties relating to newness or physical consistency in a single adjective. But for the Homeric Greeks, as for the Hanunóo, this may have been a very natural combination.

Deutscher comments (p. 93) "Conklin probably never set eyes on Gladstone's explanation ... But anyone comparing their analyses might be forgiven for thinking that Conklin simply lifted his passage wholesale from *Studies on Homer and the Homeric Age.*"

14.3.4 Linking language structure to technology

Gladstone not only recognized that Homer's seemingly chaotic use of colour vocabulary reflected a system based mainly on properties other than hue, which modern colour vocabularies are based on, but he understood the reason for that: modern colour categories are a product of modern technology. Gladstone wrote (*JM*: 539–540):

> ... much of our varied experience in colour is due to chemistry, and to commerce, which brings to us the productions of all the regions of the world. Mere Nature, at any one spot, does not present to us a full and well-marked series of the principal colours such as to be habitually before the mind's eye.

In Homer's time (*SHHA3*: 488):

> The artificial colours, with which the human eye was conversant, were chiefly the ill-defined, and anything but full-bodied, tints of metals. The materials, therefore, for a system of colour did not offer themselves to Homer's vision as they do to ours. Particular colours were indeed exhibited in rare beauty, as the blue of the sea or the sky. Yet these colours were, so to speak, isolated fragments ... the eye may require a familiarity with an ordered system of colours, as the condition of its being able closely to appreciate any one of them.

Any Western child today learns colours in connexion with plastic toys, alphabet books, and the like which present contrasting examples of highly-saturated primary hues. Homeric Greeks were not exposed to such stimuli.

In the light of modern knowledge, Gladstone's comments seem spot on. People are often puzzled by the fact that many languages lack a word for "blue", when the daytime sky offers such a clear example. But (setting aside the issue of racial differences in perception, cf. 14.2.3 above), there is evidence (Kristol 1980) that even some modern European dialect speakers may not see the sky as a thing with a nameable colour (and after all, the sky is not a thing). According to Van Brakel (1993: 115), "The most plausible explanation for the ubiquity of common colour meanings in twentieth-century languages is ... that it reflects the spread of cultural imperialism and common technology, in particular the invention of artificial dyes."

Even the study of colour terminologies by Berlin and Kay, who in general are much more interested in innately-determined features of language structure than in culture-dependent features, recognizes that "to a group ... who possess no dyed fabrics, color-coded electrical wires, and so forth, it may not be worthwhile to rote-learn labels for gross perceptual discriminations such as green/blue, despite the psychophysical salience of such contrasts" (Berlin and Kay 1969: 16) – though this was not a central or widely-noticed aspect of Berlin and Kay's theory. (Those less committed than Berlin and Kay to the concept of innate semantic structure might doubt whether the green/blue contrast will necessarily be psychologically salient for a group such as described.)

Gladstone's discussion implies a testable hypothesis about correlations between the technological resources of a society and an aspect of its language structure. "The art ... of dyeing was almost ... unknown" to the Homeric Greeks, so they did not have a hue-based colour vocabulary of the modern European type. By implication, then, other cultures with little experience of artificial pigments will likewise lack a hue-based colour system, whereas cultures which do have that technology, even if they are otherwise little advanced technically, will have a hue-based system.

We do not suggest that Gladstone spelled this out as an explicit hypothesis. There might have been little point in his doing so, because probably he would not have been in a position to test it. But the hypothesis is implicit in his writing; and we can test it.

Testable hypotheses linking non-linguistic features of a society with aspects of its language structure, while obviously desirable if one is keen to establish the scientific credentials of linguistics, have been strikingly rare in the history of that subject. The tendency has been the other way: to assume that any kind of society can have any kind of language. For instance Sapir was making essentially the latter point, in vivid wording, when he wrote ([1921] 1963: 219) "When it comes to linguistic form, Plato walks with the Macedonian swineherd, Confucius with the head-hunting savages of Assam." The earliest point we know of when testable language-type/society-type correlations entered the mainstream of linguistic discourse was with Peter Trudgill's work beginning in the 1980s (e.g. Trudgill 1989) on links between language complexity and the size and openness of societies.

Dyeing was not entirely unknown to the Homeric Greeks, but it was known as an exotic art practised by neighbouring societies to the east. The adjective *porphyreos*, discussed above, derives from *porphyra*, a marine mollusc which yields a dark-red dye;[15] the dye was called *phoinix*, which was also the word for "Phoenician", because the process of making and using it was associated with that people. (The Romans called the dye "Tyrian purple", from Tyre in the present-day Lebanon.) It is striking that even the simple technique of staining ivory is explicitly associated by Homer (*Iliad* iv.141) with the Carians and Maeonians, non-Indo-European peoples of Asia Minor. According to J.J. Hummel and E. Knecht (1910: 744), "The Phoenician and Alexandrian merchants imported ... dyestuffs into Greece, but we know little or nothing of the methods of dyeing pursued by the Greeks and Romans" – in view of the general articulateness of the two latter peoples, it seems safe to conclude that even in the classical period this technology was not well developed among them. Since it must surely take time for a novel technology to remould basic vocabulary, it is reasonable to see Homeric colour terms as the product of a dyeless culture: and Gladstone tells us that these terms are not hue-based.[16]

MacLaury (1992) offers many examples of other languages of technically-unsophisticated cultures whose "colour" vocabularies are not hue-based. Unfortunately he does not give detail on the technologies traditionally available to the respective cultures, and we are not qualified to do so. What we can do is examine the other leg of the hypothesis, which predicts that the language of a society at an early stage of civilization, if it has acquired the art of dyeing, should have a hue-based colour vocabulary. We have tested this by looking at colour words in the Chinese *Book of Odes*.

14.3.5 Old Chinese as a test case

The *Book of Odes* is a good match in terms of date and genre to the Homeric epics. Both are the earliest literary products of their respective civilizations. The *Odes* are believed to have been composed at different times from the tenth to seventh centuries BC (in Chinese terms, during the Zhou dynasty); Homer, if he was a single individual, probably lived in the eighth century BC (Lane Fox 2008:

---

15 It is possible therefore that the compound *haliporphyros* mentioned on p. 272 meant, not "sea-coloured", but "dyed with genuine *porphyra* dye from the sea".

16 One might object that the Minoans, before the Homeric period, knew the art of painting in many colours (as anyone who has seen the frescos from Knossos in the Iraklion Museum could confirm). But, first, Minoan civilization was separated from Homer by a dark age during which many arts were lost; and, probably more important, figurative painting does not lead the mind to consider colour contrasts, as dyeing does. Faced with a polychromatic picture, the obvious thing to think or talk about is what it depicts; with dyed fabrics there is not much for a non-expert to discuss other than their colours.

381–384), and cast into final form poetic material much of which may have originated well before that time. (The two sets of writings do not match in terms of quantity; the *Odes* comprise just 305 songs or poems, many of which are very short.)

However, unlike the Greeks of Homer's time, Zhou dynasty Chinese were familiar with the art of dyeing. And as predicted, the use of colour terms in the *Book of Odes* seems much more "normal" by modern European standards than Homer's usage.

The basic colour terms for the Chinese were the so-called 五色 *wǔ sè* "Five Colours": 玄 *xuán* or 黑 *hēi* "black", 朱 *zhū* or 赤 *chì* "red", 青 *qīng* "green, blue", 白 *bó* "white", 黃 *huáng* "yellow".[17] There are 71 occurrences of these words in the *Odes* (not counting separately cases where a word is reduplicated or a line is repeated with or without variations).[18] Among these occurrences, 23 – almost one in three – refer to garments, fabric, spun yarn, red (therefore presumably dyed) leather, or directly to dye.[19]

In the balance of cases where these words apply to things that are not artificially coloured, the choice of colour word seems entirely normal to the European reader. The breakdown is:

24 references to fauna, including eight to horses (mainly "yellow", which seems a natural enough way to describe bay horses) and five occurrences of 黃鳥 *huáng niǎo* "yellow bird", thought to be a name for the oriole

11 references to flora (blooms, leaves)

4 human hair in old age ("yellow")

3 stones

6 miscellaneous (yellow liquid poured as a libation – millet wine?; white dew; white clouds; Black King (apparently a name); and a reference to a horse as black and yellow that seems not to describe its natural coat colours (it may indicate flanks blackened with sweat and legs covered with the yellow mud of North China).

---

17 Axel Schuessler (2007: s. vv.) notes that *xuán* was replaced by *hēi* as the basic word for "black" during the Zhou period, and suggests that the same may have been true of *zhū* and *chì* for "red" (which seem to be used interchangeably in the *Odes*).
18 We also omit places in Odes 155 and 233 where standard texts read 青 *qīng* but Bernhard Karlgren (1942: 146) gives reason to believe that the graph is borrowed to represent a different, non-colour word.
19 We include here two cases in Ode 98 where colour words are applied to 充耳 *chōng ěr* "ear stoppers". Karlgren points out (1950: 63 note a) that knowledge of the nature of this important element of Zhou-dynasty apparel was already lost by the Han dynasty, so we cannot now know whether they were made of fabric or perhaps stone such as jade, whose colour is natural rather than artificial.

The only choice of colour term which strikes us as even slightly surprising is one reference in Ode 261 to 豹 *bào*, translated variously as "panthers" or "wild cats", as red. But we do not know precisely what colour the big cats in China 3000 years ago were, and it is not hard to imagine that the fur of some may have been rufous enough to be called "red" rather than "yellow".

Apart from the above words for the "Five Colours", many other colour words occur in the *Odes*; we have not systematically examined their use, but it is noticeable that several, possibly most, of them are written with the "silk" radical (e.g. 素 *sù* "white", 綠 *lù* "green"), suggesting that at the time the graphs were created these were perceived as words specially relevant to dyed fabrics.[20]

We find nothing at all that might suggest that any of these words, the Five Colours or the others, were used to denote light-qualities other than hue (together with the senses "black" and "white"). If the early Chinese colour sense had been as different from ours as Gladstone believed Homer's colour sense was, it is implausible that so many uses of colour words should read so naturally to 21st-century eyes.[21]

Thus Gladstone's implicit hypothesis relating colour terms to technology passes at least one test involving data that would have been unfamiliar to him (and which have not been examined, to our knowledge, by those who have discussed colour terms recently). Many respected theories in the social sciences have achieved less, in terms of empirical predictions about data unknown to the theorist.

14.4 Intellectual advance depends on a receptive audience

If Gladstone had written what he did about Homer's vocabulary in the 1950s–1970s rather than a century earlier, expressing himself in the academic idiom of that time rather than of his own, his name might now appear in every introductory linguistics textbook. As it is, although *SHHA3* has occasionally been

---

20 By giving *sù* and *lù* the same glosses as we have given for two of the Five Colours, we do not imply that these were simple synonyms; it may be, for instance, that *lù* was a specific shade of *qīng*.

21 Since Gladstone remarks (*SHHA3*: 479–81) on the surprising fewness of places where Homer refers to the colours of horses, it should for completeness be pointed out that the Chinese *Odes* also contain numerous specialized terms for horses which are claimed by the commentary tradition to refer to particular colours or patterns of colour. We do not pursue this point, partly because it is not clear in which direction it tends with respect to our overall argument, and partly because these words are long-obsolete and the meanings attributed to them sometimes strain credulity. For instance, would any language really have a simple one-syllable word for a "horse with white left hind leg", the meaning traditionally assigned to 騜 *zhù*?

mentioned in specialist works (e.g. by Berlin and Kay, who appear (1969: 148) to share the misunderstanding that Gladstone believed the Homeric Greeks were colour-blind), Gladstone's scientific writings have largely been ignored, until Deutscher has now made them widely known but in a way that perpetuates that misunderstanding. Gladstone's writing about language is a striking example of the principle that intellectual advance requires not only individuals who produce good ideas but also an audience ready to receive them.

Over the decades during which Gladstone was writing about Homer's vocabulary, he was first a leading backbencher, and then from 1859 successively Chancellor, Leader of the House, Leader of the Opposition, and Prime Minister, in a parliament which at the time was the ultimate political authority over almost a quarter of humanity. It is not every political figure of Gladstone's stature, to say the least, who finds time to make significant contributions to science. When one does, we ought not to be grudging in celebrating the fact.

And studying how even such a figure can find his intellectual contributions shuffled aside when they are awkward to digest should make us alert to the greater danger that good ideas produced by more obscure names may receive similar treatment today.

Chapter 15
Minds in Uniform:
How generative linguistics regiments culture,
and why it shouldn't

15.1 Trivializing cultural differences

Practitioners of theoretical linguistics often think of their subject as exempt from the ethical implications which loom large in most branches of social studies. Publications in linguistic theory tend to share the abstract formal quality of mathematical writing, so people imagine that linguistics is as ethically neutral as maths. They are wrong. One of the most significant (if doubtless unintended) functions of modern generative linguistic theory is to create a spurious intellectual justification for a poisonous aspect of modern life which has become widespread for non-intellectual reasons: the trivialization of cultural differences between separate human groups. People nowadays do not merely see the cultures that exist today as fairly similar to one another (which, because of modern technology, they often are), but they fail to recognize even the possibility of deep cultural differences. They do not conceive of how alien to us, mentally as well as physically, the life of our predecessors was a few centuries ago, and the life of our successors in time to come may be.

Most people with this shortsighted outlook hold it out of simple ignorance But generative linguistics is creating reasons for saying that it is the correct outlook. Cultures really are not and cannot be all that diverse, if we believe the message of Steven Pinker's *The Language Instinct* (Pinker 1995), and of the linguists such as Noam Chomsky from whom Pinker draws his ideas.

15.2 An earlier consensus

It is ironic that the linguistics of recent decades has encouraged this point of view, because when synchronic linguistics got started, about the beginning of the 20th century, and for long afterwards, its main function was – and was seen as – helping to demonstrate how large the cultural differences are between different human groups. The pioneer of synchronic linguistics in North America was the anthropologist Franz Boas, who was explicit about the fact that cultural differences often go deeper than laymen at the time tended to appreciate:

... forms of thought and action which we are inclined to consider as based on human nature are not generally valid, but characteristic of our specific culture. If this were not so, we could not understand why certain aspects of mental life that are characteristic of the Old World should be entirely or almost entirely absent in aboriginal America. An example is the contrast between the fundamental idea of judicial procedure in Africa and America; the emphasis on oath and ordeal as parts of judicial procedure in the Old World, their absence in the New World. (Boas [1932] 1940: 258)

It is indicative that, in Britain, the first chair of linguistics to be established was located at the School of Oriental and African Studies, an institution which had been founded to encourage study of the diverse cultures of the non-Western world. Standard undergraduate textbooks of linguistics emphasized the significance of structural diversity among languages as a mirror of intellectual diversity among cultures, for instance H.A. Gleason wrote ([1955] 1969: 7–8):

In learning a second language ... [y]ou will have to make ... changes in habits of thought and of description of situations in many ... instances.... In some languages, situations are not analyzed, as they are in English, in terms of an actor and an action. Instead the fundamental cleavage runs in a different direction and cannot be easily stated in English.

And this idea that human cultural differences can run deep was widely accepted as uncontroversial by educated people whose special expertise had nothing particularly to do with anthropology or with linguistics. To take an example at random from recent reading, when the historian W.L. Warren discussed the 12th-century Anglo-Norman king Henry II's dealings with the neighbouring Celtic nations of Wales, Ireland, and Scotland, he found it important to begin by explaining fundamental conceptual differences between Celtic and post-Carolingian-European world-views.

Institutions (such as kingship) which look at first sight familiar were in fact differently put together and informed by different traditions and habits. We are so accustomed to seeing social institutions closely integrated with political institutions ... that it is difficult to comprehend the development of a far from primitive and reasonably stable society in which political institutions were of comparatively minor importance.... [In England and Continental Europe] Political order was ... made the groundwork of social stability and progress. But this pattern was not inevitable. The Celtic world found an alternative to political peace as the basis for an ordered social life. (Warren 1973: 151–152)

15.3 Globalization concealing cultural diversity

In the 21st century, developments in our own Western societies have meant that the idea of deep differences between cultures is much less well understood.

Joseph Henrich et al. have thought it necessary to shock readers into an awareness of how diverse the assumptions of different cultures can be (and hence how dangerous it is to base universal theories of human psychology on experiments using almost exclusively Western university students as subjects), by describing two societies of New Guinea:

> the Etoro believe that for a boy to achieve manhood he must ingest the semen of his elders. This is accomplished through ritualized rites of passage that require young male initiates to fellate a senior member ... In contrast, the nearby Kaluli maintain that male initiation is only properly done by ritually delivering the semen through the initiate's anus, *not* his mouth ... To become a man in these societies, and eventually take a wife, every boy undergoes these initiations. [Comparable practices] ... were not uncommon among the traditional societies of Melanesia and Aboriginal Australia ... as well as in Ancient Greece and Tokugawa Japan. (Henrich et al. 2010a: 61)

What for one culture is the ultimate wickedness can be in another culture the right and proper thing to do. (British forces in Afghanistan currently are having to be taught that paedophilia is a cultural norm in parts of that country: Farmer 2011.) There simply is not any universal social pattern of which separate cultures represent separate, perhaps imperfect realizations. As Henrich et al. (2010b) put it, those interested in human nature need to be made aware that "Most people are not WEIRD [Western, educated, industrialized, rich, and democratic]".

We all know that there are many ways in which our modern circumstances make it difficult for people to understand the possibilities of cultural diversity. Because of technology, people increasingly live clustered together in towns – we understand that the majority of human beings in the world are now urban- rather than rural-dwellers, for the first time in human history – and modern media are tending to link the populations of the world together into a single "global village". Youngsters in different countries, whose parents or grandparents might have had scarcely any cultural reference points in common, nowadays often spend much of their time listening to the same pop songs and watching the same films. In the past, the chief way in which educated Europeans encountered the details of civilizations radically different from their own was through intensive study of the classics; you cannot spend years learning about ancient Greece or Rome and still suppose that modern Europe or the USA represent the only possible models for successful societies, even if you happen to prefer the modern models. But in recent decades the number of schoolchildren getting more than (at most) a brief exposure to Latin or Greek has shrunk to a vanishingly small minority in Britain and in Hungary, and (doubtless) elsewhere also. Perhaps most important of all, the internet and the World Wide Web have brought about a sudden foreshortening of people's mental time horizons. While the usual way for a student to get information was through a library, it was about as easy for him to look at a fifty- or hundred-year-old book as a two- or three-year-old one. Now that everyone uses the Web, the pre-Web world is becoming relegated to a shadowy existence. Everyone knows it was there, any adult remembers chunks of it, but in practice it just is not accessible in detail in the way that the world of the last few years is. And when Tim Berners-Lee invented the Web in 1993, urbanization and globalization had already happened. So, nowadays, it really is hard for rising generations to get their minds round the idea that the way we live now is not the only possible way for human beings to live.

If this is hard, then so much the more reason for academics to put effort into helping people grasp the potential diversity of human cultures. After all, even someone who is thoroughly glad to have been born in our time, and who feels no wistfulness about any features of past or remote present-day societies, surely hopes that life for future generations will be better still. We do not meet many people who find life at the beginning of the 21st century so wonderful in all respects that improvement is inconceivable. But how can we hope to chart positive ways forward into the future, if we have no sense that there is a wide range of alternatives to our current reality? If external circumstances nowadays happen to be making it difficult for people to understand that cultures can differ widely, then explaining and demonstrating this becomes a specially urgent task for the academic profession.

15.4 Generative linguistics as a theory of human nature

Unfortunately, generative linguistics is doing just the opposite of this. Linguists like Steven Pinker and Noam Chomsky have been giving us spurious, pseudo-intellectual reasons to believe that human monoculture really is inevitable. And although, scientifically speaking, their arguments are junk, our modern external circumstances have caused them to receive far more credence than they deserve.

For a full justification of the statement that the generative linguistic theory of human nature is junk, we must refer readers to *The "Language Instinct" Debate* (Sampson 2005), already cited at various points in the present volume. Pinker and other generative linguists deploy a wide range of arguments to make their point of view seem convincing; *The "Language Instinct" Debate* goes through these arguments systematically and analyses the logical fallacies and false premises which in each case destroy their force. We have no space to recapitulate all that here. What matters for present purposes is to explain how the generative linguists' account of human nature relates to the question of cultural diversity.

On the face of it one might not see much link between a technical theory about structural universals of language, and ideas about the nonexistence of genuine cultural diversity with respect to vital areas such as law or government. A typical finding of generative linguistics (see e.g. Chomsky 1968: 51) is that grammatical rules in all languages are "structure-dependent", in the sense discussed on p. 244 above. So for instance, a language might have a grammar rule which turns statements into questions by shifting the main verb to the beginning, as many European languages have: the English statement *The man that you were talking about is in the kitchen* becomes the question *Is the man that you were talking about in the kitchen?* – where the concept "main verb", which picks out the word *is* in this case, is a concept that depends on the grammatical structure of the whole sentence. But (the claim is) no human language has *or could have* a rule that forms questions by moving the first verb of the statement, so that instead of asking *Is the man that you were talking about in the kitchen?* you would ask *Were the man that you talking about is in the kitchen?* From an abstract, computational point of view, identifying the first verb is a much simpler operation to define than identifying the main verb, so you might think it should be a commoner kind of rule to find among the languages of the world. But identifying the first verb in a sentence is an operation which is independent of the grammatical structure into which the individual words are grouped; so, instead of being a common type of rule, according to generative linguistics it never occurs at all.

Many people can accept this idea that there are universal constraints on the diversity of grammatical rules, as an interesting and possibly true finding of technical linguistic theory, without feeling that it threatens (or even relates in any way to) humanly-significant aspects of cultural diversity. Grammar in our languages is like plumbing in our houses: it needs to be there, but most people really are not interested in thinking about the details. The humanly significant things that happen in houses are things that happen in the dining room, the drawing room, and undoubtedly in the bedrooms, but not in the pipes behind the walls. Many generative linguists undoubtedly see themselves as cultivating a subject that is as self-contained as plumbing is: they themselves are professionally interested in language structure and only in language structure.

But the leaders of the profession do not see things that way at all. For Pinker, and for Chomsky, language structure is interesting because it is seen as a specially clear kind of evidence about human cognition in a far broader sense. The fact that grammar is a rather exact field makes it relatively easy to formalize and test theories about grammatical universals. Other aspects of culture which may have greater human significance often have a somewhat woolly quality that makes it harder to pin them down mathematically or scientifically. But the value of generative linguistics, for the leaders of the field, lies in the light it sheds on these broader areas of cognition and culture.

So, for instance, Chomsky used linguistics to argue that the range of humanly-possible art forms is fixed by our biology: if a lot of modern art seems rubbishy and silly, that may be because we have already exhausted the biologically-available possibilities, leaving no way for contemporary artists to innovate other than by "Mockery of conventions that are, ultimately, grounded in human cognitive capacity" (Chomsky 1976: 125). And similarly, Chomsky felt, the general human enterprise of scientific discovery is limited to trying out a fixed range of theories which our biology makes available to us, and which can by no means be expected to include the truth about various topics – he said "Thinking of humans as biological organisms ... it is only a lucky accident if their cognitive capacity happens to be well matched to scientific truth in some area" (Chomsky 1976: 25).

Likewise, although the bulk of Pinker's book *The Language Instinct* is obviously about language, what it leads up to is a final chapter, "Mind Design", which uses what has gone before as the basis for a far more wide-ranging account of the fixity of human cognition and culture. Pinker refers at length to a book by the social anthropologist Donald Brown, *Human Universals* (D. Brown 1991), in order to argue that alongside Chomsky's "UG" or Universal Grammar we need to recognize a "UP", or Universal People – behind the apparent diversity of human cultures described by anthropologists lie hundreds of cultural universals, which Pinker specifies via a list of headings that stretches over several pages. In an important sense, human beings don't really have different cultures – in the picture Pinker presents, human beings share one culture, but with superficial local variations (just as, from Chomsky's point of view, we do not really speak different languages – for Chomsky it would be more accurate to say that we all speak essentially one language, though with superficial local differences – Chomsky 1991: 26). And having established his reputation with *The Language Instinct*, Pinker in his most important subsequent books, *How the Mind Works* (1997) and *The Blank Slate* (2002), moves well beyond language to develop in a much more general way this idea that human cognitive life is as biologically determined as human anatomy.[1]

---

1 We should add that Steven Pinker has by now produced a large body of writings which also include some very valuable contributions: for instance his analysis (Pinker 2011) of how violence in society has declined with the growth of civilization. For that matter we by no means disagree with everything that Pinker says in *The Blank Slate*. But what Pinker says about language and the human faculty of reason is, in our view, deeply mistaken.

Furthermore, it is clear that it is these broader implications which have allowed generative linguistics to make the impact it has achieved on the intellectual scene generally. We often hear findings that by this or that measure Noam Chomsky is the world's most influential living intellectual (see, for instance, an international survey published in October 2005 by the magazine *Prospect – Prospect* 2005). No-one could conceivably attain that status merely via analysis of grammatical structure, no matter how original. In Chomsky's case, of course, his status derives in large part from his interventions in concrete political affairs, which are arguably a rather separate matter from his theoretical positions. But Steven Pinker himself attained a very respectable 26th position in the same *Prospect* poll, and Pinker is not known for specific political activities. So far as the general public is concerned, the importance of generative linguistics is not to do with language.

15.5 Cognitive constraints and cultural universalism

Once one grants the idea that biology makes only a limited range of cultural possibilities available to us, it is a short step to saying that a unique set of optimal social arrangements can be identified which in principle are valid for all humans everywhere. We can't expect that primitive, economically-backward human groups will have found their way to that optimal ideal, because their circumstances are not conducive to exploring the alternatives that do exist. But the picture which Chomsky offers, when he discusses biological limits to the ranges of possible scientific theories or genres of art, is that once society grows rich enough to allow people to escape

> the social and material conditions that prevent free intellectual development ... Then, science, mathematics, and art would flourish, pressing on towards the limits of cognitive capacity (Chomsky 1976: 124–125)

– and he suggests that we in the West seem now to have reached those limits. Third World tribes might live in ways which fail fully to implement the universally ideal human culture, but we Westerners are in a position to be able to identify the right way for humans to live – the way that is right for ourselves, and right for Third World tribespeople too, though they don't know it yet.

Certainly, the idea that there is no unique optimal way of life, and that humans ought to be permanently free to experiment with novel cultural arrangements in the expectation that societies will always discover new ways to progress, has historically been associated with the belief that the contents of human cognition are not given in advance. The founder of the liberal approach in politics, which holds that the State ought to limit its interference with individual subjects as narrowly as possible in order to leave them free to experiment, was John Locke; and, classically, Locke (1690: II, §1.6) argued that:

> He that attentively considers the state of a child, at his first coming into the world, will have little reason to think him stored with plenty of ideas, that are to be the matter of his future knowledge. It is by degrees he comes to be furnished with them.

Logically it makes sense for those who believe in biologically-fixed innate ideas to place a low value on the possibilities of cultural diversity and innovation.

The trouble is, in reality there are no biological constraints imposing specific, detailed structure on human cognitive life. And someone who believes in cognitive universals, in a situation where none exist, is almost bound to end up mistaking the accidental features of his own culture, or of the dominant culture in his world, for cultural universals.

15.6 "Universal grammar" means European grammar

In the case of linguistics this mistake is very clear. From the early years of generative grammar onwards, sceptics repeatedly objected that generative linguists were merely formalizing structural features of English, or features shared by most Indo-European languages, and assuming that they had identified universals of language structure. Generative linguists often denied this, and argued that the initial over-emphasis on English was just a temporary consequence of the theory having been born in an English-speaking country. But, even though by now a far wider range of languages are regularly discussed in the generative literature, the sceptics' charge remains true. Exotic languages are observed through English-language spectacles.

Sometimes this emerges from the very terminology of the field. Consider how generative linguists discuss the incidence of subject pronouns. In North-West European languages, such as English, German, and French, it is roughly true that every finite verb has an explicit subject – even when the identity of the subject would be obvious from the context alone, a pronoun has to appear. But we don't need to go beyond the Indo-European language family to find languages where that is not so: in (Classical or Modern) Greek, for instance, the verb inflexion shows the person and number of the subject, and it is fairly unusual to include a subject pronoun as well. Generative linguists call languages like Greek "Pro-Drop" languages (see e.g. Rizzi 1982, Neeleman and Szendrői 2007). The implication of "Pro-Drop" is transparent: in "Universal Grammar" (or in other words, in English) verbs have subject pronouns, so a language like Greek which often lacks them must be a language in which the pronouns that are universally present at an underlying level are "dropped" at the surface.

In the case of Greek and other European "Pro-Drop" languages, this Anglocentric view of the situation is at least consistent, in the sense that normally these languages do contain features showing what the subject pronoun would be, if it were present. But if we go beyond Europe, we find languages where even that is not true. In Classical Chinese, verbs commonly lack subjects; and there is no question of inferring the identity of missing subjects from verb inflexions, because Chinese is not an inflecting language. A European who hears this might guess that the difference between Classical Chinese and European languages is that our languages use formal features to identify subjects explicitly, while Chinese identifies them implicitly by mentioning situational features from which verb subjects can be inferred. But that is not true either: as we saw in chapter 1, often in Classical Chinese the subject of a verb *cannot* be inferred. A standard puzzle for Europeans who encounter Classical Chinese poetry is ambiguity about whether a poet is describing events in his own life, or actions of some third party. Because our own languages are the way they are, we feel that there must be an answer to this question; when a Chinese poet writes a verb, let's say the word for "see", surely in his own mind he must either have been thinking "I see" or thinking "he sees"? But that just forces our own categories of thought onto a language where they do not apply. To the Chinese themselves, asking whether the poet meant "I see" or "he sees" is asking a non-question. In English we can say "He saw her" without specifying whether he was wearing glasses or saw her with his naked eye. In Classical Chinese one could, and often did, say "Saw her" without specifying "I saw" or "he saw".

How can the implications of the term "Pro-Drop" be appropriate, if there are languages whose speakers not only frequently do not use pronouns but frequently do not even have corresponding concepts in their mind?

Pro-Drop is only one example of the way that generative linguistics mistakes features that happen to apply to the well-known languages spoken in our particular time and part of the world for features that are imposed on all human languages by human biology. But the point is far more general.

Consider David Gil's account of Riau Indonesian (e.g. Gil 2001), which we examined in chapter 1. When native speakers of this dialect are talking casually and naturally, their grammar has features that make it difficult to map on to the alleged structural universals discussed by generative linguistics. But when the speakers are challenged to think consciously about their language, for instance by translating from English into Malay, they switch to a formal version of Malay which looks much more like the kind of language which textbooks of theoretical linguistics discuss. One might imagine that this formal Malay reflects speakers' true underlying linguistic competence, while the colloquial dialect is a kind of reduced, distorted language-variety relevant only to studies of performance. But according to Gil it is the other way round. The colloquial language-variety represents the speakers' real linguistic heritage. Formal Malay is a more or less artificial construct, created in response to the impact of Western culture, and containing features designed to mirror the logical structure of European languages. So, naturally, formal Malay looks relatively "normal" to Western linguists, but it is no real evidence in favour of universals of grammar – whereas colloquial Riau dialect is good evidence *against* linguistic universals. Speakers use the formal variety when thinking consciously about their language, because politically it is the high-prestige variety; but it is not their most natural language.

Analogous situations occur with many Third World languages, Consequently, generative linguists tend systematically to study artificial languages created under Western cultural influence under the mistaken impression that they are finding evidence that alien cultures are much the same as ours.

15.7 Honest and dishonest imperialism

What generative linguistics is doing here is describing the diverse languages of the world as if they were all variations on a pattern defined by the dominant language or language-group – but at the same time pretending that this does not amount to Anglocentrism or Eurocentrism, because the fixed common pattern is defined not by a particular language or language-family, but by a hypothetical innate cognitive structure shared by all human beings. In a similar way, 21st-century internationalists are doing at least as much as 18th- and 19th-century imperialists did to impose their particular preferred cultural norms on people to whom those norms are alien; but the modern internationalists pretend that this does not count as cultural imperialism, because the favoured norms are presented not as arbitrary preferences, but as principles allegedly valid for all peoples at all times (even though many of them were thought up only quite recently).

The empire-builders of the nineteenth century did not think or speak in those terms. They were well aware that different peoples had genuinely different and sometimes incompatible cultural norms, and that there were real conflicts to be resolved between the principle that indigenous cultures should be respected, and the principle that government should guarantee to alien subjects the same rights that it guaranteed to members of the governing nation. A well-known example is suttee (nowadays sometimes spelled *sati*), the Hindu practice of burning a dead man's widow on his funeral pyre. When the British took control of India, they tried to avoid interfering with most native customs, but as an exception they banned suttee. On one famous occasion a group of male Hindus protested about this to Sir Charles James Napier (1782–1853), who is reported to have replied:

> You say that it is your custom to burn widows. Very well. We also have a custom: when men burn a woman alive, we tie a rope around their necks and we hang them. Build your funeral pyre; beside it, my carpenters will build a gallows. You may follow your custom. And then we will follow ours.

Notice that there was no suggestion here of suttee violating some universal code of human rights, which the Hindus could in principle have known about before the British arrived. It wasn't that at all: Napier saw Hindu and British moral universes as incommensurable. Within the Hindu moral universe, burning widows was the right thing to do. Within the British moral universe, burning anyone alive was a wrong thing to do. The British had acquired power over the Hindus, so now the Hindus were going to be forced to play by British rules whether they agreed with them or not.

We can reasonably debate and disagree about where the right balance lies between respecting alien cultures, and seeking to modify those cultures when they involve systematic oppression or cruelty. But the bare minimum we owe to other cultures, surely, is at least to acknowledge that they are indeed different. If powerful outsiders tell us that aspects of the culture we grew up in are unacceptable to them, so they are going to change these whether we like it or not, then we shall probably resent that and try to resist. But we should be humiliated far worse, if the outsiders tell us and our fellows that we had not got a genuinely separate culture in the first place – the patterns they are imposing on us are the universal cultural patterns appropriate to all human beings, and if our traditional way of life deviated in some respects that was just because we were a bit muddled and ignorant. That is the attitude which present-day internationalism implies and generative linguistics supports.

Of course, there is no doubt that Noam Chomsky in particular would indignantly deny that. He is frequently eloquent in denouncing imperialism. But his comments on specific political issues, and the logical consequences of his abstract theorizing, are two very different things. What is really poisonous about the ideology that emerges from generative linguistics is that it creates a rationale for powerful groups to transform the ways of life of powerless groups while pretending that they are imposing no real changes – they are merely freeing the affected groups to realize the same innate cultural possibilities which are as natural to them as they are to everyone else, because we human beings all inherit the same biologically-fixed cultural foundations.

As Larissa Macfarquhar (2003) put it in a *New Yorker* profile of Chomsky:

> Chomsky ... has never been attracted to the notion that psychological originality or cultural variety is essential to what it means to be human. Politically, though, this has always been a dangerous move (the Jacobin move), for it allows the theorist not to take seriously any argument that departs from rationality as the theorist defines it. There can be no disagreement, then, only truth and error ...

15.8 Vocabulary and culture

It seems obvious that the institutions a society evolves for itself, and the kinds of fulfilment its members seek, will have a great deal to do with the structure of concepts encoded in its language. Consider for instance the central role of the concept of "freedom" or "liberty" in European life. The history of European political thought, from the classical Greeks to today, has been very largely about how best to interpret the ideal of freedom and how to maximize the incidence of freedom. When Europeans assess the quality of their individual lives, they tend to do so in significant part by assessing how much freedom they enjoy. Europeans were able to assign this central role to the concept of freedom, because they spoke languages which encoded the concept from a very early period. Latin *liber*, and Greek *eleutheros*, both derive from the same Indo-European root, which originally meant "people" (as the German cognate *Leute* does today). The semantic transition from "belonging to the people" to "free" originally came about because those born into an ethnic group were free men while those brought in as captives from elsewhere were slaves; the fact that this same semantic transition shows up in both the Italic and the Greek branches implies that the "freedom" concept dates back before the historical period most of the way to Proto-Indo-European.[2] Because the concept of "freedom" corresponded to a common word familiar to any speaker, no doubt originally in a relatively down-to-earth, unsophisticated sense, it was available for thinkers from Greeks in the Classical world through to Dante, Locke, and many others in recent centuries to invest with the much greater weight of significance and emotional importance that we associate with it today.

---

2 English *free* and German *frei*, together with Welsh *rhydd*, represent a similar semantic transition in a different Indo-European root, and again the fact that the transition is reflected both in Germanic and in Celtic suggests that the "freedom" sense is old – though in this case there is apparently an argument that one subfamily may have borrowed it from the other after Germanic and Celtic had separated.

We can see how culturally conditioned this development was, if we compare Europe with China. Chinese civilization is older than ours, and for most of the last 3000 years, until the Industrial Revolution, any neutral observer would have had to judge Chinese civilization as more complex and sophisticated than that of Europe. But, as it happens, the large battery of concepts which the Chinese language made available to its speakers included no root at all comparable to our word *free*. When Chinese intellectuals began to examine and translate Western thought in the nineteenth and early twentieth centuries, they had to adapt a compound term used in a distantly-related sense, *zì yóu* 自由, to stand for the European concept (see Huang 1972: 69);[3] and we understand that Chinese readers had difficulty in grasping that Europeans saw this idea as positive – for the Chinese a good society was one in which individuals subordinated themselves to the collectivity. Philosophy in traditional China was predominantly political philosophy, but Chinese political thought was not concerned with individual freedom, and individual Chinese who assessed the quality of their lives did not use that measure.[4] Arguably, this contrast remains highly relevant for understanding the differences between China and the West today.

This interdependence between vocabulary and social institutions seems a familiar, uncontroversial idea. But generative linguistics has no room for it. The generative view of vocabulary is explained in Pinker's *Language Instinct*

---

3 The original meaning of *zì yóu* was something like "follow[ing] one's own bent", with no political connotation. Interestingly, when the standard (pre-Communist) Chinese dictionary-encyclopaedia *Cí Hǎi* offers a definition for the modern, political sense of *zì yóu* (Shu et al. 1938: section *wei*, p. 221), from a Western point of view it rather misses the point by saying "not subject to *unlawful* constraint" (our translation, and our italics) – but law is a main source of potential threats to freedom.

4 The sole reference we find in Fung Yu-lan's standard *Short History of Chinese Philosophy* (Fung 1948) to a term corresponding to "free, freedom" in Chinese thought before the onset of Western influence is a single passage in the 3rd–4th-century Xiang–Guo commentary on chapter 1 of the *Zhuang-zi* (Fung, p. 229), which at several points uses *xiāo-yáo* 逍遙 or just *yáo* (Karlgren 1957: entries 1149m, 1144k) in a sense translated by Fung as "happiness and freedom" or just "freedom". (In the edition of the *Zhuang-zi* on our shelves, some of these instances of *yáo* appear instead as the visually-similar and much commoner word *tōng* 通, Karlgren entry 1185r, which means something entirely different; Fung evidently, and doubtless correctly, takes *tōng* to be a scribal error for *yáo*.) The basic meaning of *(xiāo)-yáo* was "to saunter about, be at ease", and in Fung's interpretation of the Xiang–Guo passage it refers there to freedom in a psychological sense: the nirvana-like state of mind of one who has relinquished all desires. Even if we accept Fung's interpretation of this isolated passage, the usage there is a far cry from freedom in the political sense. Note by contrast how implausible it is that a history of European philosophy would fail to include abundant references to free will and political freedom.

by reference to Jerry Fodor's theory of a language of thought. As we have seen, Fodor holds that we understand utterances in an ordinary spoken language by translating them into an internal language of thought which is fixed by human genetics; and because the language of thought is inherited biologically rather than evolved culturally, it is universal. The languages of different societies do not truly differ in their vocabularies: they all encode the same innate set of concepts. If European languages all have a word for "free" and Chinese traditionally had no such word, Fodor might explain that by saying that the European languages happen to use a single word for a compound of universal concepts which traditional Chinese would have needed to spell out via a paraphrase – rather as German has a single word *Geschwister* for a concept which English has to spell out as a three-word phrase, "brothers and sisters".

Here we are putting words into Fodor's mouth: Fodor does not actually discuss specific cases of vocabulary difference, which is perhaps quite wise of him. Pinker does, though. Indeed, he gives the specific example of "freedom" as an instance of a concept which all human beings possess, whether or not it is encoded in their language (Pinker 1995: 82). But if one insists that members of a major world civilization, which over millennia neither used a word for a particular concept nor adopted institutions which reflected that concept, nevertheless had the concept in their minds, then surely we have left science behind and entered the realm of quasi-religious dogma.

If Fodor and Pinker are right, vocabulary differences would be superficial things. They would not amount to reasons for societies to equip themselves with significantly different institutions, or for their members to pursue significantly different goals.

(Incidentally, even if we did accept Fodor's and Pinker's idea that vocabulary is innate, it would not follow that it is universal. It might seem more plausible that vocabulary should vary with individuals' ancestry. Chinese might not only lack some concepts that European languages contain, and vice versa, but yellow men, or black men, would be unable to learn some white words even when exposed to them, and white men would be unable to learn some yellow words or black words. After all, it is clear that the human brain did not cease to evolve biologically after the time when our species began to diverge into distinct races, and indeed we know now that it has continued to evolve in recent times (P. Evans et al. 2005, Mekel-Bobrov et al. 2005); so why would the brain modules responsible for the language of thought be exempt from biological evolution? We have seen no hint of this concept of racially-bound vocabulary in the writings of generative linguists, but the most plausible reason for that is merely that they fear the consequences of taking their ideas to this logical conclusion. The generative linguists want to be influential; they want to dominate their corner of the academic map, so that the research grants and attractive jobs keep coming. You do not achieve that by raising the possibility that coloured people might be genetically incapable of fully understanding English.)

15.9 Universalist politics

If all human minds shared the same biologically-fixed stock of concepts, then it might make sense to say that there is one system of social ideals which can be deduced by studying our innate cognitive mechanisms, and which is valid for all human beings everywhere and at all times, whether they realize it or not. Increasingly, we find that politics these days is operated as if that idea were true. (Cf. Phillips 2006: 63–78.)

For instance, in 2005 we in the European Union narrowly avoided adopting a Constitution whose text laid down a mass of detailed rules covering aspects of life (for instance, labour relations, housing policy, the treatment of the disabled, etc.), which traditionally would have found no place in a constitution. A normal State constitution confines itself to specifying basic rules about how the organs of the State interrelate, what the limits of their respective powers are, how their members are chosen and dismissed, and so forth. Detailed rules about relationships between private employers and employees, say, would evolve over time through the continuing argy-bargy of political activity within the unchanging framework of the basic law. But, if human culture is built on the basis of a limited range of concepts that are biologically fixed and common to all human beings, then perhaps it should be possible to work out an ideal set of rules for society in much more detail, in the expectation that they will remain ideal in the 22nd and 23rd centuries – after all, human biology is not likely to change much over a few hundred years.

We escaped the European constitution, thanks to the voters of France and the Netherlands – though the mighty ones of the European project seem still to believe that the constitution was a good idea, and have been quietly attempting to revive it. But there are plenty of other examples where laws are being changed in the name of hypothetical universal principles, although the laws in question have worked unproblematically for long periods and the populations affected have no desire for change.

Thus, consider what has been done over the last few years to the island of Sark, which is a constitutionally-separate dependency of the British Crown a few miles off the northern coast of France. Sark is one of the world's smallest States, with a population of about 600, and politically it was until very recently a remarkable feudal survival, with a constitution that must have been on the old-fashioned side even when the island was settled in the 16th century. In 2004 Sark was forced by European Union pressure to remove the provisions in its laws which prescribed the death penalty for treason, although the Serquois population protested loudly that they believed treason should remain punishable by death. And later a couple of rich newcomers found that the laws of Sark did not suit them, so in 2008 they used the European Convention on Human Rights to get the constitution overturned and transformed into a standard modern democratic system.

Until a few decades ago, we in Britain had the death penalty for more crimes than just treason, and debate continues about whether we were wise to give it up. The USA retains the death penalty today. Surely it is obvious that this is the kind of issue on which we can expect different cultures to differ, not one that can be settled in terms of hypothetical universal principles? It is understandable that the Serquois take a more serious view of treason than the English do: they had the experience within living memory of being invaded and occupied by enemy forces, something which England has happily been spared for almost a thousand years. Of course, if one believes in detailed universal principles underlying human culture, then local accidents of history may be neither here nor there. But, for those of us who disbelieve in a detailed biologically-fixed substratum for culture, it is expected that differences of historical experience of this kind will lead to differences in present-day cultural frameworks, and it is right and proper that they should be allowed to do so.

As for the constitution: the fact that the Serquois would prefer to keep it does not matter. The fact that in a face-to-face society of 600 men, women, and children there are better ways available to individuals to register their opinions than marking a cross on a slip of paper once every few years doesn't matter. The culture of Sark is being changed over the heads of the Serquois; but instead of being presented as a case of two powerful people selfishly forcing 600 powerless people to change their ways, which is the truth of it, we are asked to see it as a case of the Serquois finally achieving rights which have been unjustly witheld from them for centuries.

We could give other examples from more distant areas of the world which are more serious (though perhaps not quite as absurd) as the defeudalization of Sark.[5] The general point is that we are moving at present from a world in which

---

5 Consider for instance the way in which Britain has recently been eliminating the residual dependence of ex-colonial West Indian jurisdictions on the English legal system, and setting them up with fully-independent legal frameworks of their own, but in doing so has been careful to provide the newly-independent legal systems with entrenched rules against outlawing homo-

312 — Minds in Uniform

everyone recognizes that cultures are different, though powerful cultures some-times impose their will on weaker ones and modify them, to a world where that still happens but the powerful nations or groups pretend that the basic princi-ples of culture are everywhere alike, so that if they interfere with alien cultures they are not essentially changing them – merely allowing them to be what they were trying to be anyway, although in some cases they didn't realize it.

Politicians do not often state their assumptions at this level of philosophical abstraction; but a recent British Prime Minister, Tony Blair, made explicit remarks on the topic, in a valedictory essay on the lessons of his ten years as premier. Justifying his foreign policy, he wrote (Blair 2007):

> There is nothing more ridiculous than the attempt to portray "democracy" or "freedom" as somehow "Western" concepts which, mistakenly, we try to apply to nations or peoples to whom they are alien. There may well be governments to whom they are alien. But not peoples.... These values are universal.

The ex-Prime Minister was in error. The concepts of democracy and freedom are specific cultural creations, in the same way that the game of chess or the Apple Macintosh operating system are. They may be excellent ideas, but they are not "universal" ideas. If the political leaders of the English-speaking world are taking it for granted now that only tyrannical governments stand in the way of culturally-remote populations realizing essentially the same structure of political ideals as ours, because that structure is innate in everyone, this may explain a great deal about recent overseas interventions and their unhappy out-comes.

(We have dealt with the non-universality of the freedom concept in the pre-vious section. In the case of democracy, one might have thought that a general awareness of European intellectual history would have been enough to show how culture-specific the concept is. Or consider the debates which have occurred in China since the promulgation of "Charter 08" which called for that country to "join ... the mainstream of civilisation" by "recognising universal values"

---

sexual activity. It is clear that cultures are very diverse in their attitudes to homosexuality, which was a serious criminal offence in Britain itself not many decades ago. Europeans have changed their views on this, but many African-descended cultures seem to have a specially strong horror of homosexuality. If we are serious about giving other peoples their indepen-dence, we have to accept that their cultures will embody some different choices from ours on issues like this. But instead, the new internationalists announce that alien nations are required to conform culturally to a set of principles which are alleged to be universally valid – and which, just by coincidence, happen to match the principles embraced at the moment by the world's most powerful nations. Setting people free, but requiring them to use their freedom in approved ways, is not setting them free.

(*Economist* 2010, 2011). Whether or not values such as freedom of speech or democratic election of governments deserve to *become* universal, the debates have only made sense because as a matter of fact these and various other Western ideals did not play a part in Chinese thinking over the vast majority of China's three-thousand-year history. Many leading Chinese explicitly deny that they should have a place in China now (*Economist* 2013b).)

There is a clear parallel between this new imperialism of universal rights, and the generative-linguistics concept of universal cognitive structure. Obviously, we do not suggest that the sort of people who decide to impose adult suffrage on the island of Sark are doing so because they have been reading Noam Chomsky's *Syntactic Structures* and got a bit over-excited. Probably they have never heard of Noam Chomsky or Steven Pinker. But the link is that intellectuals such as Chomsky and Pinker are creating a philosophical climate within which the new imperialism of the 21st century becomes justifiable.

Without that philosophical climate, the new imperialism is just a product of ignorance – because people these days learn so little about cultures that are distant from our own, they genuinely fail to appreciate that human cultures can be extremely different, and consequently when they spot something somewhere far away from Western metropolises which looks out of line, they take it to indicate a pathological deviation that needs to be normalized. That attitude could be cured by better education. But if most of the principles of human culture are determined by the shared genetic inheritance of our species, then where there are cultural differences it becomes reasonable to infer that one of the cultures really is pathological in the relevant respect. And, since it is difficult for any member of an established, successful culture to believe that his own familiar way of life is diseased, the alien culture is assumed to need curing – for its own good.

15.10 Abandoning the touchstone of empiricism

The ideology which is emerging from generative linguistics does not only involve new and surprising ideas about the biological determination of cognition. It also embodies new and surprising ideas about how we decide what is true.

If a set of popular ideas are factually mistaken, traditionally we expect that sooner or later they will be abandoned because people see that the evidence refutes them. In the case of generative linguistics, though, this routine safety-mechanism of scientific advance is not working, because, as we have seen, one component of the generative approach is an explicit claim that empirical evidence is not relevant. Since linguistics is about things happening in speakers' minds, the generativists argue, if you want to find out how the grammar of your language works what you should do is look into your mind – consult your intuitions as a speaker, rather than listening to how other people speak in practice. How people actually speak is linguistic "performance", which the generativists see as an imperfect, distorted reflection of the true linguistic "competence" within speakers' minds. Besides, a linguist's intuition gives him access to information about the precise construction he happens to be interested in at the time – even if this is in fact a good grammatical construction, one might have to listen out for a very long time before one was lucky enough to hear a speaker use it in real life.

We have been here before. In the Middle Ages, people used intuition to decide all sorts of scientific questions: for instance, they knew that the planets moved in circular orbits, because the circle is the only shape perfect enough to suit a celestial object – and when empirical counter-evidence began coming in, they piled epicycles on epicycles in order to reconcile their intuitive certainty about circles with the awkward observations. Since Galileo, most of us have understood that intuitive evidence is no use: it misleads you. The planets in reality travel in ellipses. And even though language is an aspect of our own behaviour rather than a distant external reality, intuitive evidence is no more reliable in linguistics than it is in astronomy. As we saw in chapter 13, some of the mistakes that generative linguists have made by relying on intuitive evidence have been breathtakingly large.

15.11 Intuition-based politics

Parallel errors are occurring in current affairs. Again and again in the contemporary world we find political decisions which crucially affect people's ways of life being made on a basis of intuition, when empirical evidence is available but is ignored.

A good example is foreign aid. To many people in the present-day West it ranks as an unquestionable axiom that the best way to help African and other Third-World societies out of grinding poverty is to step up the level of aid payments which our governments hand over to their governments.

In reality, there has been abundant argument based on hard evidence, from economists like the late Lord (Peter) Bauer in England and William Easterly in the USA, that foreign aid doesn't work. (See e.g. P.T. Bauer 1981, Easterly 2006.) It is a good way of politicizing recipient societies and diverting the efforts of their populations away from developing successful independent and productive ways of life towards striving to become unproductive government clients; and it is a good way of turning Third World governments in turn into clients of Western governments, so that the direct control of the age of empires is replaced by a looser, less overt form of imperialism. But as a method of making the average African less poor: forget it.

We know what would genuinely improve the lot of the average African: free trade, which would allow individual Africans to build up businesses producing the agricultural goods which their economies are ready to produce, and selling them to Western markets free of tariff barriers such as the scandalous European Common Agricultural Policy, which at present actively prevents Third World residents from making a living in the only ways that are realistically open to many of them. Free trade is not enough – poor countries also need decent government – but it is a necessary condition. Free trade would permit the growth of genuinely independent societies in the Third World, shaped through the inhabitants' own initiatives and choices.

But that is probably not going to happen, because we in the West intuitively know that foreign aid is the answer. It hasn't achieved much over the last fifty years, and the economic logic suggests that it never could – but who cares about empirical evidence and argument, when the thought of our tax money going in foreign aid gives us a warm, virtuous glow inside ourselves, and that is what counts? Commercial trading relationships feel intuitively like a cold-hearted area of life, not something that we ought to be imposing on people as poor and powerless as the residents of sub-Saharan Africa. The Doha Round of international trade negotiations, launched in 2001, was intended principally to give Third World countries freer access for exports to the EU and the USA; but within a few years it had well-nigh collapsed with little achieved, and how many in the West even noticed? Not many. In 2012 *The Economist* argued that it was unreasonable to allow failure to agree freer trade in agriculture, "an industry that makes up only 7% of world trade", to interfere with progress towards freer trade between industrial nations – to which representatives of a number of Third World countries very reasonably responded that this amounted to saying "that poorer countries must abandon their agenda because richer economies are not willing to make the very same tough political decisions they ask of the developing world", and pointed out that agriculture accounted for more than sixty per cent of exports from some developing countries (*Economist* 2012).

Foreign aid is one area where public policy is nowadays based on intuition rather than on empirical evidence, to an extent that we believe would not have happened fifty or a hundred years ago. Let us give one more, smaller-scale example: the recent fate of foxhunting in England.

For hundreds of years, riding horses to follow dogs hunting foxes has been a central component of the culture of various rural parts of England. Not only does it provide glorious exercise for all ages and both sexes in winter, when other outdoor possibilities are few, but the organizations created to manage local hunts have also been the focus of much other social activity in remote areas; the dances where the girls have the best opportunity to dress up and show themselves off are typically the Hunt Balls. In 2004, in the face of passionate objections by members of hunting communities, foxhunting was made illegal, with no compensation for the thousands of hunt servants and others whose livelihoods were abolished at a stroke, by Members of Parliament most of whom are town-dwellers and scarcely know one end of a horse from the other. The true motive for this legislation was that hunting is associated with features of rural society that the then governing party instinctively dislikes – a local Master of Fox Hounds will often (though by no means always) be an aristocrat living in a large old house. But that sort of thing could not be openly stated as a reason for legal interference with people's longstanding way of life, so instead it was argued that hunting is unnecessarily cruel. This is a testable claim. Foxes in a farming area are pests whose numbers have to be controlled somehow, and it is an open question whether hunting with hounds is a specially cruel way to do it. The Government set up an enquiry under Lord Burns to answer the question; rather to Government's surprise, perhaps, the Burns Report published in 2000 found that banning foxhunting would have no clear positive effect on the incidence of cruelty (it might even increase cruelty), and it would have other consequences which everyone agrees to be adverse.[6]

So the empirical evidence was there: how much influence did it have on the parliamentary process which led to the ban? None at all. The people who made the decisions were not interested in empirical evidence. Foxes look like sweet, cuddly, furry creatures, and parliamentarians intuitively knew that hunting them was wrong. Many country folk had the opposite intuition, but how seriously could one take them? Faced with a choice between a peasant type in cheap clothes and a rural accent, versus a well-spoken Member of Parliament in an expensive dark suit, it is obvious which one has authoritative intuitions and which one has mere personal opinions.[7]

---

6 See <www.huntinginquiry.gov.uk/>. In July 2006 a survey on the practical effects of the Hunting Act appeared to show that its consequences for fox welfare have indeed been negative, with many foxes now wounded by shotguns rather than cleanly killed (Clover 2006).

7 To be fair to him, Tony Blair, who as Prime Minister pushed the hunting ban through, saw it a few years later as "a fatal mistake":

> I started to realise that this wasn't a small clique of weirdo inbreds delighting in cruelty, but a tradition, deeply embedded by history and profound community and social liens, that was integral to a way of life (Blair 2010: 304–306)

If Blair did not appreciate this before, it was not for want of people trying to explain it.

Likewise, if we in the West with our comfortable houses and air-conditioned cars know intuitively that foreign aid is the way to rescue Africans from poverty, isn't it clear to everyone that our intuitions are more authoritative than those of some African living in a thatched hut and wearing a grubby singlet, who might prefer the chance to find wider markets for his cash crops?

Well, to the present authors it isn't clear. But then we are among those eccentrics who still believe in empirical evidence.

We have offered two examples of the way in which decisions that crucially impact on people's ways of life are these days being made in terms of intuition and arguments from authority, rather than in terms of hard, reliable evidence. Obviously we are not suggesting that this is happening because of generative linguistics. Most people who are influential in decisions about foreign aid, foxhunting, or many other current-affairs issues that we could have used as illustrations, will be people who have never given a thought to generative linguistics or to the picture of human cognition which is derived from it. But what that theory does is to provide an intellectual rationale for these political developments. While people in political life were moving purely as a matter of fashion away from reliance on empirical evidence toward reliance on intuition and argument from authority, one could point out how irrational this fashion is. Even those who were caught up in the tide of fashion, if they understood what they were doing, might with luck be persuaded to turn back to the firm ground of empirical evidence; they would have found no explicit arguments to justify the fashionable trend. What generative linguistics has been doing is supplying those missing arguments. It has begun to create a climate of intellectual opinion that makes it possible for people openly to say in so many words, "Yes, we are basing decisions on intuition rather than on evidence, and we are right to do so. Empirical argument is outdated 20th-century thinking – we are progressing beyond that."

Incidentally, we also appreciate that many readers will find examples like foxhunting, or the governance of a tiny island with a three-figure population, unimportant and almost frivolous relative to the profundity of the abstract political principles under discussion. That mismatch is entirely intentional. When political principles are discussed and illustrated by reference to major policy issues crucially affecting the welfare of tens of millions, it is very natural and often happens that the passions which readers have understandably invested in the concrete issues make it difficult for them to think coolly about the abstract underlying principles. We hope that by discussing the topic of this chapter largely in terms of minor, remote issues, it will be easier for readers to recognize that (irrespective of the rights or wrongs of the Sark way of life, or of foxhunting) it is vitally important to acknowledge that cultures can be deeply different, and that knowledge must be tested empirically.

Moving from reliance on empirical science to reliance on intuition and arguments from authority is not progress. It is a reversion to the pre-Enlightenment Middle Ages. That is why it is so important to explode the false claims of generative linguistics.

15.12 New evidence for language diversity

Happily, if we treat generative linguistics as a scientific theory rather than a matter of blind faith, then it is easily exploded. We have said that we have no space here to rehearse all the detailed arguments of Sampson (2005). But some of the most recent findings by non-generative linguists are so destructive for generative theory that the older and more technical debates become almost beside the point.

Until recently, the consensus among linguists of all theoretical persuasions was that known human languages seem to be roughly comparable in the expressive power of their grammars. Languages can differ in the nature of the verbal constructions they use in order to express some conceptual relationship, but we did not find fundamental structures of thought that certain extant languages were just incapable of expressing. And that is crucial for the generative theory of human cognition. If our cognitive structures are biologically fixed, then all our languages should be equally capable of clothing those structures in words. A sceptic might respond that there is another possible explanation: all the languages we know about have emerged from a very long prehistoric period of cultural evolution, so there has been ample time for them to develop all the constructions they might need – simpler, structurally more primitive languages must once have existed, but that would have been long before the invention of writing. Still, the generative camp might have seen this as a rather weak answer.

It began to look a lot stronger, with the publication in 2000 of Guy Deutscher's *Syntactic Change in Akkadian* (Deutscher 2000). Akkadian was one of the earliest written languages in the world; as we saw in 10.13 above, Deutscher shows that we can see it developing in the Old Babylonian period (ca 2000–1500 BC), under the pressure of new communicative needs, from a state in which it contained no subordinate complement clauses into a later state where that construction had come into being. If the general grammatical architecture of human languages were determined by human biology, it is hard to see how a logical resource as fundamental as the complement clause could possibly be a historical development. It ought to be one of the universal features common to all human languages at all periods.

Then, in 2005, Daniel Everett published his description of the Pirahã language of the southern Amazon basin. On Everett's account, Pirahã is in a number of respects quite astonishingly primitive, lacking not only all types of subordinate clause and indeed grammatical embedding of any kind, but also having no quantifier terms such as "all" or "most", no words for even low numbers, and many other remarkable features. We expressed caution, earlier (p. 91), about whether all aspects of Everett's interpretation of his data will ultimately prove correct, but even if only a fraction of his claims survived criticism that would surely be enough to refute the belief that languages are alternative suits of clothing for a universal set of thought-structures.

And the idea that all human languages are equally complex seemed to fall to pieces as soon as it was treated as a fallible hypothesis open to serious examination. See e.g. various papers in Miestamo et al. (2008) or Sampson, Gil, and Trudgill (2009).

In face of findings like these, it seems indisputable that early-20th-century scholars such as Franz Boas or H.A. Gleason were right about language diversity, and scholars like Pinker and Chomsky are just mistaken.

15.13 Conclusion

The truth is that languages are cultural developments, which human groups create freely, unconstrained except in trivial ways by their biology, just as they create games, or dances, or legal systems. The game of cricket is not encoded in an Englishman's genes – and nor is the English language. Linguistics gives us no serious grounds for believing in a model of human cognition according to which we are limited culturally to realizing one or other of a fixed range of possibilities. We are free to invent new cultural forms in the future, just as we have so abundantly done in the past.

We owe it to ourselves, to our descendants, and perhaps above all to our Third World neighbours to reject any ideology that claims to set boundaries to this process of ever-new blossoming of the human spirit. Just as our lives have risen above the limitations which constrained our ancestors, so we must leave those who come after us free to rise above the limitations which restrict us.

References

Allen, Grant. 1879. *The Colour-Sense: its origin and development. An essay in comparative psychology*. (London: Trübner; our page references are to 2nd edn, 1892.)

Ammon, Ulrich. 1994. Code, sociolinguistics. In R.E. Asher (ed.), *Encyclopedia of Language and Linguistics*, 2: 578–581. Oxford: Pergamon.

Aronoff, Mark. 1976. *Word Formation in Generative Grammar*. Cambridge, Mass.: MIT Press.

Arppe, Antti and Juhani Järvikivi. 2007. Take empiricism seriously! In support of methodological diversity in linguistics. *Corpus Linguistics and Linguistic Theory* 3: 99–109.

Ayala, F. J. 1995. Evolution, the theory of. *Encyclopaedia Britannica*, 15th edn, 18: 855–883.

Babarczy, Anna, John Carroll, and Geoffrey Sampson. 2006. Definitional, personal, and mechanical constraints on part of speech annotation performance. *Natural Language Engineering* 12: 77–90.

Bailkin, Jordanna. 2005. Color problems: work, pathology, and perception in modern Britain. *International Labor and Working-Class History* 68: 93–111.

Ballasy, Nicholas. 2010. White House science czar says he would use "free market" to "de-develop" the United States. <cnsnews.com/node/75388> (accessed 2 Jan 2012).

Bangalore, Srinivas. 2000. A lightweight dependency analyzer for partial parsing. *Natural Language Engineering* 6: 113–138.

Bangalore, Srinivas, Anoop Sarkar, Christine Doran, and Beth Ann Hockey. 1998. Grammar and parser evaluation in the XTAG project. In John Carroll (ed.), *Proceedings of Workshop on the Evaluation of Parsing Systems*, 1st International Conference on Language Resources and Evaluation, Granada, Spain, 26 May 1998 (Cognitive Science Research Papers 489, University of Sussex).

Bard, Ellen Gurman, Dan Robertson, and Antonella Sorace. 1996. Magnitude estimation of linguistic acceptability. *Language* 72: 32–68.

Basilico, David. 1996. Head position and internally headed relative clauses. *Language* 72: 498–532.

Bauer, Laurie. 1990. Be-heading the word. *Journal of Linguistics* 26: 1–31.

Bauer, P. T. 1981. *Equality, the Third World and Economic Delusion*. London: Weidenfeld & Nicolson.

Baxter, William H. 1992. *A Handbook of Old Chinese Phonology*. Berlin: Mouton de Gruyter.

Bayer, Samuel. 1996. The coordination of unlike categories. *Language* 72: 579–616.

Beare, John. 1906. *Greek Theories of Elementary Cognition from Alcmaeon to Aristotle*. Oxford: Clarendon Press.

Beck, Jacob. 1972. *Surface Color Perception*. Ithaca, N.Y.: Cornell University Press.

Behme, Christina. 2013. Review of Massimo Piattelli-Palmarini et al. (eds), *Of Minds and Language. Journal of Linguistics* 49: 499–506.

Belasco, S. 1950. Variations in color and length of French [a]: a spectrographic study. *Language* 26: 481–488.

Bellmer, Elizabeth Henry. 1999. The statesman and the ophthalmologist. *Annals of Science* 56: 25–45.

Berlin, Brent and Paul Kay. 1969. *Basic Color Terms*. Berkeley and Los Angeles, Calif.: University of California Press.

Bernstein, Basil. 1971. *Class, Codes and Control*, vol. 1: *Theoretical Studies Towards a Sociology of Language*. London: Routledge & Kegan Paul.

Berwick, Robert C. and Noam Chomsky. forthcoming. The biolinguistic program: the current state of its evolution and development. To be in Anna Maria Di Sciullo and Calixto Aguero (eds), *Biolinguistic Investigations*. Cambridge, Mass.: MIT Press. Downloaded 26 Jun 2013 from <www.unifi.it/offertaformativa/allegati/uploaded_files/2010/200007/B005357/berwick-chomsky.pdf>.

Biber, Douglas and Edward Finegan. 1991. On the exploitation of computerized corpora in variation studies. In Karin Aijmer and Bengt Altenberg (eds), *English Corpus Linguistics: studies in honour of Jan Svartvik*, 204–220. London: Longman.

Bisang, Walter. 2009. On the evolution of complexity: sometimes less is more in East and mainland Southeast Asia. In Sampson, Gil, and Trudgill (2009: 34–49).

Black, Ezra, Steve Abney, Dan Flickinger, Claudia Gdaniec, Ralph Grishman, Phil Harrison, Don Hindle, Robert Ingria, Fred Jelinek, J. Klavans, Mark Liberman, Mitch Marcus, S. Roukos, B. Santorini, and Tomek Strzalkowski. 1991. A procedure for quantitatively comparing the syntactic coverage of English grammars. In *Proceedings of the Speech and Natural Language Workshop, Defence Advanced Research Projects Agency (DARPA), February 1991, Pacific Grove, Calif.*, pp. 306–311. San Francisco: Morgan Kaufmann.

Blair, Anthony C. L. 2007. What I've learned. *The Economist* 2 Jun 2007, p. 30.

Blair, Anthony C. L. 2010. *A Journey*. London: Cornerstone.

Bloomfield, Leonard. 1933. *Language*. New York: Holt.

Boas, Franz. 1911. Introduction to *Handbook of American Indian Languages*, Bureau of American Ethnology, Bulletin 40, part I, 1–83. Washington, D.C.: Government Printing Office. Reprinted in one volume with J.W. Powell, *Indian Linguistic Families of America North of Mexico*, Lincoln, Neb., 1966.

Boas, Franz. 1932. The aims of anthropological research. Reprinted in Boas, *Race, Language and Culture*, 243–259; New York: Free Press, 1940.

Bod, Rens and Remko Scha. 1996. Data-oriented language processing: an overview. *ILLC Research Report LP-96-13*, Institute for Logic, Language and Computation, University of Amsterdam. Reprinted in Sampson and McCarthy (2004: 304–325).

Bod, Rens, Remko Scha, and Khalil Sima'an (eds). 2003. *Data-Oriented Parsing*. Stanford, Calif.: CSLI Publications.

Boden, Margaret A. 2008. Odd man out: reply to reviewers. *Artificial Intelligence* 172: 1944–1964.

Boeckx, Cedric. 2006a. *Linguistic Minimalism: origins, concepts, methods, and aims*. Oxford: Oxford University Press.

Boeckx, Cedric. 2006b. Review of Postal, *Skeptical Linguistic Essays*. *Journal of Linguistics* 42: 216–221.

Boltz, William G. 1999. Language and writing. In Michael Loewe and Edward L. Shaughnessy (eds), *The Cambridge History of Ancient China: from the origins of civilization to 221 B.C.*, 74–123. Cambridge: Cambridge University Press.

Bornstein, Marc H. 1973. Color vision and color naming. *Psychological Bulletin* 80: 257–285.

Bowie, Jill, Sean Wallis, and Bas Aarts. 2012. The perfect in spoken British English. In Bas Aarts, Joanne Close, Geoffrey Leech, and Sean Wallis (eds), *The Verb Phrase in English: investigating recent language change with corpora*, 318–352. Cambridge: Cambridge University Press.

Briscoe, Edward J. 1990. English noun phrases are regular: a reply to Professor Sampson. In J. Aarts and W. Meijs (eds), *Theory and Practice in Corpus Linguistics*, 45–60. Amsterdam: Rodopi.

Briscoe, Edward J. and John A. Carroll. 2002. Robust accurate statistical annotation of general text. In *Proceedings of the 3rd International Conference on Language Resources and Evaluation*, Las Palmas, Canary Islands, 5: 1499–1504.

Briscoe, Edward J., John A. Carroll, Jonathan Graham, and Ann Copestake. 2002. Relational evaluation schemes. In *Proceedings of the Workshop "Beyond Parseval – towards improved evaluation measures for parsing systems"*, 3rd International Conference on Language Resources and Evaluation, Las Palmas, Canary Islands, 4–8.

British Medical Journal. 1881. Colour-blindness. *British Medical Journal*, 30 Apr 1881.

Broadbent, Donald E. 1973. *In Defence of Empirical Psychology*. London: Methuen.

Brown, Donald E. 1991. *Human Universals*. New York: McGraw-Hill.

Brown, Penelope. 2002. Language as a model for culture: lessons from the cognitive sciences. In Richard G. Fox and Barbara J. King (eds), *Anthropology Beyond Culture*, 169–192. Oxford: Berg.

Cardie, Claire and R. J. Mooney. 1999. Guest editors' introduction to the special issue on Machine Learning and Natural Language. *Machine Learning* vol. 1, no. 5.

Carlson, Gregory N. and Thomas Roeper. 1981. Morphology and subcategorization: case and the unmarked complex verb. In Teun Hoekstra, Harry van der Hulst, and Michael Moortgat (eds), *Lexical Grammar*, 123–164. Dordrecht: Foris.

Carnie, Andrew. 2002. *Syntax: a generative introduction*. Oxford: Blackwell.

Carroll, John A. and Edward J. Briscoe. 1996. Apportioning development effort in a probabilistic LR parsing system through evaluation. In *Proceedings of the ACL/SIGDAT Conference on Empirical Methods in Natural Language Processing*, University of Pennsylvania, 92–100.

Chen, Matthew Y. and William S.-Y. Wang. 1975. Sound change: actuation and implementation. *Language* 51: 255–281.

Cheshire, Jenny and Viv Edwards. 1993. Sociolinguistics in the classroom: exploring linguistic diversity. In Milroy and Milroy (1993: 34–52).

Chipere, Ngoni. 2003. *Understanding Complex Sentences*. London: Palgrave Macmillan.

Chomsky, Noam. 1956. Three models for the description of language. *IRE Transactions on Information Theory* IT-2.113–24. Reprinted in R. Duncan Luce, Robert R. Bush, and Eugene Galanter (eds), *Readings in Mathematical Psychology*, 2: 105–24; New York: Wiley, 1963.

Chomsky, Noam. 1957. *Syntactic Structures*. 's-Gravenhage: Mouton.

Chomsky, Noam. 1959. Review of B.F. Skinner, *Verbal Behavior*. *Language* 35: 26–58. Reprinted with new preface in L.A. Jakobovits and M.S. Miron (eds), *Readings in the Psychology of Language*, 142–171; Englewood Cliffs, N.J.: Prentice-Hall, 1967.

Chomsky, Noam. 1964. *Current Issues in Linguistic Theory*. 's-Gravenhage: Mouton.

Chomsky, Noam. 1965. *Aspects of the Theory of Syntax*. Cambridge, Mass.: MIT Press.

Chomsky, Noam. 1968. *Language and Mind*. New York: Harcourt, Brace & World.

Chomsky, Noam. 1976. *Reflections on Language*. London: Temple Smith.

Chomsky, Noam. 1981. *Lectures on Government and Binding*. Dordrecht: Foris.

Chomsky, Noam. 1991. Linguistics and cognitive science: problems and mysteries. In Asa Kasher (ed.), *The Chomskyan Turn*, 26–53. Oxford: Blackwell.

Chomsky, Noam. 2007a. Of minds and language. *Biolinguistics* 1: 9–27.

Chomsky, Noam. 2007b. Approaching UG from below. In Uli Sauerland and Hans-Martin Gärtner (eds), *Interface + Recursion = Language?*, 1–29. Berlin: Mouton de Gruyter.

Christie, Agatha. 1939. *Murder is Easy*. Glasgow: Collins. Our page reference is to the London: Fontana edition, 1960.

Clover, Charles. 2006. "More foxes wounded" since hunt Act. *Daily Telegraph* 28 Jul 2006, p. 13.

Cole, Barry L. 2003. Review of Donald McIntyre, *Colour Blindness: causes and effects. Clinical and Experimental Optometry* 86: 194.

Collier, George A. 1973. Review of Berlin and Kay (1969). *Language* 49: 245–248.

Collins, Michael. 1997. Three generative, lexicalised models for statistical parsing. In *Proceedings of the 35th Annual Meeting of the Association for Computational Linguistics and 8th Conference of the European Chapter of the Association for Computational Linguistics, 7–12 July 1997, Madrid.* San Francisco: Morgan Kaufmann.

Conklin, Harold C. 1955. Hanunóo color categories. *Southwestern Journal of Anthropology* 11: 339–344. Reprinted in Hymes (1964: 189–192).

Cowart, Wayne. 1997. *Experimental Syntax: applying objective methods to sentence judgments.* Thousand Oaks, Calif.: SAGE Publications.

Crafts, Nick. 1996. "Post-neoclassical endogenous growth theory": what are its policy implications? *Oxford Review of Economic Policy* 12: 30–47.

Creel, H. G. 1936. On the nature of Chinese ideography. *T'oung Pao* 2nd series, 32: 85–161.

Culy, Christopher. 1998. Statistical distribution and the grammatical/ungrammatical distinction. *Grammars* 1: 1–13.

Curtiss, Susan. 1977. *Genie: a psycholinguistic study of a modern-day "wild child".* New York: Academic Press.

Dalke, Anne. 2010. "All grammars leak". Posted on the "Serendip" forum (serendip.brynmawr. edu/exchange/node/7645) on 14 June 2010.

Daniels, Norman. 2003. Reflective equilibrium. *Stanford Encyclopedia of Philosophy*, <www. science.uva.nl/~seop/entries/reflective-equilibrium/>.

DeGraff, Michael. 2001. On the origin of creoles: a Cartesian critique of Neo-Darwinian linguistics. *Linguistic Typology* 5: 213–310.

Descartes, René. 1641. Letter to Mersenne of 22 Jul 1641. In C. Adam and P. Tannery (eds), *Œuvres de Descartes* (*Correspondance*, vol. iii), 414–418. Paris: Léopold Cerf, 1899.

Deutscher, Guy. 2000. *Syntactic Change in Akkadian: the evolution of sentential complementation.* Oxford: Oxford University Press.

Deutscher, Guy. 2011. *Through the Language Glass: why the world looks different in other languages.* London: Arrow Books.

Easterly, William. 2006. *The White Man's Burden: why the West's efforts to aid the Rest have done so much ill and so little good.* New York: Penguin.

The Economist. 2010. The debate over universal values. *The Economist* 2 Oct 2010, pp. 65–66.

The Economist. 2011. Universalists v. exceptionalists. *The Economist* 25 Jun 2011, pp. 15–16.

The Economist. 2012. Goodbye Doha, hello Bali. *The Economist* 8 Sep 2012; and see Letter to the Editor, *The Economist* 6 Oct 2012.

The Economist. 2013a. Has the ideas machine broken down? *The Economist* 12 Jan 2013, pp. 20–23.

The Economist. 2013b. Mixed messages. *The Economist* 29 Jun 2013, p. 68.

Eddy, William A. 1879. The evolution of a new sense. *The Popular Science Monthly*, 16: 66–71.

Edwards, Jane. 1992. Design principles in the transcription of spoken discourse. In Jan Svartvik (ed.), *Directions in Corpus Linguistics: Proceedings of Nobel Symposium 82*, 129–144. Berlin: Mouton de Gruyter.

Edwards, Viv. 1993. The grammar of Southern British English. In Milroy and Milroy (1993: 214–235).

Ehrman, Madeline E. 1966. *The Meanings of the Modals in Present-Day American English*. The Hague: Mouton.

Eisikovits, Edina. 1987. Variation in the lexical verb in inner-Sydney English. *Australian Journal of Linguistics* 7: 1–24. Reprinted in Trudgill and Chambers (1991: 120–142).

Ellis, Nick C. and Diane Larsen-Freeman. 2006. Language emergence: implications for applied linguistics – introduction to the special issue. *Applied Linguistics* 27: 558–589.

Elsness, Johan. 1997. *The Perfect and the Preterite in Contemporary and Earlier English*. (Topics in English linguistics 21.) Berlin: Mouton de Gruyter.

Enfield, Nick J. 2012. Language innateness. *Times Literary Supplement* 26 Oct 2012, p. 6.

Evans, Nicholas and Stephen C. Levinson. 2009. The myth of language universals: language diversity and its importance for cognitive science. *Behavioral and Brain Sciences* 32: 429–492.

Evans, Nicholas, Dunstan Brown, and Greville G. Corbett. 2002. The semantics of gender in Mayali. *Language* 78: 111–155.

Evans, Patrick D., Sandra L. Gilbert, Nitzan Mekel-Bobrov, Eric J. Vallender, Jeffrey R. Anderson, Leila M. Vaez-Azizi, Sarah A. Tishkoff, Richard R. Hudson, and Bruce T. Lahn. 2005. *Microcephalin*, a gene regulating brain size, continues to evolve adaptively in humans. *Science* 309: 1717–1720, 9 Sep 2005.

Everett, Charles Carroll. 1869. *The Science of Thought*. Our page reference is to the 1891 edition, Boston, Mass.: Hall and Whiting.

Everett, Daniel L. 2005. Cultural constraints on grammar and cognition in Pirahã: another look at the *Design Features* of human language. *Current Anthropology* 46: 621–646.

Faarlund, Jan Terje. 2010a. Review of Sampson, Gil, and Trudgill (2009). *Language* 86: 748–752.

Faarlund, Jan Terje. 2010b. Letter to *Language*. *Language* 86: 757.

Farmer, Ben. 2011. Accept paedophilia as part of Afghan culture, British troops told. *Daily Telegraph* 14 Jan 2011, p. 22.

Fillmore, Charles J. 1968. The case for case. In Emmon Bach and R.T. Harms (eds), *Universals in Linguistic Theory*, 1–88. New York: Holt, Rinehart and Winston.

Fodor, Jerry A. 1975. *The Language of Thought*. New York: Thomas Y. Crowell.

Fodor, Jerry A. and Jerrold J. Katz (eds). 1964. *The Structure of Language: readings in the philosophy of language*. Englewood Cliffs, N.J.: Prentice-Hall.

Foster, Jennifer. 2007. Real bad grammar: realistic grammatical description with grammaticality. *Corpus Linguistics and Linguistic Theory* 3: 73–86.

Frank, Michael C., Daniel L. Everett, Evelina Fedorenko, and Edward Gibson. 2008. Number as a cognitive technology: evidence from Pirahã language and cognition. *Cognition* 108: 819–824.

Frege, Gottlob. 1918. Der Gedanke: eine logische Untersuchung. *Beiträge zur Philosophie des Deutschen Idealismus* 1: 58–77. Translated by A.M. and Marcelle Quinton as "The thought: a logical inquiry", *Mind* 60: 289–311, 1956; reprinted in Peter F. Strawson (ed.), *Philosophical Logic*, 17–38, Oxford: Oxford University Press, 1967.

Fries, Charles C. 1952. *The Structure of English: an introduction to the construction of English sentences*. New York: Harcourt Brace.

Fung Yu-lan. 1948. *A Short History of Chinese Philosophy*. New York: Macmillan.

Gage, John. 2000. *Colour and Meaning: art, science and symbolism*. London: Thames and Hudson.

Gazdar, Gerald J. M. 1988. Applicability of indexed grammars to natural languages. In Uwe Reyle and Christian Rohrer (eds), *Natural Language Parsing and Linguistic Theories*, 69–94. Dordrecht: Reidel.

Gil, David. 1994. The structure of Riau Indonesian. *Nordic Journal of Linguistics* 17: 179–200.

Gil, David. 2001. Escaping Eurocentrism: fieldwork as a process of unlearning. In Paul Newman and Martha Ratliff (eds), *Linguistic Fieldwork*, 102–132. Cambridge: Cambridge University Press.

Gil, David. 2005. Word order without syntactic categories: how Riau Indonesian does it. In Andrew Carnie, Heidi Harley, and Sheila Ann Dooley (eds), *Verb First: on the syntax of verb initial languages*, 243–263. Amsterdam: John Benjamins.

Gil, David. 2009. How much grammar does it take to sail a boat? In Sampson, Gil, and Trudgill (2009: 19–33).

Gildea, Daniel and Daniel Jurafsky. 2002. Automatic labeling of semantic roles. *Computational Linguistics* 28: 245–288.

Gladstone, William Ewart. 1858. *Studies on Homer and the Homeric Age*, 3 vols. Oxford: Oxford University Press.

Gladstone, William Ewart. 1869. *Juventus Mundi: the gods and men of the heroic age*. London: Macmillan.

Gladstone, William Ewart. 1877. The colour-sense. *The Nineteenth Century* 2: 366–388.

Gladstone, William Ewart. 1879. On epithets of movement in Homer. *The Nineteenth Century* 5: 463–487.

Gleason, Henry A. 1955. *An Introduction to Descriptive Linguistics*. Our page reference is to the revised edition, London: Holt, Rinehart and Winston, 1969.

Goodluck, Helen and Susan L. Tavakolian. 1982. Competence and processing in children's grammar of relative clauses. *Cognition* 7: 85–95.

Gordon, Peter. 2004. Numerical cognition without words: evidence from Amazonia. *Science* 306: 496–499.

Gordon, Robert J. 2012. Is US economic growth over? Faltering innovation confronts the six headwinds. (Policy Insight no. 63.) Centre for Economic Policy Research, September 2012.

Graddol, David G. 2004. The future of language. *Science* 303: 1329–1331.

Graves, Norman. 2004. John Miller Dow Meiklejohn: educationist and prolific textbook author. *Paradigm* 2 (8), October 2004, <faculty.ed.uiuc.edu/westbury/paradigm/vol2/Graves.doc>.

Gross, Maurice. 1979. On the failure of generative grammar. *Language* 55: 859–885.

Guinness Superlatives. 1956. *The Guinness Book of Records*, 2nd edn. London: Guinness Superlatives.

Hagège, Claude. 1976. *La Grammaire générative: réflexions critiques*. Paris: PUF.

Hamilton, William. 1859. *Lectures on Metaphysics*, ed. by Rev. H. L. Mansel and J. Veitch, vol. 1. Boston, Mass.: Gould and Lincoln.

Handscombe, Richard J. (ed.). 1967a. *The Written Language of Nine and Ten-Year Old Children*. (Nuffield Foreign Languages Teaching Materials Project, Reports and Occasional Papers 24.) Leeds: Leeds University.

Handscombe, Richard J. (ed.). 1967b. *The Written Language of Eleven and Twelve-Year Old Children*. (Nuffield Foreign Languages Teaching Materials Project, Reports and Occasional Papers 25.) Leeds: Leeds University.

Hanks, Patrick. 2013. *Lexical Analysis: norms and exploitations*. Cambridge, Mass.: MIT Press.

Hannan, James. 2009. *God's Philosophers: how the medieval world laid the foundations of modern science*. London: Icon Books.

Harris, John. 1991. Conservatism versus substratal transfer in Irish English (revised version). In Trudgill and Chambers (1991: 191–212).

Haspelmath, Martin. 2010. Framework-free grammatical theory. In Bernd Heine and Heiko Narrog (eds), *The Oxford Handbook of Grammatical Analysis*, 341–365. Oxford: Oxford University Press.

Hauser, Marc D., Noam Chomsky, and W. Tecumseh Fitch. 2002. The faculty of language: what is it, who has it, and how did it evolve? *Science* 298: 1569–1579.

Helpman, Elhanan. 2004. *The Mystery of Economic Growth*. Cambridge, Mass.: Belknap Press.

Henrich, Joseph, Steven J. Heine, and Ara Norenzayan. 2010a. The weirdest people in the world? *Behavioral and Brain Sciences* 33: 61–135.

Henrich, Joseph, Steven J. Heine, and Ara Norenzayan. 2010b. Most people are not WEIRD. *Nature* 1 Jul 2010, p. 29.

Hill, Archibald A. (ed.). 1962. *Proceedings of the Third Texas Conference on Problems of Linguistic Analysis in English (May 9–12, 1958), Austin*. Austin, Tex.: University of Texas Press.

Hirschberg, Julia. 1998. "Every time I fire a linguist, my performance goes up", and other myths of the statistical natural language processing revolution. Invited talk, 15th National Conference on Artificial Intelligence (AAAI-98), Madison, Wis.

Hockett, Charles F. 1950. Peiping morphophonemics. *Language* 26: 63–85.

Hockett, Charles F. 1965. Sound change. *Language* 41: 185–204.

Hockett, Charles F. 1968. *The State of the Art*. The Hague: Mouton.

Hoffman, Thomas. 2007. "Good is good and bad is bad": but how do we know which one we had? *Corpus Linguistics and Linguistic Theory* 3: 87–98.

Hopper, Paul J. 2011. Emergent grammar. In James Gee and Michael Handford (eds), *Routledge Handbook of Discourse Analysis*, 301–314. London: Routledge.

Householder, Fred W. 1973. On arguments from asterisks. *Foundations of Language* 10: 365–376.

Howell, James. 1662. *A New English Grammar, Prescribing as certain Rules as the Language will bear, for Forreners to learn English*. London: T. Williams, H. Brome, and H. Marsh.

Howell, Peter and Keith Young. 1990. Speech repairs: report of work conducted October 1st 1989–March 31st 1990. Department of Psychology, University College London.

Howell, Peter and Keith Young. 1991. The use of prosody in highlighting alterations in repairs from unrestricted speech. *Quarterly Journal of Experimental Psychology* 43A: 733–758.

Huang, Philip C. 1972. *Liang Ch'i-ch'ao and Modern Chinese Liberalism*. Seattle: University of Washington Press.

Huck, Geoffrey J. and Younghee Na. 1990. Extraposition and focus. *Language* 66: 51–77.

Hughes, Arthur and P. Trudgill. 1996. *English Accents and Dialects: an introduction to social and regional varieties of English in the British Isles*. London: Arnold.

Hummel, J. J. and E. Knecht. 1910. Dyeing. In *Encyclopædia Britannica*, 11th edn, 3: 744–755. New York: Encyclopædia Britannica Company.

Huxley, Sir Julian. 1961. The new divinity. *The Twentieth Century* 170: 9–16.

Hymes, Dell (ed.). 1964. *Language in Culture and Society: a reader in linguistics and anthropology*. New York: Harper & Row.

Jackendoff, Ray. 1993. *Patterns in the Mind: language and human nature*. Hemel Hempstead, Herts.: Harvester Wheatsheaf.

Johansson, Sverker. 2005. *Origins of Language: constraints on hypotheses.* Amsterdam: John Benjamins.

Jones, Peter E. 1995. Contradictions and unanswered questions in the Genie case: a fresh look at the linguistic evidence. *Language and Communication* 15: 261–280.

Joseph, Brian D. 2002. The Editor's department: Endgame. *Language* 78: 615–618.

Joseph, Brian D. 2008. The Editor's department: "Last scene of all ..." *Language* 84: 686–690.

Jowett, Benjamin. 1875. *The Dialogues of Plato*, 2nd edn, vol. 5. Oxford: Oxford Univesity Press.

Kahane, Henry R. and Renée. 1950. The position of the actor expression in colloquial Mexican Spanish. *Language* 26: 236–263.

Karlgren, Bernhard. 1942. *Glosses on the Kuo Feng Odes. Bulletin of the Museum of Far Eastern Antiquities*, Stockholm, 14: 71–247.

Karlgren, Bernhard. 1950. *The Book of Odes: Chinese text, transcription and translation.* Stockholm: Museum of Far Eastern Antiquities.

Karlgren, Bernhard. 1957. *Grammata Serica Recensa. Bulletin of the Museum of Far Eastern Antiquities*, Stockholm, 29: 1–332.

Katz, Jerrold J. 1964. Analyticity and contradiction in natural language. In Fodor and Katz (1964: 519–543).

Katz, Jerrold J. 1981. *Language and Other Abstract Objects.* Totowa, N.J.: Rowman & Littlefield.

Katz, Jerrold J. and Jerry A. Fodor. 1963. The structure of a semantic theory. *Language* 39: 170–210. Reprinted in Fodor and Katz (1964: 479–518).

Keenan, Edward L. and Bernard Comrie. 1977. Noun phrase accessibility and Universal Grammar. *Linguistic Inquiry* 8: 63–99.

Kepser, Stephan and Marga Reis (eds). 2004. *Linguistic Evidence: empirical, theoretical and computational perspectives.* Berlin: Mouton de Gruyter.

Kilgarriff, Adam. 2007. Grammar is to meaning as the law is to good behaviour. *Corpus Linguistics and Linguistic Theory* 3: 195–198.

Kristol, Andres M. 1980. Color systems in modern Italy. *Language* 56: 137–145.

Krotov, Alexander, Robert Gaizauskas, and Yorick Wilks. 1994. Acquiring a stochastic context-free grammar from the Penn Treebank. In *Proceedings of the Third Conference on the Cognitive Science of Natural Language Processing, Dublin*, 79–86.

Kübler, Sandra, and Heike Telljohann. 2002. Towards a dependency-oriented evaluation for partial parsing. In *Proceedings of the workshop "Beyond Parseval – Towards improved evaluation measures for parsing systems"*, LREC 2002, Las Palmas, 2 Jun 2002, pp. 9–16.

Labov, William. 1963. The social motivation of a sound change. *Word* 19: 273–309. Reprinted in Labov (1978: 1–42).

Labov, William. 1970. The study of language in its social context. *Studium Generale* 23: 30–87. Our page reference is to the reprint in Labov (1978: 183–259).

Labov, William. 1973. The boundaries of words and their meanings. In Charles-James N. Bailey and Roger W. Shuy (eds), *New Ways of Analyzing Variation in English*, 340–373. Washington, D.C.: Georgetown University Press.

Labov, William. 1975. Empirical foundations of linguistic theory. In Robert Austerlitz (ed.), *The Scope of American Linguistics*, 77–133. Lisse: Peter de Ridder. Also published separately as *What is a linguistic fact?*, Lisse: Peter de Ridder; our page references are to the latter.

Labov, William. 1978. *Sociolinguistic Patterns.* Oxford: Blackwell.

Lakatos, Imre. 1970. Falsification and the methodology of scientific research programmes. In Imre Lakatos and Alan Musgrave (eds), *Criticism and the Growth of Knowledge*, 91–195. Cambridge: Cambridge University Press.

Lane Fox, Robin. 2008. *Travelling Heroes: Greeks and their myths in the epic age of Homer*. London: Allen Lane.

Langendoen, D. Terence. 1969. *The Study of Syntax*. New York: Holt, Rinehart & Winston.

Langendoen, D. Terence. 1997. Review of Sampson (1995). *Language* 73: 600–603.

Lass, Roger. 1994. Proliferation and option-cutting: the strong verb in the fifteenth to eighteenth centuries. In Dieter Stein and Ingrid Tieken-Boon van Ostade (eds), *Towards a Standard English 1600–1800*. (Topics in English Linguistics 12.) Berlin: Mouton de Gruyter.

Laurence, Stephen and Eric Margolis. 2001. The Poverty of the Stimulus Argument. *British Journal for the Philosophy of Science* 52: 217–276.

Lee, Lillian. 2000. Review of Manning and Schütze (1999). *Computational Linguistics* 26: 277–279.

Leisi, Ernst. 1974. *Der Wortinhalt*, 5th edn. Heidelberg: Quelle & Meyer.

Lenneberg, Eric H. 1967. *Biological Foundations of Language*. New York: Wiley.

Lenneberg, Eric H. and John M. Roberts. 1956. *The Language of Experience: a study in methodology*. (Indiana University Publications in Anthropology and Linguistics, Memoir 13.) Baltimore: Waverly Press.

Levelt, Willem J. M. 1983. Monitoring and self-repair in speech. *Cognition* 14: 41–104.

Levenshtein, V. I. 1966. Binary codes capable of correcting deletions, insertions, and reversals. *Soviet Physics – Doklady* 10: 707–710 (translation of Russian original published in 1965).

Levin, Beth and Malka Rappaport Hovav. 2005. *Argument Realization*. Cambridge: Cambridge University Press.

Lewis, John D. and Jeffrey L. Elman. 2001. Learnability and the statistical structure of language: poverty of stimulus arguments revisited. In *Proceedings of the 26th Annual Boston University Conference on Language Development*. Somerville, Mass.: Cascadilla Press.

Lewis, Martha Blanche. 1947. *Teach Yourself Malay*. London: English Universities Press.

Liddell, Henry George and Robert Scott. 1855. *A Greek–English Lexicon*, 4th edn. Oxford: Oxford University Press.

Lin Dekang. 2003. Dependency-based evaluation of Minipar. In Anne Abeillé (ed.), *Treebanks*, 317–329. Dordrecht: Kluwer.

Liu, James J.Y. 1962. *The Art of Chinese Poetry*. Chicago: University of Chicago Press.

Locke, John. 1690. *An Essay Concerning Human Understanding*. Everyman edition, London: Dent, 1961.

Lorenz, Gunter. 2001. Standard English in the light of corpus evidence: aspect rules or probabilities? Paper given at the 22nd ICAME Conference, Louvain-la-Neuve, Belgium, May 2001: <sites.uclouvain.be/cecl/events/icamepr.htm#standard>.

Maas, Utz. 2009. Orality versus literacy as a dimension of complexity. In Sampson, Gil, and Trudgill (2009: 164–177).

Macfarquhar, Larissa. 2003. The Devil's accountant. *The New Yorker* 31 Mar 2003, 64–79.

McKinnon, Timothy, Peter Cole, and Gabriella Hermon. 2011. Object agreement and "pro-drop" in Kerinci Malay. *Language* 87: 715–750.

MacLaury, Robert E. 1992. From brightness to hue: an explanatory model of color-category evolution. *Current Anthropology* 33: 137–163.

McWhorter, John H. 1998. Identifying the creole prototype: vindicating a typological class. *Language* 74: 788–818.

McWhorter, John H. 2001a. The world's simplest grammars are creole grammars. *Linguistic Typology* 5: 125–166. Reprinted in McWhorter, *Defining Creole*, 38–71; Oxford: Oxford University Press, 2005.

McWhorter, John H. 2001b. What people ask David Gil and why: rejoinder to the replies. *Linguistic Typology* 5: 388–412.

Magerman, David M. 1995. Statistical decision-tree models for parsing. In *Proceedings of the 33rd Annual Meeting of the Association for Computational Linguistics, 26–30 June 1995, Cambridge, Mass.*, pp. 276–283. San Francisco: Morgan Kaufmann.

Magnus, Hugo Friedrich. 1877. *Die geschichtliche Entwickelung des Farbensinnes*. Leipzig: Veit.

Mair, Victor H. 1994. Buddhism and the rise of the written vernacular in East Asia. *Journal of Asian Studies* 53: 707–751.

Mallory, James P. and Douglas Q. Adams. 1997. *Encyclopedia of Indo-European Culture*. London: Fitzroy Dearborn.

Malotki, Ekkehart. 1983. *Hopi Time: a linguistic analysis of the temporal concepts in the Hopi language*. Berlin: de Gruyter.

Mann, Randall. 2013. Whatever. In André Naffis-Sakely and Julian Stannard (eds), *The Palm Beach Effect*, 119–122. London: CB Editions.

Manning, Chris D. and Hinrich Schütze. 1999. *Foundations of Statistical Natural Language Processing*. Cambridge, Mass.: MIT Press.

Margolis, Eric and Stephen Laurence. 2012. In defense of nativism. *Philosophical Studies* 26 Jun 2012: <link.springer.com/article/10.1007%2Fs11098-012-9972-x>.

Màrquez, Lluís, Mihai Surdeanu, Pere Comas, and Jordi Turmo. 2005. A robust combination strategy for semantic role labeling. In *Proceedings of the Human Language Technology Conference and Conference on Empirical Methods in Natural Language Processing (HLT/EMNLP 2005)*, Vancouver, 2005, pp. 644–651; <dl.acm.org/citation.cfm?id=1220656>.

Maspero, Henri. 1955. *La Chine antique*. Paris: Imprimerie Nationale.

Meiklejohn, John Miller Dow. 1886. *The English Language: its grammar, history, and literature*. 23rd edn, London: Alfred M. Holden, 1902.

Mekel-Bobrov, Nitzan, Sandra L. Gilbert, Patrick D. Evans, Eric J. Vallender, Jeffrey R. Anderson, Richard R. Hudson, Sarah A. Tishkoff, and Bruce T. Lahn. 2005. Ongoing adaptive evolution of *ASPM*, a brain size determinant in *Homo sapiens*. *Science* 309: 1720–1722, 9 Sep 2005.

Mendenhall, William. 1967. *Introduction to Probability and Statistics*, 2nd edn. Belmont, Calif.: Wadsworth.

Meteer, Marie, et al. 1995. *Dysfluency Annotation Stylebook for the Switchboard Corpus*. <www.ldc.upenn.edu/myl/DFL-book.pdf>.

Meurers, W. Detmar. 2007. Advancing linguistics between the extremes. *Corpus Linguistics and Linguistic Theory* 3: 49–55.

Miestamo, Matti, Kaius Sinnemäki, and Fred Karlsson (eds). 2008. *Language Complexity: typology, contact, change*. Amsterdam: John Benjamins.

Miller, George A. and Patricia M. Gildea. 1987. How children learn words. In *Scientific American*, September 1987. Reprinted in William S.-Y. Wang (ed.), *The Emergence of Language: development and evolution*, 150–158. New York: W.H. Freeman.

Miller, Jim and Regina Weinert. 1998. *Spontaneous Spoken Language: syntax and discourse*. Oxford: Clarendon Press.

Milroy, James and Lesley (eds). 1993. *Real English: the grammar of English dialects in the British Isles*. London: Longman.

Mortimer, Sir John. 1993. *Dunster*. Harmondsworth, Mddx: Penguin.

Müller, Stefan. 2008. *Head-Driven Phrase Structure Grammar: eine Einführung* (2nd revised edn). Tübingen: Stauffenburg Verlag.

Neeleman, Ad and Kriszta Szendrői. 2007. Radical pro drop and the morphology of pronouns. *Linguistic Inquiry* 38: 671–714.

Newmeyer, Frederick J. 2003. Grammar is grammar and usage is usage. *Language* 79: 682–707.

Nickerson, Dorothea. 1940. History of the Munsell color system and its scientific application. *Journal of the Optical Society of America* 30: 575–586.

Norman, Jerry. 1988. *Chinese*. Cambridge: Cambridge University Press.

Nunnally, Thomas E. 2002. Review of Moon, *Fixed Expressions and Idioms in English*. *Language* 78: 172–177.

Office of Population Censuses and Surveys. 1991. *Standard Occupational Classification*, vol. 3: *Social Classifications and Coding Methodology*. London: Her Majesty's Stationery Office.

Pearson, Karl. 1896. Mathematical contributions to the theory of evolution. III. Regression, heredity, and panmixia. *Philosophical Transactions of the Royal Society* series A, 187: 253–318.

Perera, Katharine. 1984. *Children's Writing and Reading: analysing classroom language*. Oxford: Blackwell, in association with André Deutsch.

Pérez-Leroux, Ana Teresa. 1995. Resumptives in the acquisition of relative clauses. *Language Acquisition* 4: 105–138.

Phillips, Melanie. 2006. *Londonistan*. London: Gibson Square.

Piattelli-Palmarini, Massimo (ed.). 1980. *Language and Learning: the debate between Jean Piaget and Noam Chomsky*. London: Routledge and Kegan Paul.

Pinker, Steven. 1995. *The Language Instinct: the new science of language and mind*. London: Penguin.

Pinker, Steven. 1997. *How the Mind Works*. London: W.W. Norton.

Pinker, Steven. 1998. Posting 9.1209, 1 Sep 1998, on the LINGUIST List: <linguistlist.org/issues/9/9-1209.html>.

Pinker, Steven. 2002. *The Blank Slate*. London: Allen Lane.

Pinker, Steven. 2011. *The Better Angels of our Nature: a history of violence and humanity*. London: Penguin.

Pinker, Steven and Paul Bloom. 1990. Natural language and natural selection. *Behavioral and Brain Sciences* 13: 707–727.

Planck, Max. 1949. *Scientific Autobiography and Other Papers*. New York: Philosophical Library.

Pole, William. 1878. Colour blindness in relation to the Homeric expressions for colour. *Nature* 24 Oct 1878, 676–679.

Popper, Karl Raimund. 1968. *The Logic of Scientific Discovery* (revised English translation of 1934 German original). London: Hutchinson.

Prantl, Carl. 1849. *Aristoteles über die Farben*. Munich: Christian Kaiser.

Prinz, Jesse J. 2012. *Beyond Human Nature: how culture and experience shape our lives*. London: Allen Lane.

Prospect. 2005. Intellectuals. Online at <www.prospectmagazine.co.uk/prospect-100-intellectuals>.

Pulleyblank, Edwin G. 1995. *Outline of Classical Chinese Grammar*. Vancouver: UBC Press.

Pullum, Geoffrey K. 2007. Ungrammaticality, rarity, and corpus use. *Corpus Linguistics and Linguistic Theory* 3: 33–47.

Pullum, Geoffrey K. and Barbara C. Scholz. 2002. Empirical assessment of stimulus poverty arguments. In Ritter (2002: 9–50).

Pullum, Geoffrey K. and Deirdre Wilson. 1977. Autonomous syntax and the analysis of auxiliaries. *Language* 53: 741–788.

Quine, Willard van Orman. 1951. Two dogmas of empiricism. *Philosophical Review* 60: 20–43. Reprinted as chapter 2 of Quine, *From a Logical Point of View*, 2nd edn, New York: Harper & Row, 1963.

Quirk, Randolph, Sidney Greenbaum, Geoffrey N. Leech, and Jan Svartvik. 1985. *A Comprehensive Grammar of the English Language*. London: Longman.

Ridley, Matt. 2011. *The Rational Optimist*. London: Fourth Estate.

van Rijsbergen, Cornelis Joost. 1979. *Information Retrieval*, 2nd edn. London: Butterworths.

Ritter, Nancy A. (ed.). 2002. *A Review of the Poverty of Stimulus Argument*. A special issue of *The Linguistic Review*, vol. 19, nos. 1–2.

Rivero, Maria-Luisa. 1975. Referential properties of Spanish noun phrases. *Language* 51: 32–48.

Rivers, William Halse Rivers. 1901. Vision. In Alfred Cort Haddon (ed.), *Reports of the Cambridge Anthropological Expedition to the Torres Straits*, vol. 2: *Physiology and Psychology*, 8–140. Cambridge: Cambridge University Press.

Rizzi, Luigi. 1982. *Issues in Italian Syntax*. Dordrecht: Foris.

Roeper, Thomas and Muffy E. A. Siegel. 1978. A lexical transformation for verbal compounds. *Linguistic Inquiry* 9: 199–260.

Rohlf, F. James and Robert R. Sokal. 1981. *Statistical Tables*, 2nd edn. San Francisco: W.H. Freeman.

Romer, Paul M. 1986. Increasing returns and long-run growth. *Journal of Political Economy* 94: 1002–1037.

Romer, Paul M. 1990. Endogenous technical change. *Journal of Political Economy* 98: S71–S102.

Romer, Paul M. 1994. New goods, old theory, and the welfare costs of trade restrictions. *Journal of Development Economics* 43: 5–38.

Rood, David S. 1975. The implications of Wichita phonology. *Language* 51: 315–337.

Rosemont, Henry. 1974. On representing abstractions in Archaic Chinese. *Philosophy East and West* 24: 71–88.

Ross, John R. 1979. Where's English? In Charles J. Fillmore, Daniel Kempler, and William S.-Y. Wang (eds), *Individual Differences in Language Ability and Language Behavior*, 127–166. New York: Academic Press.

Ruppenhofer, Josef, Michael Ellsworth, Miriam R.L. Petruck, Christopher R. Johnson, and Jan Scheffczyk. 2006. *FrameNet II: extended theory and practice*. Berkeley, Calif.: International Computer Science Institute.

Ruse, Michael. 1973. *The Philosophy of Biology*. London: Hutchinson.

Russell, Lord (Bertrand). 1957. Mr. Strawson on referring. *Mind* n.s. 66: 385–389. Reprinted in Aloysius P. Martinich (ed.), *The Philosophy of Language*, 4th edn, 243–246; Oxford: Oxford University Press, 2001.

Sag, Ivan. 2010. English filler-gap constructions. *Language* 86: 486–545.

Sagart, Laurent. 1999. *The Roots of Old Chinese*. Amsterdam: John Benjamins.

Sampson, Geoffrey. 1975. The evidence for linguistic theories. Chapter 4 of Sampson, *The Form of Language*, London: Weidenfeld & Nicolson; a version reprinted in Sampson (2001: chapter 8).

Sampson, Geoffrey. 1979. *Liberty and Language*. Oxford: Oxford University Press.

Sampson, Geoffrey. 1980a. *Making Sense*. Oxford: Oxford University Press.

Sampson, Geoffrey. 1980b. Popperian language acquisition undefeated. *British Journal for the Philosophy of Science* 31: 63–67.

Sampson, Geoffrey. 1984. *An End to Allegiance*. London: Temple Smith.

Sampson, Geoffrey. 1987. Evidence against the "grammatical"/"ungrammatical" distinction. In Willem Meijs (ed.), *Corpus Linguistics and Beyond*, 219–226. Amsterdam: Rodopi. A version reprinted in Sampson (2001: chapter 10).

Sampson, Geoffrey. 1995. *English for the Computer: the SUSANNE corpus and analytic scheme*. Oxford: Clarendon Press.

Sampson, Geoffrey. 1997. Depth in English grammar. *Journal of Linguistics* 33: 131–151. Reprinted in Sampson (2001: chapter 4).

Sampson, Geoffrey. 1998. Consistent annotation of speech-repair structures. In A. Rubio et al. (eds), *Proceedings of the First International Conference on Language Resources and Evaluation, Granada, Spain, 28–30 May 1998*, 2: 1279–1282.

Sampson, Geoffrey. 2000a. The role of taxonomy in language engineering. *Philosophical Transactions of the Royal Society* series A, 358: 1339–1355.

Sampson, Geoffrey. 2000b. A proposal for improving the measurement of parse accuracy. *International Journal of Corpus Linguistics* 5: 53–68.

Sampson, Geoffrey. 2001. *Empirical Linguistics*. London and New York: Continuum.

Sampson, Geoffrey. 2002. Exploring the richness of the stimulus. In Ritter (2002: 73–104).

Sampson, Geoffrey. 2005. *The "Language Instinct" Debate*. (Revised and enlarged edition of a book first published as *Educating Eve*, 1997.) London and New York: Continuum.

Sampson, Geoffrey. 2006. *Love Songs of Early China*. Donington, Lincs.: Shaun Tyas.

Sampson, Geoffrey. 2007. Summary response. *Corpus Linguistics and Linguistic Theory* 3: 57–71.

Sampson, Geoffrey and Anna Babarczy. 2008. Definitional and human constraints on structural annotation of English. *Natural Language Engineering* 14: 471–494.

Sampson, Geoffrey, David Gil, and Peter Trudgill (eds). 2009. *Language Complexity as an Evolving Variable*. Oxford: Oxford University Press.

Sampson, Geoffrey, Robin Haigh, and Eric S. Atwell. 1989. Natural language analysis by stochastic optimization. *Journal of Experimental and Theoretical Artificial Intelligence* 1: 271–287.

Sampson, Geoffrey and Diana F. McCarthy (eds). 2004. *Corpus Linguistics: readings in a widening discipline*. London and New York: Continuum.

Sapir, Edward. 1921. *Language: an introduction to the study of speech*. Reprinted London: Hart-Davis, 1963.

Sapir, Edward. 1929. The status of linguistics as a science. *Language* 5: 207–214.

Sapir, Edward. 1931. Conceptual categories in primitive languages. *Science* 74: 578.

Schleicher, August. 1848. *Zur vergleichenden Sprachgeschichte* (Sprachvergleichende Untersuchungen 1). Bonn: H.B. König.

Schoenemann, P. Thomas. 1999. Syntax as an emergent characteristic of the evolution of semantic complexity. *Minds and Machines* 9: 309–346.

Scholz, Barbara C. and Geoffrey K. Pullum. 2006. Irrational nativist exuberance. In Robert Stainton (ed.), *Contemporary Debates in Cognitive Science*, 59–80. Oxford: Blackwell.

Schuessler, Axel. 2007. *ABC Etymological Dictionary of Old Chinese*. Honolulu: University of Hawai'i Press.

Schütze, Carson T. 1996. *The Empirical Base of Linguistics: grammaticality judgments and linguistic methodology*. Chicago: University of Chicago Press.

Schütze, Carson T. 2010. Linguistic evidence and grammatical theory. *Wiley Interdisciplinary Reviews: Cognitive Science* 2 (2): 206–221.

Sekine, Satoshi and Michael John Collins. 1997. Evalb software at <www.cs.nyu.edu/cs/projects/proteus/evalb/>.

Shu Xincheng, Shen Yi, Xu Yuangao, and Zhang Xiang (eds). 1938. *Cí Hǎi* 辭海 [*Sea of Terms*]. Kunming: Zhonghua Shuju.

Siegel, Sidney and N. John Castellan. 1988. *Nonparametric Statistics for the Behavioral Sciences* (2nd edn). New York: McGraw-Hill.

Simon, Herbert A. 1962. The architecture of complexity. *Proceedings of the American Philosophical Society* 106: 467–482. Reprinted in Simon, *The Sciences of the Artificial*, 84–118; Cambridge, Mass.: MIT Press, 1969.

Skinner, B. F. 1957. *Verbal Behavior*. New York: Appleton-Century-Crofts.

Smith, Nelson Voyne. 1999. *Chomsky: Ideas and Ideals*. Cambridge: Cambridge University Press.

Sokal, Alan and Jean Bricmont. 1997. *Impostures intellectuelles*. Paris: Odile Jacob. Translated as *Fashionable Nonsense: postmodern intellectuals' abuse of science*, New York: Picador, 1998.

Stafleu, Frans Antonie. 1971. *Linnaeus and the Linnaeans*. Utrecht: A. Oosthoek's Uitgevers-maatschappij.

Stefanowitsch, Anatol. 2007. Linguistics beyond grammaticality. *Corpus Linguistics and Linguistic Theory* 3: 57–71.

Stenström, Anna-Brita. 1990. Lexical items peculiar to spoken discourse. In Jan Svartvik (ed.), *The London–Lund Corpus of Spoken English*. Lund: Lund University Press.

Stockwell, Robert P., Paul Schachter, and Barbara Partee. 1973. *The Major Syntactic Structures of English*. New York: Holt, Rinehart and Winston.

"Swift Redux". 2001. A modest proposal. *ELSNews* 10.2 (Summer 2001): 7.

Tadmor, Uri. 2009. Loanwords in the world's languages: findings and results. In Martin Haspelmath and Uri Tadmor (eds), *Loanwords in the World's Languages: a comparative handbook*, 55–75. Berlin: de Gruyter Mouton.

Tarkington, Booth. 1914. *Penrod*. New York: Doubleday, Page & Co. Our page reference is to the New York: Grosset & Dunlap edn, n.d. (?1955).

Taylor, John R. 2012. *The Mental Corpus: how language is represented in the mind*. Oxford: Oxford University Press.

Taylor, Lolita, Claire Grover, and Edward J. Briscoe. 1989. The syntactic regularity of English noun phrases. In *Proceedings of the Fourth Conference of the European Chapter of the Association for Computational Linguistics, UMIST (Manchester), April 1989*, 256–263.

Thompson, Sandra A. and Yuka Koide. 1986. Iconicity and "indirect objects" in English. *Journal of Pragmatics* 11: 399–406.

Thurgood, Graham and LaPolla, Randy J. (eds). 2003. *The Sino-Tibetan Languages*. London: Routledge.

Tomasello, Michael. 2003. *Constructing a Language: a usage-based theory of language acquisition*. Cambridge, Mass.: Harvard University Press.

Tottie, Gunnel. 1991. *Negation in English Speech and Writing*. San Diego: Academic Press.

Trudgill, Peter. 1989. Interlanguage, interdialect and typological change. In Susan Gass, Carolyn Madden, Dennis Preston, and Larry Selinker (eds), *Variation in Second Language Acquisition*, vol. 2: *Psycholinguistic Issues*, 244–253. Clevedon, Som.: Multilingual Matters.

Trudgill, Peter. 1990. *The Dialects of England*. Oxford: Blackwell.

Trudgill, Peter and Jack K. Chambers (eds). 1991. *Dialects of English: studies in grammatical variation*. London: Longman.

Van Brakel, Jaap. 1992. Comment on MacLaury. *Current Anthropology* 33: 169–172.

Van Brakel, Jaap. 1993. The plasticity of categories: the case of colour. *British Journal for the Philosophy of Science* 44: 103–135.

Vanneck, Gerard. 1958. The colloquial preterite in modern American English. *Word* 14: 237–242.

de Villiers, Jill G., Helen B. Tager Flusberg, Kenji Hakuta, and Michael Cohen. 1979. Children's comprehension of relative clauses. *Journal of Psycholinguistic Research* 8: 499–528.

Visser, F.Th. 1973. *An Historical Syntax of the English Language*, part III, 2nd half. Leiden: E.J. Brill.

Warren, W.L. 1973. *Henry II*. London: Eyre Methuen.

Warsh, David. 2006. *Knowledge and the Wealth of Nations: a story of economic discovery*. New York: W.W. Norton.

Wasow, Tom and Jennifer Arnold. 2005. Intuitions in linguistic argumentation. *Lingua* 115: 1481–1496.

Welmers, William E. 1950. Notes on two languages in the Senufo group. *Language* 26: 126–146 and 494–531.

Wexler, Ken. 2012. Language innateness. Letter to the Editor, *Times Literary Supplement*, 19 Oct 2012.

White, Morton G. 1950. The analytic and the synthetic: an untenable dualism. In S. Hook (ed.), *John Dewey: Philosopher of Science and Freedom*, 316–330. New York: Dial Press. Reprinted as chapter 14 of Leonard Linsky (ed.), *Semantics and the Philosophy of Language*, Urbana, Ill.: University of Illinois Press, 1952.

Whitney, William Dwight. 1885. *The Life and Growth of Language*, 5th edn. London: Kegan Paul, Trench, & Co.

Whorf, Benjamin Lee. 1940. Science and linguistics. *MIT Technology Review* 42: 229–231. Reprinted in John B. Carroll (ed.), *Language, Thought, and Reality: selected writings of Benjamin Lee Whorf*, 207–219; Cambridge, Mass.: MIT Press, 1956.

Wierzbicka, Anna. 1996. *Semantics: primes and universals*. Oxford: Oxford University Press.

Wilson, George. 1855. *Researches on Colour-Blindness*. Edinburgh: Sutherland & Knox.

Winford, Donald. 1985. The syntax of *fi* complements in Caribbean English Creole. *Language* 61: 588–624.

Wittgenstein, Ludwig. 1953. *Philosophical Investigations*. Oxford: Blackwell.

Xue, Nianwen and Martha Palmer. 2004. Calibrating features for semantic role labeling. In *Proceedings of the Conference on Empirical Methods in Natural Language Processing (EMNLP 2004), Barcelona, 2004*, 88–94.

Yngve, Victor H. 1961. The depth hypothesis. In Roman Jakobson (ed.), *Structure of Language and its Mathematical Aspects*, Providence, Rhode Island: American Mathematical Society, 130–138. Reprinted in Fred W. Householder (ed.), *Syntactic Theory I: Structuralist*, 115–123; Harmondsworth, Mddx: Penguin, 1972.

Zwaan, Rolf A. and Anton J. Nederhof. 1990. Some aspects of scholarly communication in linguistics: an empirical study. *Language* 66: 553–557.

Index

Technical terms are indexed only for passages where they are defined.

Aarts, B. 215n
Abney, S. 218–219
Adams, D.Q. 289n
Ahlqvist, A. ix
Akkadian 19, 91–92, 199, 318
Allen, G. 272–273, 276
ambiguity and vagueness 11, 58, 198
Ammon, U. 136n
analytic v. synthetic 87–89
Anderson, J.R. 309
Arabic 247
Aranda *see* Arunta
argument from authority 84, 239, 318
Aristotle 134, 285
Arnold, J. 252
Aronoff, M. 81
Arppe, A. 105, 249, 251–252
Arunta 282
Atwell, E.S. 220
Austrian economics 113
automatic parsing 218–236
Ayala, F.J. 62
ayam makan phenomena 10–11, 15, 17–18, 198

Bailkin, J. 273
Baker, P. 150n
Ballasy, N. 113
Bangalore, S. 219, 222–223
Bard, E.G. 251
Basilico, D. 259
Bassa 285
Bauer, L. 81
Bauer, P.T. 314
Baxter, W.H. 188n, 194
Bayer, S. 260
Beare, J. 285
Beck, J. 284
behaviourism 242
Behme, C. 109
Belasco, S. 264
Bellmer, E.H. 275, 280

Berlin, B. 283, 285, 291, 295
Berners-Lee, T. 299
Bernstein, B. 136–138, 145, 148
Berwick, R.C. 21n
bi-directional attachment 126
Biber, D. 251
Bisang, W. 17, 197–198
Black, E. 218–219
Blair, A.C.L. 312, 316n
Bloom, P. 111
Bloomfield, L. 149, 185
Boas, F. 18, 281–282, 296–297, 319
Bod, R. 105
Boden, M.A. 82
Boeckx, C. 65, 246n
Boltz, W.G. 198
Bornstein, M.H. 276
Bowie, J. 215n
Bricmont, J. v
Briscoe, E.J. 76, 220, 222–223, 229, 234–235
British National Corpus vii, 29, *and* passim
Broadbent, D.E. 240
Brown Corpus vii, 251, 258
Brown, D.E. 115, 259, 301
Brown, J.G. 113–114
Brown, P. 111
Bruno, G. 84
Burns, T. 316

Cameron, D.W.D. 241
Cardie, C. 253
Carlson, G.N. 81
Carnie, A. 65, 78, 79n
Carroll, J.A. ix, 48, 220, 222–223, 229, 234–235
Castellan, N.J. 208, 264n
de Cervantes, M. 257
Chambers, J.K. 205
Charles II of England 81
Chaucer, G. 100
Chen, M.Y. 264

Cheshire, J. 211–212
CHILDES Corpus 246n
Chinese 13–19, 91–92, 184, 186–200, 217, 264, 292–294, 304, 308–309
Chipere, Ng. 30n, 92
Chomsky, A.N. 6 *and* passim
Christie, A. 212n
CHRISTINE Corpus vii–viii, 93, 119, *and* passim
Clover, C. 316n
Cohen, M. 176
Cole, B.L. 273
Cole, P. 12
Collier, G.A. 283
Collins, M.J. 219, 223
Comas, P. 50n
competence *see* performance v. competence
Comrie, B. 169
conducive contexts 174
Confucius 13–15, 18–19, 187, 198, 291
Conklin, H.C. 288–290
constituent 26n
Copestake, A. 220
Corbett, G.G. 259
Cowart, W. 79, 249
Crafts, N. 113
Creel, H.G. 16n
creole 184–201, 259
critical period 148–153, 185
Culy, C. 76, 84, 96–97
Curtiss, S. 148, 242
Czech 247

Dalke, A. 7
Dalton, J. 274
Daniels, N. 98n
Dante 307
Darwin, C.R. 114–115, 279–280
data-oriented parsing 105
deep branching 159
DeGraff, M. 185
demographically-sampled speech vii, 119–120, 136, 202
dependency grammar 2, 220
depth 159n
Descartes, R. 238
descriptive adequacy 65

descriptive v. normative empiricism 237–243
descriptive v. prescriptive linguistics 97–98
Deutscher, G. 19, 91, 199–200, 270–276, 279–280, 286–287, 290, 295, 318
Diesling, M. 259
direct v. indirect speech 127–128
discourse items 123
Doran, C. 219
Dunster construction 66, 74–75, 93

Easterly, W. 314
economic growth 112–118
Eddy, W.A. 273
edit distance 34, 224–225
Edwards, J. 24, 54, 120
Edwards, V. 204, 211–212
Ehrman, M.E. 258
Einstein, A. 287
Eisikovits, E. 129, 204–205, 214
elaborated code *see* restricted v. elaborated codes
Ellis, N.C. 7n
Ellsworth, M. 51n
Elman, J.L. 245n
Elsness, J. 202, 215–216
embedding index 138–152
emergentist linguistics 7n
endogenous growth theory 112–118
Enfield, N.J. 111
Esperanto 25, 184
Evans, N. 111, 259
Evans, P.D. 309
Everett, C.C. 8, 15
Everett, D.L. 91, 288, 319
Eversley, J. 150n

Faarlund, J.T. 109, 199
Farmer, B. 298
Fedorenko, E. 288
Fillmore, C.J. 51
Finegan, E. 251
Flickinger, D. 218–219
Fodor, J.A. 20–21, 88–89, 107, 114, 117, 309
formtag 32
Foster, J. 106
frame semantics, FrameNet 51n

Francis, W.N. 251
Frank, M.C. 288
Frege, G. 9
French 84, 201, 247, 256, 264, 303
Fries, C.C. 263
functiontag 32
Fung Yu-lan 308n

Gaelic 207
Gage, J. 273
Gaizauskas, R. 73n
Galileo 314
Gazdar, G.J.M. ix, 107
Gdaniec, C. 218–219
GEIG (Grammar Evaluation Interest Group)
    metric 218–236
Geiger, L. 277
Genie 148, 242
German 10, 20, 99–100, 105, 287, 303, 307,
    309
ghost node 33, 72n, 139
Gibson, E. 288
Gil, D. 10–13, 15, 91, 186–197, 304–305, 319
Gilbert, S.L. 309
Gildea, D. 50n
Gildea, P.M. 246n
Gladstone, W.E. 269–295
Gleason, H.A. 285, 297, 319
von Goethe, J.W. 285
gold-standard analysis 218
Goodluck, H. 176
Gordon, P. 288
Gordon, R.J. 115n
Graddol, D. 6–7, 108
Graham, J. 220
grammatical idiom 38, 139
Graves, N. 2
Greek 9–10, 80, 269–295, 298, 303–304,
    307
Greenbaum, S. 202, 205, 215
Greenberg, J.H. 257
Grishman, R. 218–219
Gross, M. 7, 240, 253
Grover, C. 76
guest node 33
Guo Xiang 308n

Hagège, C. 267
Haigh, R. 220
Hakuta, K. 176
Hamilton, W. 278–279
Handscombe, R.J. 156
Hanks, P. 247
Hannan, J. 239n
Hanunóo 288–290
Harris, J. 207, 214
Harrison, P. 218–219
Haspelmath, M. 23
Hauser, M.D. 109
Hegel, G.W.F. 281
Heine, S.J. 298
Helpman, E. 112
Henrich, J. 298
Henry II of England 297
Hermon, G. 12
hidden complexity *see* overt v. hidden
    complexity
Hill, A.A. 83
Hindle, D. 218–219
Hirschberg, J. 253–255, 265
Hockett, C.F. 7n, 264
Hockey, E.A. 219
Hoffmann, T. 104–105, 250–251
Holdren, J. 113
Holmgren, A.F. 273
Homer 269–295
Hopper, P.J. 7n
Householder, F.W. 7, 70, 84
Howell, J. 7
Howell, P. 124–125
Huang, P.C. 308
Huck, G.J. 260
Hudson, R.R. 309
Hughes, A. 216n
Hummel, J.J. 292
Humphries, B. 106
Hungarian 9, 12, 16, 19, 100
Huxley, J. 278–279
Hymes, D. 289

Igbo 65
indexed grammars 107
indirect object 33
indirect speech *see* direct v. indirect speech

Indonesian *see* Malay/Indonesian
Ingria, R. 218–219
innate ideas 238
introspection, intuition 78, 82–83, 239, 248
Italian 65, 68

Jackendoff, R. 91, 115
Järvikivi, J. 105, 249, 251–252
Jelinek, F. 218–219
Jespersen, J.O.H. 93
Johansson, S. 110
Johnson, C.R. 51n
Jones, P.E. 242
Joseph, B.D. 255, 266–267
Jowett, B. 278
Jurafsky, D. 50n

Kahane, H.R. and R. 264
Kant, I. 2
Karlgren, B. 189–192, 293n, 308n
Karlsson, K. 319
Katz, J.J. 61, 88–89
Kay, P. 283, 285
Kay, P. 291, 295
Keenan, E.L. 169
Kepser, S. 248–249, 252
Kilgarriff, A. ix, 103–104
Klavans, J. 218–219
Knecht, E. 292
Koide, Y. 101
Kristol, A.M. 290
Krotov, A. 73n
Kübler, S. 219–220
Kuhn, T.S. 134
Kunwinjku 259
Kwakiutl, Kwak'wala 18–19, 281

Labov, W. 80, 81n, 83, 216, 288
Lahn, B.T. 309
Lakatos, I. 152
Lamarck, chevalier de 279–280
Lamb, C. 278
Lancaster–Oslo/Bergen (LOB) Corpus vii
Lane Fox, R. 292–293
Langendoen, D.T. 28, 78

language of thought 20–21, 89n, 107, 114, 309
LaPolla, R.J. 188
Larsen-Freeman, D. 7n
Lass, R. 213
Latin 9–10 *and* passim
Laurence, S. 21n, 108–109, 117n
leaf-ancestor metric 34, 218–236
Lee, L. 253
Leech, G.N. vii, 27, 202, 205, 215
Lees, R.B. 251, 264
Legge, J. 14–15, 18–19
Leisi, E. 20
Lenneberg, E.H. 148–149, 151, 185, 286
Levelt, W.J.M. 124–125
Levenshtein, V.I. 224–225
Levenshtein distance *see* edit distance
Levin, E. 51
Levinson, S.C. 111
Lewis, J.D. 245n
Lewis, M.B. 189
lexical-functional grammar 21
Liberman, M. 218–219
Liddell, H.G. 289
lifelong learning 149, 153, 185
Lin Dekang 28
lineage 34, 220
Linnaeus, C. vii, 54, 62
Liu, J.J.Y. 17–18
Locke, J. 238, 242, 303, 307
Lodge, D.J. 92
London–Lund Corpus 120n–121n, 125
Lorenz, G. 215n
LUCY Corpus viii, 29n, 155, *and* passim

Maas, U. 10
McCarthy, D.F. vii, 253
Macfarquhar, L. 307
McKinnon, T. 12
MacLaury, R.E. 285–286, 289, 292
McWhorter, J.H. 185–?188, 193–197
Magerman, D.M. 219
Magnus, H.F. 273, 275–277, 280n
Mair, V.H. 16n
Malay/Indonesian 10–13, 91–92, 184, 186–187, 189–193, 195, 197n, 200, 304–305
Mallory, J.P. 289n

Malotki, E. 287
Mann, R. 69n
Manning, C.D. 220
Marcus, M.P. 28, 218–219
Margolis, E. 21n, 108–109, 117n
Màrquez, Ll. 50n
Marshall, A. 112
Marx, K. 104n
Maspero, H. 192
mathematical logic 8, 51, 86–87, 90
mediaeval logic 134
Meiklejohn, J.M.D. vi, 1–5, 22, 64, 93
Mekel-Bobrov, N. 309
Mendenhall, W. 144, 151
Meteer, M. 55
Meurers, W.D. 106
Miestamo, M. 319
Miller, G.A. 246n
Miller, J. 119, 126, 138, 158–159, 170n
von Mises, L.H.E. 113
Moon, R. 266
Mooney, R.J. 253
Morris, A. ix
Morris, W. 2
Mortimer, J.C. 66–68, 74–75
Müller, S. 95, 99–100
Munsell set 285–286

Na Younghee 260
Napier, C.J. 306
nativism 238
Nederhof, A.J. 255
Neeleman, A. 303
negative information 65, 79n
Newmeyer, F.J. 76, 78, 94, 266
Newton, I. 114–115, 287
Nickerson, D. 285
non-target-like 180
Norenzayan, A. 298
Norman, J. 187–188
normative empiricism *see* descriptive v.
     normative empiricism
Norwegian 84–85, 99
Nunnally, T.E. 78, 266

Orbán, V. 241
overt v. hidden complexity 197

Palmer, M. 50n
Parseval competitions 218–220, 236
parsing 218–236
Partee, B. 6n–7, 51
Pearson, K. 279n
Penn Treebank 28
Perera, K. 157, 167n–168n
Pérez-Leroux, A.T. 181
performance v. competence, performance
     deviation 70, 78, 82, 127, 130–131, 314
Petruck, M.R.L. 51n
Phillips, M. 310
Piattelli-Palmarini, M. 244
pidgin 184–186, 200–201
Pinker, S. 22–23, 111, 114–115, 148, 240,
     270n, 296, 299–302, 308–309, 313,
     319
Pirahã 91–92, 319
Planck, M. 267
Plato, Platonism 15, 61, 278, 291
Pole, W. 273
Ponca 18–19
Popper, K.R. 5–6, 195n, 256
positive *any more* 80, 241
poverty of the stimulus 244
Prantl, C. 285n
predicate *see* subject and predicate
prescriptive *see* descriptive v. prescriptive
Prinz, J.J. 110–111
Pro-Drop 303–304
probabilistic theory 5n
programming languages 25
Propp, V.Ja. 116
Proto-Indo-European 307
Pulleyblank, E.G. 188, 194
Pullum, G.K. 95–99, 106, 111, 244–247, 258

Quine, W. van O. 88–89
Quirk, R. 202, 205, 215

Radford, A. 258
Rahman, A. ix
Rappaport Hovav, M. 51
rationalism 238
raw corpus vii
Rawls, J.B. 98n
Reading Emotional Speech Corpus 120n

reflective equilibrium 98n
Reis, M. 248–249, 252
relational grammar 21
restricted v. elaborated codes 136
Ricardo, D. 112
Ridley, M. 113, 116
van Rijsbergen, C.J. 223
Rivero, M.-L. 257
Rivers, W.H.R. 276
Rizzi, L. 303
Roberts, J.M. 286
Robertson, D. 251
Roeper, T. 81
Rohlf, F.J. 264n
Romer, P.M. 112–117
Rood, D.S. 264–265
rootrank tag 37–38
Rosemont, H. 16n
Ross, J.R. 81–82, 109
Roukos, S. 218–219
Ruppenhofer, J. 51n
Ruse, M. 105
Russell, B.A.W. 90

s-unit 29, 120
Sag, I. 6n, 109
Sagart, L. 195n
Santorini, B. 218–219
Sapir, E. 6, 49n, 70, 282, 286–288, 291
Sarkar, A. 219
de Saussure, F.M. 1
Scha, R. 105
Schachter, P. 6n–7, 51
Scheffczyk, J. 51n
Schleicher, A. 281
Schoenemann, P.T. 111, 117
Scholz, B.C. 111, 244–245
Schuessler, A. 187, 293n
Schütze, C.T. 64–65, 248–252
Schütze, H. 220
Schumpeter, J. 113
Scott, R. 289
Sekine, S. 223
semantic role labelling 50n
semantically-unpredictable derivation 193, 195–198
Shakespeare, W. 4

Shen Yi 308n
Shona 285
Shu Xincheng 308n
Siegel, M.E.A. 81
Siegel, S. 208, 264n
Sima'an, K. 105
Simon, H.A. 22
Sinnemäki, K. 319
skeleton parsing 53–54
Skinner, B.F. 242
Smith, N.V. 109
Sokal, A. v
Sokal, R.R. 264n
Sorace, A. 251
species 62
speech repairs 124–125
speech-codes 136
Stafford, G.H. 151n
Stafleu, F.A. 62
steady state 148–149, 152–153, 185
Stefanowitsch, A. 85n, 98–102
Stenström, A.-B. 123
Stockwell, R.P. 6n–7, 51
structure-dependence 22, 244, 300
Strzalkowski, T. 218–219
subject and predicate 134
Surdeanu, M. 50n
SUSANNE Corpus and parsing scheme vii–viii, 27–28, *and* passim
Svartvik, J. 202, 205, 215
Svensson, J. 206
"Swift Redux" 223
Switchboard Corpus 55
syntactically Markovian constructions 125–127
synthetic *see* analytic v. synthetic
Szendrői, K. 303

Tadmor, U. 188
Tager Flusberg, H.B. 176
tagma 26n
tagmatag 72n
Tarkington, B. 210, 212n
Tavakolian, S.L. 176
Taylor, J.R. 12
Taylor, L. 76
Telljohann, H. 219–220

theorem 87
Thompson, S.A. 101
Thurgood, G. 188
Tishkoff, S.A. 309
Tomasello, M. 110
Tottie, G. 206
Trask, L. ix, 215n
tree-adjoining grammar 21
treebank vii, 24, 27, 54
Trudgill, P. 142–143, 203, 204, 208n, 216n, 291, 319
Turmo, J. 50n

unary branching 159–160
Universal Grammar 22–23, 90, 107–111, 115, 148, 184, 199, 201, 239–240, 242, 301, 303
Universal People 301

Vaez-Azizi, L.M. 309
vagueness *see* ambiguity and vagueness
Vallender, E.J. 309
Van Brakel, J. 284, 286, 289–291
Vanneck, G. 215–216n
Veblen, T.B. 83
verb group 32
Villiers, J.G. de 176
Visser, F.Th. 207, 215n, 217
VP (verb phrase) 32, 134

Wallis, S. 215n
Wang Wei 17
Wang, W.S.-Y. 264
Warren, W.L. 297
Warsh, D. 112
Wasow, T. 252

Watson, J.B. 242
Wedgwood Benn, A. 125
Weinert, R. 119, 126, 138, 158–159, 170n
Welmers, W.E. 263–264
Welsh 307n
Wexler, K. 111
White, M.G. 88
Whitney, W.D. 149
whiz-deletion 43n
Whorf, B.L. 286–288
wide branching 159
Wierzbicka, A. 114
Wilks, Y.A. 73n
Williams, H. 69n
Wilson, D. 258
Wilson, G. 274
Winford, D. 259
Wittgenstein, L. 88–89
wordrank tag 37–38
wordtag, wordtagging vii n, 48, 123–124, 128–129
Wundt, W. 248

X-bar theory 21
Xiang Xiu 308n
Xu Yuangao 308n
Xue Nianwen 50n

Yngve, V.H. 159n
Young, K. 124–125

Zandvoort, R.W. 93
Zhang Xiang 308n
Zhuang Zi 308n
Zwaan, R.A. 255

www.ingramcontent.com/pod-product-compliance
Lightning Source LLC
Chambersburg PA
CBHW061041110426
42740CB00050B/2528